D1795848

THE BRUTE WITHIN

OTHER TITLES IN THE SERIES INCLUDE

Kant's Empirical Realism
Paul Abela

Against Equality of Opportunity
Matt Cavanagh

Causality, Interpretation, and the Mind
William Child

Metaphor and Moral Experience
A. E. Denham

Semantic Powers
Meaning and the Means of Knowing in Classical Indian Philosophy
Jonardon Ganeri

Kant's Theory of Imagination
Bridging Gaps in Judgement and Experience
Sarah L. Gibbons

Of Liberty and Necessity
James A. Harris

The Grounds of Ethical Judgement
New Transcendental Arguments in Moral Philosophy
Christian Illies

Projective Probability
James Logue

Understanding Pictures
Dominic Lopes

Wittgenstein, Finitism, and the Foundations of Mathematics
Mathieu Marion

Truth and the End of Inquiry
A Peircean Account of Truth
C. J. Misak

The Good and the True
Michael Morris

Hegel's Idea of Freedom
Alan Patten

Nietzsche and Metaphysics
Peter Poellner

The Ontology of Mind
Events, Processes, and States
Helen Steward

Things that Happen Because They Should
A Teleological Approach to Action
Rowland Stout

The Brute Within

Appetitive Desire in Plato and Aristotle

HENDRIK LORENZ

CLARENDON PRESS · OXFORD

OXFORD
UNIVERSITY PRESS

Great Clarendon Street, Oxford OX2 6DP

Oxford University Press is a department of the University of Oxford.
It furthers the University's objective of excellence in research, scholarship,
and education by publishing worldwide in

Oxford New York

Auckland Cape Town Dar es Salaam Hong Kong Karachi
Kuala Lumpur Madrid Melbourne Mexico City Nairobi
New Delhi Shanghai Taipei Toronto

With offices in

Argentina Austria Brazil Chile Czech Republic France Greece
Guatemala Hungary Italy Japan Poland Portugal Singapore
South Korea Switzerland Thailand Turkey Ukraine Vietnam

Oxford is a registered trade mark of Oxford University Press
in the UK and in certain other countries

Published in the United States
by Oxford University Press Inc., New York

British Library Cataloguing in Publication Data

Data available

Library of Congress Cataloging in Publication Data

Lorenz, Hendrik.
The brute within : appetitive desire in Plato and Aristotle / Hendrik Lorenz.
  p. cm.
Includes bibliographical references and index.
1. Plato. 2. Aristotle. 3. Soul. 4. Desire. I. Title.
B395. L66 2006   128'.3—dc22   2005034938

Typeset by Newgen Imaging Systems (P) Ltd., Chennai, India
Printed in Great Britain
on acid-free paper by
Biddles Ltd, King's Lynn, Norfolk

ISBN 978–0–19–929063–5

To Evin

Fashion a single kind of multicoloured brute with a ring of many heads that it can grow and change at will—some from gentle, some from savage animals. Then fashion another kind, that of a lion, and another of a human being. But make the first much the largest and the other second to it in size. Now join the three of them into one, so that they somehow grow together naturally. Then, fashion around them the image of one of them, that of a human being, so that anyone who sees only the outer covering and not what's within will think it's a single creature, a human being.

(Plato, *Republic* 9, 588 C 7–E 1)

Appetite is like a brute animal, and spirit perverts rulers even when they are the best of men.

(Aristotle, *Politics* 3.16, 1287ª30–2)

Acknowledgements

I started work on the topic of this book as a graduate student at Oxford in 1996. The bulk of the book was written at Princeton between 2002 and 2004. In the course of thinking and writing about Plato's and Aristotle's psychological theories, I have been helped by many individuals. Michael Frede was the most wonderful thesis adviser I could have wished for, and has over the years remained a source of invaluable advice, encouragement, and inspiration. Others who have significantly contributed to the process of working out the overall interpretation that underlies the book include Susanne Bobzien, Lesley Brown, Myles Burnyeat, David Charles, Alan Code, John Cooper, Gail Fine, Christopher Gill, Terence Irwin, Thomas Johansen, Benjamin Morison, Jozef Müller, Christof Rapp, David Sedley, and Matthew Strohl. Lesley Brown, John Cooper, Corinne Gartner, Alexander Nehamas, and Jessica Moss read various versions of the book's type-script and supplied me with comments that helped me greatly in preparing it for publication. The Department of Philosophy at Princeton provided a supportive and highly conducive environment, and a full year of academic leave in 2003–4 accelerated the book's completion. Finally, Corinne Gartner helped by checking the book's references and by preparing the *Index Locorum*.

Some of the material presented in this book has already been published elsewhere. Earlier versions of parts of Chapters 2 and 4 have appeared as 'Desire and reason in Plato's *Republic*' in *Oxford Studies in Ancient Philosophy* XXVII (2004), 83–116. A few pages of Chapter 3 have appeared in an essay called 'The analysis of the soul in Plato's *Republic*', in Gerasimos Santas (ed.), *The Blackwell Companion to Plato's Republic* (Oxford: Blackwell, 2005). Much of Chapter 10 has appeared, in German, as 'Die Bewegung der Lebewesen bei Aristoteles', in Klaus Corcilius and Christof Rapp (eds.), *Beiträge zur Aristotelischen Handlungstheorie* (Stuttgart: Steiner, 2006) Thanks are due to Oxford University Press, Blackwell Publishing, and Steiner-Verlag for their permission to reprint this material.

Contents

Introduction 1

PART ONE: APPETITE AND REASON IN PLATO'S *REPUBLIC*

Introduction 9
1. Parts of the Soul 13
2. The Argument for Tripartition 18
3. Partition 35
4. The Simple Picture 41

PART TWO: BELIEF AND APPEARANCE IN PLATO

Introduction 55
5. Imitation and the Soul 59
6. Belief and Reason 74
7. Below Belief and Reason 95

PART THREE: *PHANTASIA* AND NON-RATIONAL DESIRE IN ARISTOTLE

Introduction 113
8. Preliminaries 119
9. *Phantasia*, Desire, and Locomotion 124
10. Desire without *phantasia* 138
11. The Workings of *phantasia* 148
12. *Phantasia* and Practical Thought 174
13. Reason and Non-rational Desire 186

Conclusion 202
Bibliography 208
General Index 215
Index Locorum 221

Introduction

According to the elaborate and extremely ingenious psychological theory that Plato presents in the *Republic*, human motivation comes in three distinct forms. Only one of the three forms of motivation originates from reason. The other two are in some sense non-rational. They derive on the one hand from spirit, which motivates us to seek esteem and avoid humiliation, and on the other hand from appetite, which impels us to pursue pleasure, such as the pleasure we tend to experience as we satisfy our bodily needs. Reason has its own attachments, including a desire to discover how things are and why they are the way they are, not with a view to benefits that such understanding may bring, but simply for its own sake. The distinct forms of motivation can interact harmoniously, with each one of them fulfilling its proper function. The person whose motivations are disposed in this harmonious way is, according to Plato's theory, virtuous. But the forms of motivation can also conflict, even in such a way that psychological conflict and division of mind become long-standing and deeply engrained.

The theory serves to describe and explain a variety of dispositions of character, virtuous as well as vicious ones. It enables Socrates, the *Republic*'s main speaker, to formulate at least a preliminary answer to one of the dialogue's key questions: what is justice? It also has profound implications for the development and maintenance of good character. It informs and guides the *Republic*'s programme of education, with its emphasis not only on intellectual excellence, but also on the early establishment of appropriate habits of attachment and response. Moreover, the theory evidently plays a central role in the *Republic*'s condemnation of drama and epic poetry. The discussion of the effects of poetry on the soul, in *Republic* 10, takes into account the fact that human motivation comes in three forms, but strongly emphasizes the contrast between the rationality of one of the forms of motivation and the non-rational, often irrational and destructive, character of the other forms.

This book has two main purposes. One of these is to shed light on the contrast between rational and non-rational motivation in Plato's of the tripartite soul. What is distinctive about rational motivation, and in what sense are the other forms non-rational? Non-rational motivation is in some ways the more difficult topic, because it is unclear what cognitive resources the theory makes available to account for it. It may seem that Plato fails to offer a coherent view of it. Many readers of the *Republic* have thought that rational resources are needed to account for the cognitive achievements involved in even the lowest of the theory's three forms of motivation, appetitive desire. I shall concentrate on appetitive desire, in part because its stubborn attachment to whatever happens to give us pleasure makes for a maximally stark contrast with the desires of reason, which spring from the distinctively human drive to act as is best overall.

Plato likens not only appetite, but also spirit, to a brute animal concealed within the human form (*Republic* 9, 588 C 7–E 2). But he takes spirit to have an affinity to reason that appetite lacks. In a cultural environment that is properly informed by the appreciation of genuine value, spirit can acquire and maintain a delicately nuanced practical outlook (note *Republic* 4, 440 B 9–C 4), so that, on that basis, it impels the well-conditioned person to pursue as admirable and praiseworthy those things, and only those things, that reason impels them to pursue as best overall. Spirit may even come to be disposed so as to find it admirable and praiseworthy to be the sort of person who pursues precisely those things that reason selects, and to pursue them precisely to the point that reason prescribes. It is not surprising, then, that Plato assigns spirit to reason as its natural helper and ally (*Republic* 4, 441 A 2–3, 441 E 4–5; *Timaeus* 70 A 2–C 1). It is a brute, at least in part because it cannot itself engage in the distinctively human activity of reasoning about what is best. But it is a highly educable brute, and it can be *humanized* to a very considerable extent.

Appetite's stubborn and inflexible attachment to whatever happens to give a person pleasure renders psychological conflict ineliminable. What gives us pleasure is under reason's control much less than what is regarded as admirable and praiseworthy in a given cultural environment. For one thing, what gives us pleasure is in large part determined by brute physiological facts about the constitution and condition of our body. Eating something now will give a hungry person pleasure regardless of whether or not they think it is now overall best to eat. Moreover, Plato thinks that appetite has an inbuilt tendency towards excess, in that the pleasures experienced in satisfying appetitive desires tend to engender new, and even more intense, appetitive desires that aim at renewed or amplified pleasurable experiences (*Republic* 4, 442 A 7–8).[1] For these reasons, Plato thinks that even in the well-disposed, virtuous soul, reason and spirit will need to watch over appetite, and will on occasion need to 'weed out' inappropriate desires that appetite will give rise to (*Republic* 4, 442 A 4–B 3; *Republic* 9, 589 A 6–B 6). Appetite's attachment to what in fact gives us pleasure is unreformable. What appetite motivates us to pursue can be reformed only by reforming what in fact gives us pleasure, within the rather stringent limits imposed by physiological facts. There is thus something ineliminably and unreformably brutish about appetite, not only about how it functions, but also about what it motivates us to pursue.

One thing that appetite and spirit have in common—anyhow on the interpretation that I shall offer—is that both of them are capable of generating fully formed motivating conditions without being capable of engaging in the activity of reasoning. I shall argue that Plato offers a coherent and relatively detailed view of the cognitive resources that are involved in the formation of appetitive desire.

---

[1] Cf. Aristotle, *Nicomachean Ethics* 3.12, 1119^{b}7–10.

These resources are available to spirit as well as to appetite, and I shall from time to time draw attention to ways in which my discussion seems to me to shed light on Plato's conception of spirit as well as on his conception of appetite. However, this book does not offer, and is not meant to offer, anything like a complete study of spirit, either as Plato or as Aristotle conceives of it. It *is* meant to offer, on the other hand, a reasonably complete study of appetite, as Plato conceives of it. On the view of appetite that I shall present, it is clearly and coherently conceived of as a non-rational form of motivation, in a way that contrasts interestingly and defensibly with rational motivation, as Plato conceives of that.

While the *Republic* is the text in which Plato introduces and argues for the theory of the tripartite soul, it is not the only Platonic dialogue that contains discussion of that theory. The *Timaeus*, a later text, provides an outline of it that is in many ways strikingly similar to its statement in the *Republic*. There is at least one notable difference, though, and I shall consider its significance for and impact on the theory. My view is that the substance of it as it is presented in the *Republic* remains intact. I therefore think that it is legitimate to speak simply of Plato's theory of the tripartite soul.

My second main purpose is to draw attention to what seems to me to be a close connection between Plato's and Aristotle's psychological theories. It is fairly well known that Aristotle adopts Plato's conception of human desire as coming in three distinct forms with little or no modification.[2] It is less widely appreciated that the key concept Aristotle employs in explaining non-rational motivation—*phantasia*, that is—has significant Platonic antecedents. Aristotle is unfortunately not as clear as one would wish him to be about what *phantasia* is and how it is involved in non-rational motivation. We do not have a comprehensive discussion by him concerning the topic. There are a considerable number of relevant discussions and remarks in the *De Anima*, in the *De Motu Animalium*, and in the collection of texts known as the *Parva Naturalia*. Some of these shed a good deal of light on *phantasia*, so that it is possible to make a reasonably detailed and, I think, plausible case for a rather specific view of what Aristotle takes *phantasia* to be and how he takes it to be involved in non-rational motivation. On this view, it is a powerful cognitive capacity that enables the retention and retrieval of sensory impressions and that is much like thought. One crucial thing that it enables a subject to do is to envisage prospective courses of action, including ones which the subject is, or

---

[2] Aristotle accepts that human desire comes in three forms, namely wish (βούλησις), spirit (θυμός), and appetite (ἐπιθυμία); see, for instance, *De Anima* 2.3, 414^{b}2; 3.9, 432^{b}5–6; *Eudemian Ethics* 2.10, 1225^{b}24–6; *Nicomachean Ethics* 3.2, 1111^{b}10–26. Wish is a rational form of desire, springing from thoughts to the effect that something or other is good and worth caring about (*Nicomachean Ethics* 3.4; 5.9, 1136^{b}7–9; *Rhetoric* 1.10, 1369^{a}3–4); spirit and appetite are non-rational. Appetites are desires that are directed at pleasure, flowing simply from beliefs or representations to the effect that something or other is a source of pleasure (cf. *De Anima* 2.3, 414^{b}3–6). Unfortunately, Aristotle says little about spirit as a distinctive form of motivation. Like Plato (*Republic* 4, 441 B 3–C 2), he treats anger, conceived of as a distress-involving desire for retaliation, as a case of spirited desire (e.g. at *Nicomachean Ethics* 7.6, 1149^{a}24–^{b}26).

can come to be, motivated to pursue. The Platonic antecedents of *phantasia* include the low-level sensory memory which Socrates in the *Philebus* defines as the preservation of perception and whose role it is to put a hungry, thirsty, or otherwise depleted subject in cognitive contact with the appropriate replenishing process (*Philebus* 34 A 10–35 D 6), but also—though less directly— the non-rational thoughts and beliefs that the *Republic* associates with even the lowest form of motivation, appetitive desire (*Republic* 9, 571 D 1–5; 10, 603 A 1–2).

It is not just, however, that Aristotle's notion of *phantasia* has significant Platonic antecedents, and that a study of these antecedents can illuminate at least some aspects of how Aristotle conceives of *phantasia*. There is also, it seems to me, a rather striking and noteworthy structural similarity between Aristotle's theory of human motivation and Plato's theory of the soul as tripartite, anyhow as it is presented in the *Timaeus*. So as to be able to capture that similarity in a suitably succinct and memorable manner, it will be useful to introduce somewhat schematically two views of what is involved in, and required for, thinking, or at any rate the kind of well-informed and properly guided thinking characteristic of experts when they deal with matters that fall within their field of expertise. Following ancient usage, I shall refer to these two views as Empiricism on the one hand and Rationalism on the other.

Empiricism is the view that thought, even expert thought, rests on nothing other than sensory experience: that is to say, on repeated cognitive encounters with perceptible objects, and on information supplied by the senses and retained by memory. Rationalism is the view that thought, especially expert thought, goes significantly beyond mere sensory experience, in that it involves, and requires, grasping intelligible (and imperceptible) items of some kind or other (for instance, Platonic forms or Aristotelian natures). While the two labels derive from Hellenistic debates between medical schools that primarily concerned the knowledgeable thinking of the expert doctor,[3] both of the competing views had deep roots in earlier philosophical conceptions of what is involved in thinking. This is obvious so far as Rationalism is concerned.[4] In reconstructing the origins of Empiricism, on the other hand, we are unfortunately limited to rather unsatisfactory

---

[3] Galen offers a clear and succinct statement of the disagreement, saying about medical expertise that 'some say that experience (ἐμπειρία) alone suffices for the art, whereas others think that reason (λόγος), too, has an important contribution to make'; *De Sectis Ingredientibus* 1, translated as in Galen, *Three Treatises on the Nature of Science*, trans. R. Walzer and M. Frede (Indianapolis, Ind.: Hackett, 1985). Members of the two groups, Galen goes on, are called Empiricists (ἐμπειρικοί) and Rationalists (λογικοί) respectively. He adds that the Empiricists are also known as μνημονευτικοί— 'memorists', to use a term coined by Michael Frede—no doubt because of their heavy reliance on memory in accounting for thought; M. Frede, 'An empiricist view of knowledge: memorism', in S. Everson (ed.), *Companions to Ancient Thought 1: Epistemology* (Cambridge: Cambridge University Press, 1990), 227.

[4] For discussion concerning some of the philosophical underpinnings of Rationalism, see J. Allen, *Inference from Signs: Ancient Debates about the Nature of Evidence* (Oxford: Oxford University Press, 2001), 91–7.

evidence.[5] Nevertheless, it is relatively clear both that Empiricism does have roots in fifth- and fourth-century philosophical theorizing,[6] and that Plato and Aristotle are familiar with at least some of the forerunners of Empiricism. For present purposes, it will suffice to exhibit the single most important piece of evidence in both regards.[7] This is a remark Socrates makes in his intellectual autobiography as presented in Plato's *Phaedo*. One thing he was wondering about as a young man, Socrates says, is whether it is blood, air, or fire that we think with, or whether it is none of these, but in fact the brain, 'which supplies the perceptions of hearing, seeing, and smelling, from which come memory and belief, and from memory and belief which has become stable, comes knowledge?' (*Phaedo* 96 B 3–9).[8] On this last view, both ordinary thought—mere belief—and expert thought—belief that has achieved stability—seem to depend on nothing but sense-perception on the one hand and memory on the other. Socrates does not credit any particular thinker with this theory, but there is some indication that it belongs to Alcmaeon of Croton (in southern Italy), a shadowy fifth- or even sixth-century figure who may have been a practising doctor as well as a philosopher.[9]

There are, moreover, important points of contact between Empiricism and the Atomist tradition beginning in the fifth century with Leucippus and Democritus. Aristotle complains repeatedly that Democritus, among other predecessors, failed to distinguish between thought and perception.[10] Our evidence suggests that Democritus tried to explain all forms of awareness in terms of streams of fine films of atoms—the so-called images (εἴδωλα)—that objects (artefacts, plants, animals, and the like) emit continuously and that, in turn, generate awareness of the object in question when they reach the soul atoms of a living thing capable of awareness. If so, Democritus' theory does not treat thought as *depending on* sense-perception, or on sense-perception and memory. Rather, it treats thought as being *exactly like* sense-perception, the only difference being that in sense-perception images reach the soul after entering the body through the appropriate sense-organ, whereas in thought images reach the soul directly, perhaps because thought-images are finer

[5] For more detailed discussion concerning the philosophical background of Empiricism, see Frede, 'An empiricist view', 234–40, to which the present paragraph is indebted.

[6] For what it is worth, Galen records that the Empiricists themselves regard their school as originating with a fifth-century Sicilian physician called Acron, about whom, unfortunately, we know next to nothing (*Subfiguratio Empirica*, 43).

[7] Further evidence is Polus' view, mentioned in Plato's *Gorgias* (462 B 10–C 3) and in Aristotle's *Metaphysics* (A 1, 981ª3–5), that experience produces art or expertise (τέχνη)—which in the context of the *Gorgias* is best understood as the view that expertise arises simply from experience. Note that the *Gorgias* indicates that Polus presented this view in a treatise. Socrates' contrasting view is, of course, that genuine expertise requires the ability to offer appropriate explanatory accounts (465 A 2–6). Note also the intriguing first chapter of Hippocrates' *Praecepta*, according to which 'reasoning (λογισμός) is memory which collects things grasped with perception'.

[8] Translations of Plato are taken from Plato, *Complete Works*, ed. J. Cooper (Indianapolis, Ind.: Hackett, 1997), with some modifications, the more significant ones of which are noted.

[9] C. Huffman's entry on Alcmaeon in the *Stanford Encyclopedia of Philosophy* (Summer 2004 Edition) contains relevant and valuable discussion; see especially 2.2.

[10] *De Anima* 1.2, 404ª27–31 and 405ª8–13, with 3.3, 427ª17–ᵇ8.

or thinner than sense-images.[11] However, one key feature that Democritus' theory seems to have in common with Empiricism is that it makes do without a dichotomy of sense and intellect as two fundamentally distinct cognitive capacities that put us in touch with two fundamentally distinct kinds of objects. For the Empiricist, what is needed to account for cognition in all its forms are simply the senses themselves and the retention by memory of information supplied by the senses. For Democritus, cognition in all its forms can be explained just in terms of streams of images, some finer or thinner than others, reaching the soul in different ways—by different routes, as it were.[12] It is intriguing to note, incidentally, that Aristotle's discussion of prophetic dreams takes Democritus' theory as a starting-point, so as to improve on it (*De Divinatione per Somnum* 2, 463^{b}31–464^{a}24).

What is relatively clear, in any case, is that Plato and Aristotle are familiar with theories of cognition that either are Empiricist in character, or at least share Empiricism's aspiration to account for thought without appealing to a specifically intellectual capacity which puts us in touch with items that are fundamentally different in kind from perceptible objects. I can now return to what I take, and shall argue, to be a structural similarity between Plato's theory of the soul as tripartite and Aristotle's theory of motivation. This is that both theories exhibit a conception of human motivation that combines aspects of both Empiricism and Rationalism in one integrated theory. On this conception, it is a fact of human psychology that fully formed motivating conditions can arise with no cognitive resources other than sensory capacities being employed at the time. That is to say, only sense-perception and the retrieval of sensory impressions are in play. Other cases of human motivation, however, are not just, in this sense, a matter of sensory experience, because they crucially involve the active use of distinctively rational resources, such as the ability to apprehend intelligible forms, or the ability to grasp means–end relations. Plato's and Aristotle's conceptions of motivation and of the practical cognition involved in it are, I shall attempt to show, remarkably continuous. Writing about them together will, I hope, enable readers to appreciate this continuity, and to achieve a clearer and richer understanding of both of them. Given that the subject matter is difficult and in some respects rather unfamiliar, any increase in clarity will, I trust, be most welcome.

---

[11] I am following C. Taylor's suggestion in his *The Atomists: Leucippus and Democritus* (Toronto: University of Toronto Press, 1999), 204.

[12] Note Philoponus' report in his *De Anima* commentary (35, 12): 'Democritus says that the soul is partless and is not a thing equipped with a plurality of powers, claiming that thought and sense-perception are the same thing and that they are manifestations of one power.'

PART ONE

APPETITE AND REASON IN PLATO'S *REPUBLIC*

Introduction

In Part I, I shall offer an interpretation of Plato's theory of the tripartite soul as it is presented in the *Republic*. Two groups of claims are central to my interpretation. The first group concerns partition of the soul as such. Plato's theory, I shall argue, holds the embodied human soul to be a composite of a number of distinct and specifiable items. The theory takes it that impulses to act arise, not from the soul as a whole, but, in each case, specifically from some part of it. It is, moreover, part of the theory that while the embodied human soul can give rise to a desire for, and a simultaneous aversion to, one and the same thing, no individual part of the soul can by itself give rise to motivational conflict of this particular kind.

My second group of claims focuses on the lowest of the theory's three parts of the soul, appetite. I shall argue that it is part of Plato's theory that appetite is non-rational in the strong sense of lacking the capacity for reasoning. At the same time, the theory takes appetite, like the other parts of the soul, to be capable of giving rise to fully formed impulses to act, so that it can, all by itself, get a person to behave in some specific way or other. It can, for example, get Leontius to run towards a pile of corpses lying by the side of the road, so as to take a close look at them (*Republic* 4, 439 E 5–440 A 4). The notion of a part of the soul that is incapable of reasoning, but capable of giving rise to episodes of behaviour, even to episodes of human behaviour, sets the scene for the book's central theme: the idea, shared by Plato and Aristotle, that while reason can, all by itself, motivate a person to act, parts or aspects of the soul other than reason are equipped with non-rational cognitive resources that are sufficient for the generation of fully formed motivating conditions.

My main argument for the non-rationality of appetite, as Plato conceives of it, depends on my view of what Platonic soul-partition comes to. My argument, in a nutshell, is this. According to my view of partition, no individual soul-part can give rise to a desire for, and a simultaneous aversion to, one and the same thing. Plato conceives of appetite as being naturally attracted to pleasure (*Republic* 4, 439 D 6–8). If appetite is rational, it is capable of forming reasoned desires for what it takes to be better in the long run, and of forming reasoned aversions to what it takes to be worse in the long run. If so, it is vulnerable to just the kind of motivational conflict that Platonic soul-partition rules out at the level of individual soul-parts. For appetite's nature will saddle it with desires for pleasures that it may, if it is rational, at the same time be averse to, on the grounds that pursuing the pleasure in question would be worse in the long run. Therefore, Plato's theory of the tripartite soul is coherent only if he conceives of appetite as non-rational.

Chapter 1 is introductory. It lays out in some detail what the rest of Part 1 is meant to establish, against the background of recent and not so recent literature on Plato's psychological theory. Chapter 2 offers an in-depth discussion of the *Republic*'s argument for tripartition of the soul. The main purpose of that discussion is to argue for my view of what Platonic soul-partition comes to. Plato's argument for tripartition depends crucially on what is standardly referred to as the Principle of Opposites, which says that the same thing cannot at the same time do opposites in the same respect and in relation to the same thing. I shall argue that the context of the overall argument makes it clear that what this principle is supposed to mean is that the same thing cannot at the same time be the proper subject of opposite predicates that apply in the same respect and in relation to the same thing. I shall show, moreover, that Plato takes desire for, and aversion to, one and the same thing to exemplify a pair of opposite predicates that apply in the same respect and in relation to the same thing. He plainly accepts, furthermore, that it is a common occurrence for someone to desire, and *at the same time* to be averse to, one and the same thing. According to my interpretation, he is committed to the view that such motivational conflicts always reveal a partition of the soul, with one part being the proper subject of the desire, and another part being the proper subject of the aversion. He is also committed to the view that if a part of the soul is incomposite, it cannot itself harbour such motivational conflicts. And it can be shown that he conceives of the three parts of the soul that are argued for in *Republic* 4 as incomposite.

Chapter 3 defends my interpretation of Platonic soul-partition against the objection that a Platonic soul is not the right kind of thing for it to make sense to say of it that it genuinely has parts. It also addresses the philosophical cost of soul-partition, so understood. It does so by considering Socrates' remark in *Republic* 10 that 'it isn't easy for a composite of many parts to be everlasting if it isn't composed in the finest way, yet this is how the soul now appeared to us' (*Republic* 10, 611 B 5–7). The chapter closes with a brief glance at Aristotle's psychological theory, by considering an Aristotelian concern about soul-partition. Aristotle thinks of the soul as, among other things, a principle that accounts for the unity of the organism it ensouls. However, for something to be a genuine principle of unity, it cannot itself be a composite. For composites stand in need of unification by something else. Aristotle's position on soul-partition will be a recurring theme of this book. We shall find that Aristotle is unwilling to commit himself to the view that the human soul is a thing of parts. One question this raises is whether Aristotle can consistently accept the Platonic analysis of human desire into three kinds without accepting the Platonic analysis of the human soul into three parts. I shall turn to this question in the book's conclusion; my answer will be affirmative.

Chapter 4 completes the argument for my view of what Platonic soul-partition comes to. It does so by disarming two prima facie reasons against it. One of these is that Plato, in *Republic* 8 (553 A 1–555 B 2), seems to describe a case of motivational conflict within appetite, and he seems to have in mind just the kind of conflict that Platonic soul-partition, on my view, rules out at the level of individual soul-parts. There is good reason to think, however, that the motivational conflict that Plato is describing at 553 A 1–555 B 2 is supposed to be a conflict, not *within* appetite, but between reason and appetite, or between reason and spirit on the one hand and appetite on the other. Moreover, many scholars think that, in *Republic* 9, Plato implicitly attributes to appetite the capacity for instrumental reasoning. If they are right, this not only refutes my claim that Plato's theory holds appetite to be incapable of reasoning. It also throws in doubt my view of Platonic soul-partition. For if appetite is rational, it is vulnerable to motivational conflict of just the kind that, according to my view of partition, Plato's theory rules out at the level of individual soul-parts. So much the worse, one might think, for my view of partition. (Alternatively, so much the worse for Plato's theory.) I shall argue, however, that Plato neither says nor implies that appetite is capable of instrumental reasoning.

The chapter ends with some remarks about Plato's theory of human motivation, as it emerges from my interpretation of the argument for tripartition of the soul. One remark is forward-looking. This is that my interpretation presents Plato as operating with a conception of what is distinctive of rational motivation that is not only clear and robust, but also importantly continuous with Aristotle's conception of rational motivation. I shall turn to Aristotle's conception in Chapter 12. The main points of contact between Plato and Aristotle are, first, that rational motivation depends on thoughts to the effect that something or other is good, and, secondly, that it brings into play desires of a very special kind. These spring from, and are informed by, the subject's grasp of means–end, or 'for the sake of', relations. The formation of such desires involves the transmission of desire from A to B in such a way that B comes to be desired specifically as a means to, or for the sake of, A.

1

Parts of the Soul

In book 4 of Plato's *Republic*, as is well known, Socrates offers a complicated and somewhat problematic argument for the conclusion that the human soul, at any rate in its embodied state, consists of three parts. One question is what Socrates commits himself to in arguing, in the way he does, that the soul is composed of parts—never mind the further questions of how many parts there are, and how they are to be characterized. Now it seems to me that concerning this first question, of what a commitment to parts of the soul in this context comes to, some recent commentators have shown an objectionable tendency to downplay what is involved in the view Socrates argues for, in a way that fails to do justice to the detail of the argument in *Republic* 4,[1] and that obscures what arguably is a significant disagreement between Plato and Aristotle about the nature and constitution of the human soul.

Here is a brief and incomplete statement of the view I shall argue for. The *Republic*'s psychological theory amounts to significantly more than the claim that there are a number of different kinds or forms of human motivation. It also involves the further claims, first, that in order to account for the fact that motivations of these different kinds or forms can (and frequently do) conflict with one another, it is necessary to accept that the embodied human soul is not, as one might think it is, a single undifferentiated thing, but is in fact a composite of a number of distinct and specifiable items; and, secondly, that it is specifically from these distinct items, rather than from the soul as a whole, that human motivation, in its various forms, arises. If so, Socrates is not only offering an analysis of human motivation and of human desire. He is also adopting a substantial and problematic position on the nature and constitution of the human soul in its embodied state. Now, we might find the analysis of motivation that the discussion undoubtedly contains a great deal more appealing than the position on the nature of the soul that it argues for. We might even think that Plato made a mistake in arguing,

---

[1] T. Irwin, *Plato's Moral Theory* (Oxford: Oxford University Press, 1977), 327, offers a particularly clear statement of the kind of interpretation that I am meaning to oppose: 'For the purposes of Book 4, then, Plato's general claims about "kinds", "parts", and "things" amount to the claim that there are desires differing in kind unrecognized by Socrates.' Cf. also C. D. C. Reeve, *Philosopher-Kings: The Argument of Plato's* Republic (Princeton: Princeton University Press, 1988), 134, 163–4; and C. Shields, 'Simple Souls', in E. Wagner (ed.), *Essays on Plato's Psychology* (Lanham, Md.: Lexington Books, 2001), 137–56.

not just that there are a variety of different forms of human motivation, but also that there are a corresponding variety of different parts of the human soul. But this should not lead us to ignore or misrepresent the latter position, if we wish to arrive at a clear view of Plato's psychological theory, as well as of the history of ancient philosophical thinking about the nature of the soul.

In addition to the question of what precisely is involved in taking the human soul to be a thing of parts—a question about *partition*—there are of course further questions, perhaps ones that are more interesting to some of us, about how many such parts there are, and what can be said about them—questions about *tri*parti-tion. One common worry is that, given the criterion for partition that Socrates employs, he might wind up with more parts than just three, so that the human soul may turn out to have a structure that is significantly different from the struc-ture of his imaginary ideal city, as it is described at 372 E–434 C, presumably with the result that his accounts of justice in the city and justice in the soul will fail to be relevantly parallel. In that case Socrates and his interlocutors, as agreed at 434 E 4–435 A 4, would have to revisit, and modify appropriately, their account of the just city. It is important, in this connection, to distinguish between two different worries, both of which envisage a larger number of soul-parts than three, but only one of which arises from concerns to do with the criterion for partition that Socrates relies on. The first worry is that the parts of the soul that Socrates intro-duces in book 4 of the *Republic*—namely reason, spirit, and appetite—just are not enough to account for the huge variety of psychological phenomena that human beings actually exhibit. It is difficult to see how the Platonic tripartition of reason, spirit, and appetite can explain grief, for instance. Grief is, one might think, not a peculiar function of a single one of these three parts, the way anger, for instance, is a function of spirit, or hunger is a function of appetite. Is it, then, some kind of joint effort of cooperating parts? Or is there a special part, responsible for grief, perhaps among other things, in addition to the other three parts? These seem to be legitimate questions about Plato's psychological theory, and ones that a compre-hensive defence of the theory, if it were to be attempted, would have to address.

They are not, however, questions that arise from considerations about the crite-rion that Socrates employs in arguing for the view that there are parts of the soul. As is well known, Socrates argues for parts of the soul, roughly speaking, by appealing to certain cases of psychological conflict, and to a principle to the effect that conflicts of this kind can only be attributed to things that have distinct parts, so that the conflict in question can properly be described as a conflict between at least two parts. A second worry about too many parts, then, stems from the thought that there appear to be many psychological conflicts that cannot be properly described as conflicts between distinct Platonic parts—say, reason and appetite—but that look rather like conflicts *within* one such part or another, typi-cally appetite. It is, after all, not too difficult to see that 'bodily' desires like hunger, thirst, and sexual arousal can generate psychological conflicts all by themselves, without any involvement of reason or spirit. Moreover, Socrates evidently does not limit appetite to basic bodily desires like hunger, thirst, and sexual arousal, but also attributes to it relatively more refined desires, such as the desire for money.[2] But the more variety there is among the desires of appetite, and the more refined its desires can be, the harder it is to believe that psychological conflicts between such desires are not, as a matter of fact, quite common. And indeed several commentators[3] think that in Book 8 of the *Republic*, where Plato has occasion to describe and discuss in some detail a number of cases of psychological conflict, he describes just such a conflict between desires that he must take to be desires of one and the same part of the soul, namely appetite (553 A 1–555 B 2). So the worry is that if Plato takes conflicts between desires to reveal a partition of the soul, in such a way that distinct parts are responsible for the conflicting desires in question, he will have to accept a sub-partition at least of the appetitive part. Nor is it easy to see that just one such sub-partition will be needed; it rather seems as if the need for further subdivisions might arise over and over again. If so, the problem is not just that Plato will have to accept more than three parts of the soul, or indeed indeterminately many ones, it will also turn out that at least one of the three parts that he introduces, the appetitive part, is not actually a basic part at all, but itself a composite item, perhaps one with indeterminately many parts.

Now, it is reasonably clear that the argument is meant to demonstrate that the human soul consists of three parts—reason, spirit, and appetite. While Socrates does seem to allow that further parts may come to light in addition to the three parts he introduces (443 D 7–8), he does not even hint at the possibility that any one of the three parts he argues for might turn out to be not a basic part after all, but itself a complex or composite item, reduplicating the complexity of the soul as a whole. Moreover, if Plato thought that the appetitive part might itself be complex, there would be no reason to think that an aversion that conflicts with some desire of appetite must belong to a part of the soul different from appetite. (Likewise, if the soul is complex, there is no reason to think that in cases of conflicting desires at least one of the desires in question must belong to something other than the soul—the body, for instance.) But when the question arises whether spirit, or anger, belongs to the appetitive part, an idea that in fact seems plausible at least to Glaucon (439 E 2–4, cf. 440 E 1), the fact that spirit can oppose, and conflict with, a desire of appetite is taken to establish right away that spirit must be different from appetite (440 A 5–7). It is a presupposition of the argument that the appetitive part is basic or simple, not complex.

It would be desirable, then, to be able to show how Plato could have thought that his argument succeeds in establishing reason, spirit, and appetite as basic, incomposite parts of the human soul. The most satisfactory way of doing this

---

[2] 442 A 6–7, 580 E 5–581 A 1, 581 A 3–7, 586 D 4–5; cf. 435 D 9–436 A 3.

[3] For instance, Irwin, *Plato's Moral Theory*, 327; J. Cooper, 'Plato's theory of human motivation', *History of Philosophy Quarterly*, 1 (1984), reprinted in his *Reason and Emotion* (Princeton: Princeton University Press, 1999), 123; M. Woods, 'Plato's division of the soul', *Proceedings of the British Academy*, 73 (1987), 31.

would obviously be to offer an interpretation of the argument such that it does in fact succeed, just as Plato presumably thought it did, in establishing these three parts as basic parts of the soul. Recent writers have attempted to offer such an interpretation, roughly along the following lines.[4] If conflict between desires of one and the same part of the soul does occur, in fact quite commonly, and is acknowledged to occur by Plato, then it presumably is not conflict as such, or *mere* conflict, that constitutes Socrates' criterion for partition of the soul, but a somewhat special kind of conflict. In fact it is fairly clear that at least one of the examples of psychological conflict that Socrates uses in the argument does exemplify a somewhat special kind of conflict, exhibiting a feature that one might well think sets this kind of conflict apart from ordinary conflicts between competing desires of the appetitive part.

When Leontius attempts to resist his desire to take a close look at some corpses (439 E 5–440 A 4), he is not just experiencing a conflict between two desires, one a desire to take a close look, the other a desire not to. A description of what is going on just in these terms would miss an important feature of the situation: for Leontius seems to have an aversion not just to taking a close look at the corpses, but also to *having the desire to do so*. This latter aversion expresses itself in the anger with which he addresses what he takes to be responsible for the desire, his eyes. If so, the case is somewhat special in that it exemplifies not just a conflict between two desires that, as it were, operate on the same level, but a conflict that also involves a desiderative attitude, an aversion, to one of the conflicting desires. In other words, the conflict in question is not just a conflict between two competing first-order desires. It also crucially involves a second-order desire, namely an aversion to having a desire of the first order. Perhaps, then, it is not just any conflict between desires, but the somewhat special case that involves a second-order desire at least on one side of the conflict, that according to Plato reveals a partition of the soul? This hypothesis at any rate has the advantage that it enables us to make room for ordinary conflicts between first-order desires that belong to one and the same part of the soul; and we have seen that it looks as if Plato might need to have room for such conflicts.

Moreover, it has seemed to most recent commentators that Plato's lowest part of the soul, the appetitive part, which he refers to as non-rational, actually has some features that we, though perhaps not Plato, think of as rational, for instance the capacity for means–end reasoning.[5] If so, the question arises what precisely Plato is meaning to deny to the appetitive part when he calls it non-rational or, to

⁴ Irwin, *Plato's Moral Theory*, 327; T. Irwin, *Plato's Ethics* (Oxford: Oxford University Press, 1995), 207–9, 211–13, 216–17; A. Price, *Mental Conflict* (London: Routledge, 1995), 47–8; cf. Cooper, 'Plato's theory of human motivation', 123.

⁵ J. Annas, *An Introduction to Plato's* Republic (Oxford: Oxford University Press, 1981), 129–30; Cooper, 'Plato's theory of human motivation', 128; Irwin, *Plato's Ethics*, 282; Price, *Mental Conflict*, 60–1; M. Burnyeat, 'Culture and society in Plato's *Republic*', in G. Peterson (ed.), *The Tanner Lectures on Human Values* 20 (Salt Lake City: University of Utah Press, 1999), 227; C. Bobonich, *Plato's Utopia Recast: His Later Ethics and Politics* (Oxford: Oxford University Press, 2002), 244.

put it more dramatically, what rationality as Plato conceives of it comes to. Confronting that question, we might with some plausibility hope that Plato's concern with second-order desires could turn out to be crucial to his conception of rationality. The suggestion might be that, for Plato, second-order desires play a role in identifying reason as a part of the soul that is the source of a certain kind of value-based motivation, of first-order desires that are in a certain way sensitive and responsive to desires of a higher order, in a way the desires of appetite are not. The suggestion may seem attractive, but is not without difficulty. One obvious problem is that Plato does not seem to limit second-order desires to reason. In fact, the one passage that most clearly seems to make use of a second-order desire in arguing for a partition of the soul does not, as we have seen, concern reason at all: the partition in question is the one between Leontius' spirit and appetite, and Leontius' second-order desire—or more precisely, aversion—belongs not to his reason, but to his spirit.

For reasons that will soon become obvious, I am not in fact proposing to pursue this suggestion. It will be clear by now that a discussion of what is involved in Plato's tripartion of the soul will, in more ways than one, concern Plato's conception of reason. In what follows, I shall argue against a number of central claims that recent writers have made and that I have already stated or at least alluded to. Part of the upshot will be that second-order desires are *not* needed in specifying the kind of psychological conflict that according to Plato reveals a partition of the soul. In arguing for that conclusion, I shall attempt to show that there is a clear sense in which conflict between desires of appetite is not, as a matter of fact, very common after all, so much so that it is relatively plausible to assume both that it does not standardly occur and that Plato thought it does not standardly occur. I shall also argue that Plato does not, in fact, describe, in book 8 of the *Republic*, cases of conflict between desires that he takes to belong to one and the same part of the soul. Moreover, I shall present reasons for thinking that when Plato denies reason to the appetitive part—and also, for that matter, to the spirited part—he is presupposing a conception of reason that is perfectly recognizable and indeed attractive, though not, of course, uncontroversial.

2

The Argument for Tripartition

Many readers of the *Republic* have felt that Socrates argues for spirit as a third part of the soul simply because the ideal city he has outlined contains three classes of citizens (roughly speaking, philosophers, the military, and businesspeople), and so he needs corresponding parts of the soul. The identification of reason and appetite as somehow distinct is, on this view, a psychologically valid step, whereas the introduction of spirit rests not on psychological grounds, but on Socrates' dialectical needs in the context. It may be worth pointing out that to think this is very much to get things the wrong way around. The idea that the just city contains these particular three classes of citizens itself rests on familiar ideas about human motivation and character, ones that quite clearly predate the *Republic*. One of these ideas is that there are in human affairs three fundamental kinds of motive or incentive, three importantly different kinds of thing that people focus their attention and desires on and that they structure their minds and lives around: wealth, honour (or esteem), and wisdom; and that, correspondingly, there are three kinds of people, naturally finding themselves leading three kinds of life: the life of business or money-making, the life of political or military excellence and prominence, and, much less commonly chosen, the life dedicated to learning and the achievement of wisdom.

The idea of these three kinds of motive already appears to be in play in Plato's *Apology*, when Socrates asks an imaginary fellow citizen:

Good Sir, you are an Athenian, a citizen of the greatest city with the greatest reputation for both wisdom and power; are you not ashamed of your eagerness to possess as much wealth, reputation, and honours as possible, while you do not care for nor give thought to wisdom or truth, or the best possible state of your soul? (*Apology* 29 D 7–E 3)

The idea of three kinds of character corresponding to these three kinds of motive is clearly present in the *Phaedo*, when Socrates says that philosophers, lovers of wisdom after all, abstain from bodily desire 'not for fear of wasting their substance and of poverty, which the majority and the money-lovers fear, nor for fear of dishonour and ill repute, like the ambitious and lovers of honour' (82 B 10–C 8; cf. *Phaedo* 68 B 8–C 3). Thus when Socrates, in book 9 of the *Republic*, classifies human beings in general (not just citizens of the just city) into three kinds— philosophical, victory-loving, and profit-loving (581 C 4–5)—the idea is, to be sure, embedded in a richer psychological framework than it ever was in earlier dialogues, but it would nevertheless be a mistake to think that it is a novel idea that results specifically from the political theory of the *Republic* let alone from Socrates' dialectical concerns in *Republic* 4. It should be clear, then, that Plato, at least, thought there was good psychological reason to identify spirit as a distinct part of the soul, as the source of, for instance, desires for honour and self-assertion, and of anger at slights and insults.

Moreover, the idea of three fundamental kinds of motive, and corresponding psychological tendencies and characters, is an important part of the background to the argument for tripartition of the soul in *Republic* 4. At the outset of the argument, it is already agreed between Socrates and Glaucon that 'each one of us has within himself the same kinds and characteristics (εἴδη τε καὶ ἤθη) as the city', namely spirit (τὸ θυμοειδές), love of learning (τὸ φιλομαθές), and love of money (τὸ φιλοχρήματον) (435 D 9–436 A 3). What Socrates and Glaucon agree on at this preliminary stage is not just the familiar idea that there are in human affairs three importantly different kinds of motive, and corresponding psychological tendencies and characters. It is the stronger claim that at least for a suitable range of people, which includes Socrates, Glaucon, and others like them, each individual has all of these psychological tendencies within him or her, and so is sensitive to all of these kinds of motive.

Now, it would be a mistake to think that the Platonic analysis of human motivation into three kinds or forms is already in evidence here in a full-fledged form, before the argument for tripartition even gets started. While we do have the idea of three kinds of psychological tendency being present in each one of us, making us sensitive and responsive to three kinds of motive, we do not yet have a full account of what these tendencies are and how they operate and interact. At the same time, if Plato's purpose had been to provide no more, and no less, than an analysis of the different forms or kinds of human motivation, he could have proceeded right away with a statement of the nature and proper functioning of each one of these tendencies, arriving at a conception of three distinctive forms of motivation by fleshing out and deepening our understanding of the three tendencies that have already been identified. This would have involved specifying, perhaps among other things, what the natural objects of pursuit are for each one of these tendencies, what their proper roles are in the life of a human being, and how they involve, or fail to involve, reason. It is very much worth noting and emphasizing that this is not, in fact, how Socrates does proceed at this stage of the discussion.[1] As we shall see, Socrates goes on to argue that in order to account properly for the fact that the embodied human soul has these different tendencies, and in particular for the fact that they can, and frequently do, conflict among themselves, it is necessary to say that the soul, in which they reside, is a thing of

---

[1] Cf. Irwin, *Plato's Moral Theory*, 327: 'Plato would have done better to introduce his argument about desires at once.'

parts, in such a way that the different tendencies in question can be attributed to different parts of the soul.

Having answered what he presents as an easy question, whether the soul has in it the same kinds and characteristics as the city, Socrates goes on to raise some difficult questions:

> Do we do each of these things with the same [sc. part of ourselves],[2] or do we do them with three different (parts)? Do we learn with one (part), get angry with another, and with some third (part) desire the pleasures of food, drink, sex, and the others that are closely akin to them? Or do we act with the whole of our soul in each of these cases, when we set out after something? (*Republic* 436 A 8–B 4)

These are questions specifically about motivation, about 'setting out after something' or, as one might translate alternatively, about 'being impelled' (ὅταν ὁρμήσωμεν, 436 B 3). Socrates envisages three kinds of psychological phenomena as being involved in being motivated or impelled: having bodily desires, being angry, and learning. The first two are relatively straightforward as motivating factors or conditions, but we may be curious about how bodily desire is supposed to be related to the money-loving kind or characteristic in the soul, with which Socrates seems to associate it. Nor is it clear how he takes learning to be relevant to motivation. The thought is presumably that learning something is (or anyhow can be) a matter of actively setting out after something, namely after the knowledge or understanding one wishes to acquire, or the subject-matter one wishes to master and make available to one's understanding.[3]

It is, however, plain what the heart of Socrates' question is: given that there are, or seem to be, three ways in which humans are impelled to act or are impelled to engage in activity—experiencing bodily desire, being angry, actively learning or working out something—is it the soul *as a whole* that is on every relevant occasion responsible for motivating conditions of these three different kinds, or is it rather the case that, for each kind of motivating condition, it is specifically some part of the soul that is responsible for it?

The context of Socrates' question allows us to say something more definite about what is, or would be, involved in the soul as a whole, or alternatively some part or other of it, being responsible for motivating conditions of one kind or another. The idea is that it is either the soul as a whole or, on the alternative view, specifically some part of it, that is, strictly and accurately speaking, the bearer or subject of relevant motivating conditions—for instance, of a desire or an emotion. If it turns out that it is, in fact, specifically some part of the soul that is the bearer of (say) a desire, then it follows right away that it is not the soul *as a whole* that is the bearer of this particular desire. It does not, in that case, follow that the desire in

---

[2] Plato's Greek does not here include any word meaning 'part'. Socrates does, however, speak of the items in question as being in us (436 A 10), and in presenting the alternative view he uses the expression 'the soul as a whole' (ὅλῃ τῇ ψυχῇ). Later in book 4, he uses the word μέρος for parts of the soul (442 B 10, C 4; cf. 581 A 6).   [3] I owe this suggestion to John Cooper.

question cannot be attributed to *the soul* at all. It can be so attributed, but it should be understood that the desire belongs to the soul in virtue of the fact that it belongs specifically to the relevant part of it. Thus we might (in that case) say that the proper subject or bearer of the desire is the relevant part of the soul, and that the desire belongs to the soul derivatively, in virtue of the fact that it belongs to a part of it. To see this, let us consider the context of Socrates' question.

Within the argument for tripartition of the soul (as well as, of course, elsewhere), Socrates attributes desires to *the soul* that he clearly takes to be desires of specifically some part of it. For instance, thirst is attributed to the soul at 439 A 9–B 3.[4] He also, of course, speaks of parts of the soul as having desires (e.g. thirst at 439 B 4), and as demanding and prompting action, by pulling and dragging the soul, or the person, in the appropriate way (439 B 3–4; D 1–2). Moreover, there is good reason to think that, on Socrates' view, it is (at least for certain purposes) preferable to attribute a desire to the part of the soul that it specifically belongs to, rather than simply to *the soul*—in part, I take it, because to attribute it to the part in question is to attribute it to that to which it, strictly and accurately speaking, belongs. Considering the case of thirst and simultaneous aversion to drinking, Socrates says that it must be one thing in the soul that thirsts and a different thing that draws back from drinking; he then offers the following comparison:

In the same way, I suppose, to say of the archer that his hands at the same time push the bow away and draw it towards him is not to speak well (οὐ καλῶς ἔχει λέγειν).[5] Rather, we ought to say that the one hand pushes it away and the other draws it towards him. (*Republic* 439 B 8–C 1)

Likewise, when there are special reasons to be accurate about what precisely it is that is the bearer of a desire or an aversion,[6] to say that it is *the soul* that desires and is at the same time averse to the same thing is not to speak well, though it is not to speak falsely. Rather, we ought to say that it is one part of the soul that desires, and a different part that is averse. In so doing we properly identify the items that the motivating conditions in question, strictly and accurately speaking, belong to. And, to anticipate a bit, once we render the situation perspicuous in this way, we also see clearly that even though it involves opposition, and opposites that in a way belong to the same thing (namely, the soul), it nevertheless does not in fact violate the Principle of Opposites.

---

[4] Note also 439 D 6–8: 'We'll call the part of the soul . . . with which it lusts, hungers, thirsts, and gets excited by other appetites the non-rational, appetitive part.'

[5] Grube–Reeve in *Plato: Complete Works* overtranslate: 'it's wrong to say'. Cf. 436 C 12–D 1: 'we wouldn't consider, I think, that he ought to put it like that'. Both of these expressions (which occur in closely connected contexts) are carefully nuanced, and they stop well short of claiming that to speak in the relevant way is to speak *falsely*.

[6] Note 436 C 6–10: 'Is it possible for the same thing to be at rest and in motion at the same time and in the same respect?—Not at all.—Let's make our agreement more precise (ἀκριβέστερον) in order to avoid disputes later on.'

If this is along the right lines, we can reformulate Socrates' question at 436 A 8–B 4 in the following way. Given that there are three distinct ways in which humans are impelled to exert themselves, is it the soul as a whole that is, in every one of the three kinds of case, the bearer of motivating conditions, or is it rather that, for each kind of motivating condition, it is specifically some part of the soul that is the bearer of motivating conditions of the relevant kind? We can now see this as a question concerning the status of the three 'kinds' in the soul that Socrates and Glaucon have already identified, namely the 'spirited' kind, the learning-loving kind, and the money-loving kind. According to one candidate answer, they are features or tendencies (or something like that) of a unitary soul that, on each occasion, acts or is active as a whole. According to another view, which is the one Socrates is going to argue for, these three 'kinds' are distinct parts of a composite, parts with their own doings or ways of being active, and it is specifically to these parts, rather than to the soul as a whole, that motivating conditions of three different kinds belong. The first alternative allows the view that the embodied human soul is an incomposite item. The second alternative does not. To show the second alternative to be correct, therefore, is to show that the embodied human soul is a composite. And, as we shall see in the next chapter, Socrates makes it quite clear that he takes the argument for tripartition of the soul to show that the human soul, at least in its embodied state, is a composite of a plurality of items (611 B 5–7).[7]

To resolve his question, Socrates appeals to what I shall follow convention in calling the *Principle of Opposites* (**PO**):

It is clear that the same thing will not be willing to do or undergo opposites in the same respect, in relation to the same thing, and at the same time.   (*Republic* 436 B 8–9)

He adds that 'if we ever find this happening in the soul, we'll know that we aren't dealing with one thing but many'. That is to say that if they ever find the soul doing or undergoing opposites, in the same respect, in relation to the same thing, and at the same time, they will know that they are dealing with a plurality of items. It would not follow right away that the soul is not a single thing at all, since having unity is compatible with having, or consisting of, a plurality of parts. But it would be the case that if the soul has unity, it has unity in the way composites do.[8]

Having stated **PO**, Socrates pauses to consider two apparent counterexamples. In doing so, he introduces two ways of analysing apparent cases of simultaneous opposition. As we shall see, only one of the two analyses he offers involves a

---

[7] Note also 436 C 1–2, 443 D 6–E 2, 554 D 9–E 1, and 588 D 5–6.

[8] Plato seems to think, reasonably enough, that (in the embodied state) unity of soul, or anyhow completed unity of soul (note παντάπασιν at 443 E 1), is something to be achieved rather than something to be taken for granted. It crucially involves a harmonious ordering of reason, spirit, and appetite. See 443 D 6–E 2. For discussion concerning the importance of structure to Plato's thinking about composition, see V. Harte, *Plato on Parts and Wholes: The Metaphysics of Structure* (Oxford: Oxford University Press, 2002), chs. 3 and 4.

partition of the subject in such a way that one part of it turns out to be the bearer of one opposite and another part of it the bearer of the other opposite. We should note that it is this particular kind of analysis that Socrates applies to the opposition between desire and aversion. In doing so he makes it clear that he conceives of the parts of the soul that he is arguing for as being responsible for motivating conditions of three kinds precisely by being the bearers of relevant psychological states such as, crucially, desire and aversion.

The first prima facie counterexample that he considers involves a person standing still and moving his arms and head at the same time. Someone might say that this is a counterexample to **PO**, in that it involves the same thing (a person) doing or undergoing opposites at the same time: the same thing is at once in motion and at rest. (The qualifications 'in the same respect' and 'in relation to the same thing' are employed neither in the example's statement nor in its resolution, presumably because they are inapplicable or irrelevant.) Socrates' response is that this fails as a counterexample to **PO**: what one ought to say is *not* that the same person is at once in motion and at rest, but rather that part of the person is at rest and part of the person is in motion.[9] Once one is appropriately precise about what the bearers of the relevant predicates are, it becomes clear that a plurality of items is involved (arms, head, legs, and the like), and that only some of these are in motion while others remain at rest. Thus it is not the case that the person *as a whole* is at rest and in motion at the same time.[10] This analysis, then, involves recognizing that the subject in question is a thing of parts, and identifying relevant parts of the subject as the proper bearers of opposite predicates.

The second prima facie counterexample is presented as being more subtle (436 D 4–5) than the first one, and it seems to be designed specifically to block the kind of analysis that Socrates applied to the first apparent counterexample.[11] An object rotating on the same spot, e.g. a spinning top, seems to be *as a whole* at rest and in motion at the same time. Having seen the first example resolved as a case of one part of the subject undergoing one opposite and another part undergoing another, Socrates' imaginary opponent produces a second apparent counterexample, which is presented in a way that must, I think, be meant specifically to rule out analysis in terms of parts of the subject as the proper bearers of the opposites in

---

[9] Grammatically it would be possible to take τὸ μέν ... τὸ δέ ... at 436 D 1 as accusatives rather than nominatives, and to construe them as accusatives of respect, yielding something like '[but we should say] that the person is at rest with respect to one part, and in motion with respect to another'. However, comparison with the closely related archer passage, at 439 B 8–C 1, militates against this reading: as in the earlier passage, an expression that predicates opposites of a composite object—the person, the archer's arms—is indicated to be unsatisfactory, and is replaced by a more accurate expression that predicates one opposite of one part of the composite, and the other opposite of another part of it. (Fortunately, ἄλλη μὲν ... χείρ, ἑτέρα δέ ... , at 439 B 10, *must* be nominatives.)

[10] If so, we should distinguish between saying (about the example under consideration) that the person is at rest and in motion at the same time, and that the person *as a whole* is at rest and in motion at the same time. The former is imprecise but not false, the latter is simply false.

[11] I have learned from the extremely illuminating discussion of this passage in Bobonich, *Plato's Utopia Recast*, 226–35.

question.[12] The new example is remarkably well chosen, and it is plausibly described: we presumably do want to say about a spinning top both that the whole of it, rather than specifically some part or other of it, is in motion (rotation, that is), and that the whole of it, rather than specifically some part or other, is at rest (for instance, because it does not incline or 'wobble').

Socrates rejects this second example as a counterexample to **PO**, in a way that unfortunately is not as clear as one might wish. One thing that, however, is quite clear and that deserves emphasis is that he does *not* resort to analysis in terms of distinct bearers of opposite predicates. Rather, he qualifies the predicates 'being at rest' and 'being in motion'. This allows him to say that the same thing—the spinning top as a whole—is at rest in one respect and is at the same time in motion in another respect. He notes that a spinning top is a complex object, involving (as he puts it) something upright or vertical (εὐθύ) as well as something round (περιφερές). With respect to the vertical, Socrates says, the spinning top is at rest, since it does not incline in any direction. At the same time, he adds (somewhat obscurely), the top is 'in circular motion with respect to the round'; which may mean simply that it is rotating.[13] If so, Socrates resolves the second apparent counterexample to **PO** not by distinguishing between distinct parts of the relevant subject as being the proper bearers of opposite predicates, but rather by distinguishing between inclination as motion in one respect and rotation as motion in another respect.[14] As a result, he is in a position to say what presumably we want to say about a spinning top, namely that it as a whole is in motion and at rest at the same time; and he wants to add, reasonably enough, that it does not do or undergo these opposites in the same respect.

The discussion of apparent counterexamples to **PO** makes available two ways of resolving or analysing apparent cases of simultaneous opposition. The first of

[12] I agree here with Bobonich, ibid., 229.

[13] As Bobonich, ibid., points out (529), merely to say that the top is in circular motion is not fully to specify the kind of motion that it engages in. Revolution, too, is circular motion. So it might be that 'with respect to the round' is supposed to indicate the direction involved in the top's motion, so as to set its rotation apart from other cases of circular motion.

[14] If this is along the right lines, one might wonder why it seems to Plato worth noting that 'the vertical' and 'the round' are *in* the top (436 D 9–E 1). One might even think that this seems to suggest that Socrates is meaning to attribute the opposites of motion and rest to distinct parts of the spinning top, namely motion to 'the round' and rest to 'the vertical'. It should be noted, however, that Socrates neither says nor implies that it is specifically some part or other, but *not* the whole, of the spinning top that is in motion or at rest. To do so would be to offer an incorrect analysis, and it would also amount to an entirely unwarranted rejection of the opponent's pointed description of the top as being *as a whole* at rest and in motion at the same time (436 D 5: οἵ γε στρόβιλοι ὅλοι ἑστᾶσί τε ἅμα καὶ κινοῦνται). On the other hand, if Plato's purpose is simply to distinguish between two kinds of motion, it might seem irrelevant that straightness and roundness are somehow internal to the moving object. It certainly is relevant, however, that to be able to do what a spinning top does, an object *must* have a certain kind of complexity. A point or a vertical line, lacking the required kind of complexity, could not at once be in motion and at rest in the way a top can be. Since this may well be what Plato has in mind, his reference to the top's internal complexity is by itself no good reason to think that he is meaning to analyse the case of a spinning top by attributing motion to one part of it and rest to another.

these involves identifying parts of the subject that are the bearers of the predicates in question. The second way relies on introducing different respects in which the subject as a whole is the bearer of both predicates.[15] When Socrates turns to the case of desire and simultaneous aversion towards the same thing (in this case, drinking), he could hardly be clearer about which way he thinks this should be analysed. He says that it must be one thing in the soul that desires and pulls, and a different thing that is averse and pulls the other way (439 B 3, C 8). He then compares this to an archer's arms at once pushing and pulling the bow, which should be analysed, he thinks, as a matter of one arm pushing while the other arm is pulling. Moreover, the 'with respect to' expressions characteristic of the spinning top analysis are absent from Socrates' discussion concerning cases of opposition between desire and aversion. It is clear, then, that Socrates conceives of the parts of the soul that he is arguing for as being responsible for various kinds of motivating conditions precisely by being the subjects or bearers of psychological states such as desire and aversion.[16] Thus we can conclude that Socrates' commitment to parts of the soul is not just a commitment to the view that there are different kinds of desire, or different forms of human motivation. It crucially includes the claims, first, that the embodied human soul is a composite of a number of distinct and specifiable items and, secondly, that it is specifically from these distinct items, rather than from the soul as a whole, that human motivation, in its various forms, arises.

A central part of Plato's argument for tripartition of the soul will be construed as something like this:

(1) The same thing cannot be characterized by opposites in the same respect, in relation to the same thing, and at the same time.

(2) Desiring and being averse are opposites; desiring to φ, and being averse to φ-ing, are opposites in relation to the same thing.

(3) It happens that the soul desires to φ, and at the same time is averse to φ-ing.

∴(4) The soul has at least two parts.

Before we go on, a number of comments should be made about this part of the argument. It is a striking feature of the argument that qualification in terms of

---

[15] Price, *Mental Conflict*, 40–1, obliterates the difference between these two kinds of analysis; as does Irwin, *Plato's Ethics*, 204.

[16] T. Irwin, *Plato's Ethics*, 204–5, offers an alternative (and incompatible) interpretation, according to which soul-parts are responsible for motivating conditions less directly. On his view, as I understand it, soul-parts are properties 'by which' or 'in respect of which' the soul 'has the properties that were to be explained'. This seems to me unattractive for several reasons. First, it disregards Socrates' careful distinction between two ways of analysing apparent cases of simultaneous opposition (the archer and the spinning top modes of analysis). Secondly, if soul-parts are merely properties, we cannot take literally Socrates' talk of the embodied soul as a composite (610 B 4–6), as one thing composed of a plurality of parts (443 E 1–2). And thirdly, Socrates' (direct) attribution to soul-parts of desires and aversions, pleasures (580 D 6–7), beliefs (571 D 2, 603 A 1–2, 605 C 1–2), and emotions (604 D 7–9, 606 A 3–7) sits awkwardly with a conception of soul-parts as *properties* of the soul (or, for that matter, with a conception of them as capacities or faculties).

different respects entirely drops out of consideration just after its application in the spinning top example. Plato presumably thinks that such qualification is applicable and relevant (for instance) in the case of a spinning top's simultaneous motion and rest, but is either inapplicable or irrelevant in the case of a soul's simultaneous desire for, and aversion to, the same thing. (This is, in fact, a presupposition of the argument.) Why does he think this? The thought might well be that desire and aversion are opposites in precisely the same respect, because they either involve, or are relevantly like, movements of the soul in opposite directions, or the application of force by the soul in opposite directions[17]—as with an archer both pushing her bow away from, and pulling it towards, herself. If so, it is reasonable to think that opposition between desire and aversion towards the same thing is like opposition between motion and rest, which cannot (strictly and accurately speaking) both be predicated of the same thing at the same time, and unlike the opposition, or quasi-opposition, between non-inclination and rotation. In that case, opposition between desire and aversion toward the same thing requires analysis in terms of distinct parts of the subject.

Another remarkable and perhaps somewhat problematic aspect of the argument has already been addressed, but it may be worth revisiting briefly. It might seem that the argument contains a clear counterexample to its first premise, **PO**. **PO** says that the same thing cannot do or undergo opposites in the same respect, in relation to the same thing, and at the same time. Socrates then goes on to show that souls, or persons, sometimes do opposites in the same respect, in relation to the same thing, and at the same time—namely when they desire, and at the same time are averse to, the same thing. Is a given soul, or person, not one and the same thing? Plato need not deny that a soul, or a person, is, in a way, a single thing,[18] or that, in a way, one thing can at the same time do opposites in the same respect, and in relation to the same thing. Nor need he think that this casts doubt on the truth

---

[17] Socrates does not offer a detailed and determinate picture of precisely how desire and aversion involve motion of the soul, or application of force by it, in opposite directions. However, the text abounds with suggestive descriptions. For instance, desiring something involves one's soul's pulling the thing toward oneself (προσάγεσθαι) (437 C 2), while aversion involves the soul's pushing and driving away (ἀπωθεῖν) (437 C 8)—precisely the pair of words used of the archer at 439 B 10–C 1. Other descriptions are perhaps more promising: in the case of opposition between desire for, and aversion to, drinking, the desiring part of the soul is described as pulling the rest of the soul toward drinking (439 B 4, D 1), while the part that is averse pulls the other way (439 B 3).

[18] I reject the claim made in Bobonich, *Plato's Utopia Recast*, 254, that 'the *Republic*'s partitioning theory commits Plato to denying the unity of the person'. 'Specifically', Bobonich adds, 'it commits him to denying that there is a single ultimate subject of all of a person's psychic states and activities.' To deny that there is a single thing that is the proper, non-derivative subject of all of a person's psychological states is *not* to deny the unity of the person. This is because the first denial (which I agree is part of the *Republic*'s psychological theory) is perfectly compatible with holding that the soul, or the person considered as the subject of psychological predicates, has unity in that it is one thing composed of a plurality of parts. Ordinary intuitions concerning the unity of the person, to which Bobonich appeals, are hardly determinate enough to require specifically that the soul is incomposite, or that there is a single item that is the proper, non-derivative subject of all psychological predicates (applied to a single person).

of **PO**. This is because **PO** may well be a claim that is considerably more specific than it seems at first sight to be. It is arguably a claim about a rather specific way of being characterized by some property or other, namely being characterized by a property *as its proper subject or bearer*, rather than (for instance) being derivatively so characterized, in virtue of the fact that a part of the subject is characterized by the property in question as its proper subject.[19]

To see this, we should recall that Socrates' question is whether *we* learn, are angry, and desire certain pleasures with relevant parts of our soul or with the whole soul. The subsequent argument is, I take it, meant to answer that question *as it stands*, rather than to reject the terms in which it is couched.[20] It is instructive to consider a restatement of **PO** at 439 B 5–6. If something, Socrates says, pulls a thirsty soul away from drinking, it would have to be something distinct from that in the soul which pulls it toward drinking. 'For we said', he adds, 'that the same thing could not do opposites about the same thing *with the same (part) of itself.*' This reformulation is bound to put one in mind of the dative expressions used in the statement of Socrates' question at 436 A 8–B 4: 'with one part in us', 'with another part', 'with the whole soul'. It is exactly this kind of formulation that is needed to allow Socrates to say that one and the same soul can (and all too frequently does) do opposites in the same respect, in relation to the same thing, and at the same time—just not with the same part of itself.[21] In other words, it is exactly the kind of formulation that is needed to underwrite Socrates' continuing practice of attributing desires, aversions, and the like to subjects such as souls or persons. In effect, then, I am suggesting that we interpret the relevant dative expressions as pinpointing the proper subjects or bearers of the motivating conditions in question.[22]

---

[19] The distinction I have in mind is made by Aristotle on a number of occasions in the *Physics*. For instance, at 8.4, 254^{b}7–14, he distinguishes between things that effect motion or are in motion *incidentally* (κατὰ συμβεβηκός) (cf. καθ᾿ ἕτερον at 4.3, 210^{a}26–7) and things that effect motion or are in motion *in themselves*, or *in their own right* (καθ᾿ αὑτά). Bearing the relevant predicate incidentally or derivatively is a matter of bearing it in virtue either of belonging to something that bears that predicate, or of having a part that bears that predicate. Cf. also 4.2, 209^{a}31–^{b}1. An example that is pertinent to our purposes is at 4.3, 210^{a}29–30. Things are said to be something or other in respect of their parts (κατὰ τὰ μέρη); which is a matter of καθ᾿ ἕτερον or incidental predication. For instance, a person is said to be knowledgeable because the rational part of her soul (τὸ λογιστικόν) is. For some clarification, see B. Morison, *On Location: Aristotle's Concept of Place* (Oxford: Oxford University Press: 2002), 59–61. There is no suggestion, here or elsewhere, that incidental predication is mispredication. To call *a person* knowledgeable is a perfectly respectable thing to do, even if it is true that it is only a part or aspect of her that is knowledgeable 'in itself'.

[20] 439 D 4–8 makes this clear.

[21] Contra Bobonich, *Plato's Utopia Recast*, 530: 'The position of γε in 439B5 stresses τὸ αὐτό and emphasizes that Plato's conclusion is that the *same thing* is not acting.' If Plato's point at 439 B 5–6 were simply that it is not *the same thing* that is acting in opposite ways, the expression 'with the same part of itself' in B 5 would be otiose. On my alternative reading, the expression does important work: it *is* the same thing that is acting in opposite ways, just not with the same part of itself. The position of γε, does not settle this matter.

[22] *Theaetetus* 184 C 1–D 5 contains further support for this suggestion. The claim that we perceive perceptibles *with* the soul arguably is precisely the claim that it is the soul that is the proper subject of perception. See M. Burnyeat, 'Plato on the grammar of perceiving', *Classical Quarterly*, 26 (1976), 33–6.

We (and our souls) are (derivative) subjects or bearers of such motivating conditions in virtue of the fact that parts of our souls are the (proper) subjects or bearers of these conditions.

Just after **PO**, Socrates introduces a second principle, one about attributes and their objects or relata—for example, thirst and drink, hunger and food, and larger and smaller. The upshot of it is this: for attributes that are such as to have or imply objects or relata—for instance, desire, knowledge, and being larger—what corresponds to the simple, unqualified attribute is the simple, unqualified object or relatum. Thus, what corresponds to 'thirst' is 'drink', what corresponds to 'hunger' is 'food', what corresponds to 'larger' is 'smaller'. At the same time, what corresponds to a complex or qualified attribute is a complex or qualified object or relatum: for example, 'hot drink' goes with 'thirst combined with cold', 'cold drink' goes with 'thirst combined with heat', 'much drink' goes with 'much thirst'; and while 'knowledge' goes with 'what can be learned', 'knowledge of housebuilding' goes with 'what can be learned pertaining to housebuilding' (or something like that). While it is not difficult to see what the principle that Socrates is appealing to amounts to, it is unclear what precisely its point is in the context of the argument for tripartition.

One suggestion that has been made by a number of scholars,[23] and that seems to me to be clearly correct, is that Plato is making a point against Socrates' view of human desire, as it is presented in earlier Platonic dialogues (such as the *Meno*, the *Protagoras*, and the *Gorgias*).[24] It is part of that view that all human desire aims at 'the good' in a certain way—namely, in such a way that when a person has a desire, it always springs from, or consists in, a belief as to what it is good, or best, for them to do in the circumstances in question. If desire fails to be directed at something that is in fact good, this always involves an error of judgement (about what it is good to do) on the part of the person whose desire it is.[25] Now, the principle concerning attributes and their objects that Socrates is appealing to in our text requires that what corresponds to 'thirst' is simply 'drink', or 'drinking', but not a complex or qualified object such as 'good drink', or 'drinking as what it is good to do'. It does not, of course, follow from the principle that anyone ever has such a thing as a desire the object of which is fully specified simply as drink, or drinking. But it does follow that if someone has a desire that is fully specified simply as thirst, the object of that desire is fully specified simply as drink, or drinking.[26] And presumably there are, as a matter of fact, situations such that a desire is fully

[23] For example, N. Murphy, *The Interpretation of Plato's* Republic (Oxford: Oxford University Press, 1951), 28–9; T. Penner, 'Thought and desire in Plato', in G. Vlastos (ed.), *Plato II: Ethics, Politics and Philosophy of Art and Religion* (Garden City, NY: Anchor Books, 1971), 106–7; Irwin, *Plato's Ethics*, 206–11.   [24] *Meno* 77 B 6–78 B 2; *Protagoras* 358 B 6–D 4; *Gorgias* 468 B 1–E 5.

[25] H. Segvic, 'No one errs willingly: the meaning of Socratic intellectualism', *Oxford Studies in Ancient Philosophy*, 19 (2000), 34–40, offers a fine discussion of this Socratic view of human motivation.

[26] Contrast complex desires such as desires for drink of one kind or another—for instance, hot drink (cf. 437 D 9–E 2). Such desires would precisely not be fully specified as thirst.

specified simply as thirst. If so, the principle requires that there are in fact cases in which a desire occurs the object of which is fully specified as drink or drinking. What such a desire is for is, simply and without qualification, drinking. But this refutes what presumably is part of the Socratic view, namely that since every desire aims at the good, a full specification of what a desire is for must always include the qualification 'good' in some suitable way:[27]

> Therefore, let no one catch us unprepared or disturb us by claiming that no one has a desire for drink but rather good drink (alternatively, drink as good: χρηστοῦ ποτοῦ),[28] nor food but good food, on the grounds that everyone after all desires good things,[29] so that if thirst is a desire, it will be a desire for good drink or whatever, and similarly with the others. (*Republic* 438 A 1–5)

There is in the background a philosophically important point about the relation between desire and belief of a certain kind. This point is not made altogether clear by the discussion here, but it can without much difficulty be made clear enough at least for present purposes. The Socrates of our text is not sufficiently careful or pedantic to be precise about how the qualification 'good' is supposed to enter into proper specifications of what a desire is for. Had he been so, he would have distinguished, perhaps among other things, between specifying what a desire is for as, for example, good food—a good example of its kind—and specifying what a

---

[27] Incidentally, the present passage seems to me to be valuable, and often neglected, evidence for how Plato (anyhow by the time he writes the *Republic*) conceives of Socratic intellectualism and, in particular, of the notion of desire or 'wanting' that it relies on. The key idea is that a complete specification of what any desire is for must always appropriately include the qualification 'good', presumably so that such a specification should look like this: 'φ-ing as what it is good, or best, to do (in the circumstances)'. This idea is, to be sure, not stated in so many words in the relevant 'Socratic' dialogues, but it chimes in well with what Socrates is presented as saying in those texts. In fact, it seems to me to be suggested in the *Meno*, and to help clarify what Socrates may have in mind in a much-discussed passage in the *Gorgias*. At *Meno* 77 D 6–E 4, Socrates is meaning to argue for the view that people who desire things that are bad, but that they take to be beneficial, really desire good things: 'Is it not clear, then, that those who do not know things to be bad do not desire what is bad, but they desire those things that they believe to be good but that are in fact bad. It follows that those who have no knowledge of these things and believe them to be good clearly desire good things.' The individuals in question do not know that the things they desire (say, gold obtained in this or that way) are, in fact, bad, and hence harmful to them. What they desire, Socrates is claiming, are *not* bad things, but those things that they thought were good things (gold obtained in this or that way), and so what they desire, what their desires are for, are good things! This suggests that a proper specification of what desires are for should look like this: 'such-and-such an object as good or beneficial'. If this is Socrates' view, it is clear right away why orators and tyrants, in committing acts of injustice, can never be doing what they desire or want to do (*Gorgias* 468 B 1–E 5). For what any desire or want is for is always this or that, or doing this or that, *as what is good and hence beneficial*, and so every act of injustice cannot but deeply frustrate the very desire that prompted it. More elaborate and, to my mind, rather implausible interpretations of *Gorgias* 466–8 are offered in T. Penner, 'Desire and power in Socrates: the argument of *Gorgias* 466A–468E that orators and tyrants have no power in the city', *Apeiron*, 24 (1991), 182–97, and in Segvic, 'No one errs willingly', 5–19.

[28] Note also 439 A 5–6: οὔτε ἀγαθοῦ οὔτε κακοῦ ('neither of something good nor of something bad').

[29] πάντες γὰρ ἄρα τῶν ἀγαθῶν ἐπιθυμοῦσιν. Cf. *Meno* 77 C 1–2: οὐ πάντες, ὤριστε, δοκοῦσί σοι τῶν ἀγαθῶν ἐπιθυμεῖν;

desire is for as, for example, food as a practical good, so that the desire in question depends on (or is) a belief to the effect that, in the circumstances, it is good or best to have food. It will become clear that the psychological theory of the *Republic* treats thirst, hunger, and the like as desires that neither depend on, nor consist in, beliefs that are arrived at, or anyhow are controlled by, reason, as the beliefs of persons are. Thus it also becomes clear that the argument for tripartition specifically rejects the Socratic view of desire that is left somewhat diffusely in the background, to the effect that all human desires depend on, or consist in, reason-controlled beliefs about what it is good or best to do in the circumstances. The desires of the appetitive part, it turns out, are such that they can be had without having any such beliefs.

It would, however, be a mistake to think that the principle is introduced simply to make a point concerning the relation between desire and belief of a certain kind. In fact it is doubtful, for a number of reasons, that making such a point is the main contribution the principle is supposed to make to the overall argument. First, there is a noteworthy lack of precision, already mentioned, about what exactly the view is that is being rejected—that what any desire is for is always a good example of its kind, or something or other as what it is good to do. If Plato's focus were on Socrates' view of human desire, one would expect that view to be pinpointed with a little more precision. Secondly, 'good' is only one of several qualifications that are rejected as candidates for entering, in whatever precise way, into a proper specification of what a person desires when, and in so far as, they experience 'thirst itself'; the other qualifications that Socrates rules out are hot and cold, and much and little. 'Thirst itself', he concludes, 'isn't for much or little, good or bad, or, in a word, for drink of a particular sort. Rather, thirst itself is in its nature only for drink itself.' This conclusion plainly is broader and looser than specifically a rejection of the Socratic view of desire.

Moreover, the conclusion understood in its full breadth serves significantly to sharpen the argument for tripartition at an important stage, in the following way. Now that Socrates has made available the notion of 'thirst itself', as a desire for 'drink itself', he can offer a highly specific example, so as to reveal the partition between appetite and reason. The example is of someone who experiences 'thirst itself', thirst pure and simple, and so the second principle requires that what this desire is for be specified, simply and without qualification, as drink: 'Hence the soul of the thirsty person, in so far as he's thirsty, doesn't wish anything else but to drink, and it wants this and is impelled toward it' (*Republic* 439 A 9–B 1). At the same time, the person in question is, for some reason, averse to drinking, and since this is supposed to be a case where one and the same thing is both what a person desires and what they are averse to, we know that what they are averse to is precisely what they desire, 'drink itself', drink pure and simple. This immediately rules out a huge variety of cases as irrelevant, cases in which someone has a desire that is, to use Plato's terminology, in some way complex or qualified, and they experience some kind of conflict between desires because there is only a partial match between what they desire and what is available to them. For instance, someone experiences 'thirst combined with heat', which is or yields a desire for drink of a certain kind, and is at the same time averse to drinking, because all that is available is steaming hot coffee. It would no doubt be interesting to know what Plato thought about conflicts of this kind, but the fact is that they are not at issue at this stage of the argument. Plato makes it very clear, and his second principle enables him to do so, that the example he is offering concerns a desire for, and an aversion to, a simple, unqualified object, 'drink itself'.

Having offered the example of a desire for, and simultaneous aversion to, drinking, Socrates quickly proceeds to assign the one attitude to appetite and the other to reason. For a number of reasons, it is unclear whether this assignment is justified. Let us, for the sake of the argument, accept that Socrates' example shows that the soul has at least two parts. Why should we accept the further claim that one of the two parts that have come to light is reason, while the other is appetite? One reason why this question might arise is that in Socrates' description of psychological conflict, the two parts that are opposed to one another seem to be doing very much the same sort of thing, except that they seem to act in opposite directions: the one part pulls 'like a brute'[30] and bids or prompts the person to drink, the other part 'pulls the other way' and in the end prevents the person from drinking. It is not as if the part that gets identified as reason acts in a distinctively rational way, by relying, for instance, on language and argument: it simply resists and, as it happens, prevails. On another occasion, the roles might be reversed: the part that now resists might bid or prompt the person to act in some way or other, and the part that is now overcome might successfully resist and prevent action. Moreover, given that Socrates is going to recognize three parts of the soul, does he have grounds for thinking that the example he offers reveals the particular parts that he claims it does, namely reason and appetite, rather than, for instance, spirit and appetite? The crucial passage for answering both of these questions is this:

Doesn't that which prevents in such cases come into play—if it comes into play at all—as a result of reasoning, while what drives and drags them to drink is as a result of affections and diseases? . . . Hence it isn't unreasonable for us to claim that they are two, and different from one another. We'll call the part of the soul with which it reasons the rational part and the part with which it lusts, hungers, thirsts, and gets excited by other desires the non-rational, appetitive part, companion of certain replenishments and pleasures. (*Republic* 439 C 10–D 8)

---

[30] Like S. R. Slings's new *Oxford Classical Text* (Oxford: Oxford University Press, 2003), and unlike Burnet's old one, I read θηρίου rather than θηρίον at 439 B 4. The genitive has much better manuscript support than the accusative. And it is much more appropriate for Socrates to compare appetite to a brute animal than so to compare the thirsty person's soul. In Socrates' elaborate image of the tripartite soul at 588 B 10–E 1, appetite is represented by a multicoloured brute (588 C 7). Note also 588 E 6, 590 B 7, and 591 B 2. S. R. Slings, *Critical Notes on Plato's* Politeia (Leiden: Brill, 2005), 191, offers further discussion.

It is not only that the aversion to drinking comes about as a result of reasoning. It is also the case that the desire to drink persists regardless. The example must involve a reason for not drinking that the person in question recognizes in virtue of some bit of reasoning—drinking, for instance, would be detrimental to health in the circumstances, and health is a highly valued good. Nevertheless, his desire to drink motivates him to act in spite of this reason. Socrates' formulation in the first sentence just quoted might seem to suggest that, on his view, if a part of the soul resists desires of the appetitive part, that part is always reason. But this cannot be his view, since Leontius' desire to look at the corpses obviously belongs to the appetitive part of his soul, and that desire is resisted by *spirit*. It is probably best to suppose that what Socrates has in mind in speaking of 'such cases' is precisely the kind of case where what is resisted by some aversion is a desire that does not directly elicit a response from spirit. If spirit is concerned with honour or, more broadly, recognition by others, then there are going to be countless desires, and actions, that spirit regards as altogether indifferent, and ordinary bodily desires for food, drink, and sex will be among them. It might be the case that once reason resists a desire that spirit initially regarded as indifferent, spirit kicks in and takes the side of reason, because it would be dishonourable or disgraceful for reason to be defeated by appetite (440 A 8–B 4); but this does not affect the fact that the desire itself, independently of reason resisting it, is harmless and indifferent so far as spirit is concerned. So, the kind of case that Socrates has in mind presumably concerns some ordinary bodily desire, such as thirst when one has not had a drink in a long time, one that is, as such, altogether indifferent to spirit. If something resists appetite in such circumstances, then, Socrates is claiming, the aversion belongs to reason.

Socrates assigns the aversion to reason at least in part because it arises directly from reasoning. It might be that the reasoning in question is no more than means–end reasoning, for instance to the effect that abstaining from drinking is the way to promote health in the circumstances. By contrast, desires such as the desire to drink in the example are said to arise from 'affections and diseases' (439 D 1–2)—that is, I take it, from bodily states that the person happens to be in. However, if the reasoning in question is only means–end reasoning, one might suppose that the aversion does not ultimately belong to reason: for one might think that what resists the desire to drink is (say) a desire for health, together with the belief that drinking in the situation is detrimental to health. One might even think that the aversion to drinking arises from desire for pleasure, together with the belief that abstaining from drinking now will result in less pain and more pleasure later, or in less pain and more pleasure overall. Thus the example appears to lend itself to a Humean analysis: what confronts the desire to drink is simply another desire, with reason in its proper role of a motivationally inert slave to passion.[31]

[31] David Hume, *A Treatise of Human Nature*, 2nd edn., ed. P. H. Nidditch (Oxford: Oxford University Press, 1978), 415: 'Reason is, and ought only to be the slave of the passions, and can never pretend to any other office than to serve and obey them.'

We should reply on Plato's behalf that what confronts the desire to drink is not a general desire for health or pleasure, but specifically an aversion to drinking. As we shall see, this aversion cannot properly be understood simply as an aversion. For Plato's purposes at this stage of the argument, the aversion to drinking may well result from a desire for health or pleasure, together with reasoning about what promotes such objects of desire. It is not part of what Plato wants to say that reason motivates or resists action without desire being involved; in fact it will be made explicit later on in the *Republic* that reason has its own desires (580 D 6–7). Plato will eventually want to say that reason can generate desires all on its own, without depending in any way on the attachments of other parts of the soul. He is, as it turns out, committed to disagreeing with Hume's famous dictum that reason is, and *should be*, slave to the passions. But if one takes a look at the catalogue of corrupt souls in books 8 and 9 of the *Republic*, it becomes clear that Plato agrees that reason *can* be the slave of non-rational desires, of desires that have their origins in other parts of the soul, such as the desire for money (553 C 4–D 4). In such corrupt cases, reason will presumably still be able to generate desires and aversions, and will be able to resist desires of other parts of the soul, as when there is a temptation to obtain a small amount of money now, though the long-term cost of doing so would massively outweigh the present benefit.

It turns out, then, that Plato disagrees with Hume's conception in more ways than one. It is not just, according to Plato, that reason should not, though it can, be a slave to passion. It is also a mistake to think of reason, even in an enslaved state, as motivationally inert.[32] Even in cases where reason's overall goals and attachments are set, as they can but should not be, by non-rational desire (e.g. for wealth or bodily pleasure), it does not follow that reason could not form desires or aversions of its own, based in part on reasoning or calculation (e.g. about how to maximize wealth or pleasure).[33] Socrates' example at 439 B 3–D 2 may well involve a less than perfectly developed reason, whose overall goals and attachments are set by non-rational desire: drinking now would be pleasurable, but reason recognizes (for instance) that the pleasure of the moment would be massively outweighed by future pain, and so it forms an aversion to drinking. What crucially matters for the purposes of the argument is that this aversion arises directly from suitable reasoning. It cannot properly be understood simply as an aversion, or simply as a desire. It is a central fact about desires and aversions of this kind that they flow from and are fully controlled by reasoning. In assigning this aversion to reason, then, Plato's theory does justice to its distinctive character as a motivating condition that is fully and directly under the control of reason. Desires like the desire to drink in the example, by contrast, not only come about independently of reasoning; it is also the case that such desires may persist even when the person appreciates that there is decisive reason not to act on them. (There is

---

[32] According to Hume, *Treatise*, 415, reason is unable to generate any practical impulse, and so is unable either to cause or to hinder 'any act of volition'.

[33] Nor of course is it part of being enslaved that one lacks or loses the ability to form desires.

then a clear sense in which such desires not only are non-rational, but can be irrational: contrary to reason.)

These remarks about the argument for tripartition, incomplete though they are, will, I think, suffice for my purposes. I now want to return to the conclusions that I am meaning to argue for, first concerning partition of the soul in general and then concerning the three parts of the soul that Plato is introducing.

3

/ Partition

To recapitulate, what Socrates is meaning to establish in arguing for soul-partition is not just the view that human desire comes in three different kinds or forms. It crucially includes the further view that the embodied human soul is a composite object, composed of a number of parts which (strictly and accurately speaking) are the subjects or bearers of different kinds of motivating conditions. A careful reading of the argument for tripartition makes clear, I have argued, that Socrates is, among other things, specifically concerned to reject the idea that the phenomena of human psychology can be accounted for on the hypothesis that the human soul is incomposite. Any interpretation that fails to accommodate that concern fails to do justice to the detail of the argument.

Given that Plato is remarkably careful and explicit about what it is he is arguing for, the question arises why it has nonetheless seemed to commentators permissible, let alone attractive, to downplay Plato's position as amounting simply to the view that human desire comes in a number of different kinds. One consideration is that in speaking of the parts of the soul, Plato rarely uses the language of parthood. In fact, he does not use such language in the argument for tripartition of the soul. In the course of that argument (*Republic* 4, 436 B 6–441 C 6), he uses loose expressions such as 'kinds'. As we have seen, however, he evidently does use the language of parthood a little later on in book 4 (442 B 10, C 4). Moreover, it is already implicit in the initial statement of the question which the argument is meant to settle that according to one alternative, different kinds of impulse to act belong to different parts of the soul, whereas according to the other alternative—and here Socrates *is* explicit—they belong to the soul *as a whole*. Another consideration is equally inadequate. This is that a Platonic soul is not the right kind of thing for it to make sense to say of it that it literally has parts.[1] For that to make sense, Platonic souls would have to be spatially extended, which they are not. This manages to make two questionable assumptions at once. It is questionable whether only spatially extended objects can have parts. How about mathematical proofs,

---

[1] R. Robinson, 'Plato's separation of reason from desire', *Phronesis*, 16 (1971), 45, takes the view that the language of parthood can be used in a way that is 'informative' and 'fairly specific' only on the basis of some difference of regions in space or periods in time—and neither, he thinks, is applicable to 'the soul'.

for instance? As for Platonic souls, the *Timaeus* presents souls as spatially extended and in fact as engaging in motion,[2] and the different parts of the soul as having distinct locations in different parts of the body, with each part having its own motions (*Timaeus* 89 E 3–90 A 2). It is impossible to be entirely confident that Plato intended a literal reading of these various claims about the soul. But there is no good reason to dismiss the suggestion that in the *Timaeus* Plato introduces the idea of parts of the soul located in different parts of the body because he continues to think, for the reasons presented in *Republic* 4, that the human soul has distinct parts, each of which is able to act on its own, and to counteract other parts. For *that* to be possible, one might well think, the soul must be extended, and its different parts must occupy different places.

Like many good things, soul-partition comes at a cost. One way in which it does is indicated in *Republic* 10. Towards the end of the dialogue, Socrates turns to the immortality of the soul, and to its life after its separation from the body. In that context, he finds soul-partition problematic. 'We must not think', he says, 'that the soul in its truest nature is full of multicoloured variety and unlikeness or that it differs with itself. . . . It isn't easy for a composite of many parts (σύνθετόν τε ἐκ πολλῶν) to be everlasting if it isn't composed in the finest way, yet this is how the soul now appeared to us' (*Republic* 611 A 10–B 7). We should recall Socrates' suggestion in the *Phaedo* that anything that is composite is 'by nature liable to be divided up into its component parts,[3] and only that which is incomposite (ἀσύνθετον), if anything, is not liable to be divided up' (*Phaedo* 78 C 1–4). In making that remark, Socrates is taking issue with the view, expressed by his interlocutor Cebes, that the soul is destroyed at about the time of death by being dispersed (*Phaedo* 77 B 3–6; cf. 69 E 6–70 B 4). Socrates clearly accepts that all composite objects are at least in principle subject to decomposition. (He also accepts, I take it, that were a soul to be 'divided up', it would cease to exist. This of course is an assumption implicit in Cebes' picture.) Now it is possible for something to be in principle subject to decomposition, but never in fact to be decomposed, either for some reason or by sheer good luck. The Socrates of the *Phaedo* obviously does not want to say that souls are never in fact destroyed simply by sheer good luck on a massive scale. If he did think that the soul is a composite, we would expect him to be concerned to offer an explanation why our souls, though they are in principle subject to decomposition, nevertheless will not come apart. The *Phaedo* contains no indication at all that he feels any such concern. The best explanation for this, I suggest, is that the Socrates of the *Phaedo* sees no reason at all to think that the soul is a composite, and at the same time takes it that there are a number of admittedly

---

[2] For discussion, see D. Sedley, ' "Becoming like god" in the *Timaeus* and Aristotle', in T. Calvo and L. Brisson (eds.), *Interpreting the* Timaeus–Critias: *Proceedings of the Fourth Symposium Platonicum* (Sankt Augustin: Academia, 1997), 329–30; and T. Johansen, 'Body, soul, and tripartition in Plato's *Timaeus*', *Oxford Studies in Ancient Philosophy*, 19 (2000), 90–3.

[3] τῷ μὲν συντεθέντι τε καὶ συνθέτῳ ὄντι φύσει προσήκει τοῦτο πάσχειν, διαιρεθῆναι ταύτῃ ᾗπερ συνετέθη.

inconclusive, but nevertheless significant, considerations in favour of thinking the opposite, such as the ones offered in the affinity argument (*Phaedo* 78 C 6–79 E 6).

How can it be, one might ask, that the Socrates of the *Phaedo* sees no reason to think that the embodied human soul is a composite object? The *Phaedo* evidently accepts the possibility of psychological conflict, of a person desiring, and at the same time being averse to, one and the same thing. Socrates in the *Phaedo* acknowledges, and indeed draws attention to, the very types of conflict that the *Republic*'s argument for tripartition of the soul relies on.[4] In fact, he appeals to the same example, quoting the same *Odyssey* passage, which in the *Republic* is used to show the distinctness of spirit from reason: Odysseus addressing his heart as his considered view about how it is best to act clashes with his furious anger at Penelope's maidservants (*Phaedo* 94 D 7–E 1; *Rep.* 441 B 3–C 2). However, the *Phaedo* assigns the lower desires—those which in the *Republic* are assigned to appetite and spirit—not to the soul, but to the body. No doubt Socrates realizes that for a body to give rise to desires even of these kinds it must be ensouled, and that there must therefore be some way or other in which the soul, as it is generally responsible for the organism's life and performance of its vital functions, is also responsible for the formation of the lower desires that he is assigning to the (living) body. Nonetheless, the *Phaedo* evidently does treat the body as the bearer or subject of the lower desires, and at the same time assigns to the soul those desires that in the *Republic* are assigned specifically to reason. As a result, the Socrates of the *Phaedo* need not (and, I suggest, does not) see the occurrence of conflicts between higher and lower desires as a reason to think that *the soul* is a composite object.[5]

The Socrates of the *Republic*, by contrast, accepts that the soul, or anyhow the embodied human soul, *is* a composite. If it is a composite, however, it is in principle subject to decomposition. It should be clear that this raises serious questions about its immortality. Might the soul ever come apart? If not, why not—given that it is, as a composite, the sort of thing that is in principle subject to decomposition? If yes, could it perhaps survive being decomposed? What Socrates says at *Republic* 611 A 10–B 7 leaves open, and draws attention to, the possibility that a composite can be everlasting if it is composed in a suitably fine way. Fineness of composition might be a reason why something that in principle is subject to decomposition will not, in fact, fall apart. There is, moreover, an alternative way of preserving the immortality of the soul in light of the tripartite theory. This is to accept that the soul will be decomposed at the time of death, but to say that it survives its decomposition. It may, after all, not be essential to the soul to be a

---

[4] *Phaedo* 94 B 7–C 1: does the soul rule 'by following the affections of the body, or by opposing them? I mean, for example, that when the body is hot and thirsty the soul draws it to the opposite, to not drinking; when the body is hungry, to not eating, and we see a thousand other examples of the soul opposing the affections of the body.' Cf. *Republic* 4, 439 C 3–4.

[5] For a suggestion as to why Plato, by the time of the *Republic*, comes to assign even the lowest desires to the soul, see Ch. 7, p. 103, n. 19.

composite of reason, spirit, and appetite. It may be that in essence the soul is
nothing but reason. For reason to be separated at death from spirit and appetite
might be a bit like having a tumour removed.

The *Republic* does not decide between these options. In *Republic* 10, Socrates
confirms the tripartite theory as offering an adequate account of what the soul's
'condition is and what parts it has *when it is immersed in human life*' (612 A 5–6).
However, to see what it is 'in truth' or 'in its true nature', we must realize, Socrates
says, what it would become if it followed its love of wisdom

> as a whole, and if the resulting effort lifted it out of the sea in which it now dwells, and if the
> many stones and shells (those which have grown all over it in a wild, earthy, and stony profu-
> sion because it feasts at those so-called happy feastings on earth) were hammered off it. Then
> we'd see what its true nature is, and we'd be able to determine whether it has many parts or
> just one and whether or in what manner it is put together.   (*Republic* 611 D 8–612 A 5)

Socrates is comparing the embodied soul to the sea god Glaucus, whose body is
covered with 'shells, seaweeds, and stones that have attached themselves to him, so
that he looks more like a wild animal than his natural self' (*Republic* 611 D 3–5).
According to the picture Socrates is offering, stones and shells attach themselves to
the soul during its embodied existence. To grasp the soul's true nature, he says, we
must think what it would be like if three conditions were met: if it followed its love
of wisdom as a whole; if that effort lifted it out of the sea in which it now dwells;
and if the accretions of embodied life were removed from it. The sea presumably
stands for embodied life and the cares and concerns it brings with it. What do the
soul's accretions, those 'many stones and shells', stand for? They might represent
the desires of appetite and spirit that are characteristic of embodied life, resulting
in disorderly conditions of the soul that include the various vices. They might also
stand for appetite and spirit themselves. In either case, the soul could, after their
removal, follow its love of wisdom as a whole, without division: either because
appetite and spirit can no longer conflict with reason, or because they have been
removed from the soul altogether. In the former case, the soul would be a composite even in its true nature. But it would not, in its true nature, be liable to division
and conflict. And so one might think that, were one to see the soul in its true
nature, one would realize that its mode of composition is in fact very fine, certainly fine enough not to endanger its immortality.

The *Timaeus* settles the issue. The two lower parts of the embodied soul are
mortal, it turns out, and only reason is in fact immortal (*Timaeus* 69 C 5–D 6). At
death reason will presumably be separated, not only from the body, but also from
appetite and spirit. Nonetheless, Timaeus speaks of discarnate human intellects as
souls, rather than as parts of souls (*Timaeus* 41 D 8–42 A 3). The idea appears to
be that that each human soul in its true nature is an intellect, with appetite and
spirit being added on temporarily during periods of embodiment.

Another way in which soul-partition comes at a cost is pointed out by Aristotle
in *De Anima* 1.5. The passage that I shall quote, 411^{b}5–14, makes it clear that

Aristotle is aware of some theorists (λέγουσι ... τινες, 411ᵇ5) who take the soul to be a composite object. The problem he is raising concerns precisely this view. Towards the end of *De Anima* 1.5, he asks whether the various activities that belong to the soul—such as perceiving, judging, desiring, and the like—belong to the soul as a whole, or whether different activities belong to different parts of it (411ᵃ26–ᵇ3). To put it cautiously, the question is closely related to Socrates' question, at *Republic* 4, 436 A 8–B 4, that the argument for tripartition is intended to settle. Some people, Aristotle continues, say that the soul is a thing of parts (μεριστή), and that it thinks (νοεῖν) with one part and desires (ἐπιθυμεῖν) with another (411ᵇ5–6). If *epithumein* is understood in its technical Aristotelian use, in which it denotes appetitive desire specifically, then anyone who accepts the psychological theory of the *Republic* will in fact accept the claim Aristotle is discussing. Here is the problem that he raises for it:

What then holds the soul together, if its nature is to be a thing of parts? It could not be the body: for it rather seems that, on the contrary, the soul holds the body together, for when it departs, the body disperses and decomposes. If then something else unifies the soul, this thing would most of all be the soul. And again, the question will arise whether this thing is one or a thing of parts. If it is one, why is not the soul one right away? If it is a thing of parts, the question will be asked what it is that holds this thing together, and in this way the argument will continue *ad infinitum*.   (*De Anima* 1.5, 411ᵇ5–14)

Implicit in the argument is a distinction between two ways of being one or having unity: on the one hand, having unity by being unified or made to be one thing (μίαν ... ποιεῖ, 411ᵇ9); on the other hand, having unity in a non-derivative way. Being one non-derivatively can be contrasted, as it is at 411ᵇ11, with being a thing of parts. An assumption that the argument plainly relies on is that the unity of composite objects is derivative, in that it depends on something or other that accounts for it. The unity of incomposite objects, on the other hand, is non-derivative. The point of the argument is that if the soul is a thing of parts, its unity is derived. So its unity will have to be accounted for by appealing to some further item, and the question will arise whether this further item does not have a better claim to being the soul than the derivative item that we started out with. An infinite regress of unifiers can be avoided, by saying that the further item that has come to light is in fact non-derivatively one, and hence capable of serving as a genuine principle of unity. But this does not resolve the difficulty. For if you say that this principle of unity is in fact the soul, then the soul will no longer be, as it was held to be, the thing that activities like perceiving and desiring belong to; they will rather belong to the item that is unified by the soul (which is not yet the body). On the other hand, if you retain the idea that it is the soul that these activities belong to, you will be committed to a further item in addition to body and soul, a principle of unity that accounts for the soul's derived unity. This, to be sure, is not a knockdown argument. None of its premises, however, is to be dismissed lightly. And given how unpalatable the alternatives are that it leaves open, it does manage to put considerable pressure on the idea that the soul, the thing that activities like perceiving and desiring belong to, is a thing of parts. Why not say that the soul is non-derivatively one right away?

That the soul is incomposite is arguably Aristotle's own considered view. I shall, in due course, discuss the question whether Aristotle can consistently accept Plato's three kinds of desire and reject Platonic tripartition with its commitment to the soul's compositeness.[6] For now, let us turn to *tri*partition.

---

6 See Conclusion, pp. 202–4.

4

The Simple Picture

What has emerged from my analysis of the argument for tripartition of the soul is what I shall call the 'simple picture'. According to this picture, it is the simultaneous occurrence of a desire and an aversion towards one and the same object that, Plato thinks, reveals a partition of the soul. This simple picture is precisely what the Principle of Opposites (**PO**) makes one expect, and indeed what it requires. Nevertheless, commentators have been unwilling to accept it, for at least two reasons.[1] I shall attempt to describe these reasons in some detail, to disarm them, and in so doing to defend the simple picture.

Several readers of the *Republic* have thought that in the catalogue of corrupt forms of city and soul in books 8 and 9, there is at least one passage in which Socrates describes a conflict between desires that belong to the same part of a person's soul.[2] The passage in question is 553 A 1–555 B 2, where Socrates characterizes the oligarchic type of person, 'both how he comes to be and what sort of man he is' (note also 558 D 4–6). This is a person whom Socrates presents as being ruled by the appetitive part of his soul, which he also calls the money-loving part (553 C 5). That part's central object of desire—in this case, money—has become the *person's* central object of desire; and adopting the appetitive part's central object of desire as one's own central object of desire must be, at least in important part, what being ruled by the appetitive part comes to. The oligarchic person is hard-working, thrifty, and generally honest, leading a disciplined life dedicated to the accumulation of wealth. He enjoys a good reputation and is thought to be just by other members of his community (554 C 12).

However, the appetitive part of his soul harbours not only desires that fit harmoniously into the overall fabric of his rather carefully organized life. It also contains desires that are evil and that it would be risky or outright self-destructive to act on, such as desires to enrich oneself in unjust ways. It is characteristic of the oligarchic person, though, to be able to control such desires, so as not to act on them except in circumstances where it is safe to do so, as when he carries out a function that allows him to do injustice and get away with it—for instance, when

---

[1] For instance, Irwin, *Plato's Moral Theory*, 327, n. 18, 3; Cooper, 'Plato's theory of human motivation', 123; Irwin, *Plato's Ethics*, 205–17; Price, *Mental Conflict*, 45–8.

[2] Irwin, *Plato's Moral Theory*, 327; Cooper, 'Plato's theory of human motivation', 123; Woods, 'Plato's division of the soul', 31.

he serves as a guardian to orphans, who cannot help or defend themselves. The fact that he acts on evil desires when it is safe to do so suggests strongly that when he refrains from acting on such desires, it is not on the basis of appreciating that these desires are evil and disgraceful, or that it would be evil and disgraceful to act in such ways, but rather, as Socrates makes clear, out of fear for his good reputation, his business, his career, his possessions, and the like. But such fears do not make the evil desires go away. The desires persist, even though he is able to control them. 'Then someone like this', Socrates says (554 D 9–E 6), 'wouldn't be entirely free from internal civil war and wouldn't be one but in some way two, though generally his better desires are in control of his worse.... For this reason, he'd be more respectable than many, but the true virtue of a single-minded and harmonious soul far escapes him.'

An assumption that commentators have made at this point is that the two parties to the internal civil war that is characteristic of the oligarch are, both of them, desires of one and the same part of the soul, namely appetite. That, after all, is the money-loving part. A related assumption that (I suspect) is also common is that when Plato, in contexts such as this, uses the word *epithumia*, it means 'appetite' and thus must refer to a desire specifically of the lowest part of the soul. So when Socrates says that in the case of the oligarchic character, his better *epithumiai* are generally in control of his worse ones, it may seem as if this very way of putting things in itself makes it clear that the civil war in the oligarch's soul involves desires of the same part on both sides of the conflict.

This, then, is one reason why commentators have been unwilling to accept what I have called the simple picture. It looks as if Plato envisages conflicting desires of one and the same part of the soul—for instance, a desire to steal a large amount of money and a simultaneous aversion to precisely the same thing, stealing the money, on the grounds that, given the circumstances, it would be intolerably risky to do so. However, if there can, on Plato's view, be such conflicts between desires that belong to the same part of the soul, then the simple picture cannot be right, or else Plato would have to accept that appetite is not, after all, a basic part of the soul, but itself a composite item, and hence subject to sub-partition.

Another reason is this. It is not only that Socrates may seem to speak, pretty much in so many words, of conflicts between desires of the lowest part of the soul. It may also seem that given the way he conceives of that part, he must be prepared to accept the possibility of such conflicts. To see this, consider the passage in book 9 in which Socrates explains why he has been calling the lowest part 'appetitive' and 'money-loving' (580 D 10–581 A 1):

As for the third part, we had no one special name for it, since it's multiform, so we named it after what is biggest and strongest in it. Hence we called it the appetitive part, because of the intensity of its desires for food, drink, sex, and all the things associated with them, but we also called it the money-loving part, because such desires are most of all satisfied through money.

To be able to recognize that it is by means of money that its primary desires—those for food, drink, sex, and the like—are most of all satisfied, and to form an attachment to money on that basis, the appetitive part (one might think) needs to be equipped with (or at least have access to) suitable resources—such as, crucially, the capacity for means–end reasoning.[3] However, if it can avail itself of *such* resources, there will be circumstances in which it is bound to generate desire/aversion pairs in relation to the same thing. One and the same thing can, for instance, be an object of aversion, and may at the same time be desired as a means to the achievement of a goal that one desires; all of this can occur at the level of the appetitive part, if indeed it can rely on such resources. The oligarch would characteristically be loath to make a large-scale public donation, but might at the same time desire to do just that, on the grounds that doing so would (say) help him in cultivating a certain reputation, which in turn would open up lucrative business opportunities.

The upshot of these considerations may seem to be that the simple picture of what kind of psychological conflict reveals partition will not do, even though it is the picture that is suggested and indeed required by **PO**, anyhow on my analysis. An adequate picture, some commentators have suggested, will have to be more complicated. As we have seen already,[4] the suggestion is that it takes a special kind of conflict to reveal a partition of the soul: at least on one side of the conflict, there must be a desire of a higher order—for instance, an aversion to having the (first-order) desire on the other side of the conflict.[5] It is, after all, not just that Leontius, according to the description at 439 E 5–440 A 4, both desires to have a look at some corpses and is at the same time averse to doing so. He also seems to have a fiercely negative attitude to his own desire to look at the corpses, a desire that he associates with his eyes—and so he angrily says to them (440 A 3–4): 'Look for yourselves, you evil wretches, and take your fill of the beautiful sight!' Moreover, it may seem plausible that the appetitive part, equipped though it is with considerable cognitive resources, nevertheless is not capable of forming evaluative attitudes of the relevant kind towards desires and aversions.[6] If so, the civil war in the

---

[3] That the appetitive part of the soul can (by itself) engage in means–end reasoning is the view taken, somewhat tentatively, by Price, *Mental Conflict*, 60–1, and, very firmly, by C. Bobonich, *Plato's Utopia Recast*, 244. See also J. Annas, *An Introduction to Plato's Republic*, 129–30; Cooper, 'Plato's theory of human motivation', 128; Burnyeat, 'Culture and society in Plato's *Republic*', 227. Irwin's view is more complicated: the appetitive part may not itself be equipped with the capacity for (means–end) reasoning, but at least it has cognitive access to the rational part's reasoning, so that it can form desires for means to its ends based on its recognition of the efficiency and long-term benefit of the means in question. See Irwin, *Plato's Ethics*, 282 (cf. 214–20).

[4] See Ch. 1, pp. 15–17.

[5] Irwin, *Plato's Moral Theory*, 327; Cooper, 'Plato's theory of human motivation', 123; Price, *Mental Conflict*, 45–8. Irwin, *Plato's Ethics*, 208 (cf. 212), goes further: what is required is not just an aversion to some first-order desire or other, but an aversion to 'acting on appetite, as such'.

[6] Cf. Price, *Mental Conflict*, 47–8. Soul-partition requires not just the symmetrical relation of contrariety, but in addition the asymmetrical relation of confrontation; and the appetitive part is not capable of that: 'confronting simply lies outside its repertory'. Cf. Irwin, *Plato's Ethics*, 207: 'no appetite can itself be opposed to acting on appetite'.

oligarch's appetitive, money-loving part does not undermine its status as incomposite. For such civil war involves no desire of a higher order, just two desires that, as it were, operate on the same level: both of them, one might think, are nothing other than desires for financial gain.

Now, there are at least three serious objections to this more complicated picture. First, it is incompatible with **PO**, the principle on which the argument for tripartition is based and which is spelled out and illustrated in great detail right at the beginning of the argument. To see this, we only need to compare the civil war in the oligarch's soul, as described at 554 B 7–E 6, with the example Socrates uses, at 439 A 9–D 2, to reveal the division between reason and appetite. In both cases, there is a desire for something or other, which Socrates thinks of (I take it) as involving part of the soul pulling the rest of it towards the object of desire—drinking, or spending other people's money (554 D 6–7). And in both cases, something else in the soul is averse to the object of desire, counteracts the desire, and gets the better of it (439 C 8, 554 E 2). Moreover, in both cases Socrates takes motivational conflict to reveal that the person in question is twofold, composed of at least two parts or aspects (439 D 4, 554 D 9–E 1). This is precisely what one expects, given Socrates' commitment to **PO** and given the fact that he takes **PO** to rule out the simultaneous presence, in a single (incomposite) part of the soul, of a desire for, and an aversion to, the same thing.

Secondly, it is an important part of (at least one version of) the more complicated picture[7] that the appetitive part has the capacity for means–end reasoning, even though Socrates thinks of the part in question as lacking the capacity for reasoning (λογισμός).[8] If means–end reasoning is not supposed to be a matter of Platonic reasoning, we need a story of what Platonic reasoning is, such that means–end reasoning does not qualify. This seems a tall order, to put it mildly.[9]

---

[7] This *is* part of the version offered in Price, *Mental Conflict*. Irwin, *Plato's Ethics*, as we have seen, offers a more complicated version of the more complicated picture. Even on this view, though, the appetitive part uses practical reason to identify suitable means to achieve its aims (282), in such a way that it (appetite) forms desires for suitable means based on its recognition of their efficiency and long-term benefit (219–20). One concern is whether this can yield a sufficiently clear and robust sense in which the appetitive part is non-rational.

[8] ἀλόγιστον, 439 D 7; cf. *Tim.* 77 B 5: the third part of the soul has no share in λογισμός.

[9] One strategy might be to distinguish between (say) 'purely instrumental reasoning' (or calculation) and 'reasoning about the good'—about, that is, how it is good (or best) to act, in the circumstances—and then to suggest that Plato reserves the vocabulary of reason for the latter. However, if 'reasoning about the good' is understood in terms of what appears to be good or best to the reasoning subject, this seems to let in too much. This is because it is hard to see why the means–end reasoning that the appetitive part is taken to engage in fails to count as a case of reasoning about the good (so understood). Satisfying intense 'bodily' desires, or (better) the intense desire of the moment, may well appear to the appetitive part to be very good indeed—which is not to say that the desire in question springs from an antecedent assessment concerning the goodness of its object. If, on the other hand, it is to be understood in terms of a proper, developed conception of the good, this lets in too little: few people will ever succeed in doing a bit of Platonic reasoning. Note also that in that case, Socrates is mistaken when he calls λογίζεσθαι what the oligarch's rational part is said to do at 553 D 2–4 (namely, to reason about how to make more money, so as to satisfy the desire to be as wealthy as possible, 555 B 11).

And thirdly, there appears to be not a shred of direct, explicit evidence that it is the presence specifically of a second-order desire at least on one side of a psychological conflict that Plato takes to reveal a partition of the soul, rather than, quite simply, the simultaneity of a desire for and an aversion to the same thing. To show that Leontius does experience a second-order desire, in addition to conflicting first-order desires, is not, of course, to show that it is specifically the addition of this second-order desire that, on Plato's view, requires or warrants the relevant partition of the soul. In view of these objections, it seems (to say the least) difficult to sustain the more complicated picture.[10] We should therefore return to the considerations that have led commentators to reject the simple picture and reflect on whether they are, in fact, cogent. I shall argue that they are not.

The first point that needs to be made is that *epithumia*, in Plato, does not *mean* 'appetite' (that is, intense desire for pleasure, or—better—for something or other *as pleasant*, typically and primarily food, drink, sex, and the like). In other words, given the way Plato uses the word, it is not part of its meaning that it must refer specifically to a desire of the sort that, according to the psychological theory of the *Republic*, the lowest part alone is responsible for. It is manifestly and demonstrably false that throughout the *Republic, epithumia* means 'appetite', until in book 9 Socrates, startling readers with a bold stroke of semantic extension, introduces the idea of 'appetites' of spirit and reason. On the second page of the *Republic* (328 D 3–5), Cephalus tells Socrates that he should visit more often, 'for you should know that as the bodily pleasures wither away, my desires (ἐπιθυμίαι) for conversations [or arguments: λόγοι] and their pleasures grow'.

A little later (338 A 5–7), Socrates says about Thrasymachus that it was obvious that he thought he had an extremely fine answer and that he (intensely) desired (ἐπιθυμεῖν) to earn people's esteem by giving it. The object of Thrasymachus' desire here is precisely one of the canonical objects of spirited desire: esteem, or good reputation (εὐδοκιμεῖν).[11] Cephalus' desires for conversations or arguments may well be ones that belong to his somewhat feebly developed reason.[12] Thrasymachus' desire for esteem seems certain to be not an appetite, but a desire that, according to the *Republic's* psychological theory, belongs to the spirited part.

A passage in book 5 clearly uses the word *epithumein*, and related words, so as to mean 'to desire' or—better, I think—'to desire intensely'. In the context, Socrates wants to show that when we say that someone desires something, we mean that he desires everything of that kind, as opposed to one part of it but not another (475 B 4–6). This is illustrated by, among other types, honour-lovers and philosophers or

---

[10] The version of the more complicated picture offered in Irwin, *Plato's Ethics*, manages to avoid the second objection—in letter, though not, one might think, in spirit. Irwin's more complicated version is, however, vulnerable to the other two objections, and that is sufficient to cast serious doubt on it.

[11] 'What about the spirited part?', Socrates asks at 581 A 9–B 1. 'Don't we say that it is wholly dedicated to the pursuit of control, victory, and high esteem (εὐδοκιμεῖν)?'.

[12] Compare the democratic character's occasional desire to philosophize, at 561 D 3. D. Scott, 'Plato's critique of the democratic character', *Phronesis*, 45 (2000), 22–6, offers reasons for thinking that this, too, is a desire of reason rather than, as others have thought, of appetite.

wisdom-lovers. The honour-lover is a 'desirer' of the whole of honour; the philosophical person likewise (intensely) desires the whole of wisdom. We might compare the *Phaedo*, where Socrates says in his intellectual autobiography that when he was young, he strongly (in fact, as he says, to an amazing extent) desired (ἐπιθυμεῖν) the kind of wisdom that was natural philosophy (96 A 5–7). Even though it is not, then, part of the meaning of the word *epithumia* that it picks out all and only appetites, or all and only desires of the lowest part of the soul, Socrates still derives the name of that part from that word, simply because of the extraordinary strength and intensity of its desires for such things as food, drink, and sex (580 D 10–E 5). As a result, when we read of *epithumiai* in Plato's writings, and of conflicts between them, we are not automatically entitled to assume that the desires in question, all or even any of them, belong to the lowest part of the soul.

We should now return, briefly, to book 8, and to the oligarchic character. We remember that this is a person who characteristically experiences psychological conflict, 'though generally his better desires are in control of his worse ones' (554 E 1–E 2). Socrates also says about him that he holds his evil desires in check 'by means of some decent part of himself' (554 C 12–D 1). Moreover, this is a person who leads his life in a disciplined and careful manner, organized and structured around the pursuit of the one thing that he, as a person, is consistently attached to, money or wealth. In this regard as in so many others, the oligarchic person corresponds to the oligarchic city, which has set wealth before itself as the good (555 B 10–11).

Now, it seems difficult to resist the thought that the oligarch's pursuit of wealth has deeply affected the whole of his motivational structure—the whole of his soul, that is—crucially including its rational part, and that it is in fact the latter part that is largely responsible for the order, carefulness, and consistency that so conspicuously characterize his life. Nor is there any reason, I think, to resist this thought. When Socrates speaks of the oligarch's 'decent part', I therefore suggest, he is meaning to refer to (or at least prominently include) that person's corrupt and disoriented rational part, which is in fact the source of at least some of his better, more thoughtful, desires. We can still, on this construal, give force to Socrates' imagery of appetite being ruler and king in the oligarch's soul, and of reason being enslaved: the rule of the appetitive part consists in the fact that its central object of desire has become the person's central object of desire, and reason is enslaved because it is not free to pursue its own natural objects of desire, but is limited to the pursuit of an object that is not appropriately connected to its own proper concerns. Recall now the kind of psychological conflict that is characteristic of this type of person: conflict between desires for quick, but unjust gratification, and careful, prudent, long-term desires for the accumulation of wealth. It is not just open to us to interpret this kind of conflict as involving, on the one hand, desires of the appetitive part and, on the other hand, desires of a corrupt and disoriented reason, perhaps supported by desires of spirit, its natural ally. In fact we have strong reason to opt for an interpretation along these lines, given the background of the argument for tripartition, and in particular the role that **PO** plays in it. If so, one important consideration against the simple picture has been disarmed.

The second consideration against the simple picture was this. Plato seems to conceive of the appetitive part as being equipped with, or having access to, considerable cognitive resources such as, crucially, the capacity for means–end reasoning. If so, there will be specifiable circumstances in which it is bound to generate simultaneous desire/aversion pairs of precisely the sort that, according to the simple picture, require a partition of the soul. But this time, the partition in question will be a sub-partition within appetite. However, the evidence for the claim that Plato takes appetite to be equipped with (or have access to) the capacity for means–end reasoning is quite inconclusive. It is that Socrates, repeatedly and prominently, attributes to it love of, and (intense) desire for, money or wealth[13] and, moreover, says that he has been calling it money-loving because its primary desires (for food, drink, sex, and the like) 'are most of all satisfied through money' (580 E 2–581 A 1). Now, recognizing that money is an effective means to the fulfilment of antecedent desires, and desiring money *on those grounds*, does, I take it, require (access to) the capacity for means–end reasoning. However, to desire money is not necessarily to desire it on grounds such as these. Nor is it necessarily the case that when the appetitive part desires money, it desires it on those grounds. Socrates certainly does not say so.

What he does say not only leaves open the possibility, but on consideration suggests strongly, that given suitable habituation and acculturation in the context of a life lived in human society, the appetitive part tends to become attached to money in such a way as to form desires for it which in each case are based on, or consist in, some kind of appreciation of it as a direct source of pleasure. The fact that its primary desires are satisfied most of all through money would not, in that case, be out of place in a statement of how it is that it comes to be attached to it, or of why it is so attached. It is not only that satisfaction of bodily desires through money lends instrumental value to it. The satisfaction of such desires through money also establishes, reinforces, and sustains patterns and habits of attention, response, and attachment, both at an individual and at a communal level.[14] The appetitive part arguably lacks the cognitive resources required to form desires for money specifically as a means to the satisfaction of its primary desires. But there is

---

[13] 442 A 6–7, 553 C 5, 581 A 3–7; cf. 436 A 1–3.

[14] I have in mind the developmental and not necessarily reason-involving phenomenon Plato and Aristotle refer to as habituation (ἐθίζειν, ἐθισμός). Note, for instance, 377 A 11–378 E 4, where Socrates speaks about the crucial importance of the ways in which the souls of young children are first moulded by the stories they hear, giving rise to beliefs 'that are hard to erase and apt to become unalterable' (378 D 7–E 2). This is later referred to as education *by habits* (522 A 3–9). It plainly begins long before the age of reason, which 'some never seem to get a share of, while the majority do so quite late' (441 A 7–B 1). Cf. also 590 B 6–9, about habituating spirit 'from youth on', so as to put up with being insulted, for the sake of money and gratification of appetites. In view of passages like these, it seems reasonable to think that Plato felt it does not need pointing out that a non-rational part of the soul could (and, in the ordinary course of things, would) develop by habituation an attachment to money.

no reason to think that it cannot develop tendencies to form intense desires for things like money as its patterns of attention and attachment are moulded, from early childhood onward, under the influence of the surrounding culture.

In fact, one reason why Socrates is so deeply dissatisfied with the stories that young children are told as part of the traditional upbringing is that the inherited stories represent gods and heroes as being money-lovers and bribable (390 E 8–391 C 6). These stories must be removed, he says, as citizens must not be allowed to be money-lovers or bribable. The clear implication is that the existing culture, such as it is, inculcates an excessive attachment to money at the very beginning of the traditional course of education—at a time when, as Socrates says, young souls are most malleable and take on any pattern one wishes to impress on them (377 B 1–2).

If this is along the right lines, then the appetitive part's desire for money does not directly rest on, and is not controlled by, a proper grasp of relevant means–end relations. Rather, it is, much like its other desires, based on, or consists in, some kind of appreciation of, or attachment to, something or other (in this case, money) as a direct source of pleasure. This picture requires that money is valued directly or non-instrumentally by the appetitive part itself and by the type of person who is ruled by it. And this seems to be the view that Socrates takes of the way money is typically valued by those who, like the oligarch, value it greatly: 'Won't the money-maker say', he asks at 581 C 11–D 3, 'that the pleasure of being honoured and that of learning are worthless compared to that of making a profit, if he gets no money from them?'[15]

Socrates, then, neither claims nor implies that appetite can reason or use reason. He admittedly leaves it somewhat unclear how it is that appetite, which is not itself equipped with the capacity for reasoning, comes to be attached to money. But this gap in the *Republic's* psychological theory can, without great difficulty, be filled in a way that avoids attributing to it the claim that appetite is able to reason or to use reason. Plato may well have thought that it goes without saying that the appetitive part, as he conceives of it, can (and usually does) develop a tendency to form desires for money as its patterns of attention and attachment are moulded from early childhood onward, in a way that does not depend on any use of practical reason on its part and that, in any case, precedes acquisition of the ability to reason. If so, we are now in a position to conclude that neither of the two main reasons that have led commentators to reject the simple picture is cogent. We should, then, return to **PO** the central position in the argument for tripartition of the soul that Socrates assigns to it (at 436 B 6–437 A 8).

Tripartition of the soul, we can conclude, is not just the claim that human desire comes in three distinct kinds or forms. Nor is it just the claim that the

---

[15] Socrates (at 581 A 3–7) calls the appetitive part not only money-loving, but also *profit*-loving (φιλοκερδές), having said that 'its pleasure and love are for profit'. This, too, suggests direct, non-instrumental appreciation.

human soul in its embodied state is a composite object, composed of three distinct parts, which (strictly and accurately speaking) are the subjects or bearers of motivating conditions of three distinct kinds. To be sure, Socrates is committed to both of these claims. But tripartition also involves the remarkable further claim that while conflict between desires can, and frequently does, occur between soul-parts, it does not and cannot occur within each one of the three parts of the soul that the theory recognizes. Moreover, the precise sort of conflict between desires that is at issue can be specified without any reference to higher-order desires. It is simply a matter of a simultaneous desire for and aversion to the same thing. The theory thus involves the claim that none of the three parts of the soul that it recognizes can at once desire and be averse to the same thing.

It will be helpful to step back from the details we have been attending to, so as to make some remarks about the *Republic*'s psychological theory and its overall plausibility (or otherwise), according to the interpretation that I have presented and argued for. Suppose that what I have called the simple picture can indeed be defended effectively. One might still be reluctant to accept it because of the intuition that motivational conflict between and among desires that Plato's theory attributes to the appetitive part is, in fact, a familiar experience that occurs frequently in ordinary circumstances. We are, after all, familiar with the situation that we have intense ('appetitive') desires which cannot, in the circumstances or even in general, be satisfied at the same time. There is, for instance, nothing particularly unusual about being torn, as people say, between a persistent and forceful craving for a cigar and an intense desire to take a nap. Plato's psychological theory no doubt attributes both of these conflicting desires to the appetitive part of the soul. We should note, though, that so far as it goes, this description of conflict is quite compatible, in letter and spirit, with Plato's theory—even on the simple picture of what sort of conflict indicates a partition of soul. This is because it is neither a part nor an implication of the description that in conflicts of this kind, the person in question has, in addition to the conflicting appetites, 'appetitive' aversions to the very same things that he desires appetitively. In fact, he may very well not have.

To see this, we should bear in mind the distinctive character of the motivating conditions that Plato's theory assigns to the appetitive part. Just as appetitive desires go hand in hand with some awareness or representation of their objects as pleasant, so appetitive aversions come with some awareness of their objects as unpleasant or painful. Now, one's appetite for a nap, together with the fact that one cannot at the same time take a nap and smoke a cigar, need not (and does not, I think) make smoking a cigar (now) strike one as an unpleasant or painful thing to do. Regardless of one's intense tiredness, one may still find the thought of (now) lighting a cigar for oneself utterly delightful. One may have to decide between these two courses of action, and the decision may be a hard one to make. But such motivational conflict need not involve, at the level of the appetitive part, the simultaneous occurrence of a desire for and an aversion to the same thing that would require a subdivision of that part.

A related concern is that it may seem as if my interpretation preserves the integrity of one part of the soul at the expense of the integrity of another. For one might think the following. If reasoning about how to satisfy any desire for A identifies B as the best or most efficient means to A, then a desire for B arises, and it will belong to reason, since it results directly from reasoning.[16] But it is easy to see that there will be all sorts of situations in which such a desire will be opposed by an aversion of reason to precisely the same thing, B.[17] Suppose, for instance, that I have an aversion of reason to smoking, on the grounds that it is bad for me. I also happen to have an intense occurrent desire to have a cigarette. I do not have any cigarettes with me at the moment, but it takes just a spot of reasoning to identify what is, in the circumstances, the most efficient way of obtaining cigarettes, which is to go to the shop around the corner and buy a pack of cigarettes there. Given my aversion to smoking, I form an aversion of reason to going to the shop the moment I think of doing so. So if a desire to go there, as a means to satisfying the desire to smoke, is assigned to *reason*, that will divide it.

On the other hand, according to the interpretation of Plato's theory that I have presented and argued for, appetite is in no position to grasp the fact that going to the shop is a means to satisfying its desire to smoke. So it is hard to see how *appetite* could respond to the situation by forming a desire specifically to go to the shop around the corner.

Perhaps the thing to say on behalf of Plato's theory is something like this. It may well be the case that appetite has *some* kind of cognitive access to reason's judgement that the way to obtain cigarettes in the circumstances is by going to the shop around the corner and buying them there. This may be by way of a representation that in some way or other presents the whole course of action 'going to the shop, buying a pack of cigarettes there, and smoking a cigarette'.[18] Appetite may respond to such a representation by giving rise to a motivating condition that impels me to pursue this course of action, perhaps because the representation prominently includes a representation of smoking, which is the object of an intense, occurrent appetitive desire. This need not—and, anyhow on my view, should not—involve any recognition *on appetite's part* that going to the shop is a means to the end of smoking a cigarette. From appetite's point of view, the representation in response to which it gives rise to the relevant motivating condition need not be articulated in terms of means–end relations. And so it need not be the case that an appetitive desire specifically to go to the shop around the corner is in play. The desire I act on in going to the shop, Plato might say, is simply my appetitive desire to smoke. He might say that what explains my behaviour as I leave the house, walk down the street, and so forth, is, *not* an indeterminately large number

[16] Directly, rather than indirectly: mediated, for instance, by habituation.

[17] Cf. Irwin, *Plato's Moral Theory*, 193: 'If a desire resulting from deliberation about appetite-satisfaction belongs to the rational part, there will be conflict within the rational part; for this appetite-directed desire may conflict with desire resulting from deliberation about over-all good.'

[18] As for what such representations might be and how they might come about, see Ch. 7.

of desires to leave the house, walk down the street, and so forth, but simply the desire to smoke, together with a complex, behaviour-guiding representation that depends, at least in part, on my judgement about how most easily to obtain cigarettes.

It may well be, then, that Plato's theory (as I have interpreted it) can accommodate, and make good sense of, a broader variety of phenomena than it appears at first sight to be able to. But is this good enough? Consider the possibility of habituating a person in such a way as to come to find painful certain experiences that are naturally pleasant, such as drinking water when being dehydrated. By means of some treatment (electric shocks, or whatever), administered over time and in a carefully designed and controlled way, one could perhaps bring it about that a person comes to regard as painful, and on that basis to be intensely averse to, the very activity of drinking (even when dehydrated)—an activity that humans are naturally constituted to find pleasant and to desire intensely, and so cannot help finding pleasant and desiring intensely. If so, the appetitive part can be manipulated, as it were in the laboratory, so as to generate simultaneous desire/aversion pairs to precisely the same thing. In that case, Plato's psychological theory would have to acknowledge that the appetitive part of this unfortunate person is not in fact incomposite: it has been divided or fractured into two distinct sub-parts, and the division manifests itself whenever the person wants to drink.[19]

However, that such a sub-partition can perhaps be effected, in certain highly artificial and invasive circumstances, is not damaging to Plato's claim that the embodied human soul is tripartite. That claim arguably needs to be understood as a claim about the structure that the human soul, in tolerably ordinary and conducive circumstances, naturally acquires and maintains as the person develops and matures, and at the same time about the different kinds of psychological activities and operations that constitute the proper functions of the complex thing that is the embodied human soul. What it may or may not be possible to bring about in laboratory conditions sheds little or no light on the structure or composition that it is natural for a soul to have, and it shows equally little about the kinds of activity in performing which the embodied human soul succeeds in carrying out its various proper functions.

I want to close by signalling an advantage of the present interpretation, namely that it enables us to attribute to Plato conceptions of practical rationality and of motivation by reason that are clear, robust, and, as we shall see, in line with closely related conceptions in Aristotle's theory of motivation.[20] In that it allows us to say that the appetitive part of the soul, which Socrates calls non-rational, lacks the

---

[19] The same point could be made, arguably with more plausibility and interest, about spirit. Perhaps conditions can occur, or can be imposed, such that a person comes to have tendencies to find the same act or response both admirable and shameful, and so she might at the same time feel desire and aversion of spirit towards the same thing. Consider, for instance, the case of a person who spends some of her so-called formative years in one culture, and some in another.

[20] Aristotle's conceptions of practical thought and reason will be discussed in Ch. 12.

capacity for means–end reasoning, it relieves us of the task of working out, on Plato's behalf, a peculiar and unfamiliar conception of reasoning, such that ordinary means–end reasoning turns out, on that conception, not to qualify as reasoning. Rather, Plato's psychological theory (we can say) does treat means–end reasoning as an exercise of reason. If all goes well, such reasoning conveys a grasp of a means–end relation. In certain circumstances, though perhaps not in others, it transmits desire from a desired end to a suitable means. Desire will be so transmitted in cases in which the end, or goal, in question is desired by reason itself. Aware both of the goal's goodness or value and of the fact that some act or other may contribute to its accomplishment, reason desires to perform the act. In the same way, aversion is transmitted from undesirable outcomes to acts that, as reason recognizes, promote them or tend to bring them about. When desire is transmitted to a means from an end that is itself desired by reason, what arises in this way is a desire of a very special kind. It is a desire for something or other specifically as a means to something else. It relies directly on, and is fully and immediately controlled by, a grasp of a means–end relation. If and when reason recognizes that the means–end relation has ceased to obtain, or that the means in question is no longer the best one among available options, this desire subsides right away.

None of this is meant to suggest for a moment that Plato's theory limits reason to considering how to accomplish goals that have already been set—for instance, by non-rational parts of the soul. On the contrary, it is a central part of the theory that reason can work out and accomplish its own objectives by relying on its own distinctive resources, which enable it to grasp the true natures of things, prominently including the true nature of goodness. Moreover, it is only by doing so that reason comes to be in a position to succeed fully in performing its proper functions, namely to acquire comprehensive understanding and to direct action in a way that is informed by, and flows from, that understanding. Given a conception of reason along these lines, it is easy to see that there is a good deal of room for desire that does not directly involve the use of reason. We can and do desire things on the basis of thoughts and reflections about how good they are, or what they are good for. But we also desire things (such as food, drink, and sex) as a result of the natural constitution and functioning, in a reasonably conducive environment, of the living organisms that we are. And moreover, we can and do form tendencies to desire certain things (such as money) and be averse to others, not on the basis of our own reflections on their goodness or value, but in the course and as a result of our upbringing, of absorbing and internalizing the beliefs and attachments of the culture that surrounds us.

PART TWO

BELIEF AND APPEARANCE
IN PLATO

Introduction

My main purpose in the preceding section was to show that Plato's psychological theory holds the appetitive part of the soul to be non-rational in the strong sense of lacking the capacity for reasoning. On the other hand it is plain that the theory takes appetite to be capable, all by itself, of giving rise to fully formed motivating conditions, and hence to episodes of behaviour, even to episodes of human behaviour. One question this raises is what cognitive resources Plato's psychological theory makes available to the non-rational parts of the soul. Part 2 attempts to answer that question, focusing on the appetitive part. I shall argue that Plato's psychological theory operates with a remarkably rich conception of non-rational cognition. It takes such cognition to be centred on the senses, but not to be limited to what is presented in occurrent acts of sense-perception. Non-rational cognition, as Plato conceives of it, crucially includes memory, which he thinks of as the preservation and re-enactment of impressions originally received in acts of sense-perception. In addition, the non-rational parts of the soul have cognitive access to sensory representations that may be formed under the influence of reason. Although Plato does not offer a fully developed theory of non-rational cognition, I am meaning to show that he does supply the resources for an outline of such cognition that is coherent, defensible, and interesting. In Part 3, I shall present and interpret what I take to be Aristotle's rather more fully developed version of what in Plato remains an outline account of non-rational cognition in terms of the reception, preservation, and re-enactment of sensory impressions.

Chapter 5 is devoted to a much-discussed passage in *Republic* 10's condemnation of imitative poetry. In that passage (602 C 4–603 B 3), Socrates calls attention to various kinds of perceptual illusions, so as to identify the part of the soul that both painting and poetry appeal to. Let us call the passage the argument from cognitive conflict. I shall claim that the division of the soul that Plato has in mind in that argument is meant to divide, not *reason* into two distinct sub-parts, but *the soul* into its rational part and some part or aspect below reason. The centrepiece of my case for that view is a non-standard reading of one of the passage's key sentences (602 E 4–6); that reading is a modified version of a reading proposed by James Adam in 1902. I shall argue that we should accept my version of Adam's reading, as it is linguistically viable and superior to the standard reading from the point of view of philosophical interpretation. Part of my defence of Adam's reading appeals to some evident connections between the argument from cognitive conflict and the discussion of imitative poetry that immediately follows it. So as to state my view fully, I shall offer a detailed discussion of the place of the argument from cognitive conflict in the overall context of *Republic* 10's long and complicated argument against imitative poetry.

According to the interpretation of the argument from cognitive conflict that I shall press, it attributes beliefs to a non-rational part of the soul. The mental states that Socrates thinks of as beliefs of a non-rational part of the soul crucially involve sensory representations of apparent states of affairs and the uncritical acceptance by a non-rational part of the soul that things are the way the senses represent them as being. On the basis of that characterization, I shall suggest that a commitment to the existence of such mental states coheres well with the rest of the *Republic*'s psychological theory. In fact I think that it should be welcomed as a significant feature of that theory.

That non-rational parts of the soul are capable of forming *beliefs* is, I shall submit, a view that Plato comes to reject. The evidence for this claim is twofold. On the one hand, it is said in the *Timaeus* that appetite is 'totally devoid of belief, reasoning, and thought' (*Timaeus* 77 B 3–6). On the other hand, a number of later Platonic dialogues, most notably the *Theaetetus*, exhibit a conception of belief that emphasizes the active, reflective aspect of belief-formation or judgement. The *Theaetetus* offers a detailed discussion of what is involved in, and required for, forming beliefs, in a way that makes it clear that Plato has come to accept that forming beliefs requires the use of cognitive resources that belong to reason alone. It is the task of Chapter 6 to present and interpret the twofold evidence for thinking that Plato comes to reject the view that parts of the soul other than reason can form beliefs. Completing that task requires discussing the *Timaeus*' statement of Plato's theory of the tripartite soul. More importantly, it requires clarifying the rather difficult and controversial passage in the *Theaetetus* in which Socrates argues that belief-formation in all cases outstrips the resources of perception (*Theaetetus* 184–7). I shall argue that Socrates in that passage distinguishes between belief-formation and sense-perception as two distinct capacities of the soul, and that he denies that the resources of perception are sufficient for the formation of any belief. This distinction leaves intact a level of awareness and cognition below belief and reason. Such non-rational cognition crucially includes, but need not be limited to, what is presented in occurrent acts of perception.

The central idea behind Plato's view that belief is a distinctively rational capacity, I shall suggest, is that forming a belief is a matter of judging, and being able to judge whether something or other is, say, hard requires being able to grasp such structural facts as that hardness is different from, and the opposite of, softness. And the ability to grasp such structural facts, Plato thinks, belongs to reason alone. The upshot of *Theaetetus* 184–7, as I understand it, is that the use of reason is required for *the application of predicates*. Plato does not think, on the other hand, that reason is required for *the apprehension of perceptual features*. And so he can continue to hold that the parts of the soul below reason can be sensitive, and responsive, to what may be presented in acts of perception. He needs to say that the non-rational parts cannot themselves apply predicates. But to say this is not to say that they cannot pick out features of a situation, or that they cannot respond to such features by forming desires or aversions.

In Chapter 7, I shall argue that much, and perhaps all, of the substance of the *Republic*'s psychological theory can survive Plato's recognition that belief is a distinctively rational capacity. The *Theaetetus*' discussion of what is required for belief provides the resources for an economical explanation of the *Timaeus*' denial of belief to appetite. In the *Republic*, Plato is evidently prepared to attribute beliefs to non-rational parts of the soul, including appetite. There is good reason to think, I shall argue, that the *Theaetetus*' conception of belief as a distinctively rational capacity is innovative, superseding a less specific, and less stringent, conception of what is involved in belief that is in play in earlier Platonic writings such as the *Republic*. As a result, we shall be in a position to explain the *Timaeus*' denial of belief to appetite simply in terms of new thoughts about the nature of belief, without assuming any substantive change in Plato's theory of the tripartite soul.

One reason in favour of this interpretative strategy is the fact that the *Timaeus*' statement of Plato's theory of the tripartite soul is strikingly close, in conception and even in language, to the *Republic*'s statement of that theory. In particular, it is part of the *Timaeus*' version of tripartition that appetite can, all on its own, give rise to episodes of behaviour. Moreover, the *Timaeus* also maintains the *Republic*'s distinction between appetite's willing obedience to reason's commands and its forcible subjugation by reason and spirit.

However, the *Timaeus*' denial of belief to appetite, against the background of its robust restatement of tripartition, also calls for clarification of how appetite, as Plato conceives of it, is in a position to do what his psychological theory requires it to be able to do. It must be able to give rise to fully formed motivating conditions, and to receive commands, but also threats, from reason. I shall discuss three passages—one from the *Timaeus* and two from the *Philebus*—that show awareness of this need for clarification, and that collectively shed a good deal of light on how Plato conceives of the cognition of soul-parts below reason. The first passage (*Timaeus* 71 A 3–E 2) is of value chiefly for showing awareness of a problem. I shall call this the *Timaeus*' problem. It is that Plato's psychological theory requires that reason can affect and influence appetite by communicating with it; but that it conceives of appetite as being unable to understand, or anyhow as being such as not to care about, the predicational structures that constitute the discourse of reason. While the passage's attempt to resolve the problem is unsuccessful, I shall suggest that it foreshadows an important development in Plato's psychological theory that resolves the *Timaeus*' problem. The passage speaks obscurely of 'images and appearances' formed under the influence of reason on the liver's shiny surface, and it assumes that appetite can in some way be aware of, and be influenced by, such appearances 'painted' by reason. What the passage is, I shall suggest, groping for is the idea that the sensory imagination can play a mediating role that enables reason to affect and influence appetite by communicating with it. This idea is expressed with admirable clarity in the *Philebus*' simile of the illustrated book

(*Philebus* 38 E 12–40 C 6). I shall discuss that passage in its own right and in the larger context of the *Philebus*. I shall also call attention to its closeness, in language and conception, to the statement and attempted resolution of the *Timaeus'* problem.

Before turning to the simile of the illustrated book, however, I shall bring into play a slightly earlier passage from the *Philebus*, namely its discussion of pleasures of anticipation (32 B 9–36 C 2). That discussion offers accounts of the formation of desire and of the apprehension of prospective situations that avoid any appeal to reason and its distinctive resources. In doing so, it offers an outline account of non-rational cognition in terms of sense-perception and of the preservation and re-enactment of sensory impressions. It enables us to see how Plato can think that the non-rational parts of the soul are able not only to give rise to fully formed motivating conditions, but also to be the bearers of expectations and of forward-looking emotions such as fear (*Timaeus* 69 C 5–D 4).

What emerges from the *Timaeus* and the *Philebus*, I shall close Part 2 by arguing, is a psychological theory that preserves the *Republic's* conception of appetite as a non-rational part of the soul. More specifically, it preserves, and significantly clarifies, two key claims of the *Republic's* theory: first, that appetite can, all on its own, give rise to fully formed motivating conditions; secondly, that there are two importantly different ways of overcoming objectionable desires of appetite. The many-headed brute can be forcibly overpowered, or it can be made gentle by reason.

5

Imitation and the Soul

Plato's psychological theory plainly equips the two non-rational parts of the soul, appetite and spirit, with some cognitive resources. The motivating conditions that Socrates ascribes to them are, as we have seen, not limited to blind, undirected cravings, but prominently include fully formed impulses to pursue or avoid specific things. Leontius' appetitive part, for instance, comes to be the bearer of an intense desire to have a close look at some corpses by the side of the road, a course of action that his spirited part is vehemently averse to. In another striking passage, Socrates speaks about what appetite thinks it is doing while the person it belongs to is asleep and his reason is at rest:

Then the brutish and savage part, full of food and drink, casts off sleep and seeks to find a way to gratify itself. You know that there is nothing it won't dare to do at such a time, free of all control by shame or reason. It does not shrink from trying to have sex with [sc. the person's] mother, as it thinks (ὡς οἴεται), or with anyone else at all, whether man, god, or brute. It will commit any foul murder, and there is no food it refuses to eat. In a word, it omits no act of folly and shamelessness.   (*Republic*, 571 C 5–D 5)

As this passage makes clear, Socrates is willing to attribute thoughts to appetite. He also characterizes temperance as friendship and agreement among the parts of the soul, which obtains 'when the ruler and the ruled believe in common (ὁμοδοξῶσι) that reason should rule, and they don't engage in civil war against it' (442 C 9–D 2). He needs some idea of agreement among the parts of the soul, so as to contrast the harmonious, perfectly unified condition of soul that is justice with inferior conditions, such as the oligarch's, which involve division, conflict, and disunity. The attribution of thoughts to non-rational soul-parts seems to find its culmination in book 10 of the *Republic*, where Socrates appears to attribute beliefs to a non-rational part,[1] and to speak of it as a part or aspect of thought (διάνοια) (603 C 1–2).[2]

I want to argue in this chapter that this seems to be the case for the excellent reason that it is in fact the case. In other words, I shall try to show that the division of the soul that Socrates argues for at 602 C 4–603 B 3 is a division between reason on

[1] 602 E 8–603 D 2. The words in question are simply δόξα and δοξάζειν, rather than the compound verb ὁμοδοξεῖν that Socrates uses in book 4.
[2] Cf. also ὁμονοητικῶς at 603 C 11.

the one hand and a non-rational part on the other. There are two main reasons why this matters for present purposes. First, if book 10 divides reason into two parts, as some have thought,[3] this will yield a psychological theory that is notably different from, and in fact incompatible with, the theory that is set out and argued for in book 4, at least as I understand it. For according to that theory, reason is one of three incomposite parts of the soul. Secondly, if *Republic* 10 is indeed where Socrates' tendency to attribute quasi-intellectual states to parts of the soul below reason finds its culmination, then this makes it a good place to reflect on that aspect of the *Republic*'s psychological theory, or anyhow of its presentation.

The main text that we shall be concerned with is 602 C 4–603 B 3. This text is in many ways connected to other parts of an extraordinarily complicated argument for the conclusion that imitative poetry should not be accepted into the ideal city. Before we turn specifically to our main text, then, a few remarks should be made about the overall argument. It is long and complicated but not, I think, unclear or confused.

Imitative poetry is poetry that involves impersonation. This covers drama, both tragic and comic, as well as epic poetry, Homer prominently included. Socrates makes it clear from the start that his argument against imitative poetry relies on his psychological theory: 'Now that we have separated the parts of the soul', he says at the beginning of book 10, 'it is even clearer, I think, that imitative poetry should be altogether excluded' (595 A 5–B 1). This is the first of several references to the *Republic*'s theory of the tripartite soul, which was introduced and argued for in book 4. The first part of the present argument (595 C 8–602 C 2) is meant to establish the preliminary conclusion that neither tragic nor epic poets have any significant knowledge concerning the various sorts of things they depict or represent. The second part focuses on the harm that drama and epic poetry do to the soul (602 C 4–606 D 7).

Socrates begins that part of the argument by asking 'on which of a person's parts does it [sc. imitation] exert its power?' (*Republic* 602 C 4–5). Glaucon asks Socrates to clarify the question. Socrates does so by showing which of a person's parts it is that painting exerts its power on. In talking about painting, he is not for a moment losing sight of poetry. Nor is this mere analogy. The point that he wants to make about the specific case of the imitative art of painting is supposed to be generally valid for all forms of imitation,[4] which includes imitative poetry as well

---

[3] For instance, N. Murphy, *The Interpretation of Plato's Republic* (Oxford: Oxford University Press, 1951), app. B, 239–43; A. Kenny, *The Anatomy of the Soul* (Oxford: Oxford University Press, 1973), 22; A. Nehamas, 'Plato on imitation and poetry in *Republic* 10', in J. Moravcsik and P. Temko (eds.), *Plato on Beauty, Wisdom and the Arts* (Totowa, NJ: Rowman and Littlefield, 1982), 65–6; M. Burnyeat, 'Culture and society in Plato's *Republic*', in G. Peterson (ed.), *The Tanner Lectures on Human Values* 20 (Salt Lake City: University of Utah Press, 1999), 223–6; D. Sedley, *The Midwife of Platonism: Text and Subtext in Plato's* Theaetetus (Oxford: Clarendon Press, 2004), 113.

[4] 603 A 9–B 3: 'This, then, is what I wanted to get agreement about when I said that painting and imitation as a whole (ἡ γραφικὴ καὶ ὅλως ἡ μιμητική) produce work that is far from the truth, namely, that imitation really consorts with a part of us that is far from wisdom.'

as painting. His point is that imitation in general appeals to a base, non-rational part of the soul. This is supposed to be seen fairly easily in the case of painting, which is why he begins with it. But the point is supposed to apply to imitation in all its forms. If it does, then it is reasonable to think, on general grounds to do with imitation, that imitative poetry too appeals to a base part of the soul. But rather than relying merely on what it is reasonable to think, Socrates wants to show this to be in fact the case by detailed and specific consideration of imitative poetry in particular. Furthermore, it is not just that he thinks that imitative poetry appeals to some base part or other of the soul, as does painting. He plainly wants to go further than that, since he wants to say, as we shall see, that it is the *same* base part of the soul that both painting and imitative poetry appeal to.

Socrates next presents his long and carefully argued answer to the question which part of the person imitative poetry exerts its power on (603 C 5–605 C 3). His answer does include a characterization of the subject matter of imitative poetry, but that does not mean it loses sight of the question it is meant to answer.[5] What imitative poetry imitates, he says, is 'human beings acting voluntarily or under compulsion, who believe that, as a result of these actions, they are doing either well or badly and who experience either pleasure or pain in all this' (*Republic* 603 C 5–8). He then asks Glaucon whether a person is 'of one mind' in the varied circumstances of action—whether, that is, his thought is disposed in a single, uniform way (ὁμονοητικῶς διάκειται, 603 C 11–D 1). Uniformity of thought is contrasted with the kind of psychological conflict and opposition that has just come to light in Socrates' discussion of painting. Is it, he asks, that 'just as a person is at war with himself in matters of sight and held opposite beliefs about the same thing at the same time, so also does he fight with himself and engage in civil war with himself in matters of action?' (*Republic* 603 D 1–3).

It is worth noting carefully how he answers that question. He says that there is no need to reach agreement about the matter now, because, as he remembers, an adequate conclusion about it was attained in earlier arguments, to the effect that 'our soul is full of a myriad of such oppositions at the same time' (603 D 5–6). This would seem to be another reference to the argument for tripartition of the soul in book 4. As early in that argument as 439 C 5, Glaucon already accepts that

---

[5] According to Nehamas, 'Plato on imitation', 66–7, the discussion of painting distinguishes between two aspects of reason, having 'little if anything to do with the irrational elements in the soul'. He acknowledges that the discussion of poetry, by contrast, emphasizes the idea that poetry appeals to the 'irrational elements'. There is no real inconsistency, he suggests, because Plato has in fact changed the topic: the discussion of painting concerns its effect on the spectator, whereas at 603 B 7–605 A 6 Plato is concerned 'not with the effect of poetry on its audience, but with the subject matter of the poem itself'. However, the central concern of the discussion of painting is not what it does to the spectator, but which part of the spectator it appeals to (602 C 4–5; 603 B 1–B 3). It is precisely the same question that Socrates raises about poetry at 603 B 10–C 3, and answers at 605 A 8–C 3, to the effect that painting and poetry appeal to the same part of the soul. As we shall see, this answer is supported and prepared for by the remarks about the subject matter of poetry, at 603 B 7–605 A 6. The key idea expressed by those remarks is that it must be a non-rational part of us that takes pleasure in dramatic representations of non-rationally driven behaviour.

it happens to very many people, and very frequently, that they are, for instance, thirsty and, at the same time, averse to drinking.

Another thing that is worth noting is that Socrates treats the motivational conflicts familiar from earlier books of the *Republic* as being very much like the conflicting beliefs of book 10: both of these are cases of civil war and opposition in the soul. He does not offer the slightest indication of any theoretically significant difference or discontinuity between the conflicting beliefs of book 10 and the conflicting desires of earlier books. Furthermore, Socrates clearly contrasts, again with no notice of any difference, both conflicting desires and conflicting beliefs with having one's thought disposed uniformly.[6] At least in the case of conflicting desires, the underlying idea of what constitutes a person's mind or thought must include not just the soul's rational part, but the whole of the tripartite soul. In other words, language that one might expect to be reserved for, and limited to, the rational part of the soul is in fact used broadly and generously so as to include the whole range of human awareness and desire.

Having reminded Glaucon of the psychological conflicts that afflict people in the varied circumstances of life, Socrates proceeds to pinpoint the parts of the soul involved in such conflicts that are going to be salient to what he wants to say about imitative poetry. He does so by revisiting book 3's example of a decent man confronted with the loss of a son, brother, or friend (387 D 4–E 8). As he said then, such a person would least give in to lamentations, and bear misfortune most quietly when it strikes. The psychological theory that was not available then, but is available now, allows Socrates to add a significant detail to the picture presented in book 3. The decent man's facade of calmness and control conceals an inner struggle. He is pulled towards remembrance of the loss he has suffered, and towards grief and lamentation. He is also pulled the other way, especially so, as Glaucon agrees emphatically (604 A 4), when he is seen by his peers. Socrates can now apply the Principle of Opposites: when there are in a person two opposite pulls (ἐναντίας . . . ἀγωγῆς) in relation to the same thing and at the same time, we say that the person must have two parts (604 B 1–2). The decent man's better part follows reason and deliberation (604 D 4–5), but it is also motivated by a sense of shame: that is why it pulls away from grief much more when he is among his equals than when he is alone. It is natural, then, to suppose that this part includes both his reason and its natural ally, spirit, and so one expects the part that pulls towards grief to be appetite. Socrates eschews such specificity, for a reason that will become clear in a bit.

It is entirely appropriate for Socrates at this stage to return to the example of a bereaved decent man. It enables him to pinpoint something in the soul that in

---

[6] The adverb ὁμονοητικῶς derives from the verb ὁμονοεῖν, which means 'think alike', 'agree', and is cognate with the political term ὁμόνοια ('unanimity', 'concord'). The word is sometimes used to contrast with words denoting civil war (στάσις). The application of such words to all of the soul, not just reason, may well stem from the city/soul parallel, which perhaps weakens their impact somewhat. But it is hard to believe that Plato could have been oblivious to the presence of the root word νοεῖν, 'think', 'understand'. (My heavy-handed paraphrase is of course meant to draw attention to that presence.)

certain circumstances pulls people towards grief and lamentation. It also enables him to show that, in the case of a character-type that Glaucon can easily recognize as respectable and indeed identify with,[7] what pulls him towards lamenting is just one part of his soul, and in fact a base and non-rational part, one that is unimpressed by the demands not only of reason and custom (νόμος) (604 B 4–C 3), but even of shame (604 A 6). Given that his emphasis in discussing imitative poetry is firmly on tragedy,[8] the centrality of grief as an emotional, non-rational force in the soul is readily understandable.

Having distinguished between two relevant soul-parts, Socrates distinguishes, plainly on the basis of the former distinction, between two corresponding kinds of character: an excitable character on the one hand and a sensible, calm one on the other (604 E 1–3). The excitable character is one whose behaviour, in appropriate circumstances, is strongly influenced by the base part of soul that has been identified, at the expense of the better part. The sensible person, by contrast, is one whose better part maintains control, either because it remains victorious or because it meets no opposition. Imitative poetry focuses heavily on imitation of the excitable character-type, both because it is easier to imitate and because 'the many' greatly prefer what strikes them as familiar and readily understandable to what does not. Imitation of human action and passion in dramatic enactment on the theatre stage can obviously be enormously engaging and enjoyable. An idea that Socrates is clearly relying on, though he does not express it in so many words, is that when the action imitated is such as normally to derive from the excitable part of the soul, the part of us to which such imitation is especially engaging and enjoyable is our own excitable part. No doubt this, too, is supposed to be obvious. Reason finds nothing worth appreciating in a grown man's lamentations. From spirit's point of view, it is a disgrace for a man to behave that way (cf. 605 E 4). Any enjoyment we may get out of *such* imitation therefore must belong to a part of us below reason and spirit.

Socrates is now in a position to answer specifically with respect to poetry the question first asked at 602 C 4–5 about imitation in general, and then restated at 603 C 2–3 about imitative poetry in particular: which part of the soul does it appeal to? His answer is that it appeals to a base, non-rational part. In fact he goes out of his way to make it clear that he takes imitative poetry to appeal to the same part that painting appeals to.[9] In what must be a back-reference to 602 C 4–603 B 3,

---

[7] The respectable man is, of course, very much like Glaucon. Witness his emphatic answer, already noted, at 604 A 4; there is only one way in which Glaucon can be sure about what the decent man does when he is *all by himself* (note the heavy emphasis at 604 A 3: ἐν ἐρημίᾳ μόνος αὐτὸς καθ' αὑτόν). Recall Adeimantus' not altogether flattering suggestion elsewhere that the timocratic, spirit-ruled character-type will be much like his (and Plato's) brother Glaucon (548 D 8–9).

[8] He famously treats Homer as the first of the tragedians, 607 A 2–3.

[9] Burnyeat, 'Culture and society', accepts that poetry appeals to a non-rational part (best seen, he thinks, as 'an enlargement of book IV's appetitive part', 224). He also holds that it is reason that undergoes division in the discussion of painting, and therefore that it is an inferior part of *reason* to which painting appeals. How, then, can Socrates identify the two parts? 'As often in Plato', Burnyeat suggests, 'what begins as a parallel or analogy ends with one term dominating the other' (225). Thus

he says that imitative poetry gratifies a part of the soul 'which cannot distinguish between the large and the small but takes the same things to be large at one time and small at another' (*Republic* 605 C 1–3). It is, however, not just that imitative poetry offers enjoyment to a part of the soul that is non-rational and excitable. The same can be said about painting as well. What makes imitative poetry especially harmful, and what justifies its exclusion from the ideal city, is that it offers enjoyment to the excitable part of our nature precisely by exciting and arousing it intensely, providing it with an opportunity to assert and exert itself. In this way, Socrates says, imitative poetry feeds and strengthens the excitable part. Moreover, in doing so, he says, it destroys the rational part of the soul (605 B 4–5). This of course is an overstatement,[10] but one, I think, with precise cash value. The idea, I suggest, is that by strengthening the excitable part, imitative poetry promotes the rule in the soul of something that is not naturally suited and equipped to rule, at the expense of reason. When reason is subordinated to other parts of the soul, it cannot realize and manifest what it is, a principle to rule and direct a person's life. Thus, imitative poetry destroys reason as a ruling and directing principle, which is what it really is.[11]

Socrates' 'greatest charge' against imitative poetry (605 C 5–606 D 7) returns to decent people (ἐπιεικεῖς) and concerns them specifically. The charge is that imitative poetry harms the souls not only of 'the many', but even of decent people, except for a very small number of individuals (605 C 5–7). Even the best of us, he says, enjoy a good tragic performance, 'giving ourselves up to following it, sympathizing with the hero and taking his sufferings seriously' (605 D 3–4). He is evidently not speaking of people the best part of whose soul is in an optimal state. It is only because their best part has not, he says, been 'adequately educated by reason or habit' that it wrongly relaxes its guard over 'the lamenting part', as he now calls it (606 A 7–B 1; cf. 606 B 3–7). Moreover, it is worth noting that the character type Socrates is describing is not in fact one who has achieved the harmonious, unified disposition of the soul that is justice, but is divided and conflicted exactly like the decent man reintroduced at 603 E 4. The part of the soul that imitative poetry gratifies is one that is forcibly held down (βίᾳ κατεχόμενον) in his own private misfortunes, and has come to be hungry for the satisfaction of weeping and wailing, 'being by nature such as to desire such things' (606 A 5–6). One thing this suggests is that Socrates takes imitative poetry to be dangerous primarily to morally imperfect individuals like Glaucon. We should note in this connection Socrates' strong emphasis, towards the end of the discussion, on its relevance not only to the ideal city but also to the constitution

---

Socrates ends up, at 605 B 7–C 3, applying language to the non-rational part that is not in fact appropriate to it (226). This is ingenious but uncompelling. It rests on the view that 602 C 4–603 B 3 is best understood as yielding a division between a superior and an inferior part of reason. I shall shortly dispute that view.

[10] Cf. 589 A 1. λιμοκτονεῖν literally means 'starve to death'.

[11] For an alternative (and not incompatible) interpretation, see D. Scott, 'Platonic pessimism and moral education', *Oxford Studies in Ancient Philosophy*, 17 (1999), 35–6.

and well-being of each individual soul,[12] culminating in a direct and forceful appeal to Glaucon, in which he reminds him of the huge importance of the struggle to be good rather than bad (608 B 4–5).[13] If Socrates is right about what imitative poetry does to the soul, enjoying a tragedy has precisely the same effect on the soul as performing an act of injustice. It makes you worse and more wretched instead of better and happier.

Before completing his greatest charge, Socrates amplifies his central point—that imitative poetry strengthens non-rational forces in the soul—beyond grief to other emotional and desiderative tendencies, such as the pleasures of humour and laughter (606 C 2–9), sexual desire, and anger (θυμός) (606 D 1). All of these, he says, are forces in the soul which imitative poetry nourishes and whose rule in the soul it promotes. We can now see why Socrates never says that it is specifically the appetitive part of the soul to which imitative poetry appeals. He quite clearly wants the base and non-rational part which imitative poetry gratifies and strengthens to include, at least on occasion, the soul's spirited part. It may be somewhat surprising all of a sudden to find spirit included in the soul's inferior part, when earlier on in the argument it seemed to belong to the decent person's better part. But there is no inconsistency or confusion here. Spirit is reason's natural ally, and it will typically support reason in such conflicts as may arise between reason and appetite. It is, however, a non-rational part of the soul, and to strengthen it beyond due measure is to endanger and ultimately to overthrow reason's rule and the proper order of the soul. It is perhaps worth pointing out, then, that when Socrates in book 10 speaks of better or worse parts or aspects of soul, he is clearly not concerned to identify incomposite or basic soul-parts. Nor need he be. The fact that reason and spirit are two distinct parts of the soul that can conflict with one another does not exclude the possibility that they cooperate harmoniously on many occasions, acting in concert as a person's better part. And while spirit and appetite frequently manifest their distinctness by pulling someone in opposite directions, it remains the case that they both are distinct from reason and jointly make up the worse part of a person's soul. It is a mistake, then, to suppose that book 10 offers bipartition of the soul as a rival theory to book 4's tripartition. It is the business of book 4 to distinguish reason, spirit, and appetite from one another, laying bare the structure of the embodied human soul. Nothing in book 10 contradicts or revises any of the distinctions made in book 4.

We come at last to 602 C 4–603 B 3. As we have seen already, Socrates wants to show what kind of part or aspect of the soul it is that imitation exerts its power on. He does this, naturally enough, by demonstrating a division of the soul. The same magnitude, he says, appears 'through sight' (διὰ τῆς ὄψεως . . . φαίνεται) not to be equal from nearby and from far away (602 B 6–8). He adds other visual appearances, such as the same things looking bent when in water and straight

---

[12] 605 B 5–7, 606 B 5–8, 606 D 4–7.

[13] Note also the sense of urgency created by Socrates' switch, at 606 C 3, from first-person plural to second-person singular.

when out of water, or both concave and convex. Painters in various ways exploit our natural tendency to obtain false appearances through sight. Fortunately, we are not condemned to lead our lives in a way that is guided and ruled only by how things appear through the senses. We can rely on measurement, arithmetic, calculation, and the like so as to discover how things *are*.[14] Socrates assigns this task of discovery to reason. His next two sentences (602 E 4–9) are difficult and crucially important. Sentence 1: 'it often happens', Socrates says, 'that when this part [sc. reason][15] has done the measuring and indicates that some things are larger or smaller than or the same size as others, the opposite appears to it at the same time about the same things [alternatively: about these things]'.[16] Glaucon agrees, and Socrates says Sentence 2: 'we agreed that it is impossible for the same thing to believe opposites about the same thing at the same time'. Glaucon agrees again, and Socrates concludes that the part of the soul whose belief is contrary to the measurements could not be the same as the part whose belief is in accordance with them. The part that is opposed to measurement and reasoning is one of the base parts or aspects in us or, as he also puts it, the thing in us that is far from wisdom.[17] It is this part of our nature, Socrates thinks, that painting and imitation as a whole appeal to.

In Sentence 2, Socrates is again referring back to the argument for tripartition in book 4. It is not said explicitly there that the same thing cannot at the same time *believe* opposites about the same thing. What is said, though, is close enough, as has been seen by others.[18] The Principle of Opposites says that the same thing cannot, at the same time, do opposites in the same respect and towards the same

---

[14] Note the contrast, which is background to the present passage, between how things (e.g. a couch) appear from one perspective or another, and how they *are* at 598 A 5, and 598 B 2–3.

[15] τούτῳ must refer to reason, the reference of τούτου in the preceding line; Schleiermacher's conjecture τῷ will not do, in view of σημαίνοντι. It is reason that *indicates*, not the person.

[16] Our editions read περὶ ταὐτά ('about the same things') at 602 E 6. However, περὶ ταῦτα ('about these things') is a perfectly feasible alternative. (Plato, readers may recall, did not use accents. Greek accents are an invention of the Hellenistic period, standardly attributed to Aristophanes of Byzantium. They were not systematically added to ancient texts until the tenth century AD.) It may be helpful to anticipate the reading of the sentence that I shall favour: read περὶ ταῦτα and take the reference of 'these things' to be the various sorts of things that feature in the sensory appearances Socrates is interested in: for instance, a stick half submerged in water, or an object that appears now concave, and now convex. (Items of these sorts have again been referred to at 602 D 6–7 as 'what appears larger or smaller, or more numerous, or heavier'.) Understand the sentence as follows: 'when reason has done the measuring and indicates that some things are larger or smaller than or the same size as others, the opposites [sc. of what on each relevant occasion appears through the senses] appear to it at the same time about these things'.

[17] Nehamas ('Plato on imitation', 66), who thinks that the part that is opposed to measurement is an inferior part of reason, denies that the derogatory language Socrates applies to it undermines this view, pointing to *Philebus* 55 E 1–3, where Socrates asks, 'if one were to set apart from each art arithmetic, measuring, and weighing, might we say that the remaining part of each would be base?' It is not just, however, that Socrates calls the part in question 'base'. He also says about it that it is 'the thing in us which is far removed from wisdom' (πόρρω . . . φρονήσεως ὄντι τῷ ἐν ἡμῖν, 603 B 1–2), and later that it is 'the soul's foolish part' (τῷ ἀνοήτῳ αὐτῆς, 605 B 7). It is hard to believe that Plato wrote in such ways of a part of *reason*.

[18] Price, *Mental Conflict*, 44; Burnyeat, 'Culture and society', 224.

thing, and *assenting* and *rejecting* are agreed, at 437 B 1, to be opposites. So believing opposites about the same thing is presumably understood as assenting to and at the same time rejecting the same thing—how things appear through the senses, or the results of measuring.[19] There is, then, a reasonable path from opposite beliefs, via the Principle of Opposites, to partition of the soul. The real question is, of course, why Socrates thinks that opposite *beliefs* are involved in the circumstances he has in mind. In some way or other, he gets from opposition between what reason indicates and how things appear through the senses to opposition between beliefs. Which parts of the soul do these opposite beliefs belong to? And is it reasonable to think that the sensory appearances Socrates has in mind are or involve beliefs?[20] To answer both questions, we need to know how to interpret Sentence 1. There are at least two possibilities.

According to the standard reading of Sentence 1, it says that (it often happens that) while reason indicates that (for example) these two trees are of equal size, it at the same time appears to it that one of them is bigger than the other.[21] On this reading, the sentence says that (it often happens, that) the opposite of what reason indicates appears, and continues to appear, to reason through the senses. It is easy to see, as we read Sentence 2, that reason accepts the results of its own measuring activities, and believes that things are as it itself indicates them to be. However, Socrates thinks this kind of case involves two beliefs that are opposite to one another. And one naturally expects that the opposition between beliefs, mentioned in Sentence 2, belongs to the same thing—or pair of things, as it turns out—as the opposition between measurement and sensory appearance envisaged in Sentence 1. So if Sentence 1 assigns the sensory appearance to reason, as it does on the standard reading, one expects *both* of the opposite beliefs mentioned in Sentence 2 to belong to reason. On this view, reason believes that things are as it itself indicates them to be and, at the same time, that things are as they appear through the senses. But it is extremely difficult to see why reason would accept a sensory appearance that it has just shown to be false. All of reason, Socrates says elsewhere, is such as always to strain to know where the truth lies (581 B 6–7). Why would it, or even just part of it, accept an appearance it knows to be false: a mere appearance, an illusion? This difficulty seems sufficiently grave to send us back to Plato's text.

[19] We may note that Socrates once again presupposes that the qualification 'in the same respect' is either inapplicable or irrelevant. He thus treats believing opposites like desire and aversion, and movement and rest, rather than like rotation and non-inclination. The key idea may well be that the disagreement between the two soul-parts is complete and unqualified: one part simply accepts that things are as they appear, the other part simply rejects that this is the case.

[20] I take it to be clear that appearance does not always involve belief. Belief requires acceptance or, to echo Plato's language, assent; appearance does not. Our better part, Plato no doubt thinks, is aware of sensory appearances; but it does not always accept them. Note πιστεύειν at 603 A 4. Cf. Aristotle, *De Anima* 3.3, 428ᵃ19–24.

[21] It is how the sentence is understood by, among others, Nehamas, 'Plato on imitation'; S. Halliwell, *Republic X* (Warminster: Aris and Phillips, 1988); P. Murray, *Plato on Poetry* (Cambridge: Cambridge University Press, 1996); Burnyeat, 'Culture and society', 223.

Back to Sentence 1, then. There is another possible reading, though it is easy to miss.[22] When reason has done its measuring and is indicating that the trees are of equal size, what appears to it to be the case—the view *it* takes of the matter—is simply that the trees are of equal size. What appears to it to be the case, however, is the very opposite of how the same things appear, and continue to appear, through the senses.[23] What Sentence 1 is saying, in other words, is that (it often happens that) when reason is indicating this or that, what appear to reason are the opposites of the simultaneous sensory appearances about the things in question.[24]

As we read on, there is, as before, nothing surprising about reason putting its trust, to use Socrates' words, in measurement and calculation (603 A 4–5). It is simply going with the view it takes of the matter. But part of the soul, Socrates clearly assumes, is unmoved by measurement and calculation, and disagrees with reason about the matter at hand. His assumption is then not only that the relevant sensory appearances persist. Of course they do. He also assumes that some part of the soul assents to, or accepts, these sensory appearances. (As we have seen, this seems in fact to be required for the Principle of Opposites to be applicable.) Why assume that? On the second reading of Sentence 1, the part of our soul that goes with sensory appearances is, or may well be, non-rational. Its distinctness from reason, we can say, is made manifest by its opposition to it.

A moment's reflection on Plato's psychological theory should make it clear how natural it is to assume that the parts of us below reason *accept* sensory appearances. Non-rational soul-parts are not disengaged contemplators, but centres of motivation. They motivate a person to act energetically and decisively in pursuit of food, drink, sex, and the like, and so as to acquire, maintain, and defend a social position of esteem and respect. They could never begin to perform those functions effectively without being supplied with tolerably good information about the person's environment and, crucially, without being ready to act on that information. The text before us suggests that, just as one would expect, one way in which they get the information they need is by sensory appearances. Moreover, the lower parts cannot do what *we* can do, namely resort to measurement, arithmetic, and the like, so as to discover how things really are. For these are the resources of reason. Unlike us, then, the lower parts *are* at the mercy of how things appear through the senses (cf. 602 D 6–9). They cannot help being taken in by sensory appearances.

---

[22] A reading along these lines was proposed and argued for by James Adam in 1902. It has received little or no attention since. Note that the excision of ἅμα περὶ ταὐτά at 602 E 6, attributed to him in both Burnet's and Slings's *Oxford Classical Text* editions, is not his last word on the matter. He came to take the view, I think rightly, that it was unnecessary. See his appendix II to book 10. It does, however, seem to me easier to read the text in Adam's way if we read περὶ ταῦτα rather than, as he ended up doing, περὶ ταὐτά.

[23] That the sensory appearance in question persists is made clear by the word ἅμα ('at the same time') at 602 E 6.   [24] Reading τἀναντία φαίνεται ἅμα περὶ ταῦτα.

On the second reading of Sentence 1, then, book 10 does not divide reason into two parts. It divides the soul into reason and a non-rational part. It seems to me that in the context of 602 C 4–603 B 3, and against the general background of Plato's psychological theory, it is fairly clear that it is in this second way, or at any rate in some such way, that the sentence is meant to be understood. The result that book 10 divides the soul into reason and a non-rational part can be corroborated by additional considerations of two kinds: considerations to do with, on the one hand, the coherence of what Socrates says in book 10 alone and, on the other hand, the overall coherence of the *Republic*'s psychological theory.

I begin with book 10 by itself. We have seen already that Socrates goes out of his way (at 605 B 7–C 3) to make it perfectly clear that painting and imitative poetry 'consort with' the same part of the soul. This, of course, is precisely what he indicates as early as 603 A 9–B 3, saying that 'this is what I wanted to get agreement about when I said [sc. at 602 C 1–2] that painting and imitative art as a whole produce work that is far from the truth, namely, that [painting and imitative art as a whole] really consort with the part of us that is far from wisdom'. At the same time, Socrates leaves very little or (as I think) no room for doubt that the soul-part that imitative poetry appeals to is non-rational. He pinpoints that part by recalling (at 603 D 3–6) the motivational conflicts of earlier books, and by drawing attention to conflicting desires in the soul of a 'decent man' confronted with the loss of a son, or someone or something else he very much values. The conflicts discussed in earlier books are conflicts between, not within, soul-parts.

Nor is this one the least bit different. It is a conflict between the man's best part, which wants to follow a particular course of reasoning (604 D 4–5), and a non-rational part that cannot get its fill of remembering the loss and lamenting (604 D 7–9), and that is said, a little later, to have grown hungry for weeping and lamenting, being naturally such as to desire such things intensely (ἐπιθυμεῖν) (606 A 3–6). Presumably it does not always and in all circumstances of life naturally desire such things, but in particular kinds of circumstances, such as ones that involve some significant loss or bereavement. And no doubt its desires for weeping and lamenting will grow especially intense if, in such circumstances, it gets 'held down forcibly'. What motivates it then, I take it, is simply the pleasure[25] it expects to get out of satisfying its pent-up hunger for weeping and lamenting. Its intense desire for these things, which it desires simply because it expects them to be pleasant, is quite insensitive to considerations of advantage and even of propriety. There is only one part of the soul, according to Plato's psychological theory, which desires in this particular way: the appetitive part.

When Socrates steps back from tragedy and says what imitative poetry in general appeals to, he both confirms the central role of the appetitive part and includes

---

[25] Note ἡδονήν at 606 B 4 (this pleasure must belong primarily to the soul-part that imitative poetry gratifies). Note also the other pleasure words used in the context: χαίρειν at 605 E 5 and 606 A 7 (where it is applied specifically to the soul-part that poetry appeals to), χαρίζειν at 605 B 7, ἀρέσκειν at 605 A 3, and of course the pleasant and painful things mentioned at 606 D 2.

anger, an emotion that belongs to the spirited part and that can oppose reason no less than the desires of the lowest part can:

> And in the case of sex, anger, and all the desire-involving pains and pleasures (πάντων τῶν ἐπιθυμητικῶν τε καὶ λυπηρῶν καὶ ἡδέων) in the soul that we say accompany all our actions, imitative poetry has the very same effect on us. It nurtures and waters them and establishes them as rulers in us when they ought to wither and be ruled, for that way we'll become better and happier rather than worse and more wretched.   (*Republic* 606 D 1–7)

As I have suggested, the inclusion of anger, which belongs to the spirited part, explains why Socrates never says, throughout the discussion of what imitative art does to the soul, that the part of the soul it appeals to is specifically the appetitive part. He takes the reach of imitation to be wider than that.

The upshot of my remarks on the argument of *Republic* 10 is this, then. Socrates raises and answers the question of which part of the soul imitative poetry 'consorts with'. Initial appearances suggest that the part in question is specifically the appetitive part, but as he completes his attack on imitative poetry, he includes at least some spirited tendencies as well. He also makes it quite clear that he takes imitative poetry to appeal to the same part as does the imitative art of painting, and indeed imitative art in all its forms. He is in a position to say this consistently and legitimately only if the division of the soul argued for at 602 C 4–603 B 3 is meant to be a division between reason and a non-rational part.[26]

Moreover, it should be clear, at any rate on reflection, that if Socrates accepts in book 10 that reason is a composite of two parts, this undermines his arguments in book 4 for the distinctness of reason from appetite and spirit.[27] If reason is composed of two parts, it can at the same time be characterized by opposites in the same respect and in relation to the same thing. If so, it can not only simultaneously believe opposites about the same things, it can also desire something and at the same be averse to it. Consider the impact this would have on the argument of book 4. An especially pertinent stage of that argument is 440 E 6–441 C 6.

Socrates has just shown the distinctness of spirit from appetite, as well as spirit's natural tendency to side with reason in conflicts within the soul. The question is then whether it is nevertheless different from reason, or whether it is a part or aspect of reason (λογιστικοῦ τι εἶδος), 'so that the soul contains not three, but two parts, reason and appetite' (440 E 6–8).[28] Socrates' main argument for the

---

[26] This problem is only mitigated, not solved, by Burnyeat's interpretation ('Culture and society', 224–6). It is part of Burnyeat's view that Socrates gets carried away by the analogy or parallel between painting and poetry and ends up, at 605 B 7–C 3, misdescribing the non-rational part that poetry appeals to.

[27] This point is missed by Burnyeat. What he takes to be book 10's division of reason into two parts is, he claims, 'neither the same as, nor inconsistent with, the motivational division of book IV. The new division is an addition, meant to work alongside the earlier one' ('Culture and society', 224).

[28] It is clear, and worth pointing out, that Socrates does not want to rely merely on the experiential or phenomenological difference between rational desire and anger. He is prepared to entertain, and take seriously up to a point, the thought that (for instance) Leontius' anger at himself might be a manifestation of his *reason*!

distinctness of spirit from reason is another argument from conflict. In a verse where Odysseus is said to strike his chest and speak to his heart, Homer represents, according to Socrates, 'the part that has reasoned about better and worse as rebuking the part that is angry without reasoning, as one thing does to another' (*Republic* 441 B 6–C 2). The thought is that reason could not desire something and at the same time rebuke itself for desiring to do it, no doubt because that would involve doing opposites at the same time, in the same respect, and in relation to the same thing. (In this Homeric case, both an angry desire to punish the maids forthwith and a reasoned aversion to doing so are in play.) It is a presupposition of the argument that reason is incomposite. If it were not, there would be no reason why it could not desire something and at the same time rebuke itself for desiring it. This could simply be a matter of one part of it doing the desiring and another part doing the rebuking.

Thus, if Socrates commits himself, in discussing painting at 602 C 4—603 B 3, to the view that reason is composed of two parts, this also introduces a serious inconsistency into the psychological theory of the *Republic*. This is even more serious than it may seem, in that book 10, as we have seen, contains a number of back-references to the argument for tripartition of the soul in book 4, all of which suggest continuity and none of which as much as hints at revision.[29] I conclude, then, that an interpretation of 602 C 4–603 B 3 on which Socrates argues for a division of the soul into reason and a non-rational part is not only called for by that passage in its own right, against the general background of Plato's psychological theory. It is also required by charity. On the alternative view, Plato would have made a mess not only of *Republic* 10 by itself, but also of the psychological theory that the *Republic* as a whole presents.

I close with some comments which presuppose (reasonably, I trust) that book 10 consistently divides the soul into reason and a non-rational part and, crucially, that it attributes beliefs not only to reason, but also to a non-rational part of the soul. The argument at 602 E 4–603 A 2 assumes not only that the non-rational part that Socrates is meaning to identify is capable of acceptance, but also that it accepts sensory appearances, so that it believes that things are as they appear through the senses. This is exemplified by the belief contrary to measurement that Socrates mentions at 603 A 1. Its acceptance of sensory appearances would seem to be quite uncritical. For between appearance and acceptance there is, in its case, no room for critical reflection, for checking whether things really are as the senses present them as being. Socrates says about it that 'it cannot distinguish between (διαγιγνώσκειν) the large and the small, but takes the same things at one time to be large and at another time to be small' (*Republic* 605 B 7–C 3). Your non-rational will part take a tree to be large when you stand right before it, simply because that is how things then appear through sight from that point of view. As you look back at the same tree from far away, your non-rational part takes it to be tiny, again

---

[29] I have noted and discussed 595 B 1, 602 E 8–9, and 603 D 3–6.

simply because that is how it then appears through sight. There is thus some sense in which the non-rational part can tell apart the large from the small. When you look at a large piece of chocolate cake and a smaller one located on a table right in front of you, your non-rational part will have no trouble, and will lose no time, in distinguishing the large from the small. In a more obvious and important sense, the non-rational part really is unable, as Socrates says it is, to distinguish between the large and the small. This is because it has no idea what it really is to be large, or small, which is obviously not the same thing as appearing through sight to be large, or small, or taking up a great deal of space, or very little space, in someone's visual field.

Throughout the discussion of imitative art, Socrates refrains from highlighting just how rich and powerful non-rational cognition is or can be. The reason is obvious, of course: he wants to compare it unfavourably to the superior achievements of reason. But this agenda should not blind us to the fact that he relies on a remarkably generous notion of what in fact appears to us through the senses. He plainly does not take this to be limited to the bare presentation of sensory qualities (e.g. 'red'), but to include more complex contents, for instance that 'this is the same size as that'. Moreover, what he says leaves open the possibility that some of the ways things appear to us through the senses are acquired. We may, for example, have to learn to hear that one sound is of slightly higher pitch than another.

In attributing beliefs to the non-rational part of the soul, Socrates has in mind mental states of considerable complexity which present things as being some way or other and which, moreover, involve acceptance at a level of the soul below reason. On consideration, we may not (and will not, I think) want to call them beliefs. They do not qualify as beliefs on Plato's own considered view of belief, which, as we shall see in the next chapter, is presented in the *Theaetetus*. According to the *Republic*'s theory, they occur at a level of the soul at which it is unable to distinguish properly even between such simple things as the large and the small, because it has no adequate idea of what these things really are. So even when the non-rational part of the soul seems to say that 'this is larger than that', it does not understand what this means. On Plato's considered view of belief, I shall argue in the next chapter, the ability to form beliefs depends on the ability to grasp relations such as difference and opposition, and this in turn requires reason. If grasping the differences and oppositions between things and features requires reason, then it is only to be expected that a non-rational part of the soul is unable to distinguish properly between such things as the large and the small. However, once it becomes clear that belief is a rational capacity, it also becomes clear that only the rational part of the soul can form beliefs. This arguably is the view we find in the *Timaeus*,[30] to which we shall turn shortly.

But even if the 'beliefs' of the non-rational part in *Republic* 10 do not, on consideration, qualify as beliefs, Socrates' use of language is nevertheless readily

---

[30] Cf. Ch. 7, pp. 95–7.

understandable. They are very much like beliefs. They involve the soul's acceptance that things are some way or other. To be precise, the soul accepts that things are this way in virtue of the fact that a part of it does. We should, moreover, bear in mind the possibility that the terminology of belief and thought finds its way to the lower parts of the soul under pressure from the city–soul parallel. The transfer of expressions such as *homonoia* ('concord'; literally, 'likeness of thought') and *homodoxein* ('to agree'; literally, 'to believe alike')[31] from city to soul naturally brings with it the attribution of thought and belief to each one of the three parts of soul. Finally, it is worth noting that the *Republic*'s conception of two distinct forms of cognition—one that employs the resources of reason, and one that does not—is a bold and ground-breaking innovation. It is hardly surprising that its author is not yet in possession of terminology that is sufficiently nuanced to do full justice to the complexities of the subject matter.

---

[31] The word ὁμοδοξεῖν occurs in Socrates' statement of what temperance is, at 442 C 9–D 2. ὁμοδοξεῖν between the ruler and the ruled that reason should rule is contrasted with civil war (στασιάζειν) against reason. Glaucon replies that temperance is nothing other than what Socrates says it is, 'both in the city and in the individual' (442 D 3–4).

6

Belief and Reason

The *Timaeus* begins by refreshing our memories of the *Republic*. As Socrates summarizes what was said on the preceding day, each item in his summary points back to material in the *Republic*, although he is not offering an exhaustive summary of the *Republic*.[1] This *quasi* back-reference encourages the expectation that the *Timaeus* will have significant points of contact with the *Republic*. As far as the soul and tripartition are concerned, that expectation is in many ways borne out.

The tripartite soul reappears when Timaeus describes, at 69 C 5–72 D 3, how the created gods construct the human body and add the mortal parts of the soul to the immortal, rational part, which they have received from the demiurge. Timaeus specifies the functions of the three soul-parts[2] in ways that are strikingly similar to the corresponding statements in the *Republic*, even as far as linguistic detail is concerned.

According to Timaeus, reason is supposed to deliberate about what is advantageous for all parts of the soul, jointly and individually (*Timaeus* 71 A 1–2).[3] According to Socrates in *Republic* 4, a person is wise in virtue of a properly developed rational part, which contains knowledge of what is advantageous to each of the three parts of the soul, and to the whole of them jointly (442 C 4–7);[4] this knowledge it is supposed to put to use in deliberation (442 A 7). Located in the head as in an acropolis (*Timaeus* 70 A 6; *Republic* 8, 560 B 7), reason makes announcements to the spirited part,[5] and spirit acts on these announcements, obediently yet fiercely.[6]

---

[1] Nor does the *Timaeus* suggest that what was said on the preceding day was, or included, *precisely* Socrates' long narration of his conversation with, among others, Glaucon and Adeimantus that is the *Republic*. The *Timaeus*' occasion is 'the festival of the goddess', which must refer either to the Greater or the Lesser Panathenaea. The *Republic* is set just after the festival of Bendis, which is months away from either one of the Panathenaea. M. Burnyeat, 'Plato on why mathematics is good for the soul', in T. Smiley (ed.), *Mathematics and Necessity, Proceedings of the British Academy*, 103 (2000), 65–6, plausibly suggests that this is Plato's way of placing the *Timaeus* at a slight distance from the *Republic*, required by differences in the character and calibre of Socrates' interlocutors and the manner of exposition that is appropriate to them.

[2] These functions belong to them as a result of the purposive organizing activities of the gods that Timaeus describes. T. Johansen, 'Body, soul, and tripartition' in Plato's *Timaeus*', *Oxford Studies in Ancient Philosophy*, 19 (2000), 100, appropriately points out the passage's ἵνα ('so that') clauses as markers of divine purposiveness.

[3] περὶ τοῦ πᾶσι κοινῇ καὶ ἰδίᾳ συμφέροντος . . . βουλεύεσθαι (accepting Burnet's emended text).

[4] ἐπιστήμην . . . τὴν τοῦ συμφέροντος ἑκάστῳ τε καὶ ὅλῳ τῷ κοινῷ.

[5] παραγγέλλειν: *Timaeus* 70 B 4; *Republic* 4, 442 C 2, C 5.

[6] κατήκοος: *Timaeus* 70 A 5; ὑπήκοος: *Republic* 4, 441 E 5.

As in the *Republic*, it is spirit's role to act as reason's ally and helper in such conflicts as may arise between it and appetite.[7] It seems to be especially responsible for threats and the use of force,[8] and Timaeus evokes spirit's warlike and military associations[9] in speaking of its location, between midriff and neck, as 'the guard-house' (70 A 7–B 3). Moreover, spirit is said to be victory-loving (φιλόνικον, cf. 90 B 2), as of course it is in the *Republic* (*Republic* 9, 581 C 4, cf. 581 A 9–B1), and it is referred to as that in the soul which shares in courage.[10]

The appetitive part's function, according to Timaeus, is to give rise to desires for 'food, drink, and for things that humans require due to their bodily nature' (*Timaeus* 70 D 7–8). Similarly in the *Republic*, the lowest part primarily accounts for desires for food, drink, and sex.[11] We may wonder why Timaeus does not explicitly mention sex among its objects of desire.[12] The answer may be that in the narrative framework of the *Timaeus*, reproduction awaits the creation of women, which is not described until near the end of the dialogue, at 90 E 1–91 D 6. Moreover, the reason why Timaeus does not mention appetite's tendency to become attached to money may well be an emphasis on biological rather than cultural facts that is dictated by his assignment: to begin with the origin of the universe and conclude with the nature of human beings (*Timaeus* 27 A 3–6). It will be Critias' task to speak of human beings in their roles as citizens, and in doing so he will rely both on Timaeus' account of the origin of human beings and on Socrates' account of 'how some of them came to have a superior education' (*Timaeus* 27 A 7–B 6).

Given, then, that the conception of the soul as tripartite that we encounter in the *Timaeus* is in many ways remarkably continuous with the conception introduced in the *Republic*, it is all the more striking to find a rather dramatic innovation embedded in the conception of the soul that Timaeus presents. This is that now belief is explicitly denied to the part of the soul which is located between midriff and navel (*Timaeus* 77 B 3–6)—that is, to appetite (cf. *Timaeus* 70 D 7–E 5): 'this part', Timaeus asserts, 'is totally devoid of belief (δόξα), reasoning (λογισμός), and thought (νοῦς)'. What motivates this innovation?

I shall argue for an answer along the following lines. In a number of dialogues that are later than the *Republic*, Plato examines the *Republic*'s divisions between

---

[7] *Timaeus* 70 A 2–7: 'The part of the mortal soul that shares in courage and anger, being victory-loving, they settled nearer the head, between the midriff and the neck, so that it might listen to reason and together with it restrain by force the part consisting of desires, should it in no way want to obey willingly the command and account coming down from the citadel.'

[8] Threats are mentioned at 70 B 7. Spirit will no doubt contribute vigorously to the use of force (βία) mentioned at 70 A 5. Note the parallel between *Republic* 8, 554 D 1, βίᾳ κατέχει . . . ἐπιθυμίας, and *Timaeus* 70 A 5–6, βίᾳ τὸ τῶν ἐπιθυμιῶν γένος κατέχοι.

[9] *Republic* 4, 440 B 3, σύμμαχον; 440 E 3–4, τὰ ὅπλα.

[10] Recall *Republic* 4, 442 B 10–C 2: 'It is because of spirit that we call a person courageous, namely, when it preserves through pains and pleasures the declarations of reason about what is to be feared and what is not.'

[11] For instance, *Republic* 4, 439 D 6–7 (cf. 436 A 10–B 2); *Republic* 9, 580 E 2–5.

[12] Note, however, the presence of ἔρως among the terrible and necessary affections of the mortal part of the soul: 69 C 7–D 6. Cf. Chapter 7, p. 100, n. 10.

intelligibles and perceptibles and between corresponding modes of cognition. These texts prominently include the *Theaetetus* and the *Sophist*. One of the results of this work is an account of belief (δόξα) which makes plain that forming any belief involves, or anyhow presupposes, a grasp of intelligibles such as being, difference, and opposition, items that can be grasped by reason only. It is not that this is a new philosophical account of belief that supersedes an earlier one. There is no earlier account. But once it becomes clear that a proper account of what is involved in and required for belief shows it to be a rational capacity, it also becomes clear that cognitive states of parts of the soul other than reason cannot be beliefs, however much like beliefs they may seem to be.

The key text is *Theaetetus* 184–7. The argument contained in that text is, in a number of places, rather difficult to interpret. Though it has attracted a great deal of scholarly attention, much of its interpretation remains controversial.[13] As I understand it, it distinguishes between belief-formation and sense-perception as two distinct capacities of the soul, denying that the resources of perception are sufficient for the formation of even the most basic forms of belief. It offers an account of what is involved in, and required for, the capacity for belief, in a way that makes perspicuous that only rational subjects are capable of belief. At the same time, it leaves intact a level of awareness and cognition below belief and reason; this includes, but need not be limited to, perception.

Already my first claim about what the argument does is controversial. According to several recent interpretations, it is part of the argument that perception can by itself yield simple perceptual beliefs.[14] Now it may well seem that there is some support for this view in the text. After obtaining Theaetetus' agreement that the soul is the single thing that perceives perceptibles *through* the senses,[15] Socrates next turns to the task of persuading Theaetetus that while there may be all sorts of

---

[13] Important contributions include J. Cooper, 'Plato on sense-perception and knowledge: *Theaetetus* 184–186', *Phronesis*, 15 (1970), 123–46, repr. in his *Knowledge, Nature, and the Good* (Princeton: Princeton University Press, 2004), 43–64; M. Frede, 'Observations on perception in Plato's later dialogues', in his *Essays in Ancient Philosophy* (Oxford: Oxford University Press, 1987), 3–8; J. McDowell, *Plato*: Theaetetus (Oxford: Oxford University Press, 1973); M. Burnyeat, 'Plato on the grammar of perceiving', *Classical Quarterly*, 26 (1976), 29–51; C. Kahn, 'Some philosophical uses of "to be" in Plato', *Phronesis*, 26 (1981), 105–34; D. Modrak, 'Perception and judgment in the *Theaetetus*', *Phronesis*, 26 (1981), 35–54; D. Bostock, *Plato's* Theaetetus (Oxford: Oxford University Press, 1988); Y. Kanayama, 'Perceiving, considering, and attaining being (*Theaetetus* 184–186)', *Oxford Studies in Ancient Philosophy*, 5 (1987), 29–81; D. Frede, 'The soul's silent dialogue: a non-aporetic reading of the *Theaetetus*', *Proceedings of the Cambridge Philological Society*, 205 (1989), 20–49; A. Silverman, 'Plato on perception and "commons"', *Classical Quarterly*, 40 (1990), 148–75. Though I have benefited greatly from this body of literature, my own interpretation differs from the views put forward by all of the above, in most cases significantly. I shall signal agreements and disagreements where appropriate.

[14] One version of this is in Cooper, 'Plato on sense-perception', 131–4. I take what he calls 'labelling' to involve forming a belief as to the identity of the feature in question: 'in order to decide whether something is red one does not need to reflect, but to use the mind at the perceptual level only' (132). Another version is argued for by Modrak, 'Perception'.

[15] Burnyeat, 'Plato on the grammar of perceiving', 29–46, offers a detailed and wholly persuasive explanation of the distinction between the 'with' and the 'through' idioms at 184 B 8–E 1.

things that we can perceive through the senses, as of course he would think that there are, there are at least some things, or 'features' of things,[16] that can be grasped through none of the senses. This task has been completed by 186 A 1, where Theaetetus accepts Socrates' suggestion that 'while the soul considers some things through the bodily powers, there are others which it considers alone and through itself' (*Theaetetus* 185 E 6–7). A bit earlier Socrates presents, as evidence supporting his conclusion, the fact that Theaetetus would readily know how to answer the question of which sense one would use to check whether some things are salty—the sense of taste, of course—whereas he would be unable to say through what sense one would consider whether some things have being, are like or unlike one another, are one or two, and so forth.

In light of this contrast, one might be inclined to credit the activity of the soul through the senses, mentioned at 185 E 7, with the ability to form simple beliefs which involve no more than applying a suitable predicate (e.g. 'salty') to something or other. As the argument continues, however, it becomes clear that its contrast between two kinds of activity of the soul is supposed to be a contrast between, on the one hand, perception as it is present, to humans and non-human animals alike, right away from birth (186 B 11–C 2) and, on the other, an activity that is capable of attaining truth (186 D 2–5) and that is correctly identified as belief-formation (δοξάζειν) (187 A 7–8). (For the sake of simplicity, let us call the latter type of activity 'thought'.) Applying any predicate is, I take it, well beyond the cognitive reach of newborn infants. And Socrates' denial that perception can attain truth is reasonable only if he withholds from it the ability to form even the simplest beliefs.[17]

So the question arises whether the argument operates with a coherent conception of perception and its cognitive reach.[18] One might think that the contrast expressed at 185 E 6–7 is meant to be, not indeed between thought and what is about to be identified (at 186 D 10–E 1) as perception, but rather between two modes of thought: the soul's consideration of things through bodily powers can and typically will yield perceptual beliefs, whereas its consideration of things 'alone and through itself' concerns 'common' predicates such as being, not-being, sameness, difference, and so forth. But this cannot be what Socrates has in mind, as he will in a moment go on to contrast the activity of the soul 'itself by itself' (187 A 5–6),[19] not with some other form or mode of thought, but with *perception*,

[16] What we need for present purposes is a broad notion of something that can be grasped about, or with regard to, something, including that it has being in that it is something or other, or is with regard to something or other, or both. In using the word 'feature', I am meaning to capture that notion.

[17] Contra Cooper, 'Plato on sense-perception'. His preferred interpretation involves the idea that perception forms beliefs (131–2) but can yield neither truths nor falsehoods (143). Note the unannounced shift from 'is F'—deciding 'whether something is red' (132)—to 'appears to be F': 'in perception one notices only the colour (etc.) a thing appears to have and says nothing about what its real colour is' (143).

[18] Cooper, 'Plato on sense-perception', 132, answers in the negative: 'the most one can do is to try to render the inconsistency palatable'.

[19] I assume—naturally and reasonably, I think—that the activity of the soul 'itself by itself' (αὐτὴ καθ' αὑτήν) mentioned at 187 A 5–6 is precisely its activity 'itself through itself' (αὐτὴ δι' αὑτῆς) referred to at 185 E 6–7.

endorsing Theaetetus' suggestion that this independent activity of the soul is belief-formation. Socrates and Theaetetus are agreed, then, that belief-formation is in all cases a manifestation of the soul's independent activity. They think that without that activity no belief can be formed, and no truth attained.

It is in fact clear, anyhow on reflection, that Socrates never in the argument endorses a conception of perception which attributes to it any ability to form beliefs of any sort. To see this, we need to bear in mind the dialectical character of the argument. At its outset, Theaetetus will presumably still take it that, at least within certain limits, perception is knowledge.[20] He will quite definitely be strongly inclined to think that one can perceive all sorts of things through one's senses, that perception can yield all sorts of beliefs, and that at least in certain circumstances these beliefs are true and indeed constitute knowledge. Socrates' purpose at 184 E 4–186 A 1, which I shall call Stage 1, is not, I suggest, to persuade Theaetetus right away that perception by itself can form no belief and attain no truth. That is a hard lesson for Theaetetus to learn. Rather, Stage 1 establishes the preliminary conclusion that while the soul does certain things through the senses—which may or may not include the formation of suitable beliefs—there are features of things, crucially including being (οὐσία, 185 C 9), to which the senses provide no access. These features are not therefore grasped (λαμβάνειν, 185 B 8) through the senses, but rather by the soul's independent activity. It will be the task of the next section—Stage 2, starting at 186 A 2—to show that perception by itself can form no belief, because cognitive access to being is in fact required for the formation of any belief, including perceptual beliefs to the effect that something or other is hard, soft, or salty. Or so I shall argue in a moment, when I turn to that section of the argument.

If this outline of the overall argument is along the right lines, Socrates' remark at 185 B 9–C 2 falls readily into place. He has just claimed that one could not grasp either through hearing or through sight certain things that a sound and a colour have in common (such as being, being self-identical, and being one thing). He goes on to offer Theaetetus another piece of evidence for the view that such common features of things cannot be grasped through the senses. If it were possible, he says, 'to raise the question whether both are salty or not, you'd be ready to say (ἕξεις εἰπεῖν) what you would investigate it with: and this would appear to be neither sight nor hearing, but something else'. Being the good student he is, Theaetetus in replying substitutes a 'through' expression for a 'with' expression,

---

[20] That view has, in any case, not been disproved. At 179 C 2–D 1, Socrates acknowledges that it has not been ruled out yet: 'so long as we keep within the limits of that immediate present experience of the individual which gives rise to perceptions and to perceptual beliefs, it is more difficult to convict these latter of being untrue—but perhaps I'm talking nonsense. Perhaps it is not possible to convict them at all; perhaps those who profess that they are perfectly evident and are always knowledge may be saying what really is.' The subsequent argument against the claim that 'all things are in motion' is not decisive against the view that, perhaps within certain limits, perception is knowledge. Socrates indicates this at 183 C 1–3, saying that 'we are not going to grant that knowledge is perception, not at any rate along the line of inquiry which supposes that all things are in motion'.

answering that the sense in question is, of course, the one that operates through the tongue. No doubt Theaetetus, at this stage in the argument, thinks that perception (taste, in this case) is all that is needed to settle questions about whether suitable things are or are not salty. And no doubt Socrates is perfectly aware that Theaetetus thinks this. But Socrates himself is non-committal, *at this stage*, about just what perception on his own view can do. What he wants to show Theaetetus is that while he knows through which senses we perceive things like sounds and colours, he is at a loss as to what sense we use in grasping common features like being, identity, and difference.[21]

Even though it is not the task of Stage 1 to show that perception by itself cannot form any belief, that outcome is nevertheless already foreshadowed by Socrates' remark about investigating whether a couple of things are, or are not, salty (ἆρ' ἐστὸν ἁλμυρὼ ἢ οὔ). The first thing one would think about a sound and a colour, he has just said, is that they both are, or have being (ὅτι ἀμφοτέρω ἐστόν). In his next few sentences, at 185 A 11–B 5, the verb 'to be' does not occur again, but the predicates used—'different', 'the same', etc.—are to be heard as complementing ἐστόν ('they both are') at 185 A 9.[22] Socrates' imaginary question whether the two of them are or are not salty thus looks back to the first thought one would have about a sound and a colour. In his next question to Theaetetus (185 C 4–7), the expressions 'is' and 'is not' are lifted from, and put one in mind of, ἐστὸν ἢ οὔ ('the two of them are or are not') in the question about saltiness.[23] 'Is' and 'is not' are paraphrased by Theaetetus, doubtless with Socrates' approval, as being (οὐσία) and not-being (τὸ μὴ εἶναι). Both are agreed to be among the features of things which the soul considers, not through the senses, but by itself. Socrates thus signals, already at Stage 1, that even simple perceptual beliefs of the form '*x* is *F*' (where the value of *F* is a perceptual predicate like 'salty') involve at least one common feature, being, a feature that is grasped only by the soul's independent activity.

---

[21] 185 C 1: ἕξεις εἰπεῖν ('you'd be ready to say') contrasts with 185 D 6–7: οὐκ ἂν ἔχοιμι εἰπεῖν ('I couldn't say').

[22] I take as read L. Brown's seminal work on the complete (or, as I would put it, bare) use of εἶναι, 'to be' ('Being in the *Sophist*: a syntactical enquiry', *Oxford Studies in Ancient Philosophy*, 4 (1986), 49–70). The crucial point is that the bare use allows complementation, as paralleled by the way 'Jane is teaching', which is *not* elliptical, allows complementation into 'Jane is teaching French'. Just as the former allows the follow-up question 'teaching what?', so 'a sound and a colour ἐστόν' (185 A 9) allows the question 'are what?' To capture the complete, non-elliptical character of sentences of the form '*x* ἐστι', it is sometimes useful to translate the verb as 'have being'. It should be borne in mind, though, that such sentences, while complete in themselves, allow appropriate predicates as complements. This is precisely what occurs at *Theaetetus* 185 A 8–B 5: ἐστόν at 185 A 9 is complete, but subsequently receives a number of predicates as complements. One might compare the far less elegant analysis offered in Kahn, 'Some philosophical uses', 121–3. Kahn takes ἐστόν at 185 A 9 to signify existence: 'that sound and colour are, with no predicate in sight, must mean that they *exist*' (his emphasis). But the verb at the same time 'provides the copula for the verbless predications' that follow. So he diagnoses 'overdetermination', proposing what he calls a 'double reading' of ἐστόν.

[23] This is seen by Kanayama, 'Perceiving', 35. Cf. Burnyeat, 'Plato on the grammar of perceiving', 43, n. 40.

There is no indication, though, that Theaetetus has cottoned on to this. Near the end of the section, he says that as for the common features of things, 'it doesn't seem to me that for these things there is any special instrument at all, as there is for the others. It seems to me that it is through itself that the soul investigates the common features with regard to all things' (*Theaetetus* 185 D 6–E 2). On the view at which Theaetetus has now arrived, investigation of the common features of things requires the soul's independent activity. This is because no sense seems to provide cognitive access to them. On the other hand, the senses do provide access to such things as sounds and colours. So Theaetetus will continue to think that perception is sufficient to investigate such things, and presumably he takes this investigative activity to include the application of suitable predicates and the formation of suitable beliefs. Rather than right away taking issue with Theaetetus' newly arrived-at view, Socrates is delighted to have got him this far. As he says, Theaetetus has saved him a vast amount of talk if it seems to him that 'while the soul considers some things through the bodily powers, there are others which it considers alone and through itself' (*Theaetetus* 185 E 5–7). Once again, Socrates remains non-committal about just what, *on his own view*, the soul's consideration of things through the senses consists in or amounts to. It is not until Stage 2 that his own view becomes clear.

So as to reinforce my suggestion as to what Socrates intends to accomplish at Stage 1, it will be useful to have a somewhat more careful look at how he proceeds. Close to the beginning of Stage 1, Socrates asks Theaetetus whether he is willing to agree that 'the things you perceive through one power, you can't perceive through another? For instance, the things you perceive through hearing, you couldn't perceive through sight, and similarly those you perceive through sight you couldn't perceive through hearing?' (*Theaetetus* 184 E 8–185 A 2). Theaetetus accepts this with no hesitation (185 A 3). What they agree on is, it seems, the strong and, in fact, rather implausible claim that nothing could be perceived through more senses than one. Once that claim is accepted, sense-perception is limited to things that, like sounds and colours, are perceived specifically and exclusively through some sense or other (call them 'special sensibles'). It has rightly been pointed out[24] that what Socrates actually makes use of in what follows is something much weaker than the very strong claim that one can perceive nothing but special sensibles. What he wants to show in what follows immediately is that one could not apprehend either through hearing or through sight that a sound and a colour share certain features, because hearing provides no access to colour while sight provides no access to sound. This plainly does not require that perception is restricted to special sensibles. It only requires that there are sensibles that are in fact special sensibles and that belong to different senses.[25]

[24] Burnyeat, 'Plato on the grammar of perceiving', 47–8.
[25] As will be seen shortly, at no point of Stage 1 does Socrates employ *as a premiss* the claim that perception is limited to special sensibles.

In fact it may be that, in the context, the agreement at 184 E 8–185 A 3 is meant to amount to this weaker, but much more plausible, claim. In arguing for the view that we perceive perceptibles through the senses rather than with them, Socrates mentions various objects of perception: white and black (184 B 7–8), high and low notes (184 B 8), hot, hard, light, and sweet (184 E). When he speaks generally about 'all the things *of this kind*' (184 E 2), it is natural to take him to have in mind the various things that are perceptible specifically through some sense or other. And perhaps it is just with regard to 'all the things of this kind'— special sensibles, that is—that Socrates and Theaetetus readily agree that the things you perceive through one sense you could not perceive through another.[26] This would certainly make it easier than it would otherwise be to see why Theaetetus seems to find Socrates' suggestion quite uncontroversial.

What Socrates wants to show at 184 E 4–185 E 9 is, in his own words, that 'while the soul considers some things through the bodily powers, there are others which it considers alone and through itself' (*Theaetetus* 185 E 6–7). In the context this clearly amounts, not to the claim that there are certain thoughts which require some independent activity of the soul, but to the stronger claim that there are certain features that can *never* be grasped by perception, but only by the soul's independent activity. At 185 C 4–D 3, Socrates and Theaetetus mention a number of features (being, not-being, the different, the same, and so forth) which Theaetetus refers to as 'the common things' (τὰ κοινά) and which the soul seems to him to consider 'itself through itself' (185 D 8–E 2), in contrast to those things, mentioned earlier, for which there is, in each case, a special sense or sense-organ (185 D 7–8). Socrates' formulation at 185 E 6–7 picks up this distinction made by Theaetetus between two sorts of features. The distinction made, Socrates can go on to ask, in the argument's next section, which sort being, likeness, and so forth belong to. To say that being, for instance, belongs to the second sort, then, is to claim that it can never be grasped by perception, but only by the soul's independent activity.

Socrates offers two arguments for the view that consideration of certain features requires the soul's independent activity. The first one (184 E 4–185 B 9) draws attention to thoughts that are explicitly about objects of more senses than one, to the effect that 'these two things'[27] (a sound and a colour), taken separately or together, share some feature: having being, being different from the other, being self-identical, being two things, being one thing. Socrates is plainly right that no one sense taken singly could account for such thoughts. However, it seems clear in the context that he is taking himself to be offering evidence for thinking that such thoughts cannot be accounted for by perception *at all*, but require some activity of the soul that is additional to and distinct from its activity though the senses.[28] Even

---

[26] This is also suggested by J. McDowell ad loc.
[27] Note the duals at 185 A 9, B 2, 4, 7.
[28] 185 E 7–9 seems to me to show this.

if such thoughts cannot be accounted for by any one sense taken singly—more precisely, by the soul's activity through any *one* sense—it does not follow right away that they cannot be accounted for by perception *at all*. One might think instead that the soul can think thoughts of this kind by operating through two (or, if necessary, more) senses at once, in this case through hearing and sight. But it is not very hard to see how such a view might be resisted, so as to reach Socrates' conclusion. Two or more senses do not simply 'add up' so as to form a path of cognitive access through which the soul receives an integrated, 'synoptic' representation of the variety of things that both or all of the senses involved provide access to. That integrated representation is precisely something that the soul has to *achieve*, and it makes good sense to distinguish the soul's activity involved in and required for achieving it from its activity through the senses.[29]

The second argument (185 B 9–E 2) starts with thoughts about the same two things—a sound and a colour—that feature in the first argument.[30] It does not repeat that they are the objects of two different senses. Rather, it emphasizes that 'is' and 'is not', or being and not-being, are shared as common features not just by these two, but indeed by *all things*. Theaetetus accepts this dramatic widening of perspective when he says that in investigating the common features with regard to all things, the soul seems to him to function through itself. The key point of the second argument is that there is no sense or sense-organ that features like being, sameness, and difference can be assigned to—as there is with features like saltiness—and that this is so not only in cases that involve the apprehension of such shared features as belonging to objects of more senses than one, but quite generally in all cases.

Should Theaetetus have accepted the generalizing step? It is one thing to accept that perception cannot account for apprehending that a sound and a colour are different from one another (185 A 11). It is another matter to accept that by itself it provides no cognitive access to the fact that one colour is different from another colour. Perhaps it is true that, as Myles Burnyeat puts it, there is no such thing as an impression of being.[31] But has Socrates given Theaetetus a reason to think that there could not be a purely auditory impression of one sound being different from

---

[29] It may be objected that Socrates is missing an important distinction between two *sorts* of independent activity of the soul: on the one hand, the construction of an integrated sensory representation of one's environment, which includes the representation of common (by which I mean 'cross-modal') features such as shapes and sizes as well as, perhaps, of objects such as houses and trees; on the other hand, the construction of an integrated *conception* of things, which includes the application of suitable predicates and the formation of suitable beliefs. This, I think, is correct about the argument as it stands. However, the argument's basic commitment that perception can neither form beliefs nor attain knowledge because it does not discern being could survive a more fine-grained articulation of the soul's independent activity, distinguishing between belief-formation (strictly speaking) on the one hand and the construction of an integrated sensory representation on the other, which might then be treated as an extension of perception as Socrates conceives of it here. Notice that Socrates will shortly speak of seeing, touching, hearing, or otherwise perceiving Theodorus and Theaetetus (*Theaetetus* 192 D 3–9); so he will in fact need an extended, more generous conception of perception.

[30] These are the two things referred to as ἀμφοτέρω at 185 B 10.

[31] Burnyeat, 'Plato on the grammar of perceiving', 49.

another (cf. 185 B 4–5)? Presumably Socrates is relying on something like this: grasping that something or other has being or is different from something else (etc.) crucially involves grasping something that is one and the same thing in each and every case (namely, being, difference, etc.); and if grasping the thing in question can clearly be seen to require the soul's independent activity in some cases, this in fact shows that it must do so in all cases.[32] If so, it is plain why the second argument begins with, and then expands on, the first argument, drawing attention to the fact that 'is' and 'is not' are shared as common features not only by the two things mentioned in the first argument, but in fact by all things.

It should, in any event, be clear now that Socrates does have reason to be glad that Theaetetus accepts his conclusion on the basis of the arguments he has offered. Theaetetus has indeed saved him a considerable amount of work. On the basis of the first argument, he appears to accept, not only that features shared by objects specific to different senses cannot be grasped through any one sense, but also that they cannot be grasped through the senses at all. Further, he also seems to accept the second argument's generalizing step, which places the common features of the first argument beyond the reach of the senses quite generally in all cases. The steps Theaetetus is willing to accept are neither unintelligible nor, I think, unreasonable. They could be defended robustly and plausibly. The point is just that Theaetetus accepts them without being given arguments specifically for them, perhaps because he can see right away that and why they are correct.[33]

I now turn to the overall argument's second stage, which begins at 186 A 2. At Stage 1, as we have seen, Socrates makes available a distinction between two sorts of features, those that the soul considers through the senses and those it considers through itself. He can now rely on this distinction, so as to ask which sort being (ἡ οὐσία) likeness and unlikeness, and sameness and difference belong to. This of course is recapitulation: all of these features were mentioned at Stage 1. Without hesitation, Theaetetus assigns them, once again, to the soul's independent activity. Socrates then asks about fine and disgraceful (καλὸν καὶ αἰσχρόν), and good and bad. Theaetetus' answer is significant, in that it contains an important clue concerning the difficult question how the word 'being' (*ousia*) is used in the remainder of the argument. These things too, he says, belong to the soul's independent activity: 'They, too, seem to be pre-eminently things whose being the mind

---

[32] Cf. McDowell, *Plato*: Theaetetus, 186: 'It follows from the principle of 184e8–185a3, together with an implicit assumption about the unity of the act of thinking, that if one thinks the same thing about two items, each of which is a proper object of a different sense, then the thinking of that thing, about anything, cannot be an exercise of either of the two senses in question.' This seems to look beyond the argument at 185 A 4–9, which focuses on thoughts specifically about 'these two things', anticipating the generalizing step indicated at 185 E 1–2: 'the thinking of that thing, about anything'.

[33] We should recall that Theaetetus is a budding mathematician (note his introduction of the predicates 'odd' and 'even' at 185 D 1–2), and that the dialogue is written to eulogize him, as its preface makes clear. Theaetetus' ability to see easily and quickly that there are all sorts of things to which the senses provide no access nicely illustrates the remarks in the *Republic* as to why mathematics is good for the soul: it promotes the soul's ascent from the 'becoming' of the 'visible' world (524 C 13) to the immutable being of intelligible reality.

considers in relation to one another, reasoning[34] about things past and present with a view to things in the future' (*Theaetetus* 186 A 10–B 1).[35] The word *ousia* is introduced into the argument by Theaetetus at 185 C 9, clearly as an abstract noun corresponding to the verb *esti*, 'is', the way *to mē einai* corresponds to *ouk esti*, 'is not'. (So he might equally well have used *to einai* instead of *ousia*.) In the context there is both an uncomplemented use of *einai* (at 185 A 9) and a complemented use (at 185 B 10): a sound and a colour both have being, and if it were possible to ask whether both of them *are* salty, Theaetetus would be able to say which sense we would use to check. In this way the word *ousia* is connected, via the verb *esti*, both to something's having being (uncomplemented use) and to something's being something or other, e.g. salty (complemented use).

What does Theaetetus have in mind in speaking of the soul considering the being of such things as goodness and badness? Given the way the word *ousia* enters the discussion, we should try to understand this in terms of uncomplemented or complemented uses of 'to be'. Moreover, throughout the argument's first stage, what gets identified as the soul's independent activity is always a matter either of thinking *that* something is, or is something or other (185 A 8–9, 11–12, B 2), or of considering *whether* something is, or is something or other (185 B 4–5, 185 B 10). Against that background, we should try to understand considering the being of something in terms of considering whether it is, or is something or other. No complemented use seems relevant at 186 A 10–B 1, since we are not given a complement. Could it be, then, that considering the being of (say) goodness is considering whether it is, or has being?

For this to begin to seem plausible, one more step is required. So far in the argument, grasping features, both special sensibles and common or shared features, has always been a matter of grasping a feature 'about', or with regard to, something or other. Thus Socrates says that you could not grasp either through hearing or through sight what is common (τὸ κοινόν) with regard to the two things in question (περὶ αὐτῶν). This is a moment later picked up by Theaetetus, when he says that with regard to all things (περὶ πάντων) the soul seems to consider the common things (τὰ κοινά) 'through itself'. In the context, this must mean that it belongs to the soul's independent activity to raise and settle questions of whether something or other bears any one of the common features. We may assume, then, that when Theaetetus, just after that, speaks of the soul's 'reaching out' for such things as being, likeness, sameness, etc. (186 A 2–7), he has in mind raising and settling questions involving such common features, with regard to something or other. In other words, he has in mind considering whether something or other is

---

[34] I translate ἀναλογίζεσθαι and related words as 'reason', rather than 'calculate', simply to make perspicuous the connection of these mental acts to the rational part of the soul (λογιστικόν). I trust that nothing hangs on this: ἀναλογίζεσθαι here, and at 186 C 2–3, is in any case not a literal case of doing arithmetic; so if 'calculate' is used as a translation, this must be understood broadly and loosely, so as to mean 'reason' or 'deliberate'.

[35] This is based on McDowell's translation, which is closer to the Greek than Levett's. In particular, it captures the significance of καί at 186 A 10.

or has being, is like something else, is the same as itself, etc. These questions correspond precisely to the assertoric thoughts mentioned at 185 A 8–B 5.[36] So when we come to 186 A 10–B 1, the context certainly allows us to supply some things or other with regard to which the soul considers the being of fineness and disgracefulness, and goodness and badness. Once one sees this, it becomes attractive to think that what the soul considers in considering the being of the features in question is whether they are or have being with regard to something or other— say, with regard to a person or a law.[37] In other words, it considers whether someone or something is fine or disgraceful, or good or bad.

This construal of considering the being of (especially) goodness and badness is exactly what is needed to make sense of what Theaetetus takes to be involved in such considerations. In saying that they involve reasoning about things past and present with a view to the future, Theaetetus clearly has in mind the point made earlier in the discussion, that claims about what is good (τἀγαθά, 177 D 2) or useful[38]—for instance, concerning a piece of legislation (177 E 5)—crucially involve a view of the future (178 A 5–10). For a law to be good or useful is in important part for it to prove to be good and useful in the future. Against this background, it makes excellent sense for Theaetetus now to say that considering whether something or other is good or bad involves reasoning with a view to the future. In fact it is difficult to see any remotely plausible alternative to the current construal of what Theaetetus means by considering the being of goodness and badness, in a way that involves reasoning with a view to the future.[39]

[36] Those thoughts, of course, were thought with regard to a sound and a colour. The corresponding questions here are asked with regard to anything whatsoever, on the basis of the generalizing step taken at 185 B 9–186 A 1.

[37] For this use of 'is', see *Sophist* 263 B 11–12 (cf. 256 E 6–7). Sitting is something that is with regard to Theaetetus (περὶ σοῦ); flying is not. This is the converse of the use in play in statements of the form '*x* is *F*'. For discussion, see M. Frede, 'Plato's *Sophist* on false statements', in R. Kraut (ed.), *The Cambridge Companion to Plato* (Cambridge: Cambridge University Press, 1992), 417–23. Note also that the *Sophist*'s discussion of false statement includes a use of the word οὐσία that is a precise parallel to the use that, on my view, is in evidence at *Theaetetus* 186 A 11, B 6, and B 7: at *Sophist* 262 C 2–5 the visitor says that sounds like 'lion stag horse' would not 'indicate either an action or an inaction or the being (οὐσίαν) of something that is or of something that is not'. In the context, the latter must mean indicating that a feature or its negation has being with regard to the item in question—for instance, that it is hard or not-hard.

[38] ὠφέλιμα, 177 D 4. This is echoed at 186 C 2–3, ἀναλογίσματα πρὸς ... ὠφέλειαν ('reasonings with a view to usefulness').

[39] Kahn, 'Some philosophical uses', 124, suggests that considering the being of something here is meant to be considering its *nature*. But if one wanted to consider something's nature, why reason about past and present with a view to the future? (I agree here with Cooper, 'Plato on sense-perception', 137.) The *Theaetetus*' digression (172 C–177 C) strongly suggests what one expects in any case, namely that on Plato's view, thinking about natures involves complete disregard (in fact, dis*respect*: 173 E 4–5) for things that are specifically in past, present, or future, and focusing instead on immutable truths. The philosopher, whose thought 'tracks down by every path the entire nature of each whole among the things that are and never descends to what lies near at hand' (173 E6–174 A2), is said neither to see nor to hear the city's laws and decrees (173 D 3–4), and scarcely to know whether his next-door neighbour 'is a man or some other kind of creature' (174 B 1–4). He will doubtless care equally little about such matters pertaining to individuals in the past and in the future. Another implausible possibility is that considering the being of something is considering quite generally whether it has being at all.

Moreover, what Theaetetus says at 186 A 10–11 is not just that it belongs to the soul's independent activity to consider the being of the things Socrates asks about at 186 A 9. What he says is rather that their being, too (καὶ τούτων ... τὴν οὐσίαν), is considered by the soul by itself.[40] He must have in mind not only fine and disgraceful, and good and bad, but also the features mentioned just before at 186 A 6–7, like and unlike, and same and different. As we have seen, when we get to 186 A 6–8, what Socrates and Theaetetus agree on is plainly that it belongs to the soul's independent activity to raise and settle questions of whether something or other is like or unlike something else, is the same as itself, and is different from other things. As we come to Theaetetus' next answer, he speaks of considering the being of things and applies this expression retrospectively to like and unlike, and to the same and the different. This only makes sense if 'considering the being of like and unlike (etc.)' means much the same thing as 'reaching out for like and unlike (etc.)'. I can see only one plausible way to interpret the former expression so as to be equivalent to the latter, and it is the one I have suggested.

Socrates now has all the materials he needs in order to make the crucial move that restricts the soul's activity through the senses to awareness of perceptual features, placing the formation of any belief beyond the reach of perception.[41] The soul, he says, will perceive through touch the hardness of what is hard, and likewise the softness of what is soft. 'But their being—that they are—and their opposition to one another and, again, the being of this opposition the soul attempts to discern (κρίνειν) for us by rising to compare them with one another' (*Theaetetus* 186 B 6–9). Theaetetus agrees with this very heartily (186 B 10). What it must mean in the context is that even attempting to discern or grasp that something is (say) hard belongs to the soul's independent activity and is therefore beyond the reach of its activity through the senses. We may recall that at Stage 1, it very much looks as if Theaetetus assumes that perception by itself is perfectly capable of dealing with questions of the form 'is *x* *F*?', where the value of *F* is a perceptual predicate like 'hard'. What has he seen now that he missed then?

The first thing to say is that Socrates has drawn his attention to the fact that forming beliefs always involves making claims to the effect that something or other has being. Forming the belief that something is hard, for instance, involves affirming that hardness is or has being with regard to the thing in question. And it has been clear to Theaetetus all along that the senses provide no access to being, and that perception does not even do as much as considering whether something or other has being, let alone answering such questions affirmatively or negatively.

But to say this is plainly not yet to do justice to two prominent features of Stage 2: first, that the soul considers, or tries to grasp, the being of opposites in

---

[40] This is noticed and rightly emphasized by Kanayama, 'Perceiving', 67.

[41] ἔχε δή at 186 B 2 indicates, not (as McDowell suggests ad loc.) that Socrates thinks Theaetetus is getting ahead of himself, but that he is now ready to take a decisive step. Compare *Gorgias*, 460 A 5, with E. R. Dodds' note: 'The exclamation indicates that Socrates has now got what he wanted, the lever which will overturn Gorgias' position.'

relation to one another;[42] secondly, that the soul's independent activity includes reasoning concerning both being and usefulness.[43] Theaetetus sees right away that considering whether something is good calls into play one's grasp not only of goodness, but also of badness—and the other way around (186 A 10–B 1). After all, judgements about goodness more often than not are comparative judgements about better and worse. What Socrates points out just after that is not only that perception is aware of perceptual features, but applies no predicates. It is also that perception is *not* aware of the opposition between even perceptual features. Attempting to discern opposition, and to recognize it *as what it is*,[44] belongs to the soul's independent activity just as much as attempting to discern the being of perceptual features. It seems unlikely that Socrates simply lumps together attempting to grasp the being of hardness and softness and attempting to grasp their opposition, as though they were two unrelated things that the soul's independent activity just happens to account for. Rather, he presumably thinks that the point about opposition makes it easier to see why it is that sense-perception by itself cannot account for the application even of perceptual predicates. And surely this is, in fact, so. To be able to do as little as considering whether something is (say) hard, let alone to settle the question, you must have some grasp of the fact that hardness is the opposite of softness. This is a very basic fact about hardness. A subject that has no grasp of it is simply incompetent with regard to questions of hardness and softness. Put more generally, what I take Socrates to be drawing attention to is the fact that the ability to raise and settle questions of whether something or other bears some feature is inseparable from the ability to grasp that the feature in question is related to certain other features, and how it is related to them, for instance by opposition.

Once we appreciate the connection between being able to apply predicates and being able to grasp structural features such as opposition, it becomes perspicuous, I shall now try to show, that only rational subjects are able to apply predicates. Socrates makes it clear that he takes reasoning (ἀναλογίσματα) to be prominently

[42] 186 A 10–11: πρὸς ἄλληλα σκοπεῖσθαι τὴν οὐσίαν ('to examine their being in comparison with one another'); 186 B 6–7: τὴν ἐναντιότητα πρὸς ἀλλήλω ('their opposition to one another'); 186 B 8: συμβάλλουσα πρὸς ἀλλήλα ('comparing them with one another').

[43] 186 C: ἀναλογίσματα πρός τε οὐσίαν καὶ ὠφέλειαν ('reasonings with a view to both being and usefulness'); 186 D 2–3: ἐν δὲ περὶ ἐκείνων συλλογισμῷ ('in reasoning about those things').

[44] This, I take it, is the force of the distinction between two cognitive steps concerning opposition indicated at 186 B 6–7: [sc. κρίνειν πειρᾶται] καὶ τὴν ἐναντιότητα καὶ τὴν οὐσίαν αὖ τῆς ἐναντιότητος ('[sc. the soul attempts to discern] their opposition and, again, the being of this opposition'). The soul first attempts to discern the opposition between hardness and softness, and then to discern that opposition has being with regard to them. This is exactly parallel—hence the word αὖ ('again')—to the distinction between perceiving (or discerning) a perceptual feature (τὴν σκληρότητα . . . αἰσθήσεται, 186 B 2–3) and discerning that the relevant property has being with regard to the object in question (τὴν οὐσίαν . . . κρίνειν, 186 B 6–9). This suggests what may seem an attractive strategy for demystifying the transition from perceptual content (perceiving hardness) to low-level propositional content ('this is hard'). The same kind of transition recurs at a purely intellectual level, between discerning an intelligible object such as (say) a certain relation and recognizing it *as the relation it is*, where the latter act, but not the former, involves applying the relevant predicate. If this can be made sense of, then the transition from perception to thought might be understood in much the same way.

involved in the soul's independent activity; so prominently, in fact, that he can restate or echo the distinction between the soul's activity through the senses and its activity through itself in terms of, on the one hand, perceiving and, on the other, reasoning about what one perceives, 'with a view to both being and usefulness' (186 C 3).[45] The reference to being as well as usefulness indicates that he takes reasoning to be involved not only in settling the practical questions that Theaetetus had in mind a short while ago (at 186 A 10–B 1), but in some way or other in all cases where one asks a question and tries to answer it.[46] Now, it is of course true that one normally does not have to reason in order to be able to tell whether something is hard or soft. How, then, might reason be involved in raising and settling questions even of this sort? A number of important hints can be found in what may seem an unlikely place.[47]

In book 7 of the *Republic*, Socrates explains how it is that mathematics, if it is pursued and studied properly, has the power to draw the soul away from the domain of becoming, towards being (οὐσία) and truth. In part because of this power, he assigns to various mathematical disciplines a huge role in the education of the guardians. In order to show the beneficial effects on the soul of studying 'number and the one', Socrates distinguishes between things, or features of things, which 'summon thought' and things which do not. His examples of the former are features like largeness and smallness, thickness and thinness, hardness and softness, and lightness and heaviness.

With regard to each of these pairs, perception reports, or says (λέγει, 524 A 7), that the same thing is both opposites. For instance, it says about the same finger that it is large and small. Let your eyes rest on your little finger for a while, then switch to your ring finger, and it looks large. If you switch to the same finger from your middle finger, it looks small. Experiences likes these, Socrates says, induce puzzlement (ἀπορεῖν, 524 A 7) in the soul. Then it is likely, he goes on, 'that in such cases the soul, summoning reasoning and thought (λογισμόν τε καὶ νόησιν), first tries to investigate (πειρᾶται ἐπισκοπεῖν) whether each of the things announced to it is one or two' (*Republic* 7, 524 B 3–5). If they appear to be two, he continues, each of them appears to be different from the other and one thing. 'So if each is one, and both are two, the soul will understand (νοήσει) that the two are separate, for it would not understand the non-separate to be two, but rather one' (*Republic* 7, 524 B 10–C 1).

The question about pairs of opposites that the soul is trying to investigate in this passage is plainly an extremely simple one, preliminary to the attempt

---

[45] Note also 186 D 2–5, where the distinction between the soul's two kinds of activity is represented in terms of affections (παθήματα) on the one hand and reasoning about them (περὶ ἐκείνων συλλογισμῷ) on the other; it is in the latter, not in the former, that being and truth can be attained.

[46] I assume that οὐσίαν at 186 C 3 primarily picks up the two occurrences of the word at 186 B 6 and 7. Thus Socrates is broadening the involvement of reason from questions of goodness or usefulness to absolutely all questions.

[47] It used to be thought—for instance, by Cornford and Cherniss—that the passage I am about to turn to says much the same as *Theaetetus* 184–7. Cooper, 'Plato on sense-perception', contains a highly effective and in fact devastating attack on that view.

(mentioned at *Theaetetus* 186 B 6–9) to grasp the opposition between them. It is simply whether hardness and softness, for instance, are one or two things (or features). The passage suggests a number of ways in which reason is involved in raising and settling even such very simple questions. There is, to begin with, the soul's puzzlement at what the senses are saying when they report the same thing to be both hard and soft. We should note that this puzzlement comes well before it grasps that hardness and softness are opposites, and indeed before it grasps that they are two separate things. Socrates evidently assumes that the soul has some inchoate sensitivity to the opposition between such features as hardness and softness *before* it begins to reason about the matter in question. Moreover, it is not just that the reports of the senses puzzle the soul. They also stir it to activity, as it tries to find out how things are, beginning with the simple question of whether hardness and softness are one or two things.

Within the psychological theory of the *Republic*, the soul's impulse to find out how things are belongs to its rational part; it is a desire of reason. As Socrates says elsewhere in the *Republic*, 'it is clear to everyone that the part with which we learn is always wholly straining to know where the truth lies' (*Republic* 9, 581 B 6–7). To have reason, according to Plato's theory, is among other things to be impelled to achieve a clear and intelligible view of how things are—directly, for its own sake, and regardless of whatever may or may not result from it.[48] No doubt it is also reason that accounts for the soul's being puzzled by the confusing reports of the senses, in a way that reveals an inchoate sensitivity to structural features such as opposition. Presumably to have reason is also to have that kind of sensitivity in at least an inchoate form.

Further, in trying to find out how things are, the soul from the start shows itself to be sensitive to logical relations such as consequence and incompatibility. This is nicely illustrated in *Republic* 7. The soul right away has some awareness that if A and B are two things, they are different from each other.[49] So if it realizes that A and B are two things, the soul will understand (νοήσει) that they are separate from one another (κεχωρισμένα). Presumably it is aware that plurality entails difference and separateness; so it accepts separateness together with plurality. It would not think, Socrates goes on, that A and B are non-separate (ἀχώριστα) from one another and yet two things, no doubt because it is aware that A and B being non-separate from one another is incompatible with their being two things. Again, the soul's sensitivity to logical relations belongs, I take it, specifically to reason.

Now, it is altogether clear that there are significant differences between this *Republic* 7 passage and *Theaetetus* 184–7. For instance, perception in the former

[48] 524 C 6–8: 'in order to get clear about all this, understanding was compelled to see the big and the small, not as mixed up together, but as separate—the opposite way from sight'.

[49] 524 B 7–8: οὐκοῦν ἐὰν δύο φαίνηται, ἕτερόν τε καὶ ἓν ἑκάτερον φαίνεται; ('If they appear to be two, won't each appear to be distinct and one?'). The subject of the appearings in question is, I take it, in both cases the soul. The thought of 'two' comes with the thought that 'one is distinct from the other and either is one'.

passage *says* rather elaborate things (for instance, 'this finger is large'), whereas it is a central concern of the latter text to make it plain that perception does not even form the simplest predications. Moreover, the passages use the term 'being' (οὐσία) in importantly different ways. The *Republic* passage uses it to refer to the Forms, and that it is not so used at *Theaetetus* 185–6 is one thing about that difficult text that has by now become uncontroversial. However, the *Republic* passage does seem to me to shed a good deal of light on why it is that Socrates proceeds in just the way he does at *Theaetetus* 186 A 2–C 5. In particular, it sheds light on why he seems to think in that passage that reason is involved, in some way or other, in the application of any predicate and in the formation of any belief.

As we have seen, Socrates runs together attempting to discern being and attempting to discern opposition (186 B 6–9). What he wants to show is that discerning being is always beyond the reach of perception. Opposition is presumably brought in to help make that point. And rightly so: to discern the being of (say) hardness with regard to something involves judging that the thing in question is hard, and being competent to judge whether something is hard requires some awareness of the opposition between hardness and softness. But any such awareness, indeed even any attempt to attain it, belongs to the soul's independent activity. The same goes for attempting to find out that one perceptual feature is different from its opposite: difference, too, is a common feature that the soul investigates through itself.

The *Republic* 7 passage provides a relatively clear picture of how recognizing the difference between one perceptual feature and its opposite is a task that calls into play reason and thought (or understanding, νόησις). Recognizing the difference between (say) hardness and softness involves, to begin with, raising the question of whether they are one or two features (by which I mean, whether they are one or two types of feature); it involves recognizing that they are in fact two features, perhaps as an inference from the observation that hardness is sometimes perceived without softness being perceived at the same time, and vice versa; it also involves recognizing that hardness and softness being two features entails that they are separate and different from one another.

Now, these are cognitive acts of a very special kind. They crucially depend on, and manifest, sensitivity to such logical relations as consequence and incompatibility. And to recognize the difference between opposite features is plainly not yet to recognize their opposition. Recognizing the opposition between hardness and softness presumably involves understanding that the same thing cannot be hard and soft at the same time.[50] The recognition of opposition then both rests on antecedent reasoning—for instance, as it is involved in recognizing difference—and supports reasoning from it to the conclusion that the same thing cannot at the

---

[50] This, in any case, is suggested by the fact that Socrates takes the truth of the Principle of Opposites to be clear without argument: δῆλον ὅτι ... ('it is clear that ...') (*Republic* 436 B 9–C 2). (The discussion that follows immediately, 436 C 9–437 A 9 is not argument for, but specification of, the principle: ἀκριβέστερον ὁμολογησώμεθα ('let's make our agreement more precise'), at 436 C 9.) Note also *Republic* 375 C 6–D 1. Cf. *Theaetetus* 189 C 11–D 3.

same time bear the two features in question. Such insights, it may be worth pointing out, are very much part of ordinary cognition. They are achieved by all rational subjects in the normal course of their development. But this is not, of course, to say that they do not involve a great deal of time and effort. It is with a view to the effort involved in the ordinary cognitive development of rational subjects that Socrates says that 'reasoning regarding the being and usefulness [sc. of what is perceived] comes, when it comes,[51] with difficulty and over time, involving much trouble and education' (*Theaetetus* 186 C 2–5).

The upshot, then, is that even the simplest predications are beyond perception. If so, it is a mistake to speak of perception as *saying* things, the way the *Republic*'s main speaker does. Another result is at least as striking, against the background of the *Republic*. Even as humble an achievement as forming a belief about a perceptible object requires a contribution from reason and understanding, in part because it requires cognitive access to intelligibles such as difference and opposition. This perforates the *Republic*'s careful distinctions between 'the visible' and 'the intelligible', and between the corresponding modes of cognition (509 D 1–511 E 5). It is a magnificent piece of irony that to secure this result, Plato relies on a point made in the central books of the *Republic*: that attaining a clear view of perceptual opposites as different from one another is a task that requires reason.

I close with some remarks about the conception of belief that emerges from the overall argument. One question that arises from the distinction between perceiving and discerning being at 186 B 2–9 is the following. Suppose we accept that to be able to form the belief that something or other bears some feature, you have to have *some* grasp of such relations as difference and opposition, and *some* grasp of the feature in question being different from, and opposite to, its opposite (if it has an opposite). But this raises the question of what kind or level of grasp is minimally required for the ability to form beliefs. Obviously one does not need to have a well worked out theory of opposition in order to be able to form the belief that some rock is hard. We should note that Socrates is appropriately circumspect in formulating what is involved in the soul's independent activity. He speaks, not of grasping or knowing (for instance) the opposition between hardness and softness, but of *attempting* to discern it. The point is that perception by itself does not contain the cognitive resources needed to account even for attempts to grasp such relations, let alone for any successful grasp at whatever level of proficiency. This, of course, is all he needs in order to show that perception by itself could never amount to knowledge. He can afford to be non-committal on how much understanding is minimally required to be able to form beliefs at all. That Plato is aware of the problem is strongly suggested, it seems to me, by the long and intricate discussion of false belief at 187 C 7–200 D 2. One reason why false belief is problematic is that for something to feature in one's beliefs at all, it may seem, one has to have knowledge or understanding with regard to it. How then can one go wrong

---

[51] Reasoning does not come to all perceivers: these include non-human animals, which have just been mentioned at 186 C 1.

about it? In other words, the very grasp that is a necessary condition for belief in the first place may seem to be at the same time a sufficient condition for true belief. The problem arises in part, I suggest, from the insight that belief is an intellectual capacity in that some understanding is required for any belief. Without an account of how much understanding is needed, there is no principled way of resisting the demand that full understanding or expertise is in fact required. Plato never provides such an account.[52]

Furthermore, it may be worth pointing out that the conception of belief as a rational capacity that emerges at *Theaetetus* 184–7 fits in well with Plato's statements of what belief is at *Theaetetus* 189 E 4–190 A 7 and *Sophist* 263 D 6–264 B 4. In both cases, the main speaker—Socrates or the visitor from Elea—emphasizes the connections between belief on the one hand and thought (διάνοια) and language (λόγος) on the other. In the *Theaetetus* passage, Socrates begins by describing thought as

a talk (λόγος) which the soul has with itself about the objects under its consideration (περὶ ὧν ἂν σκοπῇ) ... It seems to me that the soul when it thinks is simply carrying on a discussion in which it asks itself questions and answers them itself, affirms and denies. (*Theaetetus* 189 E 6–190 A 2)

He goes on to describe belief (δόξα):

And when thought arrives at something definite, either by a gradual process or a sudden leap, when it affirms one thing consistently and without divided counsel, we call this its belief. So, in my view, to form a belief (δοξάζειν) is to make a statement (λέγειν), and a belief is a statement which is not addressed to another person or spoken aloud, but silently addressed to oneself. (*Theaetetus* 190 A 2–7)

Similarly, in the *Sophist* the visitor defines thought as a silent conversation (διάλογος) that the soul has with itself (263 E 3–5), and belief as the conclusion or completion of thinking (διανοίας ἀποτελεύτησις, 264 B 1) in assertion or denial (263 E 10–264 A 2). In both the *Theaetetus* and the *Sophist*, then, belief-formation is viewed as a reflective activity, as a matter of thinking about something or other in a way that yields a considered view. Moreover, by linking belief to language (λόγος) in the way he does, Plato limits belief to views that one makes explicit to oneself by articulating them in language. We may not find this account of belief satisfactory, at least as it stands. Surely there are many beliefs that are not the results of any reflective activity at all, of raising and considering a question and answering it in light of a variety of relevant factors. And presumably one can believe something without making what it is one believes explicit by articulating it

---

[52] The discussion of false belief in the *Theaetetus* raises epistemological as well as ontological problems that a satisfactory account of false belief must address (see *Theaetetus* 188 C 10–D1). The *Sophist* solves the ontological problem by offering an account of false statement (*Sophist* 261 D 1–263 D 4). Plato never returns to the epistemological problem.

for oneself. No doubt a suitably qualified and refined version of Plato's account could be developed and defended. For present purposes, though, there is no need to do this. All I want to point out is that the conception of belief as a rational capacity that, I have argued, emerges at *Theaetetus* 184–7 coheres well with what Plato's main speakers elsewhere in the *Theaetetus*, as well as in the *Sophist*, have to say about belief.[53]

We should note in addition that the reflectiveness of belief that Plato emphasizes requires, at any rate within Plato's psychological theory, that belief is rational, by which I mean that it is a capacity specifically of the rational part of the soul. But belief can be rational in this way without being reflective in all cases. In other words, beliefs can be states or dispositions of the soul's rational part without having been arrived at by reflection. Just as reason can without reflection take up attachments and desires that have their origins in parts of the soul below reason, so presumably it can also take up 'views' or representational states that originate below reason and that present something or other in, for instance, a highly attractive way. In fact, for reason to take up, or take over, the appetitive part's attachment to wealth, for instance, will, I think, typically involve reason's taking it, independently of antecedent reflection, that wealth is good (cf. *Republic* 8, 555 B 9–1).

Moreover, Plato's recognition that belief is a specifically rational capacity is not simply a result of recognizing its connections to language and thought. In the *Republic*, even perception is presented as being able to *say* things (524 A 7), and a non-rational part of the soul is referred to as a part or aspect of *thought* (διάνοια, 603 C 1–2). In fact, the passage in *Republic* 7 about things that summon the soul to being plainly assumes that the ability to say things (for instance, 'this finger is large') does not require the resources of reason. A key insight that is operative in the later dialogues is, I suggest, that saying something, or anyhow making an assertion, always requires and manifests cognitive access to intelligibles like being, difference, and opposition. In the *Republic*, as we have seen, Plato seems to think that grasping features like difference and opposition does require employing cognitive resources that belong specifically to the rational part of the soul. But he does not seem to conclude from this that only reason can make assertions, think thoughts, and form beliefs. He does not arrive at this conclusion, I suggest, because he has not arrived at the view that making assertions, thinking thoughts, and forming beliefs in every case requires and manifests cognitive access to features like being, difference, and opposition.

---

[53] Note also that the *Timaeus* assigns belief to the wholly rational world soul on the one hand and to the human's soul's immortal part on the other. Both are composed of forms of being, sameness, and difference that correspond, in each case, to intelligible and perceptible reality (35 A 1–8). When the world soul comes to be in contact with intelligibles, understanding and knowledge result; contact with perceptibles produces true belief (37 A 2–C 5). The circular motions of the human soul's immortal part are at first in severe disarray, as a result of the agitations of birth and early development. It is this disarray of reason that accounts for the occurrence of false beliefs, especially at first of false perceptual beliefs (42 E 6–44 B 1).

We should briefly return to the *Timaeus*' denial of belief to the lowest part of the soul. As we saw earlier, Timaeus says that it 'is totally devoid of belief, reasoning (λογισμός), and understanding (νοῦς)' (*Timaeus* 77 B 5). We can now see that in denying belief to it, Timaeus is at the same time indicating the grounds on which belief is being denied to it. The ability to form beliefs requires reason and understanding, and the appetitive part of the soul has neither of these.

7

Below Belief and Reason

A question that arises now is what impact, if any, Plato's recognition of the rationality of belief has on his psychological theory as it is presented in the *Republic*. Once one accepts the rationality of belief, one should obviously refrain from attributing beliefs to parts of the soul that one holds to be non-rational. It should go without saying, though, that to deny the capacity for belief to parts of the soul other than reason is *not* to deprive them of awareness and cognition.[1]

I shall argue that much, and perhaps all, of the substance of the *Republic*'s psychological theory can survive Plato's recognition that belief is a rational capacity. My argument will proceed as follows. I shall begin by making some preliminary remarks, to the effect that the *Timaeus*' denial of belief to the lowest part of the soul is primarily motivated by new thinking about the capacity for belief, rather than about the cognitive abilities of the appetitive part. I shall then go on to discuss the *Timaeus*' robust commitment to tripartite psychology. Tripartition clearly survives the recognition that belief or judgement is rational and hence unavailable to the parts of the soul below reason. However, tripartition requires that each one of the three soul-parts is equipped with the resources needed to generate its distinctive kind of motivating condition. Since these resources must in all three cases include cognitive ones, the denial of belief to non-rational soul-parts calls for clarification of what cognitive resources are available to them. I shall draw attention to passages in the *Timaeus* and in the *Philebus* that show or suggest awareness of this need for clarification,[2] and that in fact seem to me to shed a good deal of light on the cognition of the non-rational soul-parts. We should then revisit the *Republic*'s psychological theory, so as to reflect on how much (if any) of it can be preserved.

The claim in the *Timaeus* that the lowest part of the soul is altogether incapable of belief—a claim that undeniably revises what is said in the *Republic*—can on the face of it be taken in a number of ways. One way of taking it is as a revisionary

---

[1] Contra, apparently, C. Bobonich, *Plato's Utopia Recast* (Oxford: Oxford University Press, 2002). It looks as if he is meaning to infer the denial of *contentful* mental states from the denial of '*conceptualized*' mental states, claiming that the appetitive part of the soul in the *Timaeus* is not, and cannot be, a subject of 'contentful desires' (320), apparently just because it is not capable of 'conceptualization'. Cf. 296: the lower parts of the soul 'are no longer subjects at all, since they can no longer have conceptualized states'.

[2] Namely: *Timaeus* 71 A 3–E 2, *Philebus* 32 B 9–36 C 2 and 38 E 12–40 C 6.

claim about the cognitive abilities of that part of the soul: as denying to it something that, conceived of in much the same way, is attributed to it in the *Republic*. This view assumes that at least roughly the same conception of belief is in play in both dialogues.[3] Another way of taking it is as a revisionary claim about belief: as denying that belief is such as to be within the cognitive reach of something that only has the limited abilities that Plato's psychological theory assigns to the appetitive part. On this view, it may well be the case that substantially the same conception of the lowest soul-part and its cognitive abilities is in play in both dialogues.

As we have seen, Plato articulates a conception of belief as a rational capacity in dialogues that are later than the *Republic*. There is no reason to suppose that when he wrote the *Republic* he was operating with that conception. In fact there is very good reason to think the opposite. If he had been operating with that conception, Plato would hardly have attributed beliefs to a non-rational part of the soul, as he does in *Republic* 10, except perhaps as a convenient shorthand. Moreover, Plato comes to accept that belief is a rational capacity by accepting that forming any belief requires cognitive access to intelligibles, crucially including being, which are accessible to reason only. Few considerations could be more deeply foreign to the metaphysics and epistemology of the *Republic*.[4] Furthermore, the ability to say things in assertion or denial is a rational ability, Plato comes to think, for the same reason that belief is: to assert or deny something always involves attributing being, and so assertion and denial require cognitive access to intelligibles just as much as belief does. If this conception of what is involved in and required for saying something had been available to Plato when he wrote the *Republic*, he would not have written that sense-perception says something or other, only to contrast what perception says with how the soul reflects on it with the aid of reasoning and understanding. And if it had been clear to Plato when he wrote the *Republic* that the ability to form beliefs is inseparable from the ability to discern opposition, he would not have attributed any belief to a part of the soul that is unable to distinguish between (διαγιγνώσκειν) the large and the small, let alone to grasp their opposition (*Republic* 10, 605 B 7–C1).

---

[3] A view along these lines is taken by Bobonich in *Plato's Utopia Recast*. According to his interpretation of the *Republic*'s psychological theory, it involves three distinct *rational* centres, not only of motivation, but also of belief.

[4] It is worth noting, however, that this consideration *is* reflected in the *Timaeus*: the world's wholly rational soul includes portions not just of sameness and difference, but also of *being* (οὐσία), as they are divided among bodies (τῆς . . . περὶ τὰ σώματα γιγνομένης μεριστῆς) (35 A 1–6). The presence of the 'divisible' forms is plainly supposed to account for beliefs about perceptibles (37 A 2–C 3); this is an application of the principle that like is known by like. The idea is no doubt that the perceptible world manifests a certain kind of being, and that the world soul must incorporate being of the relevant kind if it is to be able to apprehend such being, and to form beliefs on the basis of that apprehension. The world soul also includes portions of 'indivisible' being, sameness, and difference, presumably to account for its ability to apprehend the intelligible world-order, which Plato takes to exist separately from the perceptible world. The human soul's rational part is composed from the same ingredients as the world soul.

These considerations defeat the view that the conception of belief as a specifically rational capacity that emerges at *Theaetetus* 184–7, and that is reflected in the *Timaeus*, is already in play in the *Republic*. Rather, it very much seems that Plato in the *Republic* uses the term *doxa* ('belief') and related terminology more loosely and broadly, so that having a *doxa* may simply be a matter of being in a representational state, a state that presents something as being some way or other, and accepting that the thing in question is that way. Neither the representational state nor its acceptance need be rational; both can belong to the soul in virtue of belonging to any part of it. The acceptance that such a 'belief' involves may be entirely uncritical, and may be no more than a disposition to act on the information contained in the representational state. If so, the inference from having 'beliefs' to being rational is illegitimate. This of course is as it should be: the *Republic*'s non-rational parts of the soul really are non-rational, though they are capable of 'belief'.

The *Timaeus* makes clear that Plato's commitment to tripartition of the soul survives his recognition that belief is a rational capacity. Timaeus assigns belief to the world soul and to the immortal, rational part of the human soul and denies it to the appetitive part. Against the background of Plato's psychological theory and the recognition of belief as rational, it is plain that spirit too is incapable of belief. At the same time, tripartition is, as we have seen, very much in evidence in the *Timaeus*.

The non-rational soul-parts of the *Timaeus* are not only able to generate their distinctive kinds of motivating conditions. Timaeus also presents them as being capable of bringing about actions all by themselves, as of course they are in the *Republic*. Spirit's role is to unleash its might when reason reports that someone else is acting unjustly, and also, Timaeus says, when it reports that an unjust act that originates 'from the desires within' is coming to pass.[5] There is no suggestion, here or elsewhere, that the appetitive part needs any support or assistance from reason so as to originate an action. Consider also Timaeus' account of the origins of land animals:

Land animals in the wild came from men who had no tincture of philosophy and who made no study of the universe, because they no longer made use of the circular motions in their heads but instead followed the lead of the parts of the soul that reside in the chest. (*Timaeus* 91 E 2–6)

The circular motions in people's heads are the movements of the same and the different that are characteristic both of the world soul, as described at 36 B 6–D 7, and of the immortal part of the human soul. Not to make use of them is not to make use of one's reason. It should also be noted that for a considerable period in the development of human beings, the immortal parts of their souls are not,

---

[5] *Timaeus* 70 B 4–5: ὡς τις ἄδικος ... γίγνεται πρᾶξις ἔξωθεν ἢ καὶ ἀπὸ τῶν ἔνδοθεν ἐπιθυμιῶν.

according to Timaeus' account, in functioning order, and during this time their souls are devoid of understanding. It is as a result of the disturbances of birth and early development, he says, that

> even today and not only at the beginning, whenever a soul is bound within a mortal body, it at first lacks understanding (ἄνους ψυχὴ γίγνεται). But as the stream that brings growth and nourishment diminishes and the soul's orbits regain their composure, resume their proper courses, and establish themselves more and more with the passage of time, their circular motions are set straight . . . They then correctly identify what is the same and what is different, and render intelligent (ἔμφρων) the person who possesses them. (*Timaeus* 44 A 7–B 7)

Thus for a considerable period in their development, the behaviour of children will depend on the functioning of their soul's non-rational parts.[6] The non-rational parts not only generate desires of distinctive kinds, but are also the bearers of emotions and other mental states such as pleasure, pain, confidence, fear, and expectation (*Timaeus* 69 D 1–4). The desires they generate are not, then, limited to blind cravings or undirected urges. Rather, they can be sufficiently determinate to be acted on. As a result, non-rational soul-parts can generate actions all on their own, so much so that humans can do much of what they do without making use of their souls' rational parts. This, at any rate, is what Timaeus says or implies.

Moreover, it is plainly part of Timaeus' account of the tripartite soul that there can be some form of communication between reason and the non-rational parts. Reason makes announcements to spirit—for instance, that someone is wronging the person—and spirit receives them and acts appropriately on them. Furthermore, Timaeus does *not* simply say that whenever appetite wants to do something objectionable, reason and spirit are jointly to overpower it. What he says is something rather more nuanced and interesting, namely that this is to happen 'should it [sc. the appetitive part] in no way want to obey willingly (ὁπότ' . . . μηδαμῇ πείθεσθαι ἑκὸν ἐθέλοι) the command and account (τῷ τ' ἐπιτάγματι καὶ λόγῳ)[7] coming down from the citadel' (*Timaeus* 70 A 6–7). It would be pointless (or worse) to say this if it were not possible for appetite willingly to obey such commands.[8] But for that to be possible, appetite must first of all be able to *receive* reason's commands. Thus there is good reason to think that the *Timaeus*' version of

---

[6] Cf. *Republic* 4, 441 A 7–B 1: children are full of anger (as well as, of course, appetite) immediately after birth; reason arrives later if at all.

[7] Zeyl translates 'the dictates of reason'. But the command and the λόγος are syntactically coordinate, and they are both said to come 'from the citadel'—which is to say, from the rational part of the soul. Given the τ' . . . καί construction, we should take 'command' and 'account' closely together: reason's command is, or comes with, a practical account, which indicates the thing to do in the circumstances, perhaps in a way that makes perspicuous why it is the thing to do (for instance, because it is what justice requires).

[8] This passage thus contains the resources needed to refute an argument against the *Timaeus*' account of tripartition in Bobonich, *Plato's Utopia Recast*, 317. The distinction between appetite willingly obeying reason and being overpowered jointly by reason and spirit underwrites and preserves the *Republic*'s distinction between the true virtue that is temperance and the oligarch's self-control.

tripartition allows and indeed requires communication between reason and the non-rational parts: reason can share information with spirit (and perhaps with appetite as well),[9] and it can issue commands to both of the non-rational parts, which they may or may not obey.

The *Timaeus'* version of tripartition, then, calls for clarification of how the soul's non-rational parts can generate fully formed motivating conditions so as to be able to originate actions all on their own, and how they can receive both commands and information from reason. I now turn to three passages—one in the *Timaeus* and two closely related ones in the *Philebus*—that seem to me to shed a good deal of light on these questions.

Passage 1 is *Timaeus* 71 A 3–E 2. This continues Timaeus' account of how the created gods put together the mortal parts of the soul and fit them into the human body. It is a difficult and ultimately, I think, unsatisfactory passage, but one that is nonetheless significant and illuminating, especially when read together with the second of the two *Philebus* passages to be discussed in the present chapter (that is, *Philebus* 38 E 12—40 C 6). One concern that the passage clearly addresses is how reason might be able to communicate with, or even to have any effect at all on, the lowest part of the soul. As we saw, what Timaeus says about spirit at 70 A 2–7 suggests that appetite is able not only to receive reason's 'commands and accounts', but also to obey them willingly. He now says that the gods knew right away that appetite 'was not going to understand [sc. reason's] account (λόγος), and even if it were to have some awareness of some accounts or other (τινῶν . . . λόγων), it was not going to be in its nature to care about them' (*Timaeus* 71 A 3–5). In emphatic juxtaposition, Timaeus then contrasts 'accounts' with images (εἴδωλα) and appearances (φαντάσματα), by which, he says, the appetitive part would be very much enticed by night and day. It is this tendency to be enticed by images and appearances, Timaeus says, that the gods exploit so as to ensure that reason can have beneficial effects on appetite. They construct the liver as a smooth and shiny organ and place it where the appetitive part of the soul is also located. They equip it with the abilities to take on bitterness and sweetness, and to contract and relax, as appropriate. It is shiny so that 'the force of thoughts carried down from the intellect (τῶν διανοημάτων ἡ ἐκ τοῦ νοῦ φερομένη δύναμις) might be impressed on it as on a mirror that receives impressions (τύπους) and returns visible images (εἴδωλα)' (*Timaeus* 71 B 3–5). By means of the liver, Timaeus says, 'the force of thoughts' can, when appropriate, frighten the appetitive part and, on other occasions, make it 'gracious and well behaved'—depending on whether it makes the liver bitter and rough, causing pain and nausea, or whether it makes it sweet and smooth.

---

[9] If spirit can receive information from reason about injustices, appetite should be able to be informed by reason about pleasures. Cf. Aristotle, *Nicomachean Ethics* 7.6, 1149ᵃ32–ᵇ1 (a passage that will be discussed in some detail in Ch. 13): spirit may be informed of an insult or slight by reason or *phantasia*; appetite may learn about the availability of something pleasant from reason or perception.

It seems clear that the liver's role is not limited to the generation of painful and pleasant feelings of some sort or other. Timaeus speaks of impressions and images, and of 'appearances painted by a gentle inspiration from thought' (71 C 3–4), but unfortunately he leaves it strikingly unclear what they might represent and how the appetitive part can be aware of them. Yet we have been led to expect that they move and entice the appetitive part in a way that 'accounts' could not. And presumably they are supposed to convey undesirable or, when appropriate, desirable prospects—as Timaeus indicates at 71 B 7, where he speaks of a *threat* issued by the force of thoughts.[10] He speaks of the force of thoughts making bilious colours appear in or on the liver (71 B 7–8), which suggests that images or appearances of the requisite kind are in some way generated on the liver's shiny surface. But this will do little or no good, unless there is some way in which such appearances are actually *seen*.

Timaeus associates the liver not only with communication downward from reason to appetite, but also with divination.[11] This involves some kind of grasp of truth that does not depend on reason. It occurs when a person's 'power of understanding is bound in sleep or by sickness, or when some sort of possession works a change in him' (*Timaeus* 71 E 4–6). Timaeus takes appearances (φαντάσματα, 71 E 8) to play a role in at least some cases of divination, where they serve to signify 'some future, past, or present good or evil' (72 A 1–2). Presumably at least some such appearances are dreams (71 D 3–4; 71 E 7). Again it seems to be part of what Timaeus has in mind that appearances that represent something or other appear on the liver's shiny, mirror-like surface (72 B 7–D 3). And again, Timaeus leaves it obscure what exactly is supposed to appear in or on the liver, and how the soul can have awareness of such appearances.

Nonetheless, a few things seem clear enough. Plato is aware of the need to clarify how reason can convey commands, threats, and the like to appetite—how it can communicate to it something that it cares about, that can stir it to action or, as the case may be, prevent it from action. This need, I suggest, arises as follows. On the one hand, Plato wants to retain appetite's ability to obey reason's commands, in order to preserve a distinction between willing obedience and

---

[10] Cf. 70 B 6–8, where Timaeus speaks of 'prescriptions and threats' coming from reason and spirit, which 'everything in the body that is perceptive' (πᾶν ὅσον αἰσθητικὸν ἐν τῷ σώματι) is supposed to perceive and obey. In speaking of 'everything in the body', Timaeus may already have in mind the idea that the appetitive part is not spatially limited to the region around the digestive organs, but also especially animates and motivates the reproductive apparatus, once that is added to the organism in the second generation (90 E 6–91 D 6). Perception and desire belong primarily to the soul and its parts, I take it, but can be attributed derivatively to the ensouled organism and also, perhaps, to the parts or regions of it that are especially associated with one soul-part or another. Thus Timaeus speaks of 'the nature around the private parts' as 'unruly and self-willed, like an animal that will not be subject to reason and, driven crazy by its desires, seeks to overpower everything else' (91 B 4–7). More strikingly still, he says that the woman's womb 'is a living thing within her with a desire for childbearing' (91 B 7–C 2). Cf. Aristotle, *De Motu Animalium* 11, 703^b 20–6.

[11] *Timaeus* 72 B 6–7: 'This, then, explains why the liver's nature is what it is, and why it is situated in the region we say—it is for the sake of divination.'

being overpowered. On the other hand, appetite is unable, given its limited cognitive abilities, to grasp the significance of reason's 'accounts', arguably because doing so requires cognitive access to intelligibles. The problem this raises is serious. One thing that is at stake is the distinction between true virtue and mere self-control.[12]

The *Timaeus'* attempt to solve the problem is less than successful. Timaeus draws attention to appetite's tendency to be engaged by 'images and appearances', which presumably include sensory experiences such as exercises of sense-perception and of the sensory imagination as, for instance, in dreaming. This coheres well with the assignment of perception to the mortal part of the soul (69 D 4–6). It also brings to mind the non-rational part's acceptance of sensory appearances in *Republic* 10. However, the *Timaeus* fails to provide a clear account of how appearances 'painted'[13] by 'the force of thoughts issuing from the intellect' can serve to make possible the communication between reason and appetite that Plato's psychological theory requires. The root of this failure is, I suggest, that Timaeus thinks of the appearances that reason generates as being *external* to the soul, being formed in some way on the liver's shiny surface. For this to work, he would need a story about how appetite can *see* the pictures that reason paints, a story he is, of course, unable to provide. But Timaeus' failure suggests a solution to the problem. The appearances that reason generates should be thought of, not as modifications of bodily organs, but as forms of awareness of a certain kind. In other words, reason's paintings should be *internal* to the soul. This, to anticipate a bit, is in fact where the *Philebus* seems to locate them. In the *Philebus*, as we shall see, Socrates presents a picture of the human soul as being constituted so that at least some of reason's accounts—ones to do with future pleasures and pains, for instance—are accompanied by sensory representations[14] that depend on them.

The main topic of the *Philebus* is 'the good' or 'the human good'. Philebus holds that what is good for humans is the same as what is good for all animals, 'to enjoy oneself, to be pleased and delighted' (11 B 4–6). Socrates' argument against this view and for his own account of the *human* good requires distinguishing between different kinds of pleasure, and showing that there are false pleasures as well as true

---

[12] Plato's psychological theory seems to presuppose—reasonably enough, I think—that the appetitive part's liability to give rise to objectionable desires and aversions is all but ineliminable. Even *lawless* desires, Socrates says, are 'probably present in everyone', adding that 'in a few people they have been eliminated entirely or only a few weak ones remain' (*Republic* 571 B 3–C 1, 572 B 2–7). What appetite cares about are pleasures and pains, and there simply is no way of guaranteeing in advance that what strikes one as pleasant and painful in the varied circumstances of life will always accurately track one's reasoned evaluations of good and bad. Thus there is an ongoing need for appetite to be watched over by reason and spirit, as Socrates makes clear at *Republic* 442 A 4–B 3; cf. 589 A 6–B 6. However, if it is indeed part of the ordinary course of things that everyone forms objectionable desires and aversions at least every once in a while, then Plato's theory does require a 'friendly' way of allaying them that leaves intact the harmonious relations among the parts of the soul that are characteristic of true virtue.   [13] 71 C 3–4: φαντάσματα ἀποζωγραφοῖ.

[14] Indeed, 'painted appearances' (φαντάσματα ἐζωγραφημένα), as Socrates calls them at *Philebus* 40 A 9.

ones. His discussion of pleasure includes a passage (32 B 9–36 C 2) in which he argues that one kind of pleasure—the pleasure of the soul by itself, which arises through expectation (προσδοκία, 32 C 4–5)—involves and depends on memory, which was included in Socrates' initial list of goods, but absent from Philebus'. This discussion, to which I turn now, offers significant clarification of how cognitive resources below belief and reason can, on Plato's view, account for the formation of determinate desires and, by doing so, for the origination of action.

Passage 2: *Philebus* 32 B 9–36 C 2. One thing that should be pointed out right away is that throughout the passage, Socrates is at pains to emphasize that the discussion applies not only to humans, but to all animals.[15] His main concern in the passage is to introduce and clarify pleasures of anticipation. These will be taken up for further consideration in the simile of the illustrated book (38 E 12–40 C 6), where Socrates relies on pleasures of anticipation to show that some pleasures are false. The passage also includes a rather elaborate discussion of desire (ἐπιθυμία)[16] and its dependence on memory, culminating in Socrates' assertion that the account has shown that 'every impulse and every desire and the rule over every animal' belongs, not to the body, but to the soul (35 D 1–3). He begins by introducing pleasures of anticipation as a distinctive kind of pleasure, to be distinguished from the kind that accompanies the occurrent restoration of an organism's natural state of harmony when that restoration involves affections in the body that are strong enough to reach and affect the soul. Socrates asks Protarchus to accept

the anticipation by the soul itself of these two kinds of experiences [sc. destruction and restoration of the harmonious state]; the expectation before the actual pleasure will be pleasant and will inspire confidence (θαρραλέον), while the expectation of pain will be frightening (φοβερόν) and painful. (*Philebus* 32 B 9–C 2)

Protarchus replies that 'this turns out to be a different kind of pleasure and pain, a kind that belongs to the soul itself separately from the body and that comes about through expectation' (*Philebus* 32 C 3–5).[17] It is worth noting that the *Timaeus*, at

---

[15] 32 E 4; 35 C 9–10, D 3, E 3; 36 B 8–9. Strictly speaking, the discussion applies to such animals as are equipped with memory, the preservation of perception (34 A 10–11). This excludes molluscs and shellfish: see 21 C 1–8. Interestingly, such creatures will turn out to lack not only expectation, fear, and pleasures of anticipation, but also the ability to form desires (ἐπιθυμίαι). Cf. Aristotle, *De Anima* 3.11, 433ᵇ31–434ᵃ5.

[16] What Socrates offers at 34 D 10–35 D 6 is not, and is arguably not meant to be, a general account of desire, but of 'bodily' desire, where what is desired is the opposite of the affection currently undergone by *the body* (35 C 9–10). This restriction seems to be indicated at 34 D 10–E 1, where Socrates (referring back to 31 E 6–32 A 8) speaks of hunger, thirst, and the like as desires *of one kind* (τινας ἐπιθυμίας). Note also his indication, at 31 E 3–4, that hunger, thirst, and the like, and the corresponding fillings or restorations, are among the 'most ordinary and well known cases' of pains and pleasures. (Contrast the more refined and less accessible pleasures mentioned at 50 E 5–52 B 8.) The discussion here plainly concentrates on pleasures that consist in anticipating and envisaging the satisfaction of bodily desires.

[17] A fuller formulation is at 39 D 1–3, where Socrates refers back to the present passage. The contrast there is between pleasures and pains of the soul 'through itself', and ones 'through the body'.

69 D 1–6, assigns to the mortal part of the soul not only perception, pleasure, and pain, as well as anger and lust, but also 'confidence' (θάρρος), fear (φόβος), and expectation (ἐλπίς). The present passage offers a relatively detailed view of what these last three psychological states are, how they arise, and how they are related to pleasure, pain, and perception.

When Socrates returns to the newly identified kind of pleasure—pleasure of the soul itself, as he calls it (33 C 5–6)—he makes a somewhat surprising claim about it: it depends in all cases on *memory*.[18] Protarchus does not understand this right away, and Socrates proceeds to explain it by providing accounts of perception, memory, and desire. Perception is or consists in a joint affection of soul and body (33 D 2–34 A 5). Memory (μνήμη) is the 'preservation of perception' (σωτηρία αἰσθήσεως, 34 A 10–11). Socrates next turns to desire, presumably because an account of desire will make clear how it is that pleasures of anticipation depend on memory. Desires like hunger and thirst, he points out, involve not only depletion, but also a desire for its opposite, replenishment. Forming that desire requires some cognitive 'contact' with its object, with what the desire is for. As Socrates says, 'something in the person who is thirsty must necessarily somehow be in contact with replenishment' (*Philebus* 35 B 6–7). Perception could not serve to provide the required 'contact' with replenishment, given that the organism's current situation is one of depletion. The only option we are left with, Socrates asserts, and Protarchus agrees, 'is that the soul makes contact with the replenishment, and it clearly must do so through memory' (*Philebus* 35 B 11–C 1).[19]

It is part of Socrates' account, not only that the ability to form desires depends on the ability to preserve sensory impressions, but also that the ability to form desires of a particular kind depends on the actual possession of suitable impressions, as preserved by memory. Socrates seems to be fully prepared to accept a consequence of his account, namely that newborn babies could not form desires like hunger or thirst, in so far as they do not yet possess the impressions that would enable them to make cognitive contact with the relevant kinds of replenishment. If someone is depleted for the first time, he asks, 'is there any way he could be in touch with

---

[18] διὰ μνήμης πᾶν ἐστι γεγονός: 33 C 6.

[19] Socrates takes the discussion to show, not only that desire requires memory, but also, and thereby, that it is the soul, not the body, that desires belong to, even bodily desires like hunger and thirst (35 C 6–7, 35 D 5–6). Protarchus, with characteristic slowness of mind, does not immediately understand: 35 C 8. What convinces him in the end is Socrates' stress on the thought that desires, or anyhow desires of this kind, are for affections opposite to the ones that the body is undergoing at the time. Protarchus seems to think (despite the preceding account of perception!) that while the body might have awareness of an affection it is currently undergoing, it could not have awareness of an affection it is not actually undergoing. It is tempting to think that Plato is re-enacting, as it were in slow motion, his own recognition that it is in all cases the soul, not the body, that is the subject of desires—the recognition, that is, that leads to the replacement of the *Phaedo*'s psychological theory with the *Republic*'s. See my *Stanford Encyclopedia of Philosophy* entry on 'Ancient theories of soul', 3.1–2, for discussion of the two theories, and of the relation between them; in, E. N. Zalta (ed.), *Stanford Encyclopedia of Philosophy* (Winter 2003 Edition).

being replenished, either through perception or memory, since he has no experience of it, either in the present or ever in the past?' (*Philebus* 35 A 6–9).

Moreover, Socrates takes himself to have shown in the discussion of desire that it is memory that drives or directs (ἐπάγειν, 35 D 1–2) towards the objects of desire. This suggests that memory plays a key role not only in providing 'contact' with the relevant object of desire, but also in guiding the organism's action or behaviour in pursuit of it. This is, to be sure, an extension of what Socrates has actually said, but a natural and easy one. If memory can supply awareness of what it is the subject wants, it is reasonable to suppose that it can also supply awareness of how to obtain the object of desire, provided the possession and preservation of suitable sensory impressions.

Finally, Socrates returns to his main topic, pleasures of anticipation. Since the expected affection is not one that the organism is currently undergoing, perception could not supply cognitive contact with it. Sensory impressions preserved by memory have to serve this function. In this way, pleasures of anticipation depend on memory, and on suitable stored sensory impressions, just as desires like hunger and thirst do. They also depend on the subject's expecting that an appropriate replenishing process will in fact come to pass (36 A 7–B 1, B 4). In that case, the subject—human or other animal—takes pleasure in remembering the affection of being replenished (36 B 4–6)—or, as we might say, in envisaging replenishment through sensory impressions stored by memory.

Throughout the passage, Socrates is clearly at pains to provide a unified account of desire and anticipatory pleasure that applies equally to humans and non-human animals. This objective yields an account that is remarkable for being resolutely Empiricist,[20] strictly avoiding any appeal to specifically intellectual or rational resources. An account along these lines is, of course, exactly what one would expect against the background of the *Timaeus*' psychological theory. It makes pleasures and pains of anticipation available to parts of the soul below reason, as they should be if Timaeus is right in assigning to the soul's mortal part such states as confidence, fear, and expectation (*Timaeus* 69 C 5–D 6). It also provides a highly suggestive outline indicating how the soul's lower parts, in spite of their limited cognitive abilities, can nonetheless generate fully formed motivating conditions and, by doing so, originate actions all on their own.

As noted already, Socrates introduces pleasures of anticipation at least in part with a view to showing that some pleasures are false. In the second *Philebus* passage that I want to discuss, in which he compares the soul to an illustrated book, he points out a connection between beliefs, which obviously can be false, and pleasures of anticipation that depend on beliefs. The suggestion then is that in some way or other, the falsity of a belief can infect a pleasure that depends on it, so that the pleasure in question, even though a real case of pleasure, is false (40 D 7–10; 42 A 7–9).

---

[20] See Introduction, pp. 4–6, for a brief account of Empiricism.

Passage 3: *Philebus* 38 E 12–40 C 6. It is immediately clear that the simile of the illustrated book applies, not to the souls of all animals, but specifically to 'our souls' (38 E 12–13). The point of comparison between the human soul and an illustrated book is twofold. Memory, perception, and further affections that Socrates leaves unspecified form sentences or accounts (λόγοι) in our souls, much in the way a scribe writes sentences into a book. Depending on whether 'the scribe in us' writes true or false sentences, we find ourselves with true or false beliefs (δόξαι) and (uttered) statements (λόγοι).[21] In addition, Socrates thinks, the introduction of a further artisan, responsible for a different kind of product, is called for: a painter or illustrator (ζωγράφος), 'who follows the scribe and paints images (εἰκόνας) in the soul of the things spoken of [sc. in the scribe's writings]' (*Philebus* 39 B 6–7).

The painter's products are in evidence, Socrates says, when in some way one 'sees' in oneself images of the objects of one's beliefs and statements.[22] Although Socrates seems to think of these images as having been 'taken away', or derived, in some way or other from 'sight or some other sense' (39 B 9), it is important that they are not simply stored or preserved impressions received in acts of perception. In the case that Socrates is mainly interested in, someone forms a false perceptual belief, misidentifying a man in the distance as a statue (38 C 5–E 7). He then continues to think of, and *visualize*, the matter, as he travels on and is, I take it, no longer able actually to perceive it (38 E 6–7). In this case, the painter's work depicts, not what the person in fact saw (a man), but what he falsely believes he saw (a statue). As Socrates says, the painter follows the scribe, and what the painter paints is true or false depending on what the scribe writes (39 C 4–5, with 39 A 3–7). The painter's works thus involve interpretation of what one saw or perceived otherwise. They depend on the rational states or dispositions that are one's perceptual beliefs.

The pair of artisans in the soul having been introduced, Socrates returns to pleasures of anticipation, referring back to Passage 2 (32 B 9–36 C 2). The pleasures and pains of the soul 'through itself' are concerned with the future, he reminds Protarchus, and then asks him whether 'those writings and paintings (ζωγραφήματα) which come to be in us, as we said earlier, are concerned only with the past and the present, but not with the future?' (*Philebus* 39 D 7–E 2). They agree that there are in the soul both writings and corresponding paintings concerning the future. Socrates overstates himself when he says that *all* of them are expectations (39 E 4–5); this is true only of those among them that concern prospects that one thinks will, or may well, come to pass (cf. 36 A 7–B 2). Here is

---

[21] The word λόγος thus does double duty here, as it naturally can: it denotes, first, the mind's articulation of its experience; secondly, the person's utterance of a belief in speech.

[22] 39 B 9–C 1: ὅταν ἀπ' ὄψεως ἤ τινος ἄλλης αἰσθήσεως τὰ τότε δοξαζόμενα καὶ λεγόμενα ἀπαγαγών τις τὰς τῶν δοξασθέντων καὶ λεχθέντων εἰκόνας ἐν αὑτῷ ὁρᾷ πως. ('When someone has taken away from sight or some other sense the things then judged and spoken of, and in a way sees in himself the images of the things judged and spoken of.')

Socrates' example of a 'painted appearance'[23] associated with, or involved in, such an expectation: 'a person often sees himself in possession of an enormous amount of gold, and of many pleasures because of it. And in addition he also sees in this inner picture himself, beside himself with delight' (*Philebus* 40 A 9–12). If the person will not in fact get the pleasure she is expecting to get, then a belief that she will get it is false. And Socrates then claims that, in this case, falsity affects not only the visualization or sensory representation that corresponds to the belief, but also the anticipatory pleasure that is involved in envisaging the pleasure she falsely believes she will get.[24]

There are several reasons why Socrates, at this stage in the dialogue, introduces not only a scribe in the soul, who is responsible for the formation of sentences or accounts, but also a painter who follows the scribe, generating visualizations or other sensory representations that depend on the scribe's accounts. One consideration is that it is simply a fact revealed by introspection that, as Socrates says, 'this is something that is going on in us' (39 C 1–2). Moreover, a role for sensory representations is required by Socrates' general claim, made in Passage 2, that pleasures of anticipation arise *in all cases* 'through memory', the preservation of perception (33 C 5–6). In the context, that claim makes it clear that pleasures of anticipation, on Socrates' view, always involve visualizations or other sensory representations. He then turns to the rather special case of anticipatory pleasures that depend on false beliefs, because he wants to show that such pleasures are false. The scribe in the soul dramatizes the formation of belief. The painter is needed to preserve the connection, to which Socrates has already committed himself, between pleasures of anticipation and sensory representations. The painter's works—the products of the sensory imagination—will no doubt rely heavily on perceptual impressions preserved by memory, at least using them as materials, though they will also involve combinations, extensions, subtractions, and the like, as required by the scribe's accounts that the painter follows. The painter's illustrations thus enable Socrates to claim consistently that all pleasures of anticipation come about through memory, even those that also depend on beliefs. Furthermore, just after Passage 3 Socrates turns to 'inflated' pleasures, which appear greater or more intense than they really are, especially when compared with pleasures and pains in the more distant future. He likens this phenomenon, familiar from the *Protagoras* (356 A 5–E 4), to distant objects looking smaller than they really are. This point is, to say the least, much helped by the introduction of the painter in the soul. With the painter in place, prospective pleasures and pains cannot only be described in sentences and accounts, but anticipated vividly and, as it were, 'pre-enacted'[25] through the sensory imagination.

---

[23] φαντάσματα ἐζωγραφημένα, 40 A 9.

[24] For discussion of what precisely Socrates' claim amounts to, see D. Frede, *Platon:* Philebus (Göttingen: Vandenhoeck & Ruprecht, 1997), 242–60.

[25] D. Frede, ibid., 235, writes of 'vorauserleben'.

From the point of view of Plato's psychological theory, we can see another reason for the presence in the human soul of a painter as well as a scribe. The pleasures of anticipation that Socrates is discussing in Passages 2 and 3 concern satisfactions of bodily desires such as hunger, thirst, and the like, as well as the acquisition of wealth. Hunger, thirst, and the like are assigned both in the *Republic* and in the *Timaeus* to the appetitive part of the soul. The *Republic*'s statement of the theory attributes to appetite a strong tendency to become attached to money, a characterization which the *Timaeus* neither repeats nor repudiates. In any case, all or most of the pleasures of anticipation that are at issue in Passages 2 and 3 concern satisfactions of desires that, according to both versions or statements of Plato's psychological theory, belong to the appetitive part of the soul. Not only that: Plato's theory assigns to the soul's appetitive part, not only desires of this kind, but also the pleasures involved in satisfying them. It is entirely natural, then, to expect that the corresponding pleasures of anticipation will also be assigned by the theory to the appetitive part. If it is appetite that takes pleasure in the body's replenishment or restoration, it should also be appetite that takes pleasure in the anticipation of such replenishment.

From the point of view of Plato's psychological theory as it is presented in the *Timaeus*, then, there is a question about the kind of case that Socrates is concerned with in Passage 3—namely, appetitive pleasures of anticipation that depend on false beliefs to the effect that something pleasant will come to pass. The question is how the agreeable prospect is going to be communicated to appetite so as suitably to excite and delight it. This of course is a version of the question that the *Timaeus*' psychological theory raises by itself: how is reason able to convey commands, threats, and the like to the mortal parts of the soul, especially to appetite? Passage 1 strongly suggests that Plato is aware of the question and attempts to answer it, by introducing the idea of images or appearances of some sort that are in some way 'painted' under the influence of reason's thinking (*Timaeus* 71 C 4–5; B 3–5). This answer, however, is unsatisfactory, I suggested, because it makes the appearances that reason generates external to the soul, apparently conceiving of them as modifications of some sort on the liver's shiny surface. In Passage 3, by contrast, Socrates introduces appearances generated under reason's influence, not as modifications of some bodily organ, but as forms of awareness of a certain sort. To be more specific, these appearances are conceived of as distinctively *sensory* forms of awareness. The introduction of such appearances is a significant development in Plato's psychological theory. It resolves the *Timaeus*' problem about appetite's ability to enjoy the benefits of receiving communications from reason.

Given the rather striking similarity both of conception and of language between Passages 1 and 3, it seems unlikely that Plato could have been unaware of the connection. It also seems unlikely that when he wrote the *Timaeus*, or anyhow Passage 1, Passage 3's conception of the human soul as containing a scribe *and* a painter was already available to him. In that case, there would have been no need for Passage 1's elaborate and unsatisfactory construction. We should note in passing, then, that we seem to have identified a reason for thinking the *Philebus* to be later than the *Timaeus*.

We should, to conclude, briefly revisit the *Republic*'s psychological theory, to reflect on how much of it can be preserved in the wake of the recognition that belief is a rational capacity. The *Timaeus*, as we have seen, takes that recognition fully into account, and yet it seems to retain much or all of the substance of the *Republic*'s theory. It preserves the *Republic*'s commitment to the view that all three parts of the soul can form, not just blind, undirected cravings, but fully formed motivating conditions, so that each one of the three parts can by itself account for actions. This commitment of the *Timaeus* is underwritten, I have suggested, by the *Philebus*' resolutely Empiricist accounts of bodily desire and the pleasures and pains of anticipation at *Philebus* 32 B 9–36 C 2—accounts that eschew any appeal to distinctively rational resources such as belief (as Plato has come to conceive of it) and instead rely exclusively on perception and the preservation of sensory impressions.

Moreover, the *Timaeus* plainly allows communication between reason and the non-rational soul-parts. Reason shares information with spirit and, presumably, with appetite. It issues to appetite both threats and commands, which appetite may or may not obey willingly. Timaeus is evidently at pains to indicate how it can be that reason can communicate in such ways with the mortal part of the soul—in particular with appetite, its cognitively more primitive part. What he says about the subject is intriguing, though not wholly successful. One thing that is fairly clear about the inordinately long and difficult sentence that extends from 71 A 3 to 71 D 4 is that Timaeus is attempting to explain the possibility of communication from reason to appetite in a way that assigns a mediating role to the sensory imagination. I have suggested that the simile of the illustrated book, at *Philebus* 38 E 12–40 C 6, indicates an important development in Plato's thinking about the sensory imagination, and about the interaction and communication between reason and appetite. If we are prepared to accept the new conception as an emendation to the *Timaeus*' psychological theory, we end up with a theory that renders intelligible how the sensory imagination can play a mediating role so as to enable reason to communicate with appetite. An account along these lines will also be available for communications between reason and spirit.

As we have seen, the *Timaeus* indicates that appetite *can* willingly obey reason's commands, though Timaeus fails to explain satisfactorily how this may come about. Appetite may also refuse to do so, in which case it is incumbent on reason and spirit jointly to overpower it.[26] This gives us the distinction we need in

[26] *Timaeus* 70 A 2–6: 'The part of the mortal soul that exhibits courage and spirit, the ambitious part, they settled nearer the head, between the midriff and the neck, so that it might listen to reason and together with it hold down by force the part consisting of appetites (βίᾳ τὸ τῶν ἐπιθυμιῶν κατέχοι γένος).'

order to retain the *Republic*'s contrast between the truly virtuous person and the oligarch, who

forcibly holds down his other desires, which are evil (βίᾳ κατέχει ἄλλας κακὰς ἐπιθυμίας). He does so, not by persuading them that it's better not to act on them or taming them by reason (οὐ πείθων ὅτι οὐκ ἄμεινον, οὐδ' ἡμερῶν λόγῳ), but by compulsion and fear, trembling for his other possessions. (*Republic* 8, 554 C 12–D 3)

This contrast does not require the idea that the appetitive part can be persuaded by *arguments* that it should abstain from some objectionable course of action. In fact, that would be very much the wrong idea to employ, as it would result in a sub-partition within the appetitive part by introducing the possibility of lack of self-control within it. What is required by the contrast is rather some way in which reason can affect the appetitive part so as to make it gently and perhaps gladly acquiesce in the better course of action. That would be a clear case of taming appetite by reason, and it would contrast in a perfectly adequate way with holding desires down 'by compulsion and fear'. The *Republic* does not say how reason can affect appetite in the requisite way. It simply assumes that it can. Acquiescence of the non-rational parts in the course of action that reason prescribes is also what is minimally required by Socrates' account of temperance in book 4: 'A person is temperate because of the friendly and harmonious relations between these same parts, namely, when the ruler and the ruled believe in common that reason should rule and they don't engage in civil war against it' (*Republic* 4, 442 C 9–D 2).

The *Timaeus*, by contrast, does attempt to explain how reason can affect appetite. 'A gentle inspiration descending from thought', Timaeus says, may 'paint' appearances (φαντάσματα) that are opposite to the threats mentioned just before in the text. When that happens, he says, the liver becomes sweet and smooth. In this way—both, I take it, by 'painting' agreeable prospects and by causing pleasant sensations—thought makes the appetitive part gentle and tame.[27] As we have seen, Timaeus leaves it obscure how thought can paint agreeable prospects and how appetite can be aware of them. But we only have to consult the *Philebus* to see how this can be. The human soul is constituted so that certain kinds of thoughts—such as beliefs about future pleasures and pains—involve, or are accompanied by, suitable exercises of the sensory imagination, through which the person 'pre-enacts' the pleasures and pains in question. The appetitive part of the soul, Timaeus tells us, is constituted so that it fails to understand, or in any event fails to be moved by, the accounts that form the contents of thoughts (*Timaeus* 71 A 3–5). But if thoughts about good or bad prospects come with sensory representations that illustrate them, it turns out that they can, after all, move even the lowest part of the soul. For as Timaeus also lets us know, the appetitive part is so constituted as to be highly sensitive, and responsive, to 'images and appearances' (71 A 5–7).

---

27 ἵλεών τε καὶ εὐήμερον, *Timaeus* 71 D 1–2. Note ἡμερῶν at *Republic* 8, 554 D 2.

What reason can do, then, in order to make appetite acquiesce in the better course of action is to draw its attention to some pleasure that may accompany that course of action, or to some pain which that course of action may help avoid. To be sure, such tactics will not always work. Whether or not they do will depend both on the strength and intensity of the occurrent appetite and on the character and motivational structure of the person in question. As we have seen, Plato's psychological theory acknowledges that everyone forms objectionable non-rational desires at least every once in a while. At the same time, the *Republic*'s theory of virtue requires that the virtuous person is able to allay bad desires in a way that leaves intact the harmonious relations among the parts of her soul that are characteristic of true virtue. Having read both the *Timaeus* and the *Philebus*, we can see how Plato can meet that requirement.

PART THREE

PHANTASIA AND NON-RATIONAL DESIRE IN ARISTOTLE

Introduction

In Part 2, I argued that a number of later Platonic dialogues, notably the *Timaeus* and the *Philebus*, enrich Plato's psychological theory by adding a reasonably well worked out conception of non-rational cognition that is centred on the senses, but not limited to what is presented in acts of sense-perception. It crucially includes memory, which Plato conceives of as the preservation and re-enactment of sensory impressions.

In Part 3, I intend to show that Aristotle employs a somewhat more developed version of this Platonic conception in attempting to account both for the motivation of non-human animals and for the non-rational forms of human motivation. Like Plato, Aristotle operates with a rich conception of non-rational cognition that involves sense-perception as well as the preservation and re-enactment of sensory impressions. One significant Aristotelian addition is a theory of associations between sensory impressions, which clarifies how non-rational cognition can involve the formation of complex and ordered sensory representations, as well as the active occurrence of action-guiding representations that are suitable and relevant to the animal's, or person's, current circumstances as these are grasped by way of the senses. Like Plato, Aristotle operates with a conception of practical rationality that is clear and defensible, though not, of course, uncontroversial. One thing that he takes to be characteristic of practical rationality is the grasp of 'for the sake of' relations, which include, but are not limited to, means–end relations. This kind of grasp, he thinks, is a prerogative of reasoning creatures, and of the rational parts or aspects of their souls. For Aristotle as for Plato, means–end reasoning is always an exercise of reason.

It may be useful to state a number of commitments that are central to both Plato's and Aristotle's psychological theories, as these emerge from the interpretations I am presenting and arguing for. For Aristotle as for Plato, human motivation springs from a number of different sources, only one of which incorporates the capacity for reasoning. The cognition involved in the non-rational forms of motivation is centred on the senses. One way in which sensory cognition is richer than it may initially appear to be is that it includes the preservation and re-enactment of sensory impressions. Moreover, it is a fact about the constitution of the human soul that the intellect and the sensory system are integrated so that at least some acts of the intellect are accompanied by exercises of the sensory imagination in and through which the subject envisages the objects of thought in a sensory mode.

This is not to say that there are no significant differences between Plato's and Aristotle's psychological theories. There are, and I shall discuss some of them in the Conclusion. The task of Part 3 is to present and interpret Aristotle's conception of non-rational motivation, and of the cognition involved in such motivation. As in Parts 1 and 2, my focus will be on appetitive motivation.

The task of Chapters 8–10 is to lay out and defend a certain view about what Aristotle takes the mental capacity that he calls *phantasia* to be, and what role he takes it to play in non-rational motivation. On that view, *phantasia* is a capacity for sensory representation that enables the representation of features and objects of various kinds that are not currently perceived by way of the senses. I shall argue that Aristotle assigns to that capacity a prominent role in the production of behaviour, and in particular in the production of purposive locomotion, because he takes it to be able to do something that perception cannot do, which is to put an animal in cognitive contact with prospective situations. Such cognitive contact, I shall argue, is required for the formation of desires that impel the animal in question to engage in goal-directed locomotion, which is the particular form of animal behaviour that is Aristotle's central concern in his writings about the motivation of animals. These writings are the *De Motu Animalium* and *De Anima* 3.9–11.

Chapter 8 introduces the 'chain of movers' passage from chapter 8 of the *De Motu Animalium* (702^{a}17–19). That passage offers a picture of the production of animal movement in which *phantasia* is given the role of 'suitably preparing' desire. Much of Part 3 is meant to shed light on why this role falls to *phantasia*, what tasks are involved in playing it, and how *phantasia* can accomplish those tasks. The chapter adds a number of preliminaries. It presents and briefly discusses the evidence for thinking that Aristotle conceives of *phantasia* as a cognitive capacity that enables both humans and non-human animals to apprehend objects of desire. It also reminds readers of Aristotle's denial of reason to the brute animals, of his interest in animal behaviour, and of his evident awareness of the considerable cognitive powers exhibited in many forms of animal behaviour.

Chapter 9 begins by noting two appearances. These in fact are commonly taken at face value in the relevant secondary literature. The first of them is that, according to the 'chain of movers' passage, forming a desire requires having some suitable *phantasia*. Secondly, Aristotle's account of animal motivation in *De Anima* 3.10–11 commits him to the view that if an animal is capable of desire, it must be capable, not only of perception, but also of *phantasia*. On my own view, which will not be fully stated until the end of Chapter 10, neither of these appearances is quite right. Nonetheless, I take both of them to contain important grains of truth. In Chapter 10, I shall attempt to extract those grains of truth. Before this can be done, however, it is necessary to get clear about what Aristotle is committing himself to in the texts pinpointed by the two appearances just stated. In the context of the 'chain of movers' passage, as well as in the entire discussion in *De Anima* 3.9–11, he is attempting to explain, *not* desire-formation or action-production in general, but the rather more specific phenomenon of the production of purposive movement from one place to another. Once this is duly taken into consideration and all relevant texts are interpreted accordingly, it becomes clear that what he is committed to, so far as non-rational motivation is concerned, is not that *phantasia* is required for the formation of every desire, but that it is required for the formation of desires that impel animals to engage in locomotion. It is specifically this Aristotelian commitment that my interpretation is meant to explain. I begin by identifying a cognitive task that animals must accomplish if they are to form desires that impel them to engage in locomotion. This is to apprehend prospective situations. For example, if a lion is to form a desire to eat a stag that it sees somewhere in its environment, it must in some way apprehend the prospect of eating the stag. This, it should be clear, is not a task that perception by itself can accomplish. A good part of Chapter 9 is meant to show that, given how Aristotle conceives of *phantasia*, it can accomplish that task.

Chapter 9 sets out an interpretation that explains why Aristotle thinks that some suitable *phantasia* is required for the formation of desires that impel animals to engage in locomotion, taking it that, so far as non-rational motivation is concerned, he is committed only to the view that *phantasia* is required for the formation of *such* desires, rather than to the stronger view that it is required for the formation of every desire. Chapter 10 completes my argument for thinking that Aristotle is committed only to the weaker one of these two views about the connection between desire and *phantasia* in non-rational motivation. It does so by offering positive reasons for thinking that he does *not* take the view that desire-formation always requires some suitable exercise of *phantasia*, and that he is committed to *rejecting* the view that every creature capable of desire must be capable of *phantasia*. The overall interpretation of Aristotle's position that I shall present and argue for also resolves two apparent contradictions in the *De Anima*, one about *phantasia* and whether there could be animals that are incapable of it, the other about self-movement and whether there are animals not capable of that. On both counts, Aristotle's answer is a clear and unqualified 'yes'.

It is in Chapter 11 that I turn to Aristotle's version of the association of ideas. The chapter begins with the question of how he can think that the cognitive achievements involved in all forms of non-human animal behaviour can be adequately explained just in terms of perception and *phantasia*. Chapters 11 and 12, it should be noted, concentrate on non-human animal behaviour as exhibiting the clearest and most straightforward case of non-rational motivation. They aim to bring out a rich and interesting conception of non-rational cognition, in which *phantasia* plays the main role. In Chapter 13, I shall take up the question of the extent to which Aristotle takes that conception to be applicable to the motivation of ordinarily developed, adult human beings.

It is plain, to Aristotle as well as to us, that many kinds of non-human animals exhibit purposive behaviour in ways that are highly sensitive to their current circumstances as they grasp them by way of their senses. Their behaviour tends to be relevant and suitable to their circumstances. For example, a hungry and normally developed lion that notices a stag in its environment will typically try to hunt it down and eat it. If Aristotle thinks that such behaviour requires the occurrence of suitable sensory representations by means of which the lion apprehends the prospect of eating the stag, he needs to explain why it is that non-human animals tend to have behaviour-guiding representations that are relevant and suitable to their circumstances. I shall argue that Aristotle's conception of sense is rich enough to enable him to explain the occurrence of *relevant* sensory representations. What he calls the perceptual part of the soul, I shall suggest, is a system of capacities centred on the capacity for sense-perception, which also includes the capacity for *phantasia*. Moreover, I shall argue that he takes it to be part of the functioning of that system of capacities that suitably constituted animals form and maintain associations or connections between sensory impressions, to the effect that the active occurrence in the animal's perceptual system of one specific representation tends to 'trigger' the active occurrence of some other specific representation. My argument for this view for the most part consists of detailed textual analysis of a number of passages from the *De Insomniis* and the *De Memoria*.

The *De Insomniis* contains a rather elaborate theory of sensory affections being preserved in the perceptual apparatus of suitably constituted and conditioned animals. Such affections are potentialities for sensory representations, and Aristotle's theory posits the existence of dispositions that obtain among them such that sensory representations tend to follow one another in certain orderly ways. It is, moreover, clear from Aristotle's discussion that he takes the formation of such dispositions to be part of the functioning of the perceptual part or aspect of the soul.

Aristotle's account of recollection in *De Memoria* 2 makes use of his theory of ordered sequences of sensory representations, and in doing so sheds light on the questions of what sorts of connections or associations he envisages, and how he thinks the dispositions that underlie them are formed and maintained. He envisages associations of a number of different kinds, such as associations between things that are temporally or spatially proximate to each other, and things that are similar, or opposite, to one another. And he thinks the underlying dispositions are formed and maintained chiefly by habituation. I shall argue that Aristotle takes the formation and maintenance of at least some such dispositions to be part of the functioning of the perceptual system of suitably constituted animals. My argument for this conclusion will be somewhat complicated, and will involve a number of claims about how he conceives of recollecting, and about certain aspects of his conception of memory. A full statement of my argument will therefore require analysis both of the discussion of remembering in *De Memoria* 1 and of the subsequent remarks in *De Memoria* 2. The upshot of my argument will be that it is part of Aristotle's conception of sense that the perceptual system of suitably constituted animals can all by itself account, not only for acts of sense-perception, but also for associating one thing with another, remembering things, and being reminded by something of something else. If so, it should be clear that, so conceived of, the perceptual system can also account for the occurrence of sensory representations that are relevant and suitable to a perceiving subject's current circumstances.

In Chapters 8–11, *phantasia* will emerge as a powerful cognitive capacity that can account for the occurrence of representations that are both indeterminately complex and relevant to the subject's current circumstances as grasped by way of the senses. On that basis, it will be easy to see why Aristotle thinks that it is at least for some purposes appropriate to treat *phantasia* as 'thinking of a sort' (*De Anima* 3.10, 433ª9–12). One crucial point of contact between thought and *phantasia* is that both can present prospective courses of action, and, in doing so, provide the cognitive underpinnings needed for the formation of desires that impel animals to engage in movement from one place to another.

However, Aristotle plainly insists that *phantasia* is different from thought, and that none of the cognitive achievements of the brute animals counts as an act of thought. Chapter 12 addresses the question of whether his denial of thought and reason to the non-human animals is coherent and well-grounded. The chapter begins with some clarificatory remarks, showing that, within Aristotle's conceptual framework, practical thought is reason's cognitive contribution to the production of action. To justify his denial of reason to the non-human animals, it is necessary and sufficient to justify his denial of practical thought to them; and this is what the chapter attempts to do. I shall provide a detailed picture of how Aristotle conceives of practical thought. I shall then argue that practical thought, so conceived of, includes a number of features that are *not* part of the conception of non-rational cognition to be described in Chapters 8–11. The key point will be that practical thought crucially includes the apprehension of 'for the sake of' relations. I shall conclude on that basis that Aristotle has a viable distinction between rational and non-rational forms of motivation. While his position invites questions of various sorts, and stands in need of development, it seems that his denial of reason to the brute animals is well-grounded and defensible.

In presenting and discussing Aristotle's conception of non-rational cognition, I shall for the most part concentrate on the cognitive resources that his psychological theory makes available to non-human animals. I shall do this in order to arrive at a maximally clear and straightforward Aristotelian conception of cognition which does not involve, and is not affected by, any distinctively rational resources. Having worked out such a conception, I shall complete Part 3 by arguing, in Chapter 13, that Aristotle takes a conception very much along these lines to be applicable to the non-rational forms of human motivation. I shall argue that even though it is part of his moral psychology that all of a human being's cognitive and motivating conditions are rational in a way, this leaves intact a clear sense in which appetite and spirit are non-rational forms of motivation, and also a clear sense in which at least some of the cognition involved in such motivation is non-rational.

I shall begin by discussing his outline account of the human soul in *Nicomachean Ethics* 1.13. In that account, he says that the part or aspect of the soul that is the source of appetitive and spirited desires is rational in an extended sense of the word. What being rational in this extended sense comes to is being able to obey, or listen to, reason. Aristotle's claim that the source of appetitive and spirited desires is rational in this sense, I shall suggest, requires no more than that there are certain ways in which reason can influence and affect appetite and spirit— for instance, by getting occurrent non-rational desires to subside, or to grow less intense. This may come about when reason redirects the person's attention from, say, the pleasure that seems imminent to some other prospective pleasure, or to some prospective pain. Aristotle does not have the *Timaeus'* problem about the possibility of communication between reason and the lower parts or aspects of the soul.[1] Perhaps taking his cue from the *Philebus'* simile of the illustrated book, he sees intellect and sense as integrated so that all acts of the intellect are accompanied by exercises of the sensory imagination in and through which the subject envisages the objects of thought in a sensory mode. As a result, his psychological theory can easily explain how it is that thoughts of, say, prospective pains or pleasures can get a grip on the non-rational part or aspect of a person's action-producing apparatus.

It should be clear, then, that Aristotle's claim that appetite and spirit can obey, or listen to, reason leaves plenty of room for a robust sense in which appetite and spirit are non-rational forms of motivation. That having been established, I shall turn to Aristotle's account of lack of self-control in book 7 of the *Nicomachean Ethics*. The passage I shall focus on is the comparison between appetitive and spirited lack of self-control in 7.6, with its suggestive claim that spirit follows reason in a way, while appetite does not. My discussion of that passage in its context is meant to offer a clear and detailed view of the sense in which Aristotle takes appetitive and spirited desires, in mature and ordinarily developed human beings, to be non-rational. It is also designed to show that Aristotle's moral psychology not only leaves room for, but in fact requires, a conception of non-rational cognition more or less along the lines of the conception to be presented in Chapters 8–11.

What will emerge from the overall discussion in Part 3 is a conception of the human soul that clearly and sharply distinguishes between reason and a non-rational part or aspect that is the source of appetitive and spirited desires. It sees reason, spirit, and appetite as integrated and interrelated in a number of ways. At the same time, it is part of the conception that both appetite and spirit can, and often do, generate and sustain fully formed impulses to act in specific ways without it being the case that thought or reason are active at the time *in any way at all*.

---

[1] For a brief statement of that problem, see Introduction to Part 2.

8

Preliminaries

We have two discussions by Aristotle of what I shall call animal motivation—the production, that is, of the kind of locomotion that is characteristic, not only of human beings in particular, but of animals in general. It is clear from both of these discussions, the *De Motu Animalium* and *De Anima* 3.9–11, that a capacity that Aristotle calls *phantasia*—often translated as 'imagination'[1]—plays a prominent role in his account of animal motivation. He plainly takes animal motivation to presuppose desire (ὄρεξις). He appears to think, moreover, that desire, in turn, presupposes *phantasia*. To see this, consider the following passage from the *De Motu Animalium* (in what follows, the 'chain of movers' passage): 'Affections suitably prepare the organic parts, desire (ὄρεξις) [sc. suitably prepares] affections, *phantasia* [sc. suitably prepares] desire; and *phantasia* arises through thought (νόησις) or through perception' (*De Motu Animalium* 8, 702ᵃ17–19).[2] It is clear, furthermore, that *phantasia*, as Aristotle conceives of it, has a cognitive aspect. Desires aim at objects,[3] and so the desiring subject needs to have some form of cognitive access to the object of desire. In other words, to desire is to desire *something*, and desiring something (whatever it may be) involves being aware of it, or anyhow representing it, as in some way attractive—for instance, as pleasant. *Phantasia* is cognitively rich enough to be able to account for an animal's awareness of suitable objects as in some way attractive. This is shown, for instance, by a passage in *De Anima* 3.10, where Aristotle says that objects of desire move an animal in virtue of a suitable thought or a suitable *phantasia* (τῷ νοηθῆναι ἢ φαντασθῆναι, 433ᵇ11–12).

---

[1] The conventional translation, as it happens, suits my interpretation remarkably well. One significant shortcoming of using 'imagination' to denote the capacity in question is that it may suggest it is limited to *visual* representations or 'visualizations'. The same, however, goes for the Greek term φαντασία, as Aristotle notes at *De Anima* 3.3, 429ᵃ2–4. A more serious shortcoming of 'imagination' as a translation of φαντασία is that it cannot be used when the Greek word denotes, not a mental capacity, but a product of its exercise—that is, a sensory representation. I shall in what follows use the word *phantasia* to denote the capacity. I shall use the same word, and also (I regret to say) the plural *phantasiai*, to refer to sensory representations.

[2] My translations from the *De Motu Animalium* are indebted to *Aristotle's De Motu Animalium*, ed. and trans. M. Nussbaum (Princeton: Princeton University Press, 1978).

[3] Cf. *De Anima* 3.10, 433ᵃ15–16: 'every desire is for the sake of something: for the object of desire is the starting point for the practical intellect.' Most of my translations from the *De Anima* are, to some degree or other, indebted to *Aristotle's De Anima: Books II and III*, trans. D. W. Hamlyn (Oxford: Oxford University Press, 1968).

Since the brute animals lack thought (νόησις, *De Anima* 3.10, 433ᵃ11–12), they must be moved by objects of desire as presented to them by *phantasia*. Moreover, it should not be the case that *phantasia* represents to animals *just anything* as being in some way attractive. If non-human animals of some species or other are to survive and live in the way characteristic of the species, it is not enough for them to be equipped with a capacity that represents any random thing as attractive. They must have a capacity that by and large *succeeds* in representing things as (say) pleasant that in fact are pleasant to them—e.g. suitable sorts of food. Thus a lion's *phantasia* of something or other—say, a stag—as pleasant will tend to be about right: the stag typically will turn out to be pleasant to the lion much as the *phantasia* in question promises it to be.

As is well known, Aristotle denies that the brutes have reason (λόγος).⁴ He therefore cannot account for the formation of *phantasiai* in non-human animals in terms of reason and its resources. Moreover, if non-human animal *phantasia* does indeed have a cognitive aspect, as one would naturally expect, the cognition in question must, on Aristotle's view, be in some sense non-rational. Now it is plain that some non-human animals have remarkable cognitive abilities. It is also plain that Aristotle is duly impressed by the cognitive abilities of non-human animals. In *Historia Animalium* 8.5, he records some relevant observations:⁵

Among animals that are wild and quadruped the deer is held to be an intelligent (φρόνιμος) one, not least because it both gives birth alongside the roads (for the wild beasts do not approach because of the humans) and, after giving birth, first eats the membrane. Also they run for the seseli and eat it before going back to their young. Further, she leads the young to their lair, habituating (ἐθίζουσα) them to the place where they should seek refuge... Further, the male when it has grown fat (and it does grow very fat during the fruit season) does not show itself anywhere but keeps away because its fatness makes it easy to catch... And when deer have been bitten by a venom-spider or something similar, they collect crabs and eat them; this is held to make a drink that is good for man too, but it is unpleasant. (*Historia Animalium* 8.5, 611ᵃ15–ᵇ23)⁶

The behaviour patterns that Aristotle is describing, in this passage and in many others like them, are fine examples of purposiveness in the animal kingdom. They frequently seem to exhibit some form of sensitivity to means–end relations: seseli, or hartwort, the herb said to be eaten by female deer after giving birth, is a medicinal

⁴ Aristotle also denies λογισμός to the non-human animals; see, for instance, *De Anima* 3.10, 433ᵃ10–12; *Metaphysics* 1.1, 980ᵇ25–8. For present purposes, I assume that, Aristotle uses the terms λόγος and λογισμός interchangeably, as Plato seems to do in the *Republic*. (Note the occurrences of both terms in *De Anima* 3.10–11 and in *Republic* 4: λογισμός at *De Anima* 433ᵃ12, 24, 25 and 434ᵃ8; λόγος at *De Anima* 433ᵇ6; λογισμός at *Republic* 4, 439 D 1, 440 B 1, 441 A 9; λόγος at *Republic* 4, 440 B 3, 5.) This, so far as Aristotle is concerned, is a slight simplification (see Ch. 12, pp. 177–8), but one which does no harm for present purposes.

⁵ I follow Balme's restoration of the manuscript ordering of books 7–9 of the *Historia Animalium*. I also accept his defence of the authenticity of book 8; see his *Aristotle:* History of Animals, *Books 7–10* (Cambridge, Mass.: Harvard University Press, 1991), 1–13.

⁶ Translations from the *Historia Animalium* are as in *Aristotle:* History of Animals, *Books 7–10*, ed. and trans. D. M. Balme, with occasional modifications.

herb that was believed to soothe post-natal disorders. 'Many other animals that are quadruped act intelligently to help themselves', he adds a little later, adducing another striking report: 'In Crete they say the wild goats when struck by arrows look for dittany: this is believed to have the effect of expelling arrows in the body' (*Historia Animalium* 8.5, 612ª3–5). His general view is that some species of non-human animals have a form of practical intelligence,[7] which they manifest by exercising foresight for the sake of self-preservation.[8] He holds that although the brute animals cannot, strictly speaking, think, many of them are equipped with a capacity that in some ways is like thinking (νόησις),[9] and that can, within limits, serve the same functions as thought (νοῦς).[10] That capacity is *phantasia*.

It would be good to know how it is that *phantasia* is supposed to be like thinking, and how far the functional equivalence of thought and *phantasia* is supposed to go. It would also be good to know why Aristotle nonetheless insists on the distinction between thought and *phantasia*. Before we turn to these questions, however, it is worth indicating that he relies on *phantasia*, not only in explaining non-human animal motivation, but also in explaining the non-rational forms of human motivation. I shall in due course offer a detailed discussion of the roles of perception and *phantasia* in Aristotle's theory of human motivation.[11] For now, a somewhat rough-and-ready sketch may suffice; a number of significant details will be filled in later.

In his discussion of animal motivation in *De Anima* 3.9–11, Aristotle distinguishes between two kinds of *phantasia*: a rational or deliberative kind on the one hand and a perceptual kind on the other: 'Every *phantasia* is either such as to involve reasoning (λογιστική) or perceptual (αἰσθητική). In the latter, then, the other animals share also' (*De Anima* 3.10, 433ᵇ29–30). Perceptual *phantasia* is conceived of so as not to involve reasoning (λογισμός). As a result, it is, as he points out, available to 'the other animals' as well—by which he means the lower, non-rational, animals. Now it is important to note that he does *not* say that human *phantasia* involves reasoning, whereas *phantasia* in non-human animals,

---

[7] They are φρόνιμα: *Metaphysics* 1.1, 980ᵇ1–5. Cf. *Historia Animalium* 8.1, 608ª13–17. For a discussion of φρόνησις in non-human animals, see J.-L. Labarrière, 'De la *phronesis* animale', in D. Devereux and P. Pellegrin (eds.), *Biologie, Logique et Metaphysique chez Aristote* (Paris: Editions du C. N. R. S., 1990). Cf. R. Sorabji, *Animal Minds and Human Morals: The Origins of the Western Debate* (London: Duckworth, 1993), 54–5.

[8] See *Nicomachean Ethics* 6.7, 1141ª26–8. Aristotle is reporting what people say; but the passages referred to in the preceding footnote suggest that he endorses this opinion.

[9] At *De Anima* 3.10, 433ª9–10, Aristotle proposes that one might 'take *phantasia* to be like a kind of thinking (ὡς νόησίν τινα)'. Cf. J.-L. Labarrière, 'Imagination humaine et imagination animale chez Aristote', *Phronesis*, 29 (1984), 20–1.

[10] 'We see that the movers of the animal are thought (διάνοια), perception, *phantasia*, decision, wish, spirit, and appetite. And all of these can be reduced to thought (νοῦς) and desire. For *phantasia* and perception hold the same place as thought: for all of these involve discernment, while they differ in ways that have been stated elsewhere.' (*De Motu Animalium* 6, 700ᵇ17–22; for a defence of the text that my translation is based on, see Ch. 9, n. 19.) The aspect of thought (νοῦς) that is relevant to motivation is specified in *De Anima* 3.10, 433ª13–15: 'These two, then, are concerned with locomotion: thought (νοῦς) and desire, but thought which reasons for the sake of something and is practical; it differs from theoretical thought in respect of the goal.'   [11] In Ch. 13.

being merely perceptual, does not. What he says is rather that *phantasia* is either rational or perceptual, and whereas *also* non-human animals share in perceptual *phantasia*, rational *phantasia* belongs to reasoning creatures alone. As a result, *both* forms of *phantasia* are available to humans.

Nor is it difficult to see why he makes perceptual *phantasia* available to humans as well as to the brute animals. Consider his characterization of rational (or deliberative, 434ᵃ7) *phantasia*. It occurs, he says,

> in animals capable of reasoning: for the decision whether to do this or that is already a task for reasoning; and one must measure by a single standard; for one pursues what is superior; hence one has the ability to make one out of many *phantasiai* (φαντάσματα).[12] (*De Anima* 3.11, 434ᵃ7–10)

The passage is not as clear as one would wish it to be, and we shall return to it in a short while.[13] For now it is sufficient to point out that the activity Aristotle is describing is one that involves both *phantasia* and reasoning and that yields a reasoned assessment of what (given some standard) it is best to do in the circumstances in question, together with a *phantasia* which, I take it, represents the favoured course of action in some appropriate way. If this activity yields a desire, as one expects it might, the desire will depend either directly on the assessment of what is best or on the *phantasia* that represents the favoured option. However, since the content of the *phantasia* itself depends on the assessment, the desire will in either case depend on it, whether directly or by way of the *phantasia*.

But not all desires—not even all human desires—are, on Aristotle's view, desires of this kind. His theory of motivation allows for desires which arise independently of one's thoughts about what it is best to do. Appetitive desires (ἐπιθυμίαι) are the clearest case in point. These are desires for pleasure, or (better) desires for something or other *as* pleasant. They flow simply from beliefs or representations to the effect that something or other is a source of pleasure. They can, Aristotle thinks, motivate us to act not only independently of, but even against, our deliberations about what it is best to do.[14] He characterizes appetitive and spirited desires as non-rational (ἄλογοι ὀρέξεις), contrasting them with rational desire (λογιστικὴ ὄρεξις).[15]

---

[12] Aristotle is here using the word φάντασμα to refer to sensory representations. I therefore 'translate' as *phantasiai*, in accordance with my policy as stated in n. 1.   [13] In Ch. 9, p. 127.

[14] Cf. *De Anima* 3.10, 433ᵃ25–6: 'Desire produces movement also against reasoning (λογισμός): for appetitive desire (ἐπιθυμία) is a kind of desire.' On the place of appetitive desire in Aristotle's moral psychology, see J. Cooper, 'Reason, moral virtue, and moral value', in M. Frede and G. Striker (eds.), *Rationality in Greek Thought* (Oxford: Oxford University Press, 1996), 98–102; reprinted in his *Reason and Emotion: Essays on Ancient Moral Psychology and Ethical Theory* (Princeton: Princeton University Press, 1999), 253–80.

[15] ἄλογοι ὀρέξεις: *Rhetoric* 1.10, 1369ᵃ4; cf. 1369ᵃ2. λογιστικὴ ὄρεξις: *Rhetoric* 1.10, 1369ᵃ2. (Note also *De Anima* 3.9, 432ᵇ4–7.) On using Aristotle's *Rhetoric* as evidence for his moral psychology, see G. Striker, 'Emotions in context: Aristotle's treatment of the passions in the *Rhetoric* and his moral psychology', in A. Rorty (ed.), *Essays on Aristotle's* Rhetoric (Berkeley: University of California Press, 1996), 286–8.

As we have seen, he seems to think that forming a desire always involves having a *phantasia* which represents (what is to be) the object of desire in some appropriate way. We shall see in the next two chapters that this in fact is his view, except for a qualification that does not affect the present point.[16] Given that his psychological theory allows for forms of human motivation that operate independently of deliberation, he cannot consistently hold that human *phantasia* is in all cases deliberative. For if it were, human motivation, dependent as it is on *phantasia*, could not be independent of deliberation in the way Aristotle holds two of its forms to be. He therefore needs to make the non-deliberative kind of *phantasia* available to humans; and in fact he does.

[16] In Ch. 10, I shall argue that Aristotle is committed only to a qualified version of the view that desire requires *phantasia*. So far as non-rational motivation is concerned, I take Aristotle to be committed only to the view that desire requires *phantasia* if it is to lead to, and to support, the production of locomotion—that is, the production of such forms of animal movement as walking, flying, and swimming. That qualification, which will be introduced and motivated in the following two chapters, does not harm the current argument. Aristotle plainly takes it that human non-rational desire can account for locomotion without deliberation being involved (see, e.g., *De Anima* 3.10, 433ª25–6; *Nicomachean Ethics* 7.3, 1147ª34–5). So, since human non-rational desire which accounts for locomotion requires *phantasia*, and since such desire can arise independently of deliberation, humans must be capable of a kind of (desire-supporting) *phantasia* that does not involve deliberation.

9

Phantasia, Desire, and Locomotion

We saw in the preceding chapter that a number of passages in Aristotle's discussions of animal motivation (in *De Anima* 3.9–11 and in the *De Motu Animalium*) suggest a close link between desire-formation and *phantasia*. Consider, for instance, the 'chain of movers' passage: 'Affections suitably prepare the organic parts, desire (ὄρεξις) [sc. suitably prepares] affections, *phantasia* [sc. suitably prepares] desire; and *phantasia* arises through thought (νόησις) or through perception' (*De Motu Animalium* 8, 702ᵃ17–19). According to this passage, thought and perception may be involved in some way or other in the production of movement, and in the formation of desire that results in it;[1] but whether or not thought or perception is involved, *phantasia* in any case plays a role in the process. It is not obvious, either from the passage itself or from its context, whether Aristotle intends any restriction on the scope of these claims. Some related claims are made at *De Anima* 3.10, 433ᵇ27–30:

In general, then, as has been said, in so far as the animal is capable of desire, so far is it capable of self-movement; and it is not capable of desire without *phantasia*. And every *phantasia* is either rational or perceptual. In the latter, then, the other animals share also.[2]

The passage seems to imply that if an animal is capable of desire, it cannot be the case that it merely has (the capacity for) perception, without having (the capacity for) *phantasia*.[3] Why should this be so? One answer, which may seem less than illuminating, can be extracted from the 'chain of movers' passage: for perception (or, for that matter, thought) to yield a desire, some appropriate *phantasia* has to be present which will 'suitably prepare' desire.[4]

---

[1] The context of the passage makes clear that Aristotle has the production of movement in mind. Among other things, the account given in the passage is offered specifically in order to explain why it is that 'it is pretty much at the same time that a creature thinks it should walk and that it walks, unless something else impedes it' (*De Motu Animalium* 8, 702ᵃ15–17).

[2] The translation is Hamlyn's, slightly adapted. In the next chapter, I shall propose a significantly different translation.

[3] For the possibility of an animal having perception without having *phantasia*, see *De Anima* 3.3, 428ᵃ8–11; cf. 2.3, 415ᵃ8–11; cf. also *Posterior Analytics* 2.19, 99ᵇ36–100ᵃ1.

[4] An account along these lines is offered in M. Nussbaum, *Aristotle's* De Motu Animalium, Essay 5: 'The role of *phantasia* in Aristotle's explanations of action'. Nussbaum thinks Aristotle is committed to the view that '*phantasia* is a necessary condition for desire' (221, 234). She attempts to explain this by relying on the idea that 'to be moved to action an animal has to become aware of something

The passage that follows immediately (*De Anima* 3.11, 433^{b}31–434^{a}5) might seem to corroborate the view that if an animal is capable of desire, it cannot, according to Aristotle, be the case that it merely has perception, without having *phantasia*. In that passage, he is discussing the question whether certain imperfect animals have *phantasia*. He says that these animals have perception, albeit by touch only. This, incidentally, makes it plain that he takes perception to be a different capacity from the relevant kind of *phantasia*—perceptual *phantasia*, that is, as opposed to rational *phantasia*, the prerogative of animals capable of reasoning.[5] For although imperfect animals have perception (by touch), it remains an open question whether they have (perceptual) *phantasia*. Since they have appetite, a form of desire, one might expect, in view of the claim made at 3.10, 433^{b}27–9, that they have *phantasia*, too. In fact, Aristotle does not disappoint that expectation, suggesting that the creatures in question have *phantasia* in an indeterminate way:[6] 'How could they have *phantasia*? Shall we say that just as they move indeterminately, so also they have these things [sc. *phantasia* and appetite],[7] but indeterminately?' (*De Anima* 3.11, 434^{a}4–5). It may seem tempting to think that Aristotle is, in the

---

qua what-it-is-called; he has to see the man as a man, not just as pale' (259). It is the role of *phantasia*, then, to enable the animal to pick things out under the appropriate substance terms. However, there is, as S. Everson has pointed out, no good reason to think that motivation requires the identification of something or other as falling under some substance term: 'I may well reach out for, or chew something, simply in virtue of its being, say, red or sweet, without any awareness at all of what that object is apart from its having that property' (S. Everson, *Aristotle on Perception* (Oxford: Oxford University Press, 1997), 164).

[5] Contra Everson, *Aristotle on Perception*, 184, n. 103: his view is that when Aristotle introduces perceptual *phantasia* at *De Anima* 3.10, 433^{b}28–30, 'this must be taken to be referring to perception'.

[6] Contra M. Wedin, *Mind and Imagination in Aristotle* (New Haven, Conn.: Yale University Press, 1988), 41: 'Apparently ready to grant them [sc. the imperfect animals mentioned at 433^{b}31–434^{a}5] pains and pleasures and, thus, perhaps even wants [*epithumian*], Aristotle hesitates over imagination. Perhaps, he suggests, they have no imagination, but are moved only indeterminately [*kineitai aoristos*] or have pains, pleasures and wants only indeterminately.' Wedin's construal of the argument relies on the assumption that, on Aristotle's view, the relevant animals are not capable of desire (ὄρεξις). In fact this assumption is spelled out in n. 20, 41: 'Notice that Aristotle carefully avoids saying they have desire [*orexis*]. In that case, as 433^{b}27–9 asserts, they would have imagination and be capable of action.' It should, however, be perfectly clear that appetite (ἐπιθυμία) is, on Aristotle's view, one of the three species of desire (ὄρεξις). Thus being capable of appetite is precisely one way of being capable of desire. See *De Anima* 2.3, 414^{b}1–6. (Cf. also 2.2, 413^{b}21–4; 3.9, 432^{b}3–7; 3.10, 433^{a}25–6; *De Motu Animalium* 6, 700^{b}22; *Eudemian Ethics* 2.7, 1223^{a}26–7.) Cf. C. Freeland, 'Aristotle on perception, appetition, and self-motion', in M. Gill and J. Lennox (eds.), *Self-Motion: From Aristotle to Newton* (Princeton: Princeton University Press, 1994), 50, n. 31: 'Since the lower-level animals possess only primitive sensory capacities and have no capacity for self-motion, Aristotle himself wonders whether they have imagination (*De an.* III.11). He writes that though the lowest animals may have appetite (*epithumia*), they do not have desire (*orexis*), for they have no images.' However, in the passage Freeland refers to, Aristotle states explicitly that the animals he has in mind *move*, albeit indeterminately (434^{a}4, cf. 433^{b}31). Since he evidently appeals to desire and *phantasia* to account for this movement, the movement in question must be self-movement. So it is a mistake to think that the relevant creatures (on Aristotle's view) lack the capacity for self-motion. Furthermore, Aristotle plainly does *not* write that the relevant kinds of animal do not have desire, nor that they lack *phantasia*.

[7] *Pace* Wedin, *Mind and Imagination*, 41, and Freeland, 'Aristotle on perception', 50, n. 31, the reference of 'these things' (ταῦτ') at 434^{a}5 certainly includes *phantasia*, back in line 4; since it is plural, it should also refer to appetitive desire in line 3, and possibly to pain and pleasure as well.

present chapters, revising an earlier claim, namely that one way in which *phantasia* and perception can be seen to be distinct is that perception is invariably present to animals of all kinds, while *phantasia* is not (*De Anima* 3.3, 428ª8–11). He thinks that all animals, having perception, also feel pleasure and pain; and he seems to think that he can infer from this that they also experience appetitive desire.[8] So if desire in fact requires *phantasia*, as it seems to do according to *De Anima* 3.10–11, then it turns out that animals of all kinds must have *phantasia*.[9]

There is a complication that should at least be noted in passing. In some passages in Aristotle's discussions of animal motivation, he mentions thought and *phantasia* as constituting alternative ways in which an animal may apprehend an object of desire, so as to be moved, or to engage in movement, in respect of place. For instance, he says that the object of desire moves without being moved, by being apprehended in thought or *phantasia* (*De Anima* 3.10, 433ᵇ11–12). Elsewhere he says that objects of pursuit and avoidance constitute the beginning of movement: 'the apprehension of these objects in thought and *phantasia* is necessarily accompanied by heating and cooling' (*De Motu Animalium* 8, 701ᵇ33–5).

So one might take it to be Aristotle's view that in some episodes of movement-production the object of desire is apprehended, not by *phantasia*, but by thought. One might then think that *phantasia* need not, according to Aristotle, be involved in every episode of movement-production, on the grounds that whatever *phantasia* may do in the production of movement can also be done by thought. It would, however, be rash to assume that in cases in which thought rouses an animal to move from one place to another, *phantasia* is not, on Aristotle's view, involved in the production of that movement. This is not the place for a detailed discussion of the roles of *phantasia* in Aristotle's conception of rational motivation. Nonetheless, it may be worthwhile and helpful to offer a few comments on the topic.

There are several passages in Aristotle's psychological writings which make it clear that, on his view, human thought in general does not function independently of *phantasia*:[10] according to the most succinct statement of this view, 'the

---

[8] For the claim that all animals have pleasure, pain, and appetite, see *De Anima* 2.3, 414ᵇ3–6; cf. 2.2, 413ᵇ21–4.

[9] Note the interpretation offered by Themistius, 122, 5–14: 'How do these animals [sc. e.g. flies and worms, line 6] desire, without *phantasia*, which we said they do not have? Pain and pleasure can be seen to be in such animals; but where there is pleasure, by all means there is also appetite (ἐπιθυμία); and where there is appetite, by all means there is also desire (ὄρεξις); and where there is desire, there is also *phantasia*; but the previous account denied *phantasia* to such animals. Shall we say that as they move indeterminately, so also they engage in *phantasia* (φαντάζεται) indeterminately? So that they have *phantasia*, but in an inarticulate and confused form, just as they have perception: for perception too they have in an incomplete and indeterminate form. Let this question then be investigated and resolved in this way.' Cf. D. Frede, 'The cognitive role of *phantasia* in Aristotle', in M. Nussbaum and A. Rorty (eds.), *Essays on Aristotle's* De Anima (Oxford: Oxford University Press, 1992), 281; and V. Caston, 'Why Aristotle needs imagination', *Phronesis*, 41 (1996), 23, n. 9.

[10] It is not, however, part of Aristotle's psychological theory that thought quite generally involves *phantasia*. He wants to say that there are beings which think without being capable of *phantasia*, for instance the prime mover (see e. g. *Metaphysics* ∧ 7, 1072ᵇ19–21). What he seems to think, then, is that the involvement of *phantasia* in thinking is not a feature of thought quite generally, but of the

soul never thinks without a *phantasia* (φάντασμα)' (*De Anima* 3.7, 431ᵃ16–17).¹¹
It is, unfortunately, far from clear what Aristotle takes *phantasia* to contribute to
human thought in general, and why he thinks some contribution from *phantasia*
is required for any thought. However, a *De Anima* passage at which we have
already taken a brief look suggests a relatively detailed view of how he takes
phantasia to be involved specifically in practical reasoning:

> Deliberative *phantasia* occurs in animals capable of reasoning: for the decision whether to
> do this or that is already a task for reasoning; and one must measure by a single standard;
> for one pursues what is superior; hence one has the ability to make one out of many
> *phantasiai*.   (*De Anima* 3.11, 434ᵃ7–10)

The passage suggests that there are at least two ways in which *phantasia* is involved
in practical reasoning. First, the 'many *phantasiai*' mentioned in the last clause are
involved in the subject's thinking about a number of alternative courses of action, in
the process of reaching a decision 'whether to do this or that'. Presumably the
thought is that *phantasiai* support the subject's activity of concretely envisaging
candidate courses of action. Moreover, *phantasia* seems to play a further role when
a person arrives at a decision to do one thing in preference to another on the basis
of deliberation. This seems to involve the production (ποιεῖν) of 'one out of many
phantasiai'. The thought would seem to be that rational motivation tends to
involve, not only a decision to prefer one course of action over others, but also the
formation of a *phantasia* that represents in an integrated way both the favoured
course of action and others that were thought worthy of consideration. However
that may be, it is in any case clear, from the passages we have just now looked at,
that Aristotle takes *phantasia* to be involved, and involved in more ways than one,
when someone is roused by thought to move from one place to another.

I return to non-rational motivation. We have noted the following appearances
that may arise from Aristotle's discussions of animal motivation.

(1) According to the 'chain of movers' passage, forming a desire requires having
     some suitable *phantasia*.
(2) The discussion at *De Anima* 3.10–11, 433ᵇ27–434ᵃ5, commits Aristotle to
     the following view: if an animal is capable of desire, it must be capable, not
     only of perception, but of *phantasia* as well.

An interpretation of Aristotle's conception of animal motivation should aim to
accommodate or at least explain these appearances. In this chapter and the next, I
shall attempt to do precisely that.

---

occurrence of thought in mortal or perishable beings. It may be relevant that Aristotle in the
De Anima occasionally restricts the validity of claims to mortal or perishable beings: for instance, at
De Anima 2.2, 413ᵃ32 and at 2.3, 415ᵃ9.

¹¹ Cf. *De Anima* 3.7, 431ᵇ2–3; 3.8, 432ᵃ3–10; *De Memoria* 449ᵇ30–450ᵃ9. For a discussion of
these passages and their relevance to action contexts, cf. Wedin, *Mind and Imagination*, 109–113.

It should be noted right away that Aristotle does not offer a discussion that clarifies fully or satisfactorily just what role, or roles, *phantasia* is supposed to play in the formation of desire and production of movement, whether or not thought is involved.[12] As a result, any interpretation that attempts to clarify Aristotle's conception must, at some point, resort to speculation. Fortunately, there is a good deal of relevant material that can guide and constrain such speculation.

A few general remarks may be helpful. I begin with a point that may appear trivial, but that nonetheless seems to me both important and easy to miss. Aristotle's topic in his discussions of animal motivation (in *De Anima* 3.9–11 and in the *De Motu Animalium*) is, not the formation of desire quite generally, nor the production of action or behaviour in general,[13] but the production of animal locomotion. This is made very clear in *De Anima* 3.9, which begins with Aristotle announcing that he has now completed his account of the soul's discernment-involving capacities, perception and thought, and is about to turn to the capacity for locomotion (432ª15–18).[14] In the course of the same chapter, he makes it plain that he conceives of animal locomotion as always being for the sake of something (ἕνεκά του, 432ᵇ13–17). In other words, in writing of animal locomotion Aristotle has in mind goal-directed locomotion.

We might compare the following programmatic statement at the beginning of the *De Motu Animalium*: 'But now we must consider in general the common explanation for moving with any kind of movement (for some animals move by flying, some by swimming, some by walking, some in other comparable ways)' (*De Motu Animalium* 1, 698ª4–7). And as in the related discussion in *De Anima* 3.9–11, also in the *De Motu Animalium* Aristotle conceives of animal locomotion as being goal-directed: 'All animals effect movement and are moved for the sake of something, so that this is the limit (πέρας) to all their movement: the thing for the sake of which (τὸ οὗ ἕνεκα)' (*De Motu Animalium* 6, 701ª15–16). In the two discussions of animal motivation that we are concerned with, then, Aristotle is discussing the formation of desire as part of a larger context which deals with goal-directed animal locomotion. What he has to say, in that larger context, about the formation of desire may not be meant to apply to all cases of desire-formation. It may be meant to apply only to the formation of desires that impel an animal to engage in locomotion—for instance, a hungry lion's desire to eat a stag that it has just spotted somewhere at some distance in its environment.[15] I shall return to this point in the next chapter.

---

[12] Cf. M. Schofield, 'Aristotle on the imagination', in M. Nussbaum and A. Rorty (eds.), *Essays on Aristotle's* De Anima, 260, n. 35: 'Aristotle's whole treatment of *phantasia* in the non-rational animals is puzzling.'

[13] Note the pervasive assumption in Nussbaum's book on the *De Motu Animalium* that Aristotle's topic in *De Anima* 3.9–11 and in the *De Motu* is how and why it is that animals are moved to *act*, or moved to *action*.

[14] Cf. the programmatic statement at *De Anima* 1.2, 403ᵇ24–8: 'The beginning of our enquiry is to present what are most of all thought to be the natural attributes of soul. The ensouled is thought most of all to differ from the unensouled in two respects, movement and perceiving. Roughly speaking, these two points about the soul have been handed down to us by our predecessors.'

[15] Cf. *Nicomachean Ethics* 3.10, 1118ª20–3.

In the remainder of the present chapter, I shall first attempt to identify a cognitive task that animals must perform if they are to engage in goal-directed locomotion. I shall then offer reasons for thinking that, within Aristotle's psychological theory, it is specifically the capacity for *phantasia* that accomplishes that task for subjects that either are unequipped with the resources of reason or at the time fail to employ those resources appropriately.

We should begin by attending to a number of features of Aristotle's general discussion, in *De Motu Animalium* 6, of animal locomotion:

> all animals effect movement and move themselves for the sake of something, so that this is the limit to all their movement: the thing for the sake of which (τὸ οὗ ἕνεκα) ... So that the object of desire and thought is the first mover; not every object of thought, but the goal (τέλος) of things that can be done. Therefore the mover is a good of this kind, but not every good; for it is a mover in so far as something else is for the sake of it, and in so far as it is the goal of things that are for the sake of something else. And it is necessary to suppose that also the apparent good holds the place of the good (ἀγαθόν), and also the pleasant: for it is an apparent good. (*De Motu Animalium* 6, 700ᵇ15–29)

The identification of the goal (τέλος), the 'thing for the sake of which' (τὸ οὗ ἕνεκα), and the good (ἀγαθόν) is introduced in *Physics* 2, in the context of a discussion of the final cause. It might be useful briefly to have a look at the discussion in *Physics* 2, so as to see what Aristotle has in mind when he mentions goals, or 'things for the sake of which'. Here is how he introduces the final cause:

> Again, [sc. something is called a cause] in the sense of the goal (τὸ τέλος): this is the thing for the sake of which (τὸ οὗ ἕνεκα), as health is that for the sake of which there is walking about. 'Why is he walking about?' We say: 'In order to be healthy.' And having said that, we think that we have given the cause. (*Physics* 2.3, 194ᵇ32–5)[16]

In general, a goal or thing for the sake of which is something that can be achieved or attained—for instance, the well balanced state of an organism or a worthwhile activity.[17] In cases of agency, someone does something or other for the sake of a goal (for instance, being healthy), and in this case the goal is a project or purpose that she wants to achieve.[18] The goal the person in question wants to achieve, Aristotle thinks, accounts for why she does whatever she does, if indeed she does what she does for the sake of the goal. For instance, Jones' purpose of being healthy accounts for his walking about, if it is the case that he is walking about for

---

[16] Cf. *Physics* 2.3, 195ᵃ23–6, for the identification of the good (τὸ ἀγαθόν) with the goal (τέλος).

[17] For more detailed analysis, see D. Charles, 'Teleological causation in the *Physics*', in L. Judson (ed.), *Aristotle's Physics: A Collection of Essays* (Oxford: Oxford University Press, 1991), esp. 101–11.

[18] For the notion that goals are things to be *achieved*, cf. *Physics* 2.6, 197ᵇ22–6: '[the expression "in vain"] is used when the thing for the sake of which does not come about through the thing which is for its sake—for instance, if walking is for the sake of emptying the bowels, and if emptying of the bowels does not follow after walking, we say that we walked in vain, and that the walking was in vain. For that is "in vain": whenever something which is naturally for the sake of something else does not achieve (περαίνειν) that for the sake of which it is.'

the sake of health. Both in *De Anima* 3.9–11 and in the *De Motu Animalium*, Aristotle applies this style of account to the production of animal locomotion.

The animal's goal, according to *De Motu Animalium* 6, is an object of thought (διανοητόν), a good of a certain kind, or an apparent good—for instance, something pleasant. This of course raises the question: what about animals that lack the capacity for thought (διάνοια)? Given that Aristotle is evidently meaning to offer a general discussion of animal locomotion (cf. *De Motu Animalium* 1, 698ª4–7), he had better have an answer to that question. And of course he does: he has said already that non-intellectual capacities (perception and *phantasia*) 'hold the same place', within his explanatory framework, as the capacity for thought (νοῦς):

> We see that the movers of the animal are thought, perception, *phantasia*, decision, wish, spirit, and appetite.[19] And all of these can be reduced to thought (νοῦς) and desire. For *phantasia* and perception hold the same place as thought: for all of these involve discernment (κριτικά), while they differ in ways that have been stated elsewhere. (*De Motu Animalium* 6, 700ᵇ17–22)

We may take it, then, that when Aristotle goes on to refer to the animal's goal as an object of thought (διανοητόν), this is a shorthand expression for the idea that the animal's goal is something it picks out in virtue of some discernment-involving capacity or other, the relevant capacities being thought, perception, and *phantasia*.

There is good reason to think, then, that Aristotle is meaning to account for the locomotion of animals by appealing to purposes that they want to achieve. His list of animal movers includes, not only thought, but also other discernment-involving capacities, namely perception and *phantasia*. By including discernment-involving capacities other than thought, he makes available cognitive resources that non-human animals can rely on in forming purposes. Given that it is animal locomotion that he is meaning to explain, he must have in mind the formation of

---

[19] I follow Torraca's *De Motu Animalium* edition in reading the full list of movers found in the group of manuscripts Nussbaum refers to as the b_2 sub-family; cf. also J. Barnes' review of Nussbaum's edition in *Classical Review*, 30 (1980), 224–5. Nussbaum's edition follows the other manuscripts, which mention neither perception at 700ᵇ17 nor spirited desire in line 18. However, if perception and spirited desire are not included in the list, it is hard to see why they show up in lines 20 and 22. If, on the other hand, they are included, we can read 19–23 as clarifying how the movers mentioned in the list are related to thought and desire: *phantasia* and perception, being discernment-involving capacities, can (within appropriate limits) occupy the same place as thought in Aristotle's explanatory framework; wish, spirit, and appetite are the forms of desire; and decision involves both thought and desire. Nussbaum defends the shorter list in 'The "common explanation" of animal motion', in P. Moraux and J. Wiesner (eds.), *Zweifelhaftes im Corpus Aristotelicum* (Berlin: Walter de Gruyter, 1983). The other members of the *b* family, she points out, agree with all of the *a* family in offering the shorter list; and it is improbable that the same shortening of the list should independently have occurred twice or several times over. However, the b_2 group evidently has a number of superior readings—which *are* accepted by Nussbaum—where all members of *a* and several other members of *b* are in agreement in offering the same inferior reading: 700ª8; 701ª19; 702ª20; cf. also 700ª26. It is, I think, difficult to account for this fact without assuming that the members of b_2 are influenced by a source that is independent of the archetype common to *a* and *b*. Once this assumption is in place, however, there is no good reason *not* to add b_2's clearly superior list of movers to the list of b_2's readings that seem to draw on that independent tradition.

purposes that motivate animals to engage in locomotion, as when a lion forms the purpose of eating a stag that it sees somewhere in its environment. Forming *such* purposes always, or at least typically, involves accomplishing the cognitive task of envisaging a prospective situation, one that does not currently obtain and that may, as a matter of fact, never come to obtain. I shall refer to this task as envisaging prospects.[20]

It should be acknowledged at once that, unfortunately, Aristotle does not say, in the *De Motu Animalium* or anywhere else, that animal locomotion always or typically involves envisaging prospects, or that animals can envisage prospects in virtue of having the discernment-involving capacities of perception and *phantasia*. He may well think, I suggest, that this goes without saying, perhaps relying on the *Philebus'* discussions of desire and anticipatory pleasure.[21] There is, however, a relevant and valuable passage in the *Nicomachean Ethics*, where Aristotle plainly does attribute the ability to envisage prospects to non-human animals, not directly in connection with purposive locomotion and desire-formation, but, rather intriguingly, in connection with pleasures of anticipation. In *Nicomachean Ethics* 3.10, his task is to identify the sorts of pleasure that the virtue of temperance and the vice of self-indulgence are concerned with. These are, he says, 'the kind of pleasures that the other animals share in, which therefore appear slavish and brutish; these are [sc. the pleasures to do with] touch and taste' (*Nicomachean Ethics* 3.10, 1118ª23–6).[22] He holds that sights, sounds, and smells are at best incidental sources of pleasure to the brute animals:

Nor is there in non-human animals any pleasure connected with these senses [sc. sight, hearing, smell], except incidentally. For dogs do not take pleasure in the scent of hares, but in the eating of them, but the scent told them that the hares were there; nor does the lion take pleasure in the lowing of the ox, but in eating it, but it perceived by the lowing that the ox was near, and it appears to take pleasure in the lowing; and similarly what pleases the lion is not the sight of 'a stag or a wild goat', but that he is going to get a meal. (*Nicomachean Ethics* 3.10, 1118ª18–23)

He accepts that animals like dogs and lions may show signs of pleasure, and in fact may experience pleasure, when they see, hear, or smell suitable things located in their environment—for instance, hares, oxen, stags, or wild goats. But he insists that in such cases they take pleasure, not in the relevant sights, sounds, and smells, but *in the prospect of eating.* The lion is pleased right away when it sees a stag,

---

[20] Could there be locomotion-effecting purposes that do not involve the apprehension of a prospect? Perhaps: your recoiling from the oven when you inadvertently put your hand on a hot surface may be driven simply by your aversion to an intensely painful experience, without any apprehension of a prospect being involved or required in addition; and it may be appropriate to say that your locomotion has a purpose, which is to avoid or stop the painful experience. However, this is hardly a standard or typical example of purposive locomotion. Moreover, it plainly does not provide a model that could serve to explain the variety of forms of animal motivation.

[21] See Chapter 7, pp. 102–4.

[22] Translations from the *Nicomachean Ethics* are indebted to those in J. Barnes (ed.), *The Complete Works of Aristotle* (Princeton: Princeton University Press, 1984), as well as to C. Rowe's translation in S. Broadie and C. Rowe, *Aristotle*: Nicomachean Ethics (Oxford: Oxford University Press, 2002).

before it hunts it down and gets its teeth into it.[23] What pleases it, though, is not the look of the stag, Aristotle thinks, but the prospect of making a meal of it. Presumably Aristotle does not think that envisaging this prospect is simply something that gives the lion pleasure. It seems safe to assume that if a lion envisages such a prospect and is pleased by it, it will also be motivated to hunt down the stag, so as to get its teeth into it. In other words, the lion will want to eat the stag, and it will engage in vigorous locomotion for the sake of this goal. What I am suggesting is simply that Aristotle recognizes, and in fact takes it to go without saying, that the purposive locomotion of animals involves and requires envisaging prospects like the one that pleases the lion in the example.

Now, envisaging prospects is, of course, a task that perception by itself cannot account for—even on Aristotle's notion of perception, which, as is well known, is remarkably generous. 'By perception', he remarks in the *De Memoria et Reminiscentia* (449^{b}13–15), 'we apprehend (γνωρίζομεν) neither what is future nor what is past, but only what is present.' Creatures endowed with perception, but no other cognitive capacity, could apprehend perceptibles presently located in their environment, but could not envisage prospects. It may come as a surprise, but there is in fact reason to think that, on Aristotle's view, there are such animals. Consider the following passage from the last chapter of the *Posterior Analytics*:

Given that perception is in them, in some animals the sensory impression persists (ἐγγίγνεται μονὴ τοῦ αἰσθήματος), in others it does not. If it does not, then the animal has no cognition (γνῶσις) apart from perceiving (either in general or with regard to the items which do not persist). But other animals can still hold sensory impressions in their soul after perceiving.[24]   (*Posterior Analytics* 2.19, 99^{b}36–100^{a}1)

The passage suggests that Aristotle takes the view that there are animal species whose members can apprehend nothing other than perceptibles presently located in their environment. Such animals will not be able to envisage prospects. It is hard to see how they could form purposes that might motivate them to engage in locomotion. This, however, may be just as it should be: some kinds of animals, after all, are stationary. They lack the capacity for purposive locomotion.[25] I shall turn to them in the next chapter.

---

[23] The Homeric passage to which Aristotle is alluding in lines 22–3 is well chosen. In that passage Menelaus, who is delighted to see Paris, is compared to a hungry lion who has come across the carcass of a stag or a wild goat. Menelaus has just seen Paris, and is pleased already; likewise, the lion has just come across the carcass, and is pleased already. The Homeric passage runs as follows: 'Menelaus saw Paris thus stride out before the ranks, and was pleased as a hungry lion that lights on the carcass of a stag or a wild goat, and devours it there and then, though dogs and youths set upon him. Even thus was Menelaus pleased when his eyes caught sight of Paris, for he deemed that now he should be revenged' (*Iliad* 3, 21–9, based on Samuel Butler's translation).

[24] Cf. Plato, *Philebus* 21 C 1–8, on certain creatures of the sea (for instance, testaceans) which have perception, but retain no memory of any kind. Interestingly, Alexander of Aphrodisias mentions testaceans as animals which (like all animals) have perception, but lack *phantasia* (*De Anima* 67, 2–3).

[25] See, for instance, *De Anima* 3.9, 432^{b}19–21: 'For there are many animals that have perception, but are stationary (μόνιμα) and unmoving throughout their lives (ἀκίνητα διὰ τέλους).' Cf. *De*

I have argued that if an animal's purpose is to motivate it to engage in locomotion, forming that purpose will, at least typically, involve envisaging a prospect. So far as rational motivation is concerned, the purpose in question is an object of thought. There is nothing mysterious about a thinking subject's ability to envisage situations that do not currently obtain: thought ranges freely over past, present, and future, and over what is actual as well as what is merely possible. Non-human animals, by contrast, are not in a position to avail themselves of the capacity for thought, so as to form purposes that may motivate them to engage in locomotion. Moreover, even human behaviour, Aristotle holds, is not always guided by thought. At the same time, he indicates that, within his explanatory framework, perception and *phantasia* 'hold the same place' as thought. This means, I assume, that perception and *phantasia* can, within appropriate limits, serve the same functions as thought. So we expect that while rational subjects can rely on thought in framing goals for action, non-rational subjects, and rational subjects who fail to make suitable use of the capacity for thought, are limited to perception and *phantasia* in forming whatever purposes they may form. Accordingly, we expect that perception and *phantasia*, jointly or individually, are cognitively powerful enough to enable subjects to form purposes that, if all goes well, get the animal in question to fly, swim, run, or otherwise travel from one place to another. Forming such purposes, however, is a task that perception by itself cannot accomplish. I shall now argue that *phantasia* can.[26]

In *Posterior Analytics* 2.19, as we have seen already, Aristotle distinguishes between animals that have perception without being able to retain sensory impressions, and animals that, apart from having perception, also have the capacity for retaining sensory impressions.[27] This distinction made, he says that animals that lack retention have no cognition apart from perceiving, either in general or with regard to the items that they do not retain. This suggests clearly and strongly that animals that have the capacity for retention have cognition apart from perceiving. It is reasonable to assume, then, that, on Aristotle's view, animals capable of retention can apprehend appropriate sorts of things that they do not at present perceive, provided that they retain suitable sensory impressions.

It is, moreover, clear that the capacity for *phantasia*, as Aristotle conceives of it, involves the capacity for retaining sensory impressions. He thinks of *phantasiai* as changes or affections (κινήσεις) that occur as a result of the activity of perception,

---

Anima 2.2, 413ᵇ2–4: 'for also living things which do not move or change in respect of place, but have perception, we call animals'; *De Anima* 2.3, 414ᵇ14–17: 'let this much be said, that those living things which have the sense of touch also have desire. As for *phantasia*, we have not yet achieved clarity, and we must look into this later. Some animals, in addition to these [sc. capacities], also have the capacity for locomotion'; *Physics* 8.7, 261ᵃ15–7; *Parts of Animals* 4.7, 683ᵇ9–10: 'Some species of testaceans are absolutely unmoving (ἀκίνητα πάμπαν), and others not quite but nearly so.'

26 In Ch. 11, I shall supplement the present chapter's argument by discussing the interaction between perception and *phantasia* in enabling the formation of desires that are sensitive and suitable to the subject's situation-specific circumstances.

27 μονὴ τοῦ αἰσθήματος, 99ᵇ36–7; αἰσθομένοις ἔχειν ἔτι ἐν τῇ ψυχῇ, 99ᵇ39–100ᵃ1.

and he takes such changes both to occur simultaneously with the activity of perception, and to be retained beyond the relevant episode of perceptual activity.[28] *Phantasiai* are like perceptions, Aristotle says, and they are able to *persist* (ἐμμένειν, *De Anima* 3.3, 429ᵃ4) beyond the activity of perception.[29]

On the basis of *Posterior Analytics* 2.19, then, we may assume that, on Aristotle's view, animals that have the capacity for retaining sensory impressions can apprehend appropriate items that they cannot currently see, hear, or otherwise perceive, provided that they retain suitable sensory impressions. We can now add a second point, namely that the capacity for *phantasia* in fact involves the capacity for retaining sensory impressions. These two views, taken together, suggest a cognitive role for *phantasia*. Animals that are capable of *phantasia* have cognition apart from perceiving: they can apprehend appropriate items that they do not currently perceive by way of their senses, provided that they retain suitable sensory impressions.

A number of passages in the *De Motu Animalium* corroborate the view that *phantasia*, as Aristotle conceives of it, enables subjects to apprehend appropriate items that are not currently present to their senses. Here is one:

> In the animal the same part can become larger and smaller and change its shape, as the parts expand on account of heat and contract again on account of cooling, and undergo qualitative changes. Qualitative changes are produced by *phantasiai*, perceptions, and thoughts. For perceptions are at once a kind of qualitative change, and *phantasia* and thought have the power of the actual things: for in a way the form, apprehended by thought, of something hot, cold, pleasant, or terrible happens to be such as each of the things themselves, and this is why we shudder and are agitated just thinking of something. All these are affections and qualitative changes.   (*De Motu Animalium* 7, 701ᵇ13–22)

Aristotle takes it that *phantasiai*, perceptions, and thoughts are capable of bringing about qualitative changes in parts of the body which may result in large-scale changes like blushing, pallor, shuddering, trembling, and the like. He is remarkably brief about why perceptions can bring about such qualitative changes: perceptions, he says, are *already* qualitative changes of a kind, and he seems to think that once this is understood, there is no difficulty in seeing how they can

---

[28] According to *De Anima* 3.3, 428ᵇ25–30, *phantasia* with respect to proper sensibles is true while perception is present, *phantasiai* with respect to common and accidental sensibles may be false (which suggests that they may also be true), both while perception is present and *while it is absent* (καὶ [sc. τῆς αἰσθήσεως] παρούσης καὶ ἀπούσης).

[29] For the connection between *phantasia* and the retention of sensory impressions, see also *De Anima* 1.4, 408ᵇ15–18, where Aristotle says that recollection is a change or motion that issues from the soul and extends to the 'changes' or 'states of rest' (μονάς) in the sense-organs. In the *De Memoria*, Aristotle picks out changes of this kind by using the term *phantasia* (φώτασμα, 450ᵇ10–11), and likens them to paintings (οἶον ζωγράφημά τι, 450ᵃ29–30) and imprints (οἶον τύπον τινὰ, 450ᵃ31). Note moreover *De Anima* 3.2, 425ᵇ24–5, with discussion in J. Freudenthal, *Über den Begriff des Wortes* phantasia *bei Aristoteles* (Göttingen: Rente, 1863), 6–8. Aristotle's discussion of dreaming is another context in which he makes explanatory use of the retention of sensory impressions: see *De Insomniis* 2, 459ᵃ24–8 and 460ᵃ32–ᵇ3.

bring about changes of the relevant kind in parts of the body.[30] The ability of *phantasiai* and thoughts to bring about such changes seems to stand in need of more explanation than perception's ability to do so. In providing this explanation, Aristotle relies on the idea that *phantasia* and thinking reproduce, or retain, something of the character of their objects. Thinking of yesterday's delicious meal can be pleasant in much the way having the actual meal was; and Aristotle wants to explain this fact by saying that thought can apprehend suitable perceptual forms and, in doing so, generate an experience that is much like the experience of having the actual meal. By generating such experiences, thought can bring about affections such as shuddering and being agitated. These are, or involve, qualitative changes in parts of the body. Aristotle thinks he can show, then, that thought has the power to bring about qualitative changes in the body: it has the power to bring about affections like shuddering and being agitated, and such affections are, or involve, qualitative changes in appropriate parts of the body.

Although Aristotle's examples concern perceptual forms being apprehended by *thought*, there is no reason at all to think that, on his view, such forms can be apprehended by thought only, and not also by *phantasia*. Rather, he is appealing to thought in order to illustrate a point that he takes to apply to *phantasia* no less than to thought. He is, after all, arguing for the claim that *phantasiai* and thoughts, no less than perceptions, can bring about qualitative changes in the body. Moreover, a later passage, which is presented as a restatement of the account offered in *De Motu* 7 and 8, confirms that the notion of forms being apprehended by a subject (for instance, the forms of something hot, cold, and the like) is meant to be applicable to the functioning, not only of thought, but also of *phantasia*. *Phantasia* as well as thought can, Aristotle holds, present such forms to the subject: 'For thinking and *phantasia*, as has been said before, present the things that are productive of affections: for they present the forms of the things that are productive [sc. of the affections]' (*De Motu Animalium* 11, 703^{b}18–20). So while perception enables an animal to apprehend things that are present to its senses, Aristotle takes both thought and *phantasia* to enable their possessors to go beyond that range.

Aristotle takes *phantasiai* to be like perceptions (*De Anima* 3.3, 428^{b}10–7; 429^{a}4–8), and he takes *phantasia* and perception to have the same range of objects.[31] As a result, *phantasia* benefits from his generous notion of what can be perceived through the senses.[32] *Phantasia* can thus apprehend, not only perceptual

---

[30] We may note in passing that this text suggests rather strongly that Aristotle conceives of perceptions as being realized in qualitative changes in appropriate parts of the body (presumably the sense-organs, including the central organ of perception). This view has been forcefully challenged in a series of articles by M. Burnyeat, beginning with 'Is an Aristotelian philosophy of mind still credible? A draft', in M. Nussbaum and A. Rorty (eds.), *Essays on Aristotle's* De Anima, 15–26. According to Burnyeat, perception as Aristotle conceives of it is a strictly immaterial activity, such that there is precisely nothing that stands to it as matter to form.

[31] *De Anima* 3.3, 428^{b}12–3: '*phantasia* is of that of which there is perception'.

[32] Sorabji, *Animal Minds and Human Morals*, 17–20, discusses Aristotle's rich notion of perception. Some passages that may serve as examples are *De Insomniis* 3, 462^{a}3 (perceiving that one is

features, but also objects like stags or humans. It should also be possible to have *phantasiai* (for instance) of being in some state or other, of performing some action, and of enjoying an experience.[33] There is, then, good reason to accept that Aristotle conceives of *phantasia* so that it is cognitively powerful enough to enable a subject to apprehend what one might, speaking loosely, refer to as *situations*— performing an action, say, or enjoying an experience. It is, of course, a further step to accept that *phantasia*, on Aristotle's view, also enables subjects to apprehend *prospective* situations (e.g. eating the stag over there). In fact, one might wonder how *phantasia*, given the way Aristotle conceives of it, can possibly account for the apprehension of prospective situations.[34] Now it should be noted that the same question arises for Socrates' accounts of desire and anticipatory pleasure at *Philebus* 32 B 9–36 C 2.[35] There it is memory, the preservation of perception, that accounts for the apprehension of objects of desire, and of prospective bodily replenishments or restorations. One might think that since sensory impressions derive from particulars—say, from a particular episode of eating a particular stag—their retention can only explain the apprehension of particular episodes that occurred in the past, but neither of types of actions (e.g. 'stag-eating'), nor of prospective actions (say, making a meal of the stag over there).

It is, however, a mistake to think that because what perceivers perceive are particular items of some sort or other, it follows that what sensory impressions represent, and what they enable a subject to apprehend, is limited to particular items of some sort or other. A perceiving subject may see Socrates, but a sensory impression that originates and derives from the encounter may represent, not Socrates, but (say) 'snub-nosed man'. Sensory impressions of this sort may not enable their subject reliably to pick out some individual or other in future

---

asleep); *Nicomachean Ethics* 9.9, 1170^{a}25–^{b}8 (perceiving that one is walking); and *Rhetoric* 1.11, 1370^{a}27–8 (perceiving an affection that one is undergoing). There are, of course, questions about how perception can account for a subject's awareness of (e.g.) being in some state or other, being engaged in some course of action, or having something happen to one. But such questions pertain to Aristotle's conception of perception, which this is not the place to discuss and elucidate.

[33] J. Cooper's review of R. Sorabji's *Aristotle on Memory, Archiv für Geschichte der Philosophie*, 57 (1975), 68–9, includes some pertinent remarks on *De Anima* 3.3, 428^{b}10–17: 'an act of imaging is here described as a "motion" that *resembles* an act of seeing or hearing or whatever. Of course, the resemblance between the two acts will be partly due to the fact that the act of imaging has for its content an image that resembles the thing originally perceived; but it is the resemblance between the two *acts* that Aristotle emphasizes in the first instance. . . . on Aristotle's theory one can explain, say, remembering how to do something as the ability to run through in one's mind the process of doing it'. According to the interpretation offered in Sorabji, *Aristotle on Memory* (London: Duckworth, 1972), 97–8, Aristotelian *phantasiai* may represent (for instance) what someone did last Monday, or the action of putting away a chisel. Cf. *De Memoria* 2, 452^{b}30–453^{a}2, about a person who remembers 'that he did something or other the day before yesterday'.

[34] Note, for instance, the question raised in D. Gallop, *Aristotle on Sleep and Dreams* (Peterborough, Ont.: Broadview Press, 1991), 160–2, about how *phantasia* can represent an action the subject is *going to* carry out, as Aristotle's discussion of divination through dreams seems to require: 'If anyone has a dream of an action that he merely intends to carry out, such a dream could hardly be due to a residue of waking perception. There could be no such residue from perception of an event that has, *ex hypothesi*, not yet occurred.'   [35] Ch. 7, pp. 102–4.

encounters.[36] However, they could support more modest, but in fact crucially important, cognitive achievements. Suitable sensory impressions of, say, some sort of food may enable a subject to represent and apprehend, not indeed some particular instance of it, but simply food of this sort. The same goes for actions. While it is of course true that lions perceive particular episodes of, say, eating stags, the sensory impressions that originate and derive from such episodes may well represent, not particular episodes, but patterns or configurations of appropriate sensory characteristics. Retaining such configurations could enable a lion to envisage the prospect of 'stag-eating' (or whatever), in a way that supports anticipatory pleasure as well as the formation of desire and the production of purposive locomotion.

[36] Note Aristotle's remark that 'a child begins by calling all men father, and all women mother, but later on distinguishes each of these' (*Physics* 1.1, 184^{a}21–^{b}14). Cf. D. Scott, *Recollection and Experience: Plato's Theory of Learning and its Successors* (Cambridge: Cambridge University Press, 1995), 124, on this passage: 'As far as the perception of particulars is concerned, we should not assume that because particulars are what we perceive, we perceive them merely as particulars, i.e., we perceive them in all their particularity.'

10

Desire without *phantasia*

In the preceding chapter, I pointed out that Aristotle's discussions of animal motivation, in *De Anima* 3.9–11 and in the *De Motu Animalium*, are concerned, not with the formation of desire or with the production of behaviour in general, but specifically with the production of animal locomotion. As a result, when Aristotle, in the context of these discussions, presents desire as being preceded and prepared by some suitable *phantasia*, as he does in the *De Motu*'s 'chain of movers' passage, this is not by itself a good reason to commit him to the view that forming any desire always requires some exercise or other of the capacity for *phantasia*. In the present chapter, I intend to show that there is in fact good reason to think that he does *not* take the view that desire always requires some suitable *phantasia*. I trust that showing this is worthwhile in its own right. It will also complete my argument for the view that, so far as non-rational motivation is concerned, he takes *phantasia* to be required specifically for the formation of desires that are such as to motivate an animal to engage in locomotion.

A number of texts in the *De Anima* commit Aristotle to the view that it is possible for an animal to be capable of desire without being capable of *phantasia*. In *De Anima* 2.3, he links the capacity for desire to the capacity for perception:

> If a living thing has the capacity for perception, it also has the capacity for desire. For desire comprises appetitive desire, spirited desire, and wish. And all animals have at least one of the senses, touch. For that which has perception, there is both pleasure and pain, and both the pleasant and the painful; and where there are these, there also is appetitive desire: for this is desire for the pleasant. (*De Anima* 2.3, 414ᵇ1–6)[1]

According to *De Anima* 2.3, then, an animal is capable of desire if it is capable of perception. In *De Anima* 3.3, Aristotle points out that there are animals that have the capacity for perception without having the capacity for *phantasia*.[2]

---

[1] A shorter version of this argument is at *De Somno* 1, 454ᵇ29–31. Cf. *De Anima* 2.3, 414ᵇ15–17.

[2] Cf. *Posterior Analytics* 2.19, 99ᵇ36–100ᵃ1. Note also the claim, at *De Anima* 3.3, 428ᵃ19–24, that *many* animals have *phantasia*. There is a problematic passage in *De Anima* 2.2, namely 413ᵇ21–4, where Aristotle claims that when certain insects are cut in two, each of the parts has perception and locomotion, 'and if they have perception, they also have *phantasia* and desire: for where there is perception, there is pain and pleasure, and where these are, there is necessarily also appetitive desire'. If so, all animals have *phantasia*, given that they have perception. Freudenthal, *Über den Begriff des Wortes* phantasia, 8, proposes to delete καὶ φαντασίαν in line 22, partly for the following

In fact, this is one of his arguments for the distinctness of *phantasia* from perception:

Furthermore, perception is invariably present [sc. in animals], but not *phantasia*.[3] If they were the same in actuality, then it would be possible for all animals to have *phantasia*; but it does not seem to be so: ants and bees, for instance, have *phantasia*, while grubs do not.[4] (*De Anima* 3.3, 428ᵃ8–11)

It is clear, then, that Aristotle says both that (1) if an animal is capable of perception, then it is capable of desire, and that (2) some animals have the capacity for perception, but lack, or anyhow seem to lack, the capacity for *phantasia*. From (1) and (2), it follows that some animals have the capacity for desire, but lack, or anyhow seem to lack, the capacity for *phantasia*. Now, since this is Aristotle's view, he had better conceive of desire and of what is required for it in such a way that an animal can be capable of desire whether or not it is capable of *phantasia*. It seems that a fragment contained in *De Anima* 3.7 offers an outline of such a conception:

(1) Perceiving, then, is like mere utterance and thought; but when something is pleasant or painful, [sc. the soul] pursues or avoids it, as it were affirming or denying it; (2) and the pleasure and pain in question are activities of the soul with the perceptual mean in relation to the good or bad as such. And this is also what the actual avoidance and desire in question are;[5]

reasons, which seem to me cogent. First, it interrupts the train of thought, since Aristotle goes on to argue for the link between perception and desire, but has nothing to say about a link between perception and *phantasia*. Secondly, the view that any animal has *phantasia*, given that it has perception, is contradicted at *De Anima* 2.3, 415ᵃ10–11, and at *De Anima* 3.3, 428ᵃ8–11.

[3] I translate ἀεί in line 8 as 'invariably', in agreement with the interpretation of the passage offered in R. D. Hicks, *Aristotle: De Anima* (Cambridge: Cambridge University Press, 1907), 461–2.

[4] All our manuscripts read οἷον μύρμηκι ἢ μελίττῃ, καὶ σκώληκι. I accept Torstrik's conjecture οἷον μύρμηκι μὲν ἢ μελίττῃ, σκώληκι δ' οὔ, and translate accordingly. Ants and bees should plainly *not* be included in a list of animals that may not be capable of *phantasia*. First, Aristotle is in fact committed to the view that bees have *phantasia*, as Hicks, on p. 462, points out: he attributes memory to them (in *Metaphysics* 1.1, 980ᵃ27–980ᵇ25), and his account of memory in the *De Memoria* makes clear that having the capacity for memory requires having the capacity for *phantasia*. Secondly, Themistius (writing in the fourth century AD) seems to have read something rather different from what our manuscripts say: 'Some animals', he writes, 'have *phantasia*, others do not: perhaps the ant and the bee, much more so the dog, the horse, and whatever animals have perception [sc. have *phantasia*], while the grub does not' (90, 6). Alexander of Aphrodisias (second–third centuries AD) mentions testaceans and grubs as examples of animals which have perception without having *phantasia* (no mention of ants and bees); *De Anima* 67.2–3. Cf. also Philoponus on *De Anima* 2.2, 413ᵇ22 (240, 11–5): ants have *phantasia*; 'but grubs, as he will say in what follows, are not seen to have *phantasia*'. (Simplicius, writing in the sixth century AD, appears to have read the text as our manuscripts have it.)

[5] At 431ᵃ12, the manuscripts are divided between τοῦτο on the one hand, and τὸ αὐτό or ταὐτόν on the other; so are the ancient commentators, with Philoponus reading τοῦτο and Simplicius reading ταὐτόν; and so are modern scholars, with Torstrik (1862) and Hicks (1907) reading τοῦτο and Ross (1961) and Hamlyn (1968) reading ταὐτό. I much prefer τοῦτο—first, because in this way we avoid what Hamlyn concedes is a 'hard saying', namely that 'actual avoidance and actual desire are the same'; and secondly because it enables us to construe the passage as expressing what seems to me a rather clear and attractive train of thought, with section (2) clarifying the relations holding among the items which figure in section (1), i.e. perception, pleasure, pain, pursuit (or desire), and avoidance (or aversion). Section (2) asserts constitutive connections both between perception and certain forms of pleasure and pain, and between those forms of pleasure and pain and

and the desiderative part or aspect (τὸ ὀρεκτικόν) is not different from the part to do with avoidance (τὸ φευκτικόν), nor either from the perceptual part (τὸ αἰσθητικόν); they are, however, different in being. (3) But to the thinking soul (τῇ διανοητικῇ ψυχῇ), *phantasiai* serve as percepts (αἰσθήματα). And when it affirms or denies good or bad, it avoids or pursues. (*De Anima* 3.7, 431ᵃ8–16)⁶

In the section marked as (1), certain forms of pursuit and avoidance are presented as arising from perceptions of something pleasant or painful.⁷ In section (2), Aristotle seems to identify the relevant forms of desire and avoidance with perceptual activities that involve pleasure or pain. It thus seems that he envisages a direct link between perceptual activity on the one hand and activity of desire or avoidance on the other. Certain forms of perceptual activity either result in, or constitute, certain forms of desiderative activity. There is no mention, in sections (1) or (2), of any contribution from *phantasia* to the formation of desire. *Phantasiai* only come in later, in section (3), when Aristotle turns to thought, apparently intending a contrast to what precedes: 'But to the thinking soul, *phantasiai* serve as percepts.'

It seems to me very much worth noting that in this whole passage, locomotion is not mentioned. By contrast, locomotion is, as we have seen, at the centre of Aristotle's attention in *De Anima* 3.9–11, and in the *De Motu Animalium*. In the preceding chapter, I argued that Aristotle assigns to *phantasia* a distinctive role in the formation of desires that account for purposive locomotion. At the same time, he may have reasons for leaving open the possibility of desires that can be explained, without appealing to *phantasia*, but simply in terms of perception, pleasure, and pain. He may also have reasons for leaving open the possibility of animals that are capable of desire, without being capable of *phantasia*. After all, there may be kinds of animals that show no sign of purposive locomotion, but that do engage in behaviour that he will want to explain in terms of cognition and desire. If so, he will be inclined to attribute to such animals the capacities for perception (minimally, touch) and desire, whereas he

certain forms of desire and avoidance. Certain forms of feeling pleasure and pain *are* forms of perceptual activity, and these forms of perceptual activity at the same time constitute desiderative states or activities. If so, perceptual activity of these forms is at once cognitive and desiderative. We might compare Aristotle's conception of decision (προαίρεσις), which similarly shares in both cognition and desire (see, for instance, *De Motu Animalium* 6, 700ᵇ23; *Nicomachean Ethics* 6.2, 1139ᵇ4–5), although the cognitive element involved in decision is intellectual, rather than (merely) perceptual.

⁶ I am grateful to David Charles for drawing my attention to this passage.

⁷ The relevant forms of pursuit and avoidance, I assume, are ones which spring specifically from appetitive desire or aversion. These, after all, are the motivating conditions which arise from awareness, or from the representation, specifically of pleasant or painful things. Accordingly, I take it that what Aristotle has in mind in section (2) are, not desire/pursuit and aversion/avoidance in general, but the particular forms of motivation that feature in section (1). One good reason for reading the passage in this restricted way is that Aristotle in section (3) turns to forms of pursuit and avoidance that arise, not from pleasant or painful perceptions, but from thoughts that affirm or deny goodness or badness.

may not see any need to attribute to them the capacity for *phantasia*. Take, for instance, sponges:[8]

It is said that sponges have perception. And there is an indication of this: for if a sponge becomes aware of an attempt being made to detach it, it contracts and it becomes difficult to remove it. It does the same thing in conditions of strong wind and waves, so that it does not get detached. Some people express doubts as to the truth of this assertion; as, for instance, the people of Torone.   (*Historia Animalium* 5.16, 548^{b}10–15)[9]

The sponge's contracting is not, we may safely assume, a matter of locomotion. Sponges no doubt are animals that Aristotle classifies as stationary, which is to say that they do not engage in locomotion.[10] So far as sponges are concerned, then, there is no locomotion that needs to be explained. Nonetheless, they are reported to engage in behaviour that Aristotle may wish to explain in terms of cognition and desire. In fact he is inclined to attribute perception to them. Given the links between perception, pleasure, pain, and desire that we find, for instance, at *De Anima* 2.3, 414^{b}1–6, it is reasonable to think that he is also inclined to attribute pleasure, pain, desire, and aversion to them,[11] and generally to animals that manifest behaviour of the kind that, at least according to some reports, sponges manifest. If so, it is open to him to explain the contracting of a sponge, when an attempt is made to detach it from its rock, simply in terms of (say) perception, pain, and aversion. He can say that the sponge perceives the occurrent process of gradually being detached as being intensely painful; that it is therefore strongly averse to it; and that this aversion expresses itself in avoidance behaviour, which involves contraction.[12] We might think that in cases such as this one there is no need to attribute to the creature in question any ability to envisage prospective situations, situations that do not currently obtain. For behaviour of the kind reportedly manifested by sponges could, it seems reasonable to think, be explained just in terms of perception and what we might call pro-attitudes or contra-attitudes to items that the animal apprehends in acts of perception—for instance, occurrent states or processes.[13]

---

[8] Philoponus (240, 22–5) suggests that sponges have tactile perception and appetitive desire, without having *phantasia*.   [9] Cf. *Historia Animalium* 1.1, 487^{b}10–12.

[10] Cf. De *Partibus Animalium* 4.5, 681^{a}16–18: 'A sponge, then, as already said, in these respects completely resembles a plant, that throughout its life it is attached to a rock, and that when separated from this it dies.' Translations from the *De Partibus Animalium* are as in J. Barnes (ed.), *Complete Works*. Cf. *Historia Animalium* 1.1, 487^{b}6–12.

[11] Aristotle thinks, I assume, that all creatures capable of desire are also capable of aversion. That he takes all creatures capable of perception to be capable, not only of appetitive desire, but also of appetitive aversion, is suggested by the inclusion of pain in the argument at *De Anima* 2.3, 414^{b}1–6. As we have seen, a form of avoidance is characterized as a perceptual activity at *De Anima* 3.7, 431^{a}8–14; Aristotle there adds that 'the desiderative part or aspect is not different from the part to do with avoidance'. Note also the remark, at *De Anima* 3.12, 434^{b}11–18, that for an animal to be preserved, it must have the sense of touch, or else it could not avoid some things and take others.

[12] As Christof Rapp pointed out to me, the explanation of the sponge's contracting may have much the same structure as the explanation of what happens when you accidentally put your hand on a very hot object.

[13] Given that sponges are not capable of *locomotion*, how should their behaviour be classified? Aristotle's discussions of animal motivation in *De Anima* 3.9–11 and in the *De Motu Animalium*

What, then, of the appearance that, according to the 'chain of movers' passage, forming a desire requires having some suitable *phantasia*? As we have seen already, that passage has its place in the context of a discussion of animal locomotion. In fact what it says is specifically meant to explain why it is that 'it is pretty much at the same time that a creature thinks it should walk (ὅτι πορευτέον) and that it walks, unless something else impedes it' (702ª15–17). We may, then, record a qualified version of the claim that the 'chain of movers' passage at first sight appeared to imply:

> (1′) Forming a desire that can support, and account for, goal-directed locomo-
> tion requires having some suitable *phantasia*.[14]

So far as non-rational motivation is concerned, we can explain Aristotle's commitment to claim (1′) in the following way. If a desire is to support, and account for, purposive locomotion, forming it involves envisaging a prospective situation. Envisaging a prospect, then, is a cognitive task that a subject must actually perform if it is to engage in purposive locomotion. Now, Aristotle takes it that there are three cognitive capacities that may be involved in the production of animal locomotion: thought, perception, and *phantasia*. Perception by itself plainly does not enable an animal to envisage prospects. At the same time, Aristotle denies the capacity for thought to non-human animals. He also holds that humans can be motivated to act, and no doubt to engage in purposive locomotion, without thought being active at the time.[15] Thus we expect that *phantasia*, as Aristotle

---

focus (reasonably enough, I think) on forms of animal movement such as flying, swimming, walking, and the like—forms of movement, that is, which involve movement of the *whole* animate organism from one place to another. Note the identification of locomotion with *progressive* motion (πορευτικὴ κίνησις) at *De Anima* 3.9, 432ᵇ13–14; cf. πορεία ('progression') at 25–6. This leaves it somewhat unclear what Aristotle wants to say about forms of behaviour which involve locomotion only of *parts* of an organism, or only changes other than locomotion. It is worth pointing out that the former case does not, for Aristotle, count as a case of movement of an organism 'in its own right' or 'as such' (καθ' αὑτό); an animal which engages in movement only with regard to some part of itself engages in movement only incidentally (κατὰ συμβεβηκός). See *Physics* 8.4, 254ᵇ7–14, and p. 27, n. 9. Aristotle's general idea is, I suggest, that if a theory can explain the complex and demanding achievement of purposive animal *locomotion*, it can surely explain the more primitive forms of animal behaviour, such as reactions to perceptual stimuli as displayed by stationary animals of various kinds.

[14] It is perhaps worth noting that Aristotle does not, either in *De Motu Animalium* 8 or anywhere else, assert in so many words that if an animal forms a desire which results in locomotion, the animal in question necessarily or invariably has some suitable *phantasia*. However, the *De Motu Animalium* is aiming to offer a general account of animal locomotion, as its second sentence makes clear (*De Motu Animalium* 1, 698ª4–7). And in that general account of animal locomotion, *phantasia* is envisaged, in the 'chain of movers' passage, as playing the role of 'suitably preparing' desire. So we have good reason to assume that, on Aristotle's view, *phantasia* is involved in the production of animal locomotion either invariably or at least so far as cases are concerned which he takes to be sufficiently central to focus on them. For the sake of simplicity, I retain (1′) as formulated above.

[15] *De Anima* 3.3, 429ª4–8: 'Because *phantasiai* persist in the animal and are like perceptions, animals do many things in ways that depend on them [sc. rather than on thought]. As for the brute animals, this is because they do not have an intellect (νοῦς). With humans, it is because their intellects are sometimes covered over by passion, disease, or sleep.' I offer a suggestion about what precisely the last sentence may mean in Ch. 13, n. 29.

conceives of it, enables an animal to envisage prospects. In Chapter 9, I offered what seem to me good reasons for thinking that, in fact, it does.

Aristotle thinks, moreover, that when thought rouses an animal to travel from one place to another, this too involves the formation, or anyhow the active occurrence, of some suitable *phantasia*.[16] He may well think that, in that, in this case too, the occurrence of some *phantasia* is required for the formation of the desire in question. In fact he may take it to be required for the very possibility of rational motivation.[17] At least for present purposes, then, we have arrived at a sufficiently clear and detailed view of why Aristotle thinks that, in general, forming a desire that impels an animal to engage in goal-directed locomotion requires the occurrence of some suitable *phantasia*.

I turn to appearance (2):

(2) The discussion at *De Anima* 3.10–11, 433^{b}27–434^{a}5, commits Aristotle to the following view: if an animal is capable of desire, it must be capable, not only of perception, but of *phantasia* as well.

It is worth noting that at *De Anima* 3.10, 433^{b}27–9, Aristotle appears to connect the capacity for desire, not only with the capacity for *phantasia*, but also with the capacity for self-movement: 'In general, then, as has been said, in so far as the animal is capable of desire, so far is it capable of self-movement (αὐτοῦ κινητικόν); and it is not capable of desire without *phantasia*.'[18] In this passage, he appears to assert general connections between the capacities for desire, for self-movement, and for *phantasia*. As we have seen, he has already noted a connection between the capacities for perception and for desire:

If a living thing has the capacity for perception, it also has the capacity for desire. For desire comprises appetitive desire, spirited desire, and wish. And all animals have at least one of the senses, touch. For that which has perception, there is both pleasure and pain, and both the pleasant and the painful; and where there are these, there also is appetitive desire: for this is desire for the pleasant.   (*De Anima* 2.3, 414^{b}1–6)

We have now come close to having to diagnose an inconsistency within the *De Anima*. Aristotle asserts, or appears to assert, that all animals have perception, minimally in the form of touch; that whatever has perception also has desire; and that whatever has desire also has the capacities for locomotion and for *phantasia*.[19] If we take him to make these claims, we have to commit him to the view that all animals are capable of locomotion and of *phantasia*. However, he states in *De Anima* 3.9 that 'there are many animals which have perception, but are stationary

---

[16] This is clear from the 'chain of movers' passage. Note also *De Anima* 3.11, 434^{a}7–10.

[17] I give more content to this suggestion in the Conclusion, pp. 205–6.

[18] This is Hamlyn's translation, slightly modified. I should reiterate that this is not how I think the passage is best understood. I shall shortly propose an alternative translation.

[19] T. Irwin, *Aristotle's First Principles* (Oxford: Oxford University Press, 1988), 304–5: 'Since perception requires desire, and desire requires appearance, perception requires appearance.' Similarly V. Caston, 'Why Aristotle needs imagination', 23, n. 9.

and unmoving throughout their lives' (*De Anima* 3.9, 432ᵇ19–21).[20] He also claims, as we have seen, that there are kinds of animals which have the capacity for perception, but lack, or anyhow seem to lack, the capacity for *phantasia* (*De Anima* 3.3, 428ᵃ8–11). One way of responding to these difficulties is to offer a developmental interpretation—for instance, something like this. There was a time in Aristotle's intellectual career when he believed that there are some animal species which lack the capacities for locomotion and *phantasia*. Some traces of this view can be detected in the *De Anima* and other texts. At a later stage in his development, Aristotle (for some reason or other) came to think that all animals are capable of locomotion and *phantasia*, at least in rudimentary and indeterminate ways. According to this developmental interpretation, Aristotle in *De Anima* 3.10–11 revises views that he committed himself to in some earlier passages of the *De Anima*.[21]

Another prima facie possibility is to take a developmental view of *phantasia*, but to insist that, so far as locomotion is concerned, what Aristotle says in the *De Anima* is consistent. One way in which this might be done is by assuming that the capacity for *self-motion*, which is mentioned at 3.10, 433ᵇ27–9, is more broadly conceived than the capacity for *locomotion*, which is denied to some animals in several places of the *De Anima* (for instance, at 3.9, 432ᵇ19–21). For there may be animals which do not move from place to place, but which are nonetheless capable of moving parts of their bodies: such animals could be regarded as being capable of self-motion, without having the capacity for locomotion.[22]

However, Aristotle does not give any indication, in the discussion in *De Anima* 3.9–11, that he intends there to be a difference between (self-) locomotion and self-motion, let alone that he intends to exploit such a difference.[23] On the contrary, he makes clear, at the beginning of 3.9, that the topic to be discussed in

---

[20] Note also *De Partibus Animalium* 4.7, 683ᵇ9–10: 'Some species of testaceans are absolutely unmoving (ἀκίνητα πάμπαν), and others not quite but nearly so.' Also *Physics* 8.7, 261ᵃ15–17: 'some living things are completely unmoving (ὅλως ἀκίνητα) due to lack of an appropriate organ—viz., plants and many kinds of animal.' Note furthermore the restriction 'as far as animals are concerned that engage in self-motion (ὅσα κινεῖται αὐτὰ αὑτά)' at *De Motu Animalium* 4, 700ᵃ7–11, and 700ᵃ21–5. Cf. *De Anima* 2.3, 414ᵇ14–19. For a discussion of Aristotle's views on the lowest forms of animal life, see G. Lloyd, *Aristotelian Explorations* (Cambridge: Cambridge University Press, 1996), 67–82.

[21] A developmental interpretation is suggested by (for instance) Irwin, *Aristotle's First Principles*, 587, n. 3. On his view, *De Anima* 3.11, 433ᵇ31–434ᵃ7, revises the earlier view expressed at *De Anima* 3.3, 428ᵃ9–11: 'These later thoughts seem to be the best.' Similarly D. Frede, 'The cognitive role of *phantasia*', in M. Nussbaum and A. Rorty (eds.), *Essays on Aristotle's* De Anima, 281, who suggests 'modification' on Aristotle's part.

[22] Cf. Irwin, *Aristotle's First Principles*, 587, n. 2, about stationary animals: 'Even though they do not move from place to place, they move parts of themselves; a sea-anemone or a shellfish, e.g., may close up and protect itself if it is poked, *HA* 487ᵇ7–11.'

[23] Note the frequent shifts, in *De Anima* 3.9–10, between 'motion' expressions (κινεῖν, κίνησις) and 'locomotion' expressions (κινεῖν κατὰ τόπον, κίνησις κατὰ τόπον), with no suggestion at all that such shifts involve a broadening or narrowing of scope: locomotion at 432ᵃ17, motion at 432ᵃ18, locomotion at 432ᵇ8, motion at 432ᵇ28, 433ᵃ7, 433ᵃ9, locomotion at 433ᵃ13, motion at 433ᵃ18, and so forth.

what follows is the self-locomotion of animals (3.9, 432^{a}7–8; ^{b}7–8; ^{b}13–4; 3.10, 433^{a}9–13). The question of what in the soul it is that *moves* the animal (432^{a}18–19) is restated a little later on as 'the question which has now arisen', namely, 'what is it that moves the animal *in respect of place*' (432^{b}7–8). Thus the text suggests very strongly that the topic Aristotle is proposing to discuss is precisely one kind of motion: the self-locomotion of animals. So if, within this discussion, he denies or attributes to certain animals the capacity for the relevant kind of motion, he should be understood as denying or attributing to them the capacity for locomotion. As a result, if we read the discussion in such a way as to commit him to the view that all animals are capable of the relevant kind of movement—locomotion, that is—we cannot avoid diagnosing an inconsistency, given that he denies the capacity for locomotion to some animals (for instance, within the very discussion we are concerned with).

Can we resolve this problem of consistency? It seems to me that we can, and also that we can make sense of Aristotle's overall position without having to resort to developmental assumptions of the kind I have sketched. I think that we can interpret *De Anima* 3.10–11, 433^{b}27–434^{a}5, so that it is compatible with the view that some animals are not capable of locomotion, and may not be capable of *phantasia*. To see that this is possible, we should note that the assertion at *De Anima* 3.10, 433^{b}27–8, is offered as a *restatement* of something that has been said before ('as has been said', 433^{b}27). There is no need to stress that Aristotle has not asserted anything like a necessary link between desire and locomotion, such that if an animal is capable of desire, it must be capable of locomotion as well. Something that has been said, by contrast, is that it is the capacity for desire that produces locomotion (*De Anima* 3.10, 433^{a}31–^{b}1). This statement, I take it, answers the question that 3.9 begins by asking: what in the soul is it that moves the animal in respect of place?[24] The question applies only to animals which are capable of locomotion. And the answer is that it is the capacity for desire that moves *them* in respect of place. I suggest that at *De Anima* 3.10, 433^{b}27–8, Aristotle is meaning to do no more and no less than to restate this point: for all animals that are capable of locomotion, it is in so far as they are capable of desire that they are capable of locomotion—which, of course, is not to say that all animals are capable of locomotion. In light of the interpretation that I am suggesting, Aristotle's Greek should be translated in something like the following way: 'In general, then, as has been said, it is in so far as the animal has the capacity for desire that it has the capacity for self-motion'.[25]

Moreover, the link between desire and *phantasia* that Aristotle describes at 433^{b}28–9 may, and I think should, be understood as restricted in scope by the

---

[24] *De Anima* 3.9, 432^{a}15–22; cf. 432^{b}7–8, 13–14.
[25] Cf. Hicks's translation: 'Thus, then, in general terms, as already stated, the animal is capable of moving itself just in so far as it is appetitive'. Similarly, Ross' paraphrase (in his *De Anima* commentary, Oxford: Oxford University Press, 1961, 315): 'To state the matter generally, it is by virtue of having desire that an animal moves itself'.

context, which is a discussion of what it is that moves the animal in respect of place. For animals which are capable of locomotion, what imparts locomotion to *them* is the capacity for desire acting in concert with the capacity for *phantasia*.[26] This, of course, is not to say that all animals are capable of *phantasia*, or that all animals which are capable of desire are also capable of *phantasia*. I propose to translate the passage as a whole in the following way: 'In general, then, as has been said, it is in so far as the animal has the capacity for desire that it has the capacity for self-motion, but in so far as it has the capacity for desire not without the capacity for *phantasia*.'

Given the interpretation that I have offered, the following problem may be raised. Aristotle asserts that it is the capacity for desire that produces locomotion (3.10, 433ᵃ31–ᵇ1). He also wants to say that some animal species have the capacity for desire, but lack the capacity for locomotion (3.9, 432ᵇ19–21, together with 2.3, 414ᵇ1–6). But then his position may seem to be vulnerable to a form of argument that he himself employs so as to counter the view that it is the capacity for perception that produces locomotion (3.9, 432ᵇ19–26).[27] The argument in 3.9 runs as follows. Many animals have the capacity for perception, without having the capacity for locomotion; and nature does nothing in vain. If it were the capacity for perception that produced locomotion, then having the capacity for perception would involve being capable of locomotion. If so, some animals would, surprisingly, have the capacity for locomotion, although their bodies do not have suitable parts to enable them actually to engage in locomotion. Nature would have endowed them with a capacity that they could never exercise; which violates the principle that nature does nothing in vain.

It appears, however, that Aristotle wants to attribute to stationary animals not only the capacity for perception, but also the capacity for desire. And if it is the capacity for desire that produces locomotion, then (Aristotle is bound to think) being capable of desire involves being capable of locomotion. Once more we arrive at the result that some animals are naturally endowed with a capacity that, naturally, they can never exercise.

One way in which Aristotle can respond to this problem is as follows. Strictly speaking, it is not the capacity for desire *as such* that produces locomotion, but that capacity as supported by a system of cognitive capacities which includes either *phantasia* or thought (or both, as in the human case). In fact, this may well be exactly what Aristotle has in mind. The primary mover of the animal is not, he holds, the capacity for desire, but the object of desire; and the object of desire produces motion by being grasped in thought or *phantasia* (3.10, 433ᵇ11–12).[28]

---

[26] Grammatically speaking, the clause ὀρεκτικὸν δὲ οὐκ ἄνευ φαντασίας at 433ᵇ28–9 may be taken as an apposition to the clause ᾗ ὀρεκτικὸν τὸ ζῷον at 433ᵇ27–8, amplifying and, I shall suggest presently, qualifying the content of the earlier clause. Reading the passage in this way, I propose to put a comma between κινητικόν and ὀρεκτικόν at 433ᵇ28, departing from the punctuation adopted by (for instance) Hicks and Ross, who both print a colon.

[27] Cf. Irwin, *Aristotle's First Principles*, 595, n. 1.

[28] πρῶτον δὲ πάντων τὸ ὀρεκτόν· τοῦτο γὰρ κινεῖ οὐ κινούμενον, τῷ νοηθῆναι ἢ φαντασθῆναι.

Thus the production of the relevant kind of motion—locomotion, that is—presupposes that the subject is capable of thought or at least of *phantasia*. It is tempting to think, then, that the clause 'having the capacity for desire not without *phantasia*' (ὀρεκτικὸν δὲ οὐκ ἄνευ φαντασίας) at 3.10, 433ᵇ28–9, is meant to place a restriction on the connection between the capacity for desire and the capacity for locomotion: the capacity for desire produces locomotion *only if* it is supported by a suitably powerful cognitive apparatus—one, that is, which minimally includes the capacity for *phantasia*.

At the beginning of *De Anima* 3.11, Aristotle raises the question of what it is that moves imperfect animals, which have perception only in the form of touch. Presumably he has not changed the subject: he is still discussing movement in respect of place, and he is wondering whether the indeterminate kind of locomotion of the relevant animal species should be explained in terms of desire and *phantasia*. As we have seen, part of his answer is that they must have appetitive desire. Moreover, he suggests that as they engage in movement in an indeterminate way, so they have *phantasia* in an indeterminate way. Aristotle is not here committing himself to the view that all animals are capable of locomotion, indeterminate or otherwise. He is discussing the question of how to explain the indeterminate form of purposive locomotion that he takes some low-level animals to exhibit. None of what he says in this context implies that all animals exhibit at least such an indeterminate form of purposive locomotion.

We may conclude that when a species of animal shows signs of purposive locomotion, even of a rudimentary and indeterminate kind, Aristotle is inclined to attribute the capacity for *phantasia* to the relevant species. At the same time, looking at species that represent the lowest forms of animal life, Aristotle may want to attribute the capacities for perception and desire to some kinds of animals which show no sign of having the capacity for locomotion. Given the connection between locomotion and *phantasia* that I argued for in Chapter 9, he may well be inclined to deny the capacity for *phantasia* to such animals.

11

The Workings of *phantasia*

It may be helpful to begin by recalling the roles perception and *phantasia* are presented as playing in the conceptual framework that Aristotle employs in his discussions of animal locomotion, in *De Anima* 3.9–11 and in the *De Motu Animalium*. Much of this conceptual framework is on display in two rather similar passages, one from *De Motu Animalium* 6, the other from *De Anima* 3.10:

> We see that the movers of the animal are thought (διάνοια), perception, *phantasia*, decision, wish, spirit, and appetite. And all of these can be reduced to thought (νοῦς) and desire. For *phantasia* and perception hold the same place as thought: for all of these involve discernment, while they differ in ways that have been stated elsewhere. (*De Motu Animalium* 6, 700ᵇ17–22)

> These two are seen to produce movement, either desire or thought (νοῦς), if one were to take *phantasia* to be like a kind of thinking (ὡς νόησίν τινα): for many follow *phantasiai* against knowledge, and in the other animals there is neither thinking (νόησις) nor reasoning (λογισμός), but there is *phantasia*. Both of these, then, can produce movement in respect of place, thought and desire—but thought which reasons for the sake of something and is practical. (*De Anima* 3.10, 433ᵃ9–14)

In both passages, Aristotle proposes to account for animal locomotion in terms of cognition and desire. He also makes clear, in these passages and in their respective contexts, that there are, on his view, different kinds of cognition, and different kinds of desire. The relevant kinds of cognition are thought or thinking (διάνοια, νόησις) on the one hand and *phantasia* and perception on the other. In the passage from *De Anima* 3.10, Aristotle suggests that we take *phantasia* to be 'like a kind of thinking'. He nevertheless implicitly insists, in the same passage, on the distinction between *phantasia* and thinking: he credits all or almost all non-human animals with *phantasia* and at the same time denies them the capacity for thinking. In the present chapter, I shall discuss some points of contact between *phantasia* and thought, hoping to shed light on what Aristotle may have in mind in suggesting that *phantasia* can be taken to be 'like a kind of thinking'. In the next chapter, I shall turn to the question of why Aristotle, in spite of whatever similarities there may be between the two, nevertheless insists on their distinctness.

Given that the forms of cognition that Aristotle makes available for the explanation of animal movement are thought, *phantasia*, and perception, the cognition involved in the purposive movement of non-human animals must on his view be explicable in terms of *phantasia* and perception alone. What I intend to do in what follows is to consider some forms of non-human animal behaviour that Aristotle observes and discusses, and to reflect on the question of how it might be that the cognition involved in such forms of behaviour can be explained simply in terms of *phantasia* and perception, as he conceives of them. My main objective will be to bring out the remarkably powerful notion of *phantasia* with which Aristotle operates. For this purpose, it will not be necessary to provide a comprehensive or exhaustive survey of the forms of behaviour that he observes and discusses. Rather, I shall focus on a few cases that seem especially helpful in showing the remarkable power of *phantasia*, as he conceives of it.

In the present chapter, as well as in the next one, I shall focus on non-human animal motivation as providing the clearest case of non-rational motivation, as Aristotle conceives of it. What I intend to bring to light is a rich and, I think, rather attractive conception of non-rational motivation that is in principle applicable both to non-human animal behaviour and to human behaviour that fails to manifest reason. In Chapter 13, I shall turn to the question of the extent to which Aristotle takes that conception to be applicable to the behaviour of adult, ordinarily developed humans.

In a passage from *Nicomachean Ethics* 3.10 that we had a look at in Chapter 9, Aristotle discusses a situation in which a predatory animal notices some suitable prey somewhere in its environment. In that passage, he is interested in the pleasure that the predator takes in such circumstances. 'What pleases the lion', he insists, 'is not the sight of "a stag or a wild goat", but that he is going to get a meal.'[1] The lion's pleasure, Aristotle thinks, is a pleasure of anticipation, and so he must take it to involve apprehending the prospect of having a meal. This makes clear that he thinks non-human animals can, in some way or other, anticipate or envisage prospects. Independently of this, it seems to be an implication of his account of animal locomotion, in *De Anima* 3.9–11 and in the *De Motu Animalium*, that non-human animals can envisage prospects. He evidently thinks that they are capable of locomotion for the sake of goals, and this capacity seems to presuppose the capacity for envisaging prospects.

It is fairly easy to see at least some ways in which perception and *phantasia* may enter into accounts of the types of animal response and behaviour that Aristotle notes in *Nicomachean Ethics* 3.10. Perception supplies the predator with the information that some suitable prey is located nearby in its environment. A *phantasia* which, in some way or other, presents the prospect of having a meal will play a role in the explanation both of the lion's pleasure of anticipation, and of its purposive locomotion towards its prey.

If Aristotle has in mind an account along these lines, as it seems clear that he does, he must assume, not only that non-human animals can envisage prospects,

---

[1] [sc. χαίρει] ὅτι βορὰν ἕξει: *Nicomachean Ethics* 3.10, 1118ª18–23.

but also that there is some mechanism which brings it about that in cases of the kind described in *Nicomachean Ethics* 3.10, animals envisage prospects that are *suitable* to the circumstances they find themselves in, whatever these may be. It is plain, after all, that there is a rather tight fit between the prospect the animal apprehends by way of *phantasia* and its current situation, which is presented to it by way of its senses. What a lion typically anticipates on seeing (say) a stag is having a meal, rather than, for instance, copulating. This fit between prospective and present situations cannot be a mere coincidence. It must stem from an ability that lions and many other kinds of animals have as a matter of being naturally constituted the way they are, namely to envisage prospects that are, more often than not, suitable to their present circumstances.

These points may be made in another way. The suggestion so far has been that, on Aristotle's view, animals with the capacity for retaining sensory impressions are capable of envisaging prospective situations, with the latter capacity playing a crucial role in purposive locomotion. However, one deficiency of the account so far offered on Aristotle's behalf is that it fails to explain the fact that non-human animals can, in appropriate circumstances, be *relied on* to behave in rather specific ways. There are circumstances in which a lion, when presented with a stag, will hunt it down and sink its teeth into it.[2] According to Aristotle's account, the lion's behaviour expresses and realizes a purpose. Forming that purpose, I have suggested, requires rather specific exercises of the capacity for *phantasia*. Thus Aristotle must, I take it, assume that there are circumstances in which lions can be relied on, when presented with some prey, to have some suitable *phantasia* that will in some way or other represent eating the prey, rather than having no *phantasia* at all, or having some quite different *phantasia*.

A theory which, like Aristotle's, proposes to account for the cognitive achievements involved in the purposive behaviour of non-human animals in terms of perception and *phantasia* should then be able to account, in these terms, not only for their ability to envisage prospective situations, but also for the fact that, given certain conditions, they can be relied on to envisage prospects that are suitable to the circumstances they find themselves in. Otherwise there would be an important gap in Aristotle's account. Now, Aristotle does not explicitly confront the question why it is that some of the brute animals can, given certain circumstances, be relied on to envisage rather specific prospects. It is nevertheless possible to make a detailed and, I hope, persuasive case for the view that perception and, in particular, *phantasia*, as he conceives of them, can, or anyhow are meant to be able to, account for an animal's ability to envisage prospects that are suitable to its

---

[2] These circumstances include, for instance, that the lion is in reasonably good health and not completely sated, and perhaps also that it has acquired appropriate levels of relevant experience and skill of the sorts that lions naturally acquire in their habitat. The difference between a healthy, hungry lion and a sick or sated one will not lie in what prospects they can envisage, but presumably in which ones they find pleasurable and thus desirable.

circumstances. Making this case will be my task in the remainder of the present chapter.

According to Aristotle's psychological theory, for any animal capable of perception and *phantasia*, it is the same part or aspect of its soul that accounts for its being capable both of perceiving and of having *phantasiai*.[3] We can see this in the first chapter of the *De Insomniis*. Aristotle begins that treatise by asking in virtue of what part or aspect of the soul it is that we have dreams and, specifically, whether dreams are affections of the part or aspect of the soul that is concerned with thinking (τὸ νοητικόν), or the one concerned with perceiving (τὸ αἰσθητικόν) (458ª33–ᵇ2).[4] At the end of the chapter, the question is answered: dreaming belongs to the part or aspect of the soul that is concerned with perceiving, in so far as it is concerned with *phantasia* (459ª21–2); for a dream appears to be a kind of *phantasia* (φάντασμα), hence to belong to the part or aspect concerned with *phantasia* (τὸ φανταστικόν), and that part or aspect is in fact the same as the part or aspect concerned with perceiving (τὸ αἰσθητικόν) (459ª14–22). It is Aristotle's view, then, that there is a part or aspect of the soul, which may be referred to as the perceptual part, that enables certain living things both to perceive and to have *phantasiai*.[5] It turns out that

---

[3] There are several passages in Aristotle's psychological writings in which he mentions μόρια τῆς ψυχῆς, a notion which I intend to capture by writing of parts or aspects of the soul. Although Aristotle is not very specific about what he has in mind in mentioning these items, a number of points are nevertheless clear. Being *a part* of the soul is contrasted with being *a soul* (*De Anima* 2.2, 413ᵇ11–16); as a result, conceiving of (for instance) whatever it is that is concerned with perceiving (αἰσθητικόν) as a part or aspect of the soul enables Aristotle to resist the view that an animal may have more souls than one, since it has something concerned with perceiving, something concerned with nutrition, and so forth. At the same time, he evidently finds the notion that the soul is a thing of parts—a composite object, that is—to be deeply and seriously problematic, as we saw in Chapter 3. The *aporia* for soul partition that is articulated at *De Anima* 1.5, 411ᵇ5–14, is never, in fact, resolved. Thus Aristotle may well have in mind a notion as weak as 'aspect'. Claims about parts or aspects of the soul may simply be claims about how the various capacities which constitute the soul are related to one another, and about which 'psychic' capacities are needed to account for a given activity or operation which living things perform in virtue of being ensouled.

[4] I assume that the expression τὸ αἰσθητικόν at 458ᵇ2 refers to a part or aspect of the soul, just as the expression τὸ νοητικόν in the same sentence. Thus the second question seems to me to be a specification of the first one, narrowing down the range of candidates to two. τὸ αἰσθητικόν has been introduced as a part or aspect of the soul in the preceding treatise, *De Somno* (which, at 453ᵇ17–20, announces the *De Insomniis*): at 454ª11–19, Aristotle mentions τὸ αἰσθητικόν as one of the items that are spoken of as parts or aspects of the soul (μόρια τῆς ψυχῆς), and later in the same chapter he refers to it as the part or aspect concerned with perceiving (τὸ αἰσθητικὸν μόριον): 'Sleep is an affection of the part or aspect concerned with perceiving, a kind of fetter and lack of movement; so that it is necessary that everything that sleeps has a part or aspect concerned with perceiving' (454ᵇ9–12). This result is assumed in the *De Insomniis*: 'Let us assume what is quite obvious, that dreaming is an affection of that which is concerned with perceiving (τὸ αἰσθητικόν), just as sleep is: for dreaming does not belong to another part or aspect of animals than sleep' (459ª11–14).

[5] It is with, or in virtue of, the αἰσθητικόν that *we* have certain cognitions: see *De Insomniis* 1, 458ᵇ2–3. In other words, the αἰσθητικόν, rather than itself doing the perceiving, enables *us* to perceive. This form of expression reflects Aristotle's view that it is 'perhaps better' to say that *we* pity, learn, or think with, or in virtue of, the soul, than to say that the soul pities, learns, or thinks (*De Anima* 1.4, 408ᵇ13–18). For more on this view, see Conclusion, pp. 203–4.

this part or aspect is, on Aristotle's view, also responsible for dreaming, and for remembering.[6]

The perceptual part of the soul is meant to account for a variety of interrelated activities in which animals engage, much as the soul as a whole, according to Aristotle's psychological theory, accounts for an even wider variety of interrelated activities. And as the perceptual part is conceived of as a part or aspect of the soul as a whole, so the activities it accounts for form a subset of the set of interrelated activities that the soul as a whole accounts for. Activities that Aristotle takes to belong to the soul, but not to its perceptual part, include digestion and thought.[7]

Now, an ordinarily developed living thing that is equipped with a perceptual soul-part is an organism with a certain structure. This will typically involve having a variety of sense-organs and a central organ of perception; I shall refer to that configuration of organs as the animal's perceptual apparatus. For animals capable of *phantasia*, this apparatus will be complex enough to support, not only the reception of sensory impressions when appropriate objects are present to its senses, but also the retention of such impressions when the objects in question are no longer present. It is part of Aristotle's psychological theory, I suggested, that the ability to retain sensory impressions enables animals to envisage prospects, and to form purposes that may impel them to engage in movement from one place to another.

There is, moreover, good reason to think that, on Aristotle's view, the perceptual part of a suitable animal's soul can account for the fact that, given certain conditions, it can be relied on to envisage prospects that are suitable to the circumstances in which it finds itself. As is clear from a number of texts in the *Parva*

---

[6] 'Memory also of intelligibles does not occur without a *phantasia*. Hence it would seem to belong incidentally to that which is concerned with thought, but in itself to the primary part or aspect concerned with perceiving (τὸ πρῶτον αἰσθητικόν)' (*De Memoria et Reminiscentia* 1, 450ᵃ12–14). This suggestion answers one of the questions posed in the first sentence of the *De Memoria et Reminiscentia*, namely 'to which of the parts or aspects of the soul does this affection [sc. remembering] occur?'

[7] I reject J. Whiting's suggestion, argued for in 'Locomotive soul: the parts of soul in Aristotle's scientific works', *Oxford Studies in Ancient Philosophy*, 22 (2002), 192–200, that thought, or at least practical thought, belongs to the αἰσθητικόν. Aristotle never says or implies that a person thinks or deliberates in virtue of the part of their soul that is concerned with *perceiving*. Nor does he ever identify the αἰσθητικόν with the νοητικόν, or its practical aspect. If thought belonged to the αἰσθητικόν, then 'αἰσθητικόν' and 'νοητικόν' would be two designations for one subject, in precisely the way Aristotle in fact takes 'αἰσθητικόν' and 'φανταστικόν' to be. That this is *not* his view is clear from the *De Insomniis* and the *De Memoria*. He begins the *De Insomniis* by asking, as we have seen, whether dreaming belongs to the part concerned with thinking (νοητικόν) or to the αἰσθητικόν. His answer is that it does *not* belong to the part responsible for belief and thought (*De Insomniis* 1, 459ᵃ8–9)—the νοητικόν, that is—but in fact to the perceiving part, with the qualification that it belongs to it in so far as it is concerned with *phantasia* (459ᵃ10–11, 21–2). In *De Memoria* 1, he notes that he is assigning memory, specifically *not* to either one of the intellectual parts (450ᵃ16–17), but to the part or aspect to which *phantasia* belongs (450ᵃ22–5). (For the moment, I am leaving aside the complication that since objects of thought are incidental objects of memory, memory belongs incidentally or derivatively also to the intellect. I shall shortly offer some comments on the role of the intellect in Aristotle's account of memory.)

Naturalia, Aristotle takes it to be part of the functioning of the perceptual part of the soul that connections or associations between sensory impressions are formed and maintained in the perceptual apparatus of suitably constituted animals.[8] As a result, he is in a position to explain an animal's ability to envisage prospects that are suitable to its present circumstances in terms of associations between sensory impressions. He may, for instance, hold that a suitably conditioned animal associates eating, presented to it by way of *phantasia*, with the look and the smell of animals of certain kinds, as presented to it by way of its senses.

In order to support, and give more content to, this suggestion, I shall discuss two texts from the *Parva Naturalia* in which Aristotle presents and employs a rather elaborate theory of ordered sequences of sensory impressions. These passages are chapter 3 of the *De Insomniis* and chapter 2 of the *De Memoria et Reminiscentia*. Both texts rely explicitly on the account of *phantasia* offered in *De Anima* 3.3.[9] According to that account, a *phantasia* is a change (κίνησις) which arises from the activity of perception; it is like the perception that produced it; and it can persist beyond the activity of perception that produced it (*De Anima* 3.3, 429ª1–5). As we shall see, both texts make clear that Aristotle takes the changes or, as I shall call them in what follows, affections[10] that constitute *phantasiai* to be in some way or other retained or preserved in the animal's perceptual apparatus.[11]

Both texts, moreover, present theories according to which it is, in suitably constituted animals, part of the functioning of the perceptual part of their souls that sensory affections are preserved in their perceptual apparatus in an orderly way, with dispositions obtaining among them to the effect that specific representations tend to become active together with, or to be followed by, other specific representations. As a result, Aristotle can account for a remarkable degree of order in the mental lives of non-human animals. Perceptual experience, he is in a position to hold, can bring it about that *phantasiai* are activated in an animal's perceptual apparatus when and as appropriate, and that *phantasiai* form ordered sequences of indeterminate duration and complexity. All of this may happen, he can add, without thought being involved *in any way at all*. The two texts present a coherent and relatively detailed view of the affections that constitute *phantasiai*, and of what accounts for the order which sequences of such affections may

---

[8] As Beare saw, the texts in question contain Aristotle's version of the 'association of ideas': *Greek Theories of Elementary Cognition from Alcmaeon to Aristotle* (Oxford: Oxford University Press, 1906), 306, 318.

[9] References to *De Anima* 3.3 are at *De Insomniis* 1, 459ª14–18, and at *De Memoria et Reminiscentia* 1, 449ᵇ30–1.

[10] Aristotle speaks both of changes and of affections (πάθος): *De Insomniis* 2, 459ª26, ᵇ5; *De Memoria* 1, 450ᵇ5, 12, 18.

[11] *De Insomniis* 2, 459ª26–7; ᵇ5–7; 3, 462ª9: ἐν τοῖς αἰσθητηρίοις ('in the sense-organs'). Cf. *De Memoria* 1, 450ª28–9: ἐν τῇ ψυχῇ καὶ τῷ μορίῳ τοῦ σώματος τῷ ἔχοντι αὐτήν ('in the soul and in the ensouled part of the body'); 2, 453ª24: περὶ τὸν αἰσθητικὸν τόπον ('around the place concerned with perception'). Note also *De Anima* 1.4, 408ᵇ17–18: recollection involves changes and 'states of rest' (μονάς) in the sense-organs (ἐν τοῖς αἰσθητηρίοις).

exhibit. For our purposes, the two texts complement each other rather nicely. In the *De Insomniis*, Aristotle goes into considerable detail concerning the material basis and underlying physiology of *phantasia*. In the *De Memoria et Reminiscentia*, he makes some very interesting remarks about what accounts for the order which sequences of sensory affections tend to exhibit.

I shall begin with chapter 3 of the *De Insomniis*. By the time we get to that chapter, Aristotle has answered the question which the *De Insomniis* begins by asking, namely what part of the soul it is to which dreams belong. His answer, as we have seen already, is that they belong to the perceptual part, in so far as it is responsible for *phantasiai*. For dreams, he holds, are *phantasiai* of a certain kind. He has also restated, and in fact amplified somewhat, the account of *phantasia* offered in *De Anima* 3.3. He has added to that account that the affections that constitute *phantasiai* are *qualitative* changes, caused by the qualitative changes that constitute perceptions (459^{b}1–7). Moreover, in chapter 3 itself he adds that these affections, or at least the active ones among them, are ongoing disturbances in the animal's perceptual apparatus: 'We must suppose that like the little eddies that form in rivers, so each of the changes [sc. sensory affections] occurs continuously (γίνεσθαι συνεχῶς). Often they remain in the same way. Often they are broken down into other shapes because of collisions' (*De Insomniis* 3, 461^{a}8–11). We should note that the retention of such affections requires that disturbances created by acts of perception are in some way or other preserved in the animal's perceptual apparatus.[12] These disturbances, moreover, are contentful. As they arrive at the central organ of perception—the heart, that is (*De Iuventute* 3, 469^{a}5–7)—they generate sensory experiences:

In blooded animals, as the blood becomes calm and separated out, the change belonging to percepts[13] from each sense-organ is preserved (σῳζομένη). This makes dreams connected (εἰρόμενα),[14] makes things appear to the dreamer, and brings it about that they seem to see on account of the changes descending from sight, to hear on account of those coming from hearing, and so on with those that proceed from the other organs. For also when one is awake, it is because of the change from there arriving at the starting point [sc. the central organ of perception] that one seems to be seeing, hearing, and perceiving.　(*De Insomniis* 3, 461^{a}25–^{b}1)[15]

---

[12] It is worth pointing out the striking closeness in conception between Aristotle's *phantasiai* and memory in Plato's *Philebus*. According to the *Philebus*, perceptions are contentful disturbances (σεισμοί) undergone jointly by body and soul (*Philebus* 33 D 5, E 11; note also πάθος at 34 A 3 and κίνησις at 34 A 4); and memory is the preservation (σωτηρία) of such disturbances (34 A 10–11).

[13] τῶν αἰσθημάτων ἡ κίνησις at 461^{a}26 is, I take it, a shorter expression for αἱ ὑπόλοιποι κινήσεις αἱ συμβαίνουσαι ἀπὸ τῶν αἰσθημάτων at 461^{a}18–19. What Aristotle has in mind is something that can be thought of either as one complex disturbance or as any number of interrelated disturbances that jointly travel from the peripheral sense-organs to the central organ of perception.

[14] Like Ross, Beare in J. Barnes (ed.), *The Complete Works of Aristotle*, and Gallop, I accept Lulofs's conjecture εἰρόμενά at 461^{a}27.

[15] My translations from the *De Insomniis* are indebted to those by Beare, in Barnes (ed.), *The Complete Works of Aristotle*, and by Gallop, in *Aristotle on Sleep and Dreams*.

One phenomenon in which Aristotle is interested is the contrast between unconnected, disorderly dreams and dreams that are well connected and life-like. His explanation of that contrast is that the heat associated with the activity of digestion generates large-scale disturbances in the relevant parts of the body, which can interfere with the more delicate disturbances that carry the contents of dreams (461ª14–25). It is in the blood of suitably constituted animals, he holds, that contentful affections originally created by acts of perception are preserved.[16] What he says suggests that he takes such affections to be preserved primarily in the blood located in the peripheral sense-organs.[17] In sleep, much of that blood travels to the heart, carrying with it affections that are contained in it. When the blood around the heart is agitated by the large-scale disturbances of digestion, the contentful affections travelling from the peripheral sense-organs to the heart may be altogether destroyed, or they may be thrown into disarray—for instance, by being broken up in collisions—so that disorderly and unconnected dreams ensue. By contrast, when the blood around the heart is relatively calm, the affections travelling to the heart may be preserved in their order and complexity, in which case they generate dreams that are coherent and life-like. Such dreams may present to the dreamer, not monstrosities, but people he or she knows,[18] or the actions and pursuits of their waking lives.[19] 'When someone is asleep', Aristotle adds,

as most of the blood travels down to its source, the changes present within it—some potentially, some actively—travel down with it. They are so disposed that in *this* change, *that* one will emerge from the blood, and as *this* one perishes, *that* one.[20] They are disposed towards one another (καὶ πρὸς ἀλλήλας δὴ ἔχουσιν) like the artificial frogs that rise to the surface of water as salt is being dissolved.[21] In a similar way, these changes are in us potentially, and become active when what arrests them is relaxed. And as they are released, they are active in the little blood that remains in the sense-organs, taking on a resemblance, as cloud-shapes do, which in their rapid changes we liken to humans and centaurs. Each of them is, as has been said, a remnant of a percept in activity (ὑπόλειμμα τοῦ ἐν τῇ

---

[16] This is not to say that on Aristotle's view the blood itself receives and preserves the affections in question. His view rather seems to be that it is *pneuma* contained in the blood that is the bearer of sensory affections. F. Solmsen, 'Greek philosophy and the discovery of the nerves', *Museum Helveticum*, 18 (1961), 172–8, and G. Freudenthal, *Aristotle's Theory of Material Substance: Heat and Pneuma, Form and Soul* (Oxford: Clarendon Press, 1995), 130–4, offer detailed discussions of this point.

[17] Note *De Insomniis* 2, 459ª24–8; ἐν τοῖς ὄμμασιν ('in the eyes'), 459ᵇ10–11; 3, 461ᵇ16–21.

[18] Coriscus, for example: 462ª2–8.

[19] *De Divinatione per Somnum* 1, 463ª23–7: 'when we are about to do something, or are in the middle of doing something, or have done something, it often happens that in dreams we find ourselves with these acts and find ourselves doing them—the reason being that the change [sc. the sensory affection that constitutes the *phantasia* in question] happens to have its path prepared (προω-δοποιημένη) as a result of our daytime beginnings.'

[20] οὕτω δ' ἔχουσιν ὥστε ἐν τῇ κινήσει τῃδὶ ἥδε ἐπιπολάσει ἐξ αὐτοῦ ἡ κίνησις, ἂν δ' αὕτη φθαρῇ, ἥδε.

[21] According to Sophonias, 37, 12–24, and Michael of Ephesus, 72, 8–19, Aristotle has in mind a number of wooden frogs that are buried in layers of salt one on top of the other. As water is added and the salt dissolves, one frog after another rises and, in rising, becomes visible.

ἐνεργείᾳ αἰσθήματος); and when the real percept has departed, it persists, and it is true that it is like Coriscus, but is not Coriscus.   (*De Insomniis* 3, 461ᵇ11–24)

The passage presents a remarkably elaborate theory of sensory affections. They are in the perceptual apparatus either potentially or actively. Active affections, I take it, are ongoing contentful disturbances. Potential affections are potentialities for such disturbances. They are arrested in some way or other, and they become active when what arrests them is removed or relaxed. Moreover, Aristotle plainly thinks that sensory affections are, or tend to be, *ordered* in certain ways, so that the activity of one particular affection is followed by the activity of another particular affection, which is followed by the activity of yet another one, and so forth.²² This is important for his account of dreaming, I suggest, because he wants to explain why dreams can represent, in a well-connected and life-like manner, complex events and processes that unfold over considerable periods of time, as when a builder dreams of building a house, or a sculptor of making a statue (cf. *De Divinatione per Somnum* 1, 463ᵃ21–30). If Aristotle's account is to be able to explain the occurrence of *such* dreams, he plainly needs to allow, not only that affections produced by acts of perception can be preserved and re-enacted, but also that the order in which such affections are received can be preserved and re-enacted. This, I submit, is exactly what he does allow in our passage.

Now, it is worth emphasizing that having dreams, no matter how complex and elaborate they may be, is not, according to Aristotle's theory, an exercise of the capacity for thinking. Nor does he think that dreams are limited to humans. He evidently thinks that some of the brute animals have dreams.²³ In fact, his explanation of connected dreams is meant to apply, not only to humans, but to blooded animals in general,²⁴ or anyhow to those among them which are capable of dreaming. Aristotle's account distinguishes sharply between dreams themselves and thoughts about dreams that a dreaming person may have—for example, the thought that the experience in question is a dream (*De Insomniis* 3, 462ᵃ28–9; 462ᵃ5–7; cf. 1, 458ᵇ15–20; ᵇ25). Such thoughts, if and when they occur, belong

---

²² The sentence in which this becomes clear (461ᵇ13–15) is, I think, often under-translated. Consider, for instance, Gallop's translation in *Aristotle: On Sleep and Dreams*: 'They are so disposed that in any given movement, one movement will rise from it to the surface; and if that one perishes, then another will do so.' (Similarly Hett's Loeb translation, and Beare in *The Complete Works of Aristotle.*) According to this translation, Aristotle's point is that there is a steady flow of sensory affections in the perceptual apparatus, such that for any given one, there is another that follows it. However, this interpretation fails to give force to the demonstrative pronouns in Aristotle's Greek. (After all, he could have written, say, ἄλλη τις κίνησις instead of ἥδε ἡ κίνησις in line 14, and ἄλλη τις instead of ἥδε in line 15.) The present sentence should be compared with a passage from the *De Memoria* which, I take it, expresses the same idea of order obtaining among sensory affections: 'Acts of recollection happen because, naturally, *this* change (ἡ κίνησις ἥδε) occurs after *that* one (τήνδε). If this is so by necessity, then plainly whenever one undergoes the earlier one, one will undergo the later one. If it is not by necessity but by habit, one will for the most part undergo the one after the other' (*De Memoria* 2, 451ᵇ10–14).

²³ *De Divinatione per Somnum* 2, 463ᵇ12–13; note also *De Insomniis* 1, 459ᵃ13–15.

²⁴ ἐν τοῖς ἐναίμοις ('in blooded animals'), *De Insomniis* 3, 461ᵃ25–6.

to the intellectual part of the soul. Dreams themselves, by contrast, Aristotle assigns to the perceptual part of the soul, in so far as it is concerned with *phantasia*. What this means is that having dreams, no matter how elaborate and 'connected' they may be, is on Aristotle's view an activity that, in and of itself, involves no more than suitable exercises of the capacity for *phantasia*. That capacity, moreover, belongs to the system of capacities that he refers to as the perceptual part of the soul.

Let me recapitulate. Aristotle thinks, I take it, that the *phantasiai* that constitute dreams can exhibit order, in that they can represent complex events and processes in a connected and life-like manner. He wants to explain the possibility of such order by appealing to dispositions among sensory affections which are in some way or other preserved in the animal's perceptual apparatus. Sensory affections, he holds, are preserved in the perceptual apparatus either as active, contentful disturbances or as potentialities for such disturbances. He takes it that such affections can, in suitable organisms, be preserved *in an orderly way*, so that the activity of one particular contentful disturbance in the animal's perceptual apparatus is, or tends to be, followed by the activity of another particular disturbance, which is or tends to be followed by the activity of another particular disturbance, and so forth. It must then be part of his psychological theory that animals capable of preserving sensory affections in an orderly way are constituted so that appropriate dispositions can be formed among sensory affections that may be preserved in their perceptual apparatus. Moreover, since at least some of the brute animals are, on his view, capable of having 'connected' dreams, his theory must make the preservation of order among sensory affections available to suitable kinds of non-human animals as well as to human beings.

We should now attempt to get a clearer view of the dispositions which Aristotle thinks can come to obtain among sensory affections in the perceptual apparatus of suitable kinds of animals. Does he offer an account of how it is that such dispositions are formed and maintained? It seems to me that we can extract at least some crucial parts of such an account from a few passages in the second chapter of the *De Memoria*.

The main topic of *De Memoria* 2 is recollecting (ἀνάμνησις, ἀναμιμνήσκεσθαι). This follows a discussion of remembering (μνήμη, μνημονεύειν, μεμνῆσθαι) in the first chapter. It is in discussing recollecting that Aristotle makes especially prominent use of his theory of ordered sequences of sensory affections. However, he also relies on that theory in specifying what is involved in remembering something. As we shall see, this turns out to be rather important for our purposes. Now it is not immediately obvious what Aristotle means either by remembering or by recollecting. Before we turn to chapter 2 and its discussion of recollection, then, I want to make some remarks about Aristotle's conception of remembering, and to draw attention to some aspects of the discussion in chapter 1 that it will be important to bear in mind as we approach chapter 2.

The objects of memory, Aristotle holds, are things that lie in the past.[25] More precisely, what can be remembered, he takes it, are things that one perceived or thought of in the past. And remembering something, he thinks, is not just a matter of having in mind something that you perceived or thought of in the past. It also involves being aware that you perceived or thought of this thing in the past (*De Memoria* 1, 449^{b}18–23; 450^{a}19–21). As a result, he takes it that when you are remembering, say, a forest fire, this involves not just the retrieval and re-enactment of sensory affections that were actively present in your perceptual apparatus at the time. It also involves your being aware, perhaps in a certain distinctive way, that you did perceive what is now being represented to you at some more or less specific time in the past, or at the very least at some time or other in the past (*De Memoria* 2, 452^{b}23–453^{a}4).

It is worth noting that this conception of memory is cognitively more demanding than Plato's in the *Philebus*, even just so far as perceptual memory is concerned. In the *Philebus*, memory (μνήμη, μεμνῆσθαι) is defined simply as the preservation of perception (34 A 10–11). One way in which memory, so understood, is employed is in putting a thirsty or otherwise depleted animal in cognitive contact with the appropriate type of replenishment, so as to enable the animal to form a desire. Socrates offers no indication that such exercises of memory as are required for the formation of desire must involve not only a re-enactment of a previously received sensory affection, but also some kind of awareness of having had past dealings with the thing in question. Plato, in the *Philebus*, seems to regard the mere re-enactment of a sensory affection preserved by the soul as an exercise of memory. Aristotle distinguishes between such mere re-enactment and re-enactment accompanied by awareness of past interaction with the thing in question. He regards only the latter as amounting to an act of remembering. The former he treats as a case of *phantasia*.

This distinction is made close to the end of chapter 1, where Aristotle responds to the difficulty of how it can be that what is remembered is not a sensory affection or appearance that, at the time, is actively present to the animal,[26] but the absent object from which that affection or appearance derives (450^{a}25–7; 450^{b}11–15). A picture of, say, the Eiffel Tower is both a picture in its own right and a representation, or 'likeness', of the Eiffel Tower. You can observe it all by itself and

---

[25] ἡ δὲ μνήμη τοῦ γενομένου ('memory is of the past'): 449^{b}15, 27–8.

[26] That what one remembers might be sensory affections preserved in one's perceptual apparatus is so abstruse a thought that I hesitate to attribute it to Aristotle even for purposes of articulating an *aporia*. Aristotle plainly uses the word φάντασμα ('*phantasia*') to refer both to sensory affections preserved in an animal's perceptual apparatus (e.g. at *De Memoria* 1, 450^{b}10) and to appearances which he takes to be involved in the active occurrence of such affections (e.g. ibid., 449^{b}31–450^{a}1, 451^{a}10). I am inclined to think, partly on the basis of the present passage, that he uses the related terminology of πάθος ('affection'), τύπος ('impression'), and the like, in the same twofold way. If so, it is open to us to interpret the difficulty discussed at 450^{b}11–451^{a}17 as dealing with the question of whether one remembers appearances that are present to one's mind at the time, or absent objects from which such appearances derive. This is a good question to ask, and Aristotle's subsequent discussion seems to me to offer a plausible and interesting answer to it.

simply as the picture it is. But you can also look at it as a representation of the Eiffel Tower. Likewise, Aristotle suggests, a *phantasia* that is involved in an act of remembering is something all by itself (αὐτό τι καθ᾽ αὑτό), and it is at the same time a representation of the thing, now absent, from which it derives (450ᵇ20–7). Correspondingly, he distinguishes between two ways of employing a *phantasia*. The soul, he thinks, can attend to the appearance involved in a given *phantasia* all by itself and simply as the appearance it is; but it can also employ a suitable *phantasia* as a representation, or 'likeness', of the particular thing from which it derives (450ᵇ27–451ᵃ2). Aristotle regards what occurs in the former case as merely an act of *phantasia*, and only what occurs in the latter case as an act of remembering.

Now, it should be clear that both ways of employing a *phantasia* involve having experiences with representational content.[27] Even to have an ordinary *phantasia* of, say, a forest fire is to have a forest fire represented to one in some way or other. *Remembering* some forest fire, as Aristotle thinks of it, goes beyond such representation. It is not just a matter of having a forest fire represented to one. It also involves being aware, perhaps in a certain distinctive way, that what is represented to one is something that one did perceive at some time in the past. Having articulated the notion of employing a *phantasia* as a representation of what it derives from, Aristotle is ready to say what he takes remembering to be: the having of a *phantasia* as a representation of the thing it derives from (φαντάσματος, ὡς εἰκόνος οὗ φάντασμα, ἕξις).[28] That is to say I take it, that remembering something is a matter of having a *phantasia* in a way that involves being aware, perhaps in a certain way, that what is represented to one is something that one perceived or otherwise experienced at some more or less specific time in the past, or at least at some time or other in the past.

Remembering, Aristotle holds, belongs to the perceptual part of the soul, in so far as it is responsible for *phantasia*.[29] This answers the last one of the three questions about remembering that the *De Memoria* begins by asking: in virtue of what part of the soul does remembering occur (449ᵇ4–5)? What it means is that remembering is, like dreaming, an exercise of the capacity for *phantasia*, which, as we have seen already, is part of the system of capacities that is the perceptual part of the soul. Given that Aristotle takes remembering to be a matter of utilizing sensory impressions in a certain way, one can readily see why he assigns the activity of remembering, via the capacity for *phantasia*, to the perceptual part of the soul. However, although the *phantasiai* that Aristotle takes to be involved in remembering

---

[27] I agree here with S. Everson, *Aristotle on Perception*, 196.

[28] I assume that what Aristotle is meaning to define is the *activity* of remembering (ἐνεργεῖν κατὰ τὸ μνημονεύειν, ἐνεργεῖν τῇ μνήμῃ), since activities are definitionally prior to capacities (*De Anima* 2.4, 415ᵃ18–20). In his definition of remembering, Aristotle may be using the word ἕξις in precisely the way Plato uses the same word in the *Theaetetus*' aviary simile. There, ἕξις is contrasted with κτῆσις (*Theaetetus* 197 B 1–4). The latter denotes possession; the former is illustrated by having a cloak on, and by holding a bird in one's hand. Note also the aorists σχῇ at *De Memoria* 1, 449ᵇ19, and σχεῖν at *Theaetetus* 197 C 9; this means something like 'to get hold of'.

[29] *De Memoria* 1, 450ᵃ22–3: τίνος μὲν οὖν τῶν τῆς ψυχῆς ἐστι μνήμη, φανερόν, ὅτι οὗπερ καὶ ἡ φαντασία ('it is clear then which part of the soul memory belongs to: the part that *phantasia* belongs to as well'). Cf. 451ᵃ16–17.

can represent an enormous variety of things, they nonetheless are subject to the limitation that they are *sensory* representations. They cannot in themselves provide cognitive contact with intelligibles such as, for instance, essences or natures.[30] At the same time, Aristotle's discussion from the start includes references to remembering, not only perceptibles, but intelligibles as well—for example, remembering some object of study (*De Memoria* 1, 449ᵇ15–23). However, if remembering in general is a matter of utilizing sensory impressions in a certain way, it is not clear how anyone can possibly remember, say, what it is to be a human being. Somewhat surprisingly, Aristotle does not explicitly flag this as a difficulty, but he does attempt to answer the question.

Every act of the human intellect, he holds, involves and requires representing features such as magnitude and time, features whose representation involves and requires suitable exercises of the capacity for *phantasia*. It is at least part of the idea that thinking anything at all, anyhow for thinkers like us, requires visualizing the objects of thought by means of the sensory imagination.[31] The visualizations in question are *phantasiai*. Aristotle rather naturally extends this idea and claims that visualizing is required, not only for grasping an object of thought in the first place, but also for subsequent acts of remembering the thing in question: 'memory also of intelligibles', he says, 'does not occur without a *phantasia*' (450ᵃ12–13). This makes acts of *phantasia* necessary for remembering intelligibles. Aristotle seems to think, however, that it also establishes that remembering in general belongs in its own right (καθ' αὑτό) to the perceptual part of the soul, in so far as it is responsible for *phantasia*, and at best incidentally to the intellect (450ᵃ13–14). In any case, Aristotle plainly does hold that remembering in general belongs in its own right to the perceptual part of the soul, and incidentally to the intellect. He also holds, relatedly, that the proper objects of memory are, as he puts it, things of which there is *phantasia*[32]—by which, I take it, he means things that *phantasia* can represent.[33] Things that cannot be grasped without *phantasia*, he adds, are incidental objects of memory. In the context, it is clear that the latter items are meant to be intelligibles. They cannot themselves be represented by the sensory affections that constitute *phantasiai*, but their grasp by the intellect requires appropriate acts of *phantasia*.

---

[30] This is because they are in themselves simply exercises of sensory capacities. They belong to the perceptual part of the soul, after all. Only acts of the intellect can provide cognitive contact with intelligibles.

[31] Cf. *De Memoria* 1, 450ᵃ4–5: καὶ ὁ νοῶν ὡσαύτως, κἂν μὴ ποσὸν νοῇ, τίθεται πρὸ ὀμμάτων ποσόν ('in the same way a person who is thinking, even if he is not thinking of something with a size, places something with a size before his eyes').

[32] 450ᵃ23–5: ἐστι μνημονευτὰ καθ' αὑτὰ μὲν ὧν ἐστι φαντασία, κατὰ συμβεβηκὸς δὲ ὅσα μὴ ἄνευ φαντασίας ('things of which there is *phantasia* are objects of memory in their own right; things which are not grasped without *phantasia* are incidental objects of memory').

[33] I should perhaps note that in writing of *phantasia* being able or unable to represent something or other, I am meaning to convey the idea that it is able or unable to provide cognitive contact with the item in question, the way sight, for instance, is able to provide cognitive contact with colours but not with flavours.

What Aristotle appears to have in mind, then, is something like this. It is after all possible to remember intelligibles, such as, for instance, what it is to be a human being. Intelligibles, however, are not remembered in their own right. Remembering intelligibles is always parasitic on remembering things that are remembered in their own right, and these are things that are represented by *phantasia*. If this is Aristotle's view, as it seems to be, he will say that what actually happens whenever someone remembers an intelligible object is that he or she in the first place remembers something that is represented by *phantasia*, and that memory *happens to be accompanied* by an act of the intellect that is the thought of the object in question, perhaps in that this act of the intellect is prompted by the relevant exercise of *phantasia*. The upshot is that things that can be represented by *phantasia* can be remembered directly and immediately, whereas intelligibles can only be remembered indirectly, in a way that is mediated by remembering things that are represented by *phantasia*. If that is Aristotle's picture, this makes at least some sense of his view that intelligibles are incidental objects of memory, and that remembering belongs to the intellect incidentally. For on that picture remembering intelligibles will always accompany, and depend on, remembering things that are represented by *phantasia*, and such acts of the intellect as may be involved in remembering will always accompany, and depend on, appropriate acts of *phantasia*.

The question remains, of course, why Aristotle adopts a picture along these lines. His adoption of some such picture is motivated, I suggest, by his acceptance of the following premisses.

(1) The proper objects of memory are things which are capable of being represented by representational items (states, processes, or whatever) which can be preserved in the animal's organism.
(2) Sensory affections are the only sort of representational items that can be preserved in an animal's organism.
(3) Sensory affections cannot represent intelligibles.

These premisses entail the conclusion that intelligibles are not among the proper objects of memory. To accept premiss (1) is to adopt a rather natural view of the functioning of memory as a matter of storing and retrieving representational items of some sort or other. Committing something to memory, on that view, crucially involves forming and retaining some sort of representation of it, and remembering it involves retrieving that representation and employing it in a certain way. As we have seen, Aristotle does embrace a view of memory along these lines.[34]

[34] The view he adopts is, incidentally, indebted to Platonic antecedents. In writing, at 450ª29–32, of 'something like a painting' (οἷον ζωγράφημά τι) being retained in the living organism, and of 'something like an imprint' (οἷον τύπον τινά) being stamped in the organism (ἐνσημαίνεται), the way seals are imprinted with signet rings (καθάπερ οἱ σφραγιζόμενοι τοῖς δακτυλίοις), Aristotle is echoing not only the *Philebus*' simile of the painter in the soul, but also the *Theaetetus*' wax block model of memory and knowledge. According to the latter, we have in our souls a block of wax, and 'we make impressions (ἀποτυποῦσθαι) upon this of everything

Given Aristotle's psychological theory, moreover, the representational items in question could either be thoughts or sensory affections. Now, we have seen that Aristotle takes sensory affections to be contentful modifications in the hylomorphic structure that is the animal's perceptual apparatus. There is nothing mysterious about how such modifications can be preserved indefinitely in the animal's perceptual apparatus. By contrast, Aristotle holds that there is no such thing as a bodily organ or apparatus of thought (*De Anima* 3.4, 429ª22–7). Thoughts are not, on his view, modifications of any kind in a bodily structure, nor are they constituted by such modifications. Since he does not take them to reside in a bodily structure in the first place, he cannot make sense of their *preservation* in a bodily structure.

On Aristotle's view, then, sensory affections are the only sort of representational item that can be preserved in the animal's organism. However, since sensory affections cannot represent intelligibles, Aristotle is compelled to accept that intelligibles are not among the proper objects of memory. He does want to say, though, that it is in a way possible to remember intelligibles. To show how, he resorts to the rather ingenious idea that intelligibles are incidental objects of memory. When you remember, say, the proof of a geometrical theorem which you studied the day before yesterday, what actually happens, Aristotle might say, is that you remember how you visualized the items mentioned in the proof (as being extended objects of such-and-such sizes and shapes) as well as how you visualized the operations performed on them (cutting them in halves, and the like). These memories are not memories *of the proof itself.* But they are, or may well be, accompanied by the thought of the proof itself, perhaps in that they may prompt an intellectual act that is the thought of the proof. If so, Aristotle can say that in a way you are remembering the proof. You are remembering it incidentally, because you are remembering how you visualized it, and that memory happens to be accompanied by the thought of the proof itself.

We should now turn to chapter 2 and its discussion of recollecting (τὸ ἀναμιμνήσκεσθαι). I begin with some linguistic points. *Anamimnēskein* is a transitive verb, meaning 'to remind'. The present infinitive *anamimnēskesthai* can be construed either as middle, 'to remind oneself, to recollect', or as passive, 'to be reminded'. Now, if one looks at the passages in the *Meno* and the *Phaedo* in which Plato presents and discusses his so-called theory of recollection,[35] it becomes clear that he strongly tends to use the infinitive form *anamimnēskesthai* in contexts in which someone actively sets out to call something to mind (middle rather than

we wish to remember among the things we have seen or heard or thought of ourselves; we hold the wax under our perceptions and thoughts and take a stamp from them, in the way we take the imprints of signet rings (ὥσπερ δακτυλίων σημεῖα ἐνσημαινομένους)' (*Theaetetus* 191 D 4–8). Aristotle adopts Plato's picture with two significant modifications. First, the generation of imprints does not depend on what one wishes to remember, but occurs simply as a matter of the ordinary functioning of the animal's cognitive apparatus. Secondly, there are, for Aristotle, no imprints of *thoughts* (450ª27–32).

35 *Meno* 81 C 5–86 C 2; *Phaedo* 72 E 1–77 A 5.

passive construal),³⁶ rather than contexts in which it just so happens that someone is reminded of something without having tried to call the thing in question to mind.³⁷ For the latter type of case, Plato uses expressions that are unambiguously passive, like *anamnēsthēnai*, whenever such expressions are available.³⁸ At the same time, it is noteworthy that Plato uses the noun *anamnēsis* both in the middle sense of recollecting and in the passive sense of being reminded.³⁹ Against that background and in light of the fact that Aristotle is echoing Plato's characterization of recollection,⁴⁰ it is reasonable to expect that when Aristotle proposes to discuss *to anamimnēskesthai*, he has in mind deliberately recollecting something, as opposed to cases in which it just so happens that something reminds someone of something else. This expectation is in fact fully borne out by the discussion in *De Memoria* 2.

Here is Aristotle's statement of what he takes recollecting to be: 'When someone recovers (ἀναλαμβάνῃ) a piece of knowledge, a perception, or that thing the having of which we said is memory, that recovery, when it occurs, is recollecting one of the things mentioned; and it turns out that this is followed by remembering and memory'⁴¹ (*De Memoria* 2, 451ᵇ2–6). This is a preliminary statement only, because he takes it to be true only with a qualification that he is not yet in a position to articulate fully. Not every case of recovering a piece of knowledge, a perception, or a *phantasia* is, he thinks, a case of recollecting. For someone can, for instance, recover a piece of knowledge, not by recollecting it, but by learning the thing in question all

---

³⁶ Note, for example, *Meno* 85 D 6–7, where Socrates asks: τὸ δὲ ἀναλαμβάνειν αὐτὸν ἐν αὑτῷ ἐπιστήμην οὐκ ἀναμιμνῄσκεσθαί ἐστιν; ('Is not one's own recovery of knowledge in oneself recollection?') Also 86 B 4: ἐπιχειρεῖν ζητεῖν καὶ ἀναμιμνῄσκεσθαι ('try to seek out and recollect'). Cf. *Phaedo* 75 E 2–7.

³⁷ This point is missed entirely by Sorabji, *Aristotle on Memory*, 40–1.

³⁸ For example, *Phaedo* 73 D 10–11: Σιμμίαν τις ἰδὼν πολλάκις Κέβητος ἀνεμνήσθη ('on seeing Simmias, one is often put in mind of Cebes'); E 6–7: καὶ Σιμμίαν ἰδόντα γεγραμμένον Κέβητος ἀναμνησθῆναι ('on seeing a picture of Simmias, [someone may] be reminded of Cebes'). At *Phaedo* 73 C 6–74 A 7, Socrates discusses cases of one thing reminding someone of another thing, in order to make certain points that he takes to apply to every case of ἀνάμνησις, crucially including active, deliberate recollection. At that stage of the discussion, Socrates is notably careful in using unambiguously passive forms of ἀναμιμνῄσκειν whenever they are available. The only ambiguous form is ἀναμιμνῄσκεται at 74 A 5. This is present tense indicative, where no unambiguously passive form is available. Cf. Aristotle, *Nicomachean Ethics* 9.4, 1166ᵇ15 (a passage mentioned by Sorabji, *Aristotle on Memory*, 99), where Aristotle says that bad people avoid being alone, because while alone they are reminded of many distressing things (ἀναμιμνῄσκονται γὰρ πολλῶν καὶ δυσχερῶν).

³⁹ The noun is to be construed in the middle sense in the slogan that learning is recollection. Passive uses are in evidence at *Phaedo* 73 D 10, E 1, and 74 A 2. The noun is clearly used in the middle sense at *De Memoria* 2, 453ᵃ15. There is an interesting passive use at *Nicomachean Ethics* 3.10, 1118ᵃ12–13: self-indulgent people take pleasure in the smells of perfumes and tasty dishes, because 'through these they are reminded of the objects of their appetites' (διὰ τούτων ἀνάμνησις γίνεται αὐτοῖς τῶν ἐπιθυμημάτων).

⁴⁰ To recollect is to recover knowledge (ἀναλαμβάνειν . . . ἐπιστήμην): *Meno* 85 D 6–7; *Phaedo* 75 E 4; *De Memoria* 2, 451ᵇ2–3. Cf. also *Philebus* 34 B 6–8.

⁴¹ With all extant manuscripts, I read τὸ rather than τῷ at 451ᵇ5. Ross and Sorabji follow Michael (*c.* AD 1090) and Sophonias (*c.* AD 1300) in reading the latter. Ross's reason for rejecting the reading of the manuscripts is that it makes μνήμην 'a mere repetition' of μνημονεύειν. This is true, but in view of the same kind of repetition at 449ᵇ4, 451ᵃ14–15, and 453ᵇ8–9, it is no good reason to abandon the reading of all manuscripts.

over again. Recollecting, Aristotle says somewhat obscurely, requires the presence within of a principle over and above that required for learning (451ᵇ9–10).

Before he can offer his full statement of what distinguishes recollecting from relearning, he must first present his theory of ordered sequences of sensory affections. Recollecting occurs, he holds, because sensory affections form ordered sequences, so that the active occurrence of some particular contentful disturbance in one's perceptual apparatus tends to be followed by the active occurrence of another such disturbance:

Acts of recollection (αἱ ἀναμνήσεις) happen because, naturally, *this* change [sc. sensory affection] occurs after *that* one (ἐπειδὴ πέφυκεν ἡ κίνησις ἥδε γενέσθαι μετὰ τήνδε). If this is so by necessity, then plainly whenever one undergoes the earlier one, one will undergo the later one. If it is not by necessity but by habit, one will for the most part undergo the one after the other. (It is a fact that some changes become more habitual with just one occurrence than others that have occurred many times. And this is why after seeing some things once, we remember better than we do after seeing other things many times.) In recollecting, then, we undergo some one or other of the earlier changes, until we undergo the one that is habitually followed by the change in question. It is for this reason also that we hunt for (θηρεύομεν)⁴² that which follows in the sequence (τὸ ἐφεξῆς), beginning in thought (νοήσαντες) with the now or with something else, and with something similar to the thing in question, something opposite to it, or something proximate to it (τοῦ σύνεγγυς). Recollection occurs for this reason: for the changes that belong to these things are in some cases the same ones, in other cases they occur together, in yet other cases the one change contains part of the other, so that after the earlier one only a little remains to be undergone. It is in this way, then, that people search, but also without searching, they are reminded in this way,⁴³ when the change in question occurs after some other one. And for the most part the change in question does occur after the occurrence of other changes of the kinds we mentioned [sc. affections belonging to items similar, opposite, or proximate to the item represented or called to mind by the affection in question].   (*De Memoria* 2, 451ᵇ10–25)⁴⁴

⁴² This is another Platonic echo, this time from the *Theaetetus*' aviary model: 197 D 1, 198 A 2, A 7.

⁴³ ζητοῦσι μὲν οὖν οὕτω, καὶ μὴ ζητοῦντες δ᾽ οὕτως ἀναμιμνήσκονται. The word order suggests strongly that Aristotle intends a contrast between ζητοῦσι ('people search') and μὴ ζητοῦντες ('without searching') rather than, as Sorabji takes it, between 'people search in this way' and 'without searching *in this way*'. (See Kühner–Gerth, *Ausführliche Grammatik der Griechischen Sprache, Zweiter Teil: Satzlehre* (Hannover: Hahnsche Buchandlung, 1904), §528.). Beare takes the sentence the way I do; Sorabji, 99, admits that his reading strains the Greek. Sorabji's problem is that if the text is read in the way it is most natural to read it, Aristotle seems to speak of *recollecting without searching*. But he repeatedly characterizes recollecting as a matter of searching (esp. 453ᵃ15–16; cf. 451ᵇ30, 452ᵃ8, and 453ᵃ12). However, ἀναμιμνήσκονται need not be construed as middle; it can just as naturally be read as passive. Sophonias (10, 1–2), for what it is worth, takes the second clause to describe a case of *being reminded* without having searched: ὅταν δὲ μὴ ζητοῦσιν ἀναμνησθῆναι τοῦ γένηται (note the passive!). The idea, I take it, is this. People search *in this way*: namely by thinking of something or other that is somehow related to the thing they are searching for—for example, something similar, opposite, or proximate to it. *In this way*, too, people, may be reminded of something without searching for it: by thinking of something or other that is somehow related to the thing in question—for example, by being similar, opposite, or proximate to it.

⁴⁴ My translations from the *De Memoria* are indebted to those by Beare, in Barnes (ed.), *The Complete Works of Aristotle*, and by Sorabji, *Aristotle on Memory*.

As we have seen, Aristotle's main topic in the chapter is recollecting, which is a matter of deliberately recalling something or other. In the passage just quoted, he is focusing on recollecting, but he also addresses being reminded of something without seeking to recall it. His theory of ordered sequences of sensory affections is, I take it, meant to explain both the fact that one thing frequently reminds us of another, and the fact that by means of suitable mental activity we sometimes manage to recollect things that we perceived or thought of in the past, but that do not now come to mind right away or without effort.

Aristotle begins by saying that the order that obtains among sensory affections is either necessary or habitual. In the subsequent discussion only habit recurs (at 451^{b}28–30 and at 452^{b}26–8). Necessity seems to drop out of consideration. It is, in any case, not easy to see how necessity might be relevant.[45] Aristotle takes it, moreover, that we tend to associate things with one another on the basis of such relations as similarity, opposition, and proximity (by which he probably means both spatial and temporal proximity). He does not address the question of how habituation and such patterns of association are interrelated. He may well think that such patterns are themselves at least in part due to habituation, in that we are used to thinking of opposites together, or to hearing thunder after seeing lightning. But he may also think that relations that obtain between suitable things can facilitate, or even bring about, the formation of habits of association, as when one comes to associate toads with frogs because they are rather similar. However that may be, it is clear that Aristotle is meaning to account for recollecting and being reminded by appealing to ordered sequences of sensory affections.[46] These are affections of the same kind as the ones that he mentions in *De Insomniis* 3. For the purposes of that text, he assumes that dispositions among sensory affections can be formed in the perceptual apparatus of suitable kinds of animals, so that active sensory affections can come to follow each other in orderly ways.[47] As we saw, he relies on that assumption in explaining how their dreams can be 'connected'. The present text adds significant detail to that picture. It says that the dispositions among sensory affections obtain either by necessity or as a result of habituation; and that sensory affections typically are so disposed that, at any rate so far as humans are concerned, things that are similar, opposite, and proximate to one another tend to be represented, or called to mind, together or in immediate succession.

[45] I shall offer a suggestion at the end of the chapter.

[46] This claim ought to be acceptable independently of my view that Aristotle is explicitly talking about being reminded at 451^{b}23–4. For also the series of associations employed in recollection will typically involve multiple cases of being reminded by something of something else (e.g. 452^{a}13–16).

[47] The *De Insomniis* comes after the *De Memoria* in Bekker's edition of Aristotle's works. This may well be in line with Aristotle's view about the order in which the two texts should be studied. The *De Sensu*, at 436^{a}5–17, sets out a programme of topics to be discussed which the *Parva Naturalia* follows loosely. In that order, memory comes right after sense-perception and precedes, among other things, sleep and waking. Dreaming, moreover, is announced as a topic to be discussed at the beginning of the *De Somno* (453^{b}17–20). There is some reason for thinking, then, that the *De Insomniis* takes as read the *De Memoria*'s rather more detailed statement of Aristotle's theory of orderly sequences of sensory affections.

A slightly later passage seems to offer a little more detail as to how things that are proximate to each other come to be associated with one another:

It is by habit that changes follow one another, *this* one after *that* one. And so when someone wants to recollect (ἀναμιμνήσκεσθαι), he will do this: he will seek to get hold of a starting point, after which the change in question will occur. And it is for this reason that from some starting point acts of recollection occur most swiftly and finely. For just as the things in question are related to one another in terms of one thing after another (ὡς γὰρ ἔχουσι τὰ πράγματα πρὸς ἄλληλα τῷ ἐφεξῆς), so also are the changes. (*De Memoria* 2, 451ᵇ28–452ᵃ2)

Aristotle thinks that we obtain sensory affections from interacting with perceptible and intelligible objects. These objects themselves exhibit order in various ways. Thunder comes after lightning, the sea after the sandy beach, the conclusion of an argument after its premisses. It is a fact about some kinds of animals, Aristotle holds, that they are able, not only to preserve sensory affections that they obtain from interacting with perceptible or intelligible objects, but also to retain these sensory affections in an orderly way, a way that reflects the order of the objects they derive from.

He is now ready to revisit the difference between recollecting and relearning:

Recollecting differs from relearning in that the person in question will be able in a certain way to be conveyed through himself (δυνήσεταί πως δι' αὐτοῦ κινηθῆναι) to what follows the starting point. When this ability is absent, and the person depends on someone or something else, he no longer remembers (οὐκέτι μέμνηται). It often happens that one is unable to be reminded, but with some searching one is able to, and finds what one is looking for. This occurs when one initiates many changes (κινοῦντι πολλά), until one initiates one that is such as to be followed by the thing in question. (*De Memoria* 2, 452ᵃ4–10)

Having presented his theory of ordered sequences of sensory affections, he can now give more content to his earlier remark that recollecting requires the presence within of a principle over and above that required for learning. What it requires, he takes it, is the presence in the person's perceptual apparatus of suitable sensory affections, and the existence of suitable dispositions among them, so that he or she will be able, by selecting an appropriate starting-point, to set off a sensory affection, or a series of such affections, so that the object in question will come to be present to his or her mind. I take it to be Aristotle's view, moreover, that where the object of recollection is intelligible rather than perceptible—say, a theorem or a definition—it will not itself be represented by the sensory affections that the person manages to excite, but those sensory affections will be accompanied by an intellectual act that is the thought of the relevant intelligible object.

It is worth pointing out that Aristotle's account contains the resources needed to distinguish recollecting, not only from relearning by being instructed, but also from relearning by rediscovering for oneself.[48] Suppose you once knew the proof of a geometrical theorem, but you subsequently forgot it. It so happens that you are unable to recollect it, but by utilizing your general knowledge of geometry you manage to work the proof out by yourself. In a way, you have recovered a piece of knowledge through yourself rather than through someone or something else. Aristotle can say, however, that you nonetheless did not *recollect* the proof because you were not 'conveyed' to it in the way that is distinctive of recollecting. For you were not conveyed all the way to it by a series of sensory affections preserved within you, so that some, or one, of these affections turned out to be accompanied by the intellectual grasp of the proof. Instead, you had to work the proof out by exercising other pieces of knowledge and hence by employing your intellect in ways other than the identification of an appropriate starting-point for recollection and the subsequent grasp of the proof itself.

Furthermore, it is important to note that, in distinguishing recollecting from relearning, Aristotle is making a fresh point about what is involved in remembering something. He says that when someone has lost the ability to be appropriately 'conveyed' to the active cognition of something or other, he or she no longer remembers the thing in question (452^a6-7). Now, what he has in mind in saying this is plainly not that in this case the person in question is not at that time performing an *act* of remembering. His point is rather that in this case the person has lost the acquired ability to remember the thing in question.[49] He also spells out what he takes to be involved in *having* the ability that we deny to someone when we say that he or she no longer remembers something or other: 'Remembering (τὸ μεμνῆσθαι) is the presence within one of the power that conveys one [sc. to the thing in question], so that one is conveyed to it from oneself *and from the changes one has within oneself, in the way described*'[50] (*De Memoria* 2, 452^a10-12). This characterization of what may be called dispositional memory[51] applies Aristotle's theory of ordered sequences of affections to memory and remembering. It is a rather complicated characterization, and it deserves careful attention. It characterizes the acquired ability to remember something as the presence within one of a power to bring about some change, or some changes. The exercise of that power results in one's being affected so that the object of memory is represented to one or is called to one's mind.

---

[48] Sorabji, *Aristotle on Memory*, 38–9, claims that Aristotle goes wrong in failing to recognize that one can relearn something through one's own efforts, 'and without depending on someone else'. On my view, that objection misfires. Aristotle does not, and need not, deny that one can relearn by oneself. He can gladly accept this, since he has the resources needed to distinguish recollecting from that kind of relearning, too.

[49] This acquired ability corresponds to the second potentiality, or first actuality, that is knowing something without contemplating it: *De Anima* 2.5, $417^a21-417^b2$; 2.1, 412^a22-3.

[50] τὸ γὰρ μεμνῆσθαί ἐστι τὸ ἐνεῖναι δύναμιν τὴν κινοῦσαν· τοῦτο δέ, ὥστ᾽ ἐξ αὐτοῦ καὶ ὧν ἔχει κινήσεων κινηθῆναι, ὥσπερ εἴρηται.

[51] The formulation is due to Sorabji, *Aristotle on Memory*, 1.

Now, Aristotle evidently does not think that having the acquired ability to remember, say, what Cebes looks like entails being able to perform a suitable act of remembering *whenever one pleases*. He thinks it happens frequently that one does not manage to activate dispositional memory. One might suppose that the case of a person who has dispositional memory but does not manage to activate it is a counterexample to Aristotle's chararacterization of dispositional memory. But this would be mistaken. His characterization of dispositional memory requires only that there is in fact some way in which it could be activated; it may be difficult for its bearer to identify that way. What he has in mind in the context is that there is some affection or other, say one that represents Cebes' companion Simmias, such that the active occurrence of *that* affection would be followed, or anyhow would tend to be followed, by the active occurrence of an affection that represents what Cebes looks like. The upshot is that Aristotle takes dispositional memory not only to involve sensory affections that are retained or preserved in the organism. He also takes it to involve—in many cases and perhaps in general—the existence of dispositions that obtain among those sensory affections, such that one specific sensory affection tends to become active together with, or in succession to, the activity of another specific sensory affection.

This, I submit, is a significant addition to the account of memory and remembering offered in chapter 1 of the *De Memoria*. In that chapter, Aristotle concentrates on the act of remembering, having little or nothing to say about dispositional memory. That chapter, moreover, has nothing to say about the question of how it is that representations that are retained in an organism are accessed and recalled. In other words, chapter 1 has nothing to say about the *transition* from having dispositional memory to the act of remembering. According to Aristotle's account, the perceptual apparatus of a suitably constituted and ordinarily developed animal will retain countless sensory affections. He tells us nothing, in *De Memoria* 1, about how and why it is that sometimes some of these countless affections come to be active in the animal's perceptual apparatus, so that the animal is remembering this or that particular thing.

Now, one might think that he takes it to be specifically by way of recollecting, as that is discussed in *De Memoria* 2, that representations retained in an organism are accessed and recalled. This, however, cannot be the whole story. First, recollecting, as he thinks of it, is a matter of deliberately recalling, and there obviously are many acts of remembering that do not involve deliberately recalling whatever the thing in question may be, as when you are remembering something because it just so happens that you are reminded of it by something else. Secondly, recollecting, as Aristotle thinks of it, is a matter of deliberately recalling in a rather specific way, namely by thinking of something else that, with some luck, puts one in mind of the thing in question.[52] So if you manage to call something to mind directly and

---

[52] Aristotle makes it very clear, throughout *De Memoria* 2, that what he thinks of as recollecting is always a matter of mentally proceeding *from something else* to the object of recollection: see, e.g., 451^{b}16–18, 18–22, 29–31, 452^{a}4–6, 8–10, 12–16, etc.

without first thinking of something else, as no doubt you sometimes do, this will not be a case of recollecting, as Aristotle thinks of it, at any rate for the purposes of *De Memoria* 2. In fact, his account of recollecting presupposes the ability to call something to mind directly, since the starting-points of many acts of recollection will be thoughts of things that one manages to call to mind directly.[53] Presumably, calling something to mind directly is supposed to be a matter simply of thinking of it, rather than of recollecting it. Thirdly, while Aristotle evidently attributes the ability to remember to some of the brute animals, he denies the ability to recollect to all of them:

> Recollecting differs from remembering not only with regard to time,[54] but also in that many of the other animals, too, have a share in remembering, whereas it may be said that, apart from humans, none of the known animals has a share in recollecting.[55] The reason is that recollecting is rather like a kind of reasoning (οἶον συλλογισμός τις). For the person who is recollecting reasons (συλλογίζεται) that he saw or heard the thing in question before, or that he was affected by it in some other such way, and recollecting is rather like conducting a search of some kind (οἶον ζήτησίς τις). To do that, however, naturally belongs only to creatures whose soul has a deliberative part as well. (And indeed deliberation, too, is a kind of reasoning.) (453ᵃ4–14)

Given how Aristotle conceives of recollecting, and how he discusses it throughout *De Memoria* 2, it is not difficult to see why he holds it to be limited to reasoning creatures. He seems to think that reason is involved in recollecting in at least two ways. First, anyone who sets out to recollect something or other believes that he or she did at some stage perceive or think of the thing in question, and Aristotle takes that belief to depend on some kind of grasp of reason. Thus I may believe that I went through Plato's argument for the tripartition of the soul, because I know that I studied book 4 of the *Republic*, and I also know that this is the text which contains that argument. Or I may believe that I heard Cebes' name at a dinner party last week, because I know that I was introduced to him by his companion Simmias. Aristotle's thought might simply be that while you are not actually remembering the thing in question, it could only be by way of some appropriate bit of reasoning that you are aware of having perceived or thought of it at some time in the past.

Secondly, once you start recollecting, you are, according to Aristotle's theory, conducting a search, or something rather like a search, for a representation that will represent the thing in question, or call it to mind (453ᵃ15–16). This will

---

[53] *De Memoria* 2, 451ᵇ18–19: διὸ καὶ τὸ ἐφεξῆς θηρεύομεν νοήσαντες ἀπὸ τοῦ νῦν ἢ ἄλλου τινός, καὶ ἀφ' ὁμοίου ἢ ἐναντίου ἢ τοῦ σύνεγγυς ('it is for this reason that we hunt for that which follows in the sequence, beginning in *thought* with the now or with something else, and with something similar to the thing in question, something opposite to it, or something proximate to it').

[54] What Aristotle has in mind, I take it, is that recollecting typically occurs some time after memory has first been established. This is because recollecting requires that the item in question has, so to speak, absented itself from one's mind, for example in that it has been forgotten, or simply in that one has not thought of it in a while. Cf. *De Memoria* 2, 451ᵃ31–ᵇ2.

[55] Aristotle offers a more confident statement of this view at *Historia Animalium* 1.1, 488ᵇ26.

require finding a suitable starting-point,[56] a thought that involves the occurrence of an active sensory affection, so that this affection is followed by another such affection that will represent or call to mind the object of recollection. Aristotle, naturally enough, associates this search for a starting-point with deliberation (453ª12–14). Like deliberation, it is a matter of having a goal and of identifying a suitable starting-point, something that one is now in a position to do with a view to achieving one's goal.

It is plain, then, that recollection, as Aristotle thinks of it, is a rather special way in which representations retained in an organism may become active, and one that, moreover, he takes to be unavailable to the brute animals. If Aristotle's account of memory is to be anything like tolerably complete, he must at least indicate how representations can become active independently of recollection, as he characterizes it in *De Memoria* 2. Furthermore, it will not do simply to point to the fact that one can sometimes call something to mind directly and without first thinking of something else, as when you exercise some piece of knowledge,[57] or when you think of the colour of your own eyes. For this would still not do justice to the fact that memory often becomes active without anything being deliberately called to mind, as when it just so happens that the scent of some flower reminds you of a walk you took during last year's summer vacation. It is, moreover, doubtful whether Aristotle is prepared to attribute to any non-human animal the ability deliberately to call something to mind, directly or otherwise. It seems that he regards directly calling something to mind as a case of thinking (*De Memoria* 2, 451ᵇ18–20), and hence as an act of the intellect. If so, it too is unavailable to the brutes. One thing that Aristotle does need to do, in any case, is to indicate a way for representations to become active which does not involve deliberately recalling the thing in question, directly or otherwise. I submit that he does precisely that when he characterizes dispositional memory as involving—in many cases and perhaps in general—the existence of dispositions among sensory affections to become active together or in succession in ways that are determined, at least in large part, by past sensory experience and habituation.

In characterizing dispositional memory in this way, Aristotle makes it clear that he takes acquiring the ability to remember, say, what Cebes looks like not simply to be a matter of retaining an appropriate sensory affection somewhere or other in one's perceptual apparatus. He also takes acquiring such an ability—in many cases and perhaps in general—to involve retaining the relevant sensory affection in a way that relates it to other such affections by way of appropriate dispositions to become active together, or in immediate succession. As a result, we can see how,

---

[56] Cf. 451ᵇ29–31: ὅταν τοίνυν ἀναμιμνήσκεσθαι βούληται, τοῦτο ποιήσει· ζητήσει λαβεῖν ἀρχὴν κινήσεως, μεθ᾽ ἣν ἐκείνη ἔσται ('when someone wants to recollect, he will do this: he will seek to get hold of a starting-point, after which the change in question will occur').

[57] Cf. *De Anima* 2.5, 417ᵇ22–4: 'Knowledge is of universals, and these in a way are in the soul itself. For this reason thinking is up to the person, and he can think whenever he wishes to (διὸ νοῆσαι μὲν ἐπ᾽ αὐτῷ, ὁπόταν βούληται).'

according to his account of memory, sensory affections can become active in a way that does not involve deliberately recalling the thing in question. This can happen when one type of sensory affection 'triggers' another type. For example, your dispositional memory of what Cebes looks like may be activated by sensory affections that actively occur in your perceptual apparatus as you see Simmias.

Moreover, Aristotle evidently holds, as we have seen, that memory and remembering belong to the perceptual part of the soul.[58] On the basis of this assignment, it is, I think, reasonable to attribute to him the view that all activities and operations that form part of the ordinary functioning of memory are exercises of capacities that belong to the perceptual part of the soul, or are exercises of one such capacity. In fact, I take this to be no more than a fuller statement of his claim that memory belongs to the perceptual part of the soul. Now, we have seen that he takes it to be part of acquiring and maintaining dispositional memory that sensory affections are retained in ways which relate them to other such affections by way of appropriate dispositions to become active together or in succession. He must take it, moreover, that acquiring and maintaining dispositional memory is part of the ordinary functioning of memory. If this is along the right lines, then it is in fact clear that Aristotle is committed to the view that preserving sensory affections in a suitably structured way is a matter of exercising capacities that belong to the perceptual part of the soul, or of exercising one such capacity. The most plausible candidate for this task is, of course, the capacity for *phantasia*. This, after all, is the capacity that accounts for the preservation of sensory affections. Moreover, Aristotle indicates a special connection between memory and *phantasia* when he says that memory belongs to the part of the soul to which *phantasia* belongs as well (*De Memoria* 1, 450ᵃ22–3).

As Aristotle is quick to point out, by assigning memory to the perceptual part rather than the intellect, he is making memory available to at least some of the non-human animals (*De Memoria* 1, 450ᵃ15–16).[59] Moreover, we have now seen that he takes it to be part of the functioning of memory, anyhow in suitably constituted animals, that sensory affections are preserved in their perceptual apparatus in a structured way, with dispositions obtaining among them to co-occur or follow one another in certain ways. By assigning memory to the perceptual part of the soul, he therefore makes the formation and maintenance of such dispositions among sensory affections available, at least in principle, to suitably constituted non-human animals. In virtue of the perceptual part of their souls,

---

[58] *De Memoria* 1, 450ᵃ22–3; 451ᵃ16–17; this is confirmed at the end of the treatise, 453ᵇ8–10. To do justice to the complexity of Aristotle's position, we should add that he takes the simple statement that memory belongs to the perceptual part of the soul to be appropriate so far as the proper objects of memory are concerned. As we saw earlier, he takes the intellect to be involved in remembering intelligibles. For present purposes, however, I can afford to limit myself to Aristotle's views on remembering the proper objects of memory; and so I disregard the complications introduced into his theory of memory by remembering intelligibles.

[59] Other texts in which Aristotle attributes memory to non-human animals include *Historia Animalium* 1.1, 488ᵇ25–6, and *Metaphysics* A 1, 980ᵇ21–7.

Aristotle is in a position to hold, such animals can preserve sensory affections in suitably interrelated ways. This may enable them, for instance, to associate one thing with another, to be reminded by something of something else, and to have ongoing representations of indeterminate duration and complexity.

This position, it should be noted, is not only one for which his psychological theory fully provides the resources. It is also one that he needs to adopt if he is to be able to account for the cognitive achievements involved in forms of non-human animal behaviour that he describes in considerable detail. Consider, for instance, his report of adult deer leading their young to their lair, habituating (ἐθίζειν) them to the place where they should seek refuge (*Historia Animalium* 8.5, 611ᵃ20–1). From the point of view of Aristotle's psychological theory, such behaviour plainly needs to be accounted for in terms of the preservation of sensory affections in orderly ways, so that the habituation of juvenile deer can be seen to equip them with appropriately complex representations that are preserved in their perceptual apparatus, so as to guide their speedy return to the lair in moments of peril.

Moreover, we saw earlier in the present chapter that Aristotle's psychological theory needs to be able to account for the suitability of a non-human animal's *phantasiai* to its current circumstances, which Aristotle must think is manifested in anticipatory pleasure as well as in purposive locomotion. What is minimally required for explaining such phenomena is what Aristotle's account of memory in fact makes available: namely, that brute animals of many kinds can form and maintain appropriate dispositions among sensory affections retained in their perceptual apparatus, so that they may associate one thing with another, or be reminded by something of something else. Thus when a lion notices a stag in its environment, its current perceptual experience may put it in mind of what it is like to eat a stag, and that representation may both occasion anticipatory pleasure and play a crucial role in impelling the lion to go after its prey.

The interpretation that I have presented and argued for gives Aristotle no more than the bare bones of an account of non-human animal cognition in terms of connections or associations between sensory impressions. To do justice to the cognitive achievements of non-human animals, such an account would no doubt require extensive supplementation and refinement. Something would, for instance, have to be said about how it is that among all the countless possible connections or associations between impressions that might be formed, such connections as are required for the animal to survive, and to get around in the world, actually get formed. Such an account might appeal to a mechanism which privileges sequences of impressions that lead to, or involve, pleasurable experiences, e.g. 'stag-eating'. But we should also bear in mind that Aristotle leaves open the possibility that at least some sequences of representations may be a matter, not of habit, but of necessity:

Acts of recollection happen because, naturally, *this* sensory affection occurs after *that* one. If this is so by necessity, then plainly whenever one undergoes the earlier one, one will undergo the later one. If it is not by necessity but by habit, one will for the most part undergo the one after the other. (*De Memoria* 2, 451^{b}10–14)

The underlying idea might well be that the perceptual apparatus of some kinds of animals is constituted so that they are predisposed to proceed from one specific type of representation to another, provided that the animal in question actually receives sensory affections of the relevant types. In other words, the idea might be that some kinds of animals are 'wired up' in such a way that their perceptual apparatus contains, as it were, 'slots' specifically for certain types of affections, in which affections of these types are stored as soon as they are received. Affections of one type will then be linked to affections of some other type, with the effect that the animal in question invariably proceeds from representations of one type to representations of another. In this way, Aristotle's Empiricism[60] about *phantasia* could turn out to be a less extreme position than it may appear to be: although an animal has to acquire by experience whatever sensory affections it needs, its nature might be such as to facilitate—or even, given a suitably conducive environment, to predetermine—the formation of such connections or associations between impressions as are required for it to be able to live in the way that is characteristic of its species.

[60] For a brief account of Empiricism, see Introduction, pp. 4–6.

12

Phantasia and Practical Thought

One of my central purposes in the preceding chapters was to bring out and emphasize the remarkable cognitive power of *phantasia*, as Aristotle conceives of it. After some preliminary remarks in Chapter 8, I argued in Chapter 9 that *phantasia* enables animals to envisage prospects without having to depend on thought or reason. It is important that *phantasia* can do this, given that Aristotle conceives of animal locomotion as purposive in a way that seems to require that animals, including many kinds which he takes to be non-rational, are capable of envisaging prospects. It is not just, however, that many kinds of animals exhibit purposive behaviour. They also form purposes that are, by and large, suitable to the circumstances they find themselves in. When a lion notices a stag, it will typically want to make a meal of it. If forming purposes of this kind involves envisaging prospects, animals (including many kinds of non-human ones) must not only be able to envisage prospects quite generally. They also must be cognitively equipped so that, given certain circumstances, they can be relied on to envisage a prospect of a certain kind, rather than not envisaging any prospect at all, or envisaging one of an altogether different kind.

In Chapter 11, I argued that, on Aristotle's view, perception and *phantasia* can account for the way in which non-rational subjects can, given certain conditions, be relied on to envisage prospects that are suitable to their circumstances. According to Aristotle's psychological theory, to be a living thing capable of perception and *phantasia* involves having a soul that includes a perceptual part—a part or aspect of the soul which, I argued, is meant to account for a broad variety of operations and activities, such as perceiving, retaining sensory impressions, envisaging prospects, having dispositional memory, remembering something, and being reminded of something by something else. Aristotle is thus in a position to accept that some kinds of non-human animals can, given certain conditions, be relied on to envisage prospects that are suitable to their circumstances; and he can account for this in terms of associations of sensory impressions, with the perceptual soul-part of suitably constituted animals enabling them to form such associations. An account along some such lines seems to me to be required by Aristotle's theory of animal motivation. A number of texts in the *Parva Naturalia*, moreover, both provide the resources needed for such an account, and suggest rather strongly that Aristotle has in mind a picture of non-human animal cognition along these lines. In the

De Memoria, he indicates that he takes the ability to be reminded of one thing by another to be part of having dispositional memory, and he assigns memory to the perceptual part of the soul, noting that in doing so he is making memory available to suitably constituted non-human animals. In the *De Insomniis*, he proposes to account for 'well-connected' representations occurring in dreams in terms of the idea that some blooded animals, including humans but not limited to them, are constituted so that sensory affections may be preserved in their perceptual apparatus in orderly ways, with dispositions obtaining among them such that appropriate sensory representations tend to follow one another in orderly sequences.

In view of the overall interpretation that I have argued for, the question arises why the cognitive achievements of which non-human animals are capable, remark-able though they are, nonetheless do not, according to Aristotle, involve, or amount to, exercises of thought or reason. It may be instructive briefly to consider the contrasting view of David Hume, who adduces instances of cognitive achieve-ments of non-human animals so as to support his claim that 'beasts are endow'd with thought and reason as well as men'.[1] Hume's examples include that of 'a dog, that avoids fire and precipices, that shuns strangers, and caresses his master' (177). With regard to such forms of behaviour, Hume asserts that 'they proceed from a reasoning, that is not in itself different, nor founded on different principles, from that which appears in human nature' (177). He explains the dog's cognitive achievements in terms of sensory impressions and inferences drawn from such impressions: for example, 'from the tone of voice the dog infers his master's anger, and foresees his own punishment' (178). To draw an inference of this kind, according to Hume, is to engage in reasoning. There is no reason to think that Aristotle and Hume disagree about the details of non-human animal behaviour as they are evident to observation. In fact, the examples that Hume offers feature rather modest achievements, especially in comparison to some of the more remarkable feats that Aristotle reports in book 8 of the *Historia Animalium*.[2] Rather, the disagreement between Aristotle and Hume is about the terms in which such and other instances of non-human animal behaviour should be explained. Hume attributes thought and reason to non-human animals so as to be able to explain their cognitive achievements in terms of inferences and exercises of reason. Aristotle, by contrast, takes it that non-human animal behaviour can be quite adequately explained without crediting the brute animals with thought or reason.[3]

---

[1] David Hume, *A Treatise of Human Nature*, 2nd edn., ed. P. H. Nidditch (Oxford: Oxford University Press, 1978), 176.

[2] Note, in particular, the reports concerning wild goats curing themselves (8.6, 612^{a}2–5), the Egyptian grey mongoose taking precautions against snakebite (8.6, 612^{a}16–21), cranes giving signals to one another (8.10, 614^{b}18–27), lions punishing offenders (8.44, 629^{b}24–7), and the quasi-calculations of dolphins (8.48, 631^{a}27–31).

[3] I am not meaning to suggest that the disagreement between Aristotle and Hume reflects a difference between ancient and modern conceptions of thought and reason. Already in antiquity there were thinkers who, like Hume, credited non-human animals with thought and reason, taking it that one could not adequately explain the cognitive achievements of many non-human animals without

Now, Aristotle's denial of thought and reason to non-human animals is controversial, and may seem problematic. For one might think that in order to offer an adequate account of the achievements of at least some non-human animals, one has to attribute thought and reason to them. Aristotle plainly takes the view that such an account can be provided without crediting non-human animals with thought or reason, and indeed he offers, or provides the resources for, an account along these lines which is relatively detailed and, I think, rather attractive. However, a critic might suggest that at least some of the cognitive achievements which Aristotle attributes to non-human animals, and which he treats as cases of perception and *phantasia*, really are manifestations of thought, or exercises of reason. To see whether Aristotle has an answer to that suggestion, and (if so) what it is, we should, I propose, attend to Aristotle's notions of thought and reason. More precisely, we should examine the roles which thought and reason, according to Aristotle, play in the production of action. On any tolerably clear view of Aristotle's conceptions of thought and reason, and of the roles he takes them to play in the production of action, it will, I think, be clear why he holds that the cognitive achievements of non-human animals, remarkable though they are, nonetheless do not amount to, or involve, exercises of thought or reason.

Let us, to begin with, return for one last time to the list of movers in *De Motu Animalium* 6: 'We see that the movers of the animal are thought (διάνοια), perception, *phantasia*, decision (προαίρεσις), wish (βούλησις), spirit, and appetite' (*De Motu Animalium* 6, 700^{b}17–18). Although this is not made explicit in the *De Motu Animalium* itself, it is nonetheless plain from the context of Aristotle's psychological writings that non-human animals have, on his view, no share in thought, decision, or wish.[4] Thus in their case the list of movers is limited to

attributing thought and reason to them. Consider, for instance, the following passage from a speech by Autobulus, in Plutarch's *De Sollertia Animalium*: '(we think) that there is no animal that does not, according to nature, have a kind of belief (δόξα τις) and reasoning (λογισμός), just as it has perception and impulse. For nature, which, as they rightly say, does everything for the sake of, and with a view to, something, did not make the animal capable of perception just to perceive when something is happening to it. Rather, there being many things that are friendly to it, and many that are hostile, it could not survive for a moment, if it had not learned to guard itself against the one, and to mix with the other. Now, perception provides to each animal cognition of both in the same way; but the acts of taking and pursuing that follow the perception of beneficial things, and the acts of fleeing and avoiding that follow the perception of destructive and painful things, could by no means occur in creatures not naturally constituted so as to reason to some extent (λογίζεσθαί τι), to discern, to remember and to pay attention' (960 D–F). Cf. also Porphyry, *De Abstinentia*, esp. book 3, which seems to be indebted to Plutarch's dialogue (but perhaps they use a common source): for instance, chapter 21 of book 3 contains a nearly identical version of the passage just quoted. While Plutarch and Porphyry supply the most prominent ancient texts concerning non-human animal rationality, they are not isolated figures in this regard: for further material and discussion, see Sorabji, *Animal Minds and Human Morals*, esp. 78–96.

[4] Aristotle denies thought to non-human animals at *De Anima* 3.3, 429^{a}4–8; 3.10, 433^{a}11–12. Decision involves thought, according to *De Motu Animalium* 6, 700^{b}23 (cf. *Nicomachean Ethics* 6.2, 1139^{b}4–5); so since non-human animals lack thought, they must lack decision as well (see also *Nicomachean Ethics* 3.2, 1111^{b}6–9; ^{b}12–13).

perception, *phantasia*, appetite, and spirit.[5] I shall concentrate on the question whether the denial to non-human animals of thought and decision is well-grounded. It will become clear that in answering that question we shall also be answering the question whether Aristotle's denial of reason to non-human animals is well-grounded.

At the beginning of his positive account of animal locomotion, Aristotle distinguishes between practical and theoretical or contemplative thought: 'These two, then, are concerned with locomotion: thought and desire, but thought which reasons for the sake of something and is practical; it differs from theoretical thought in respect of the goal' (*De Anima* 3.10, 433ª13–15).[6] It is specifically practical thought, rather than thought in general, that, Aristotle thinks, is responsible for the production of locomotion and action. What I propose to do in what follows is to draw attention to a number of features of practical thought, as Aristotle conceives of it, and then to compare practical thought, so conceived, with the practical cognition of non-human animals, as it has emerged in preceding chapters. It will become clear that there is a very considerable gap between practical thought and non-human animal cognition, so conceived. And so Aristotle's denial of practical thought to non-human animals, remarkable though their cognitive abilities may be, will turn out to be conceptually coherent.

Where will this leave us as far as the denial of reason to non-human animals is concerned? Before this question can be adequately answered, we must confront a complication. Two Greek words which are commonly translated as 'reason', 'rationality', or the like—*logos* and *logismos*—are used by Aristotle to capture related, but nevertheless distinct, notions.[7]

The word *logos* (in the relevant sense) is used by Aristotle interchangeably with the word *nous*, where the latter denotes the capacity for thought.[8] Correspondingly, the part or aspect of the soul that has *logos* (τὸ λόγον ἔχον) is the intellect *as a whole*, including the part or aspect concerned with theoretical understanding (τὸ ἐπιστημονικόν) (*Nicomachean Ethics* 6.2, 1139ª3–15). Staying close to Aristotle's usage, I shall be using the words 'reason' and 'thought' to capture this notion of *logos*.[9] As we have seen already, moreover, practical thought (πρακτικὸς νοῦς) is the

---

[5] For the attribution of spirited desire to non-human animals, see *Nicomachean Ethics* 3.2, 1111ᵇ12–13; *Eudemian Ethics* 2.10, 1225ᵇ26–7.

[6] Practical thought (πρακτικὸς νοῦς, διάνοια πρακτική) is also mentioned at *De Anima* 3.10, 433ª16 and 18; cf. also *Nicomachean Ethics* 6.2, 1139ª35–6. The latter passage indicates that the qualification 'practical', after 'reasoning for the sake of something', is not otiose: according to *Nicomachean Ethics* 6.2, 1139ᵇ1–2, thought for the sake of something is in charge, not only of action (πρᾶξις), but also of production (ποίησις).

[7] Socrates in the *Republic* seems to treat the terms λογισμός and λόγος (in the relevant sense) as synonymous. See, for instance, *Republic* 4, 440 A 9–B 7, with λογισμός at B 1 and λόγος at B 3 and B 5.

[8] *De Anima* 3.10, 433ᵇ5–10 provides a clear example.

[9] For the connection between reason (λόγος) and thought (νοῦς) in Aristotle's terminology, see also *Nicomachean Ethics* 6.2, 1139ᵇ12, where the two parts or aspects of reason are referred to as 'both parts concerned with thinking' (ἀμφοτέρων . . . τῶν νοητικῶν μορίων).

aspect of thought or reason in virtue and by way of which it contributes to the production of action: in the case of a person whose reason is well developed, practical thought will account for the apprehension both of the right goals for action, and of the ways in which those goals may properly be achieved. Accordingly, in showing what Aristotle's grounds are for denying practical thought to non-human animals, we will also account for the fact that he denies them reason. After all, we will be identifying his grounds for denying that they are endowed with the ability to reason about what to do, and in this way to employ reason in generating the motivating conditions from which their behaviour flows.

The word *logismos* and related expressions, on the other hand, are used by Aristotle in a more specific way. He identifies *logizesthai* with deliberating (βουλεύεσθαι),[10] and in so connecting it with related notions of taking counsel and devising plans, he ties the word *logismos* specifically to the domain of action. Moreover, in Aristotle's discussions of practical cognition, both in the psychological and in the ethical writings, *logismos* is limited to contexts in which some goal or other has been fixed, whether it is a very general goal such as living one's life well, or a more specific one such as recovering a certain sum of money. In such contexts, *logizesthai* is a matter of reasoning or deliberating about how to achieve the goal in question.[11] For the sake of clarity, I shall be using the expression 'deliberative reasoning' to capture Aristotle's notion of *logismos*. Since Aristotle conceives of deliberative reasoning as being prominently involved in the activity of practical thought, the discussion of practical thought in what follows will shed some more light on the role he takes *logismos* to play in the production of action.

The features of practical thought to which I wish to draw attention can be observed in the psychological writings, especially in the *De Anima*, and I shall refer to a number of passages from *De Anima* 3.9–11. But in investigating Aristotle's conception of practical thought we should also bear in mind the very detailed discussions of practical cognition which he offers in his ethical writings, especially in book 2 of the *Eudemian Ethics* and in books 3 and 6 of the *Nicomachean Ethics*. In fact the ethical writings provide a more detailed account of practical thought than the psychological writings do, but one which, so far as I can see, coheres well with the discussions in the psychological writings. My comments on practical thought, as Aristotle conceives of it, will therefore draw on the ethical writings as well as on the psychological writings.

We should begin by noting that Aristotle, time and again in both the psychological and the ethical writings, presents practical thought as having a certain structure, which involves a goal or 'thing for the sake of which' on the one hand

---

[10] *Nicomachean Ethics* 6.2, 1139ᵃ12–13: τὸ γὰρ βουλεύεσθαι καὶ λογίζεσθαι ταὐτόν. Cf. the shift from φαντασία λογιστική at *De Anima* 3.10, 433ᵇ29, to βουλευτική at 3.11, 434ᵃ7, and again to λογισμός in the same sentence.

[11] Passages in which λογισμός is presented as serving this function include *De Anima* 3.10, 433ᵃ14; 3.11, 434ᵃ7–10; *Eudemian Ethics* 2.10, 1226ᵇ21–30.

and reasoning or deliberating about how to achieve it on the other. Practical thought extends from the recognition of a goal to the origination of action for the sake of achieving it. This conception of practical thought is expressed, for instance, close to the beginning of Aristotle's positive account of animal locomotion in *De Anima* 3.10:

These two, then, are concerned with locomotion, thought and desire, but thought which reasons for the sake of something and is practical; it differs from theoretical thought in respect of the goal. Also every desire is for the sake of something: for the object of desire is the beginning of practical thought, and its last bit is the beginning of action. (*De Anima* 3.10, 433ª13–17)

A passage from *Eudemian Ethics* 2.10 contains a somewhat more detailed account:

Nobody deliberates about the goal, but it is laid down for everyone; rather, people deliberate about things which contribute to the goal (περὶ . . . τῶν εἰς τοῦτο [sc. τὸ τέλος] τεινόντων), whether *this* thing or *that* contributes to its attainment, or how *this*, when it has been decided on, will come to pass. We all continue to deliberate until we relate to ourselves the beginning of the process of change. (*Eudemian Ethics* 2.10, 1226ᵇ9–13)¹²

The passage goes on by drawing attention to an important feature of practical thought, one which is relevant to our purposes. After pointing out that decision involves deliberation, Aristotle draws the conclusion that non-human animals lack decision, since they lack deliberation:

For this reason decision is not present in the other animals, nor at every age in life, nor in a human being no matter what state he is in: for neither is deliberating and opinion about the why (ὑπόληψις τοῦ διὰ τί). Nothing prevents belief about whether something should be done, or whether something should not be done, from being present to many, but not so with belief through reasoning (δι' λογισμοῦ). For that part or aspect of the soul is deliberative which contemplates a species of cause. For the 'for the sake of which' is one of the causes. . . . That for the sake of which something is or comes to be, that we say is a cause—for instance, the recovery of money is a cause of walking, if he is walking for the sake of this. For this reason, those who do not have an aim (σκοπός) are not deliberative. (*Eudemian Ethics* 2.10, 1226ᵇ21–30)

As we have seen, practical thought crucially involves the recognition of a goal (for instance, the recovery of some sum of money), and also of things which may contribute to its achievement (for instance, going somewhere, writing a letter, making a telephone call). The present passage indicates that if deliberative reasoning is involved in a bit of behaviour in the right way, it is not only the case that the person in question is (say) going to the marketplace for the sake of recovering money, and hence in a certain sense because of recovering money. He also grasps the 'for the sake of' relation between going there and recovering the money; in this

¹² My translations from the *Eudemian Ethics* follow those in J. Barnes (ed.), *The Complete Works of Aristotle*.

case, that relation is a means–end relation.[13] He is aware of his goal of recovering money, and he recognizes that going to the marketplace is something that may contribute to the achievement of his goal. His going there depends on, first, his recognition of the goal in question and, secondly, his recognition that doing this is something that may contribute to its achievement. If he did not, in fact, aim to recover the money, or if he did not recognize that going to the marketplace is something that may contribute to that recovery, he would not be going there, except by coincidence.

Now it is important to note that there is room for the idea of a subject doing A for the sake of doing B without itself grasping the 'for the sake of' relation that in fact obtains between its doing A and its doing B. A cat which sees one end of a slowly receding shoe-lace will advance, *so as to get hold of the shoe-lace*. The cat's forward motion plainly is goal-directed: it is driven and controlled by the purpose of getting hold of the shoe-lace. There is, however, no need to assume that the cat is aware of the fact that advancing is what it needs to do in the circumstances in order to get hold of the shoe-lace. Perhaps it advances simply as a result of being naturally constituted the way it is; or as a joint product of its natural constitution and of the conditioning that cats receive in the course of their development in ordinary circumstances. In much the same way, one might well think, a lion wanting to make a meal of a stag that it sees before itself will advance, *so as to get its teeth into the stag*. This, too, does not require that the lion grasps the fact that advancing is what it needs to do in the circumstances in order to get its teeth into the stag. Perhaps it advances simply as a result of being naturally constituted the way it is; or as a joint product of its natural constitution and of the conditioning that lions receive in the course of their development in ordinary circumstances.

It is also worth noting that a subject may form a complex desire for A, B, and C, where A and B in fact are required for, and may contribute to, securing C, without being the least bit aware of the fact that A, B, and C are related in this way. Consider a hungry, ordinarily conditioned lion that sees a stag at some distance in its environment. In normal circumstances, it will try to hunt down the stag and eat it. Aristotle's theory explains the lion's behaviour in terms of perception, *phantasia*, and desire. I take it that his explanation, when fully stated, will look more or less like this. Perception supplies the lion with awareness of the stag in the distance. *Phantasia* makes the lion envisage the prospect of making a meal of the stag. It may also make the lion apprehend certain things that it

---

[13] This particular 'for the sake of' relation is one between a means and an end. Not all such relations are. Some are part–whole relations, the whole in question being a goal and the part a constituent or ingredient of it. To use one of Ackrill's examples, one may play golf for the sake of having an enjoyable holiday; J. Ackrill, 'Aristotle on *eudaimonia*', *Proceedings of the British Academy*, 60 (1974), 19. Yet another way in which one thing can be done for the sake of another is by being something that achieving a goal in the circumstances consists in, or is realized by. Someone may take a walk for the sake of getting some exercise. The forms of 'for the sake of' relations are discussed in some detail in J. Cooper, *Reason and Human Good in Aristotle* (Indianapolis, Ind.: Hackett, 1975), 19–22.

needs to do in order to get its teeth into the stag. It may do both by providing the lion with a complex representation of, say, laying hold of the stag, killing it in a certain way, and then making a meal of it. The whole of this rather elaborate prospect may become an object of desire, so that the lion can properly be described as wanting to lay hold of the stag, kill it in a certain way, and then eat it. Desire involves, or results in, bodily changes of some kind or other. These, in turn, may effect the large-scale bodily changes which constitute the lion's purposive behaviour as it pursues the stag, lays hold of it, kills it in the appropriate way, and proceeds to make a meal of it. To appeal to the lion's desire, and to the representation that gives it its content, is to render intelligible why the animal all of a sudden engages in rapid locomotion, and why it completes the episode of locomotion in the rather specific way that in fact it does. For some such story to be intelligible and explanatory, Aristotle need not assume that the representations that guide the lion's behaviour are articulated in terms of 'for the sake of' relations.[14] He only needs an account of how appropriately complex and situation-specific representations can arise in suitably constituted animals as a result of perceptual experience; and I have argued that, in fact, he is in a position to offer such an account.

The present text indicates that, by contrast, behaviour which involves deliberative reasoning in the right way will crucially involve the subject's grasping the 'for the sake of' relation that obtains between what it is they are doing and what it is for the sake of which they are doing it. This grasp manifests itself as the subject's 'opinion about the why' concerning the bit of behaviour in question. We have, then, identified an important feature of practical thought, as Aristotle conceives of it: since it involves deliberative reasoning, it includes the subject's recognition of 'for the sake of' relations.

There is another feature of practical thought that is relevant to our purposes. It is described in some detail in a passage from *Nicomachean Ethics* 3.3, which is closely related to the passage from *Eudemian Ethics* 2.10 that we have looked at:

We deliberate not about goals, but about things that contribute towards goals (περὶ τῶν πρὸς τὰ τέλη). . . . Having laid down the goal, people consider how and through which things it will come to pass. And if it appears that it comes to be through a plurality of things, they consider in addition through which thing most easily and most finely; if it is achieved through one thing, they consider how it will come to pass through that, and through which thing that in turn will come to pass, until they arrive at the first cause, which in discovery is last. (*Nicomachean Ethics* 3.3, 1112ᵇ11–20)

---

14 It should be noted that it is not part of my interpretation that 'for the sake of' relations do not in fact obtain between the lion's acts of laying hold of the stag and killing it on the one hand and the act of eating it on the other. We may well want to say that such relations do obtain, though the lion is not cognitively equipped to grasp them. After all, it may be the case that whereas the lion's attachment to eating is primitive, its interest in such things as laying hold of animals and killing them depends causally (though, I suggest, not cognitively) on the fact that doing these things, anyhow in the lion's natural habitat, is required for, and strongly tends to contribute to, eating.

It is not only that in practical thinking we identify goals and recognize things that may contribute to their achievement. We are also able to recognize any number of alternative ways in which we might promote the achievement of our goals and, what is more, we are able to assess these alternatives in relation to one another, for instance in terms of ease or fineness. The ability to recognize and assess alternatives, as an important part of practical thought, also features in the passage from *De Anima* 3.11 which is meant to explain why deliberative *phantasia* is limited to subjects that are capable of deliberative reasoning: 'Deliberative *phantasia* is present in animals capable of reasoning (for whether to do *this* or *that* is already a task for reasoning; and it is necessary to measure by one standard: for he pursues what is greater; so that he can make one out of many *phantasiai*)' (*De Anima* 3.11, 434^{a}7–10).[15]

We have now identified a number of features or aspects of Aristotle's conception of practical thought, as Aristotle conceives of it: the recognition of 'for the sake of' relations, as well as and the recognition and assessment of alternative courses of action. There is, on the other hand, no reason to think that the practical cognition of non-human animals, as Aristotle conceives of it, includes any of these features. Among them, the recognition of 'for the sake of' relations is clearly basic; it is presupposed by the others. We saw that the recognition of 'for the sake of' relations crucially involves, first, the awareness of a goal and, secondly, the recognition that (minimally) something or other may contribute to the achievement of the goal in question, in such a way that the subject forms an 'opinion about the why', an opinion that reflects his or her recognition of an action being for the sake of achieving some goal. Aristotle's conception of non-human animal cognition, as I have presented and interpreted it, does credit non-human animals with the capacity for awareness of goals, but it does not attribute to them the ability to recognize things as contributing to the achievement of goals, so as to grasp 'for the sake of' relations. Nor does Aristotle's conception of non-human animal cognition credit the brute animals with 'opinions about the why'.[16]

Consider the example of a deer crossing a stream as it tries to get back to its young. Aristotle's account, according to the interpretation I have offered, does not require that the animal recognizes that what it is doing, crossing the stream, is required for, and may contribute to, its getting back to its offspring. Nor, in general, does Aristotle's account require a grasp on the animal's part of 'for the sake of' relations. Nor does it require, or indeed allow, 'opinions about the why' on the part of the animal—opinions that would reflect the animal's recognition of its behaviour being for the sake of achieving a goal. Aristotle assumes that the cognitive achievements involved in the deer's behaviour can be accounted for in terms of perception and *phantasia* alone. He assumes, I suggested, that for many

---

[15] For some discussion of this passage, see Ch. 9, p. 127.

[16] This, of course, is as it should be, given that, at *Eudemian Ethics* 2.10, 1226^{b}21–3, Aristotle denies to the non-human animals 'opinions about the why'.

kinds of non-human animals, being capable of perception and *phantasia* involves being constituted in a way that supports the formation—through such factors as experience and habituation—of associations between sensory impressions. If so, it is open to him to say that a deer may rely on associations between impressions in forming a complex purpose such as, say, 'crossing the stream, then going through the forest by the side of the road, and then returning to the cave where the young are waiting'. This purpose may cause it to cross the stream (and so forth) without grasping in any way at all that doing so is required for, and may contribute to, getting back to its offspring.

It is not difficult to see that there may be important differences between an organism that proceeds on the basis of associations between impressions, formed by experience and habit, and an organism that can grasp 'for the sake of' relations and that can form 'opinions about the why'—opinions that reflect its cognition of an action being for the sake of a goal. For one thing, an organism of the latter kind is capable of much greater flexibility in its responses to a changing environment. Consider two organisms. Both of them are able to find their way to a location where there is a supply of fresh water. One of them can rely on practical thought; the other can only proceed by associations of impressions. Suppose that their environment changes so that no water is available any more at the location in question. The thinking organism, as soon as he or she finds out that the source of water has run dry, will also recognize that going to *this* location is no longer something that contributes to achieving the goal of drinking water, should there be such a goal. Given this recognition, the organism, in so far as it is guided by practical thought, will not go to the same location again, if its goal is to drink water. So far as the other organism is concerned, it may take a long time before the relevant associations between impressions in its perceptual apparatus cease to be effective, and cease to guide the organism's behaviour. After all, such associations are based, we said, on experience and habit, not on recognizing that some things are required for, and may contribute to, the achievement of others.

The advantages of practical thought over non-rational cognition, as Aristotle conceives of both of these, become even clearer once we take into account the recognition of alternative ways of achieving a goal, and the assessment of such alternatives in terms of some standard or other. We should also note, at least in passing, that grasping 'for the sake of' relations can not only guide and inform the pursuit of low-level objectives as they arise on a day-to-day basis. It also makes possible an integrated view of how to lead one's life overall, one that is articulated in terms of 'for the sake of' relations, which include means–end relations as well as part–whole relations.

It can, then, be shown that, given the way Aristotle conceives of practical thought on the one hand and of non-human animal cognition on the other, there is a very considerable gap between the two. And so his denial of practical thought to non-human animals, remarkable though their cognitive abilities may be, turns out to be conceptually coherent. This result also applies to the denial of decision. According to the discussions concerning decision both in the *Eudemian Ethics* and in the *Nicomachean Ethics*, it presupposes deliberation,[17] which includes the recognition of 'for the sake of' relations, the recognition of alternative ways of achieving a goal and the assessment of such alternatives in terms of some standard or other. Thus decision, as well as practical thought, can be shown to be well beyond the reach of non-human animal cognition, as Aristotle conceives of it.[18]

As for the defensibility or otherwise of Aristotle's denial to non-human animals of practical thought, and at the same time of reason and decision, I shall confine myself to the following remarks. It is clear that Aristotle's positive account of non-human animal cognition, and of non-rational cognition in general, in terms of perception and *phantasia* stands in need of substantial development. As a result, my reconstruction of that account had to be speculative to a considerable extent. However, the conception of non-rational cognition that has emerged from my interpretation is coherent, economical, and of considerable explanatory power. At the same time, a critic who wants to challenge Aristotle's denial of practical thought to non-human animals faces a daunting task, if he or she accepts Aristotle's conception of practical thought as combining the features to which I have drawn attention, namely the recognition of 'for the sake of' relations, the recognition of alternative ways of achieving a goal, and the consideration and assessment of such alternatives in terms of some standard or other. Aristotle's conception of practical thought invites questions of various sorts, which cannot be discussed here, such as what unifies the features or aspects I have pinpointed, or how he can account for the non-deliberative, but intellectual, recognition of practical goals that his theory evidently requires.[19] Nonetheless, the conception

---

[17] This point is clear already from Aristotle's definition of decision as deliberative desire (ὄρεξις βουλευτική) (*Nicomachean Ethics* 6.2, 1139ᵃ23; cf. *Eudemian Ethics* 2.10, 1226ᵇ17). For more explicit statements of the point, see (e.g.) *Nicomachean Ethics* 3.3, 1113ᵃ2–5, and *Eudemian Ethics* 2.10, 1227ᵃ3–5.

[18] Decision, as Aristotle conceives of it, presupposes not only deliberation, but wish (βούλησις) as well. This view is argued for (e.g.) by E. Anscombe, 'Thought and action in Aristotle', in R. Bambrough (ed.), *New Essays on Plato and Aristotle* (London: Routledge, 1965), 143–8, and by Irwin, *Aristotle's First Principles*, 337. Moreover, see *Eudemian Ethics* 2.10, 1226ᵇ14–17: 'decision arises from these [sc. belief and wish]: for the person who decides has both of these'. Accordingly, an action may be deliberated without being decided on: this is as it should be, if an un-self-controlled act can be deliberated (see *Nicomachean Ethics* 6.9, 1142ᵇ18–20) and is not (by definition, as it were) decided on (cf. *Nicomachean Ethics* 3.2, 1111ᵇ13–15). Since decision presupposes both wish and deliberation, the denial of decision to non-human animals is grounded both in their lacking wishes *and* in their lacking the ability to deliberate.

[19] Deliberation, or deliberative reasoning, does not exhaust practical thought, since practical thought is in charge, not only of identifying ways in which goals can be achieved, but also of determining goals in the first place. Deliberation presupposes that a goal has been fixed, and so it cannot, on pain of infinite regress, be all that there is to practical thought. Practical thought must therefore include non-deliberative recognition of goals. For discussion concerning this point, see Cooper, *Reason and Human Good in Aristotle*, 58–66; A. Mele, 'Aristotle on the roles of reason in motivation and justification', *Archiv für Geschichte der Philosophie*, 66 (1984), 124–37.

of practical thought which I have presented is, I hope, detailed and clear enough at least for present purposes. What has emerged in the course of my discussion is, it seems to me, a clearly conceived and well-grounded contrast between non-rational cognition, which humans share with other animals, and practical thought, of which humans alone are capable.

13

Reason and Non-rational Desire

There remains a question about the applicability of Aristotle's conception of non-rational cognition to adult human beings. Are not all of a reasoning creature's cognitive and motivating conditions affected by rationality?[1] In some ways they may well be, I shall argue on Aristotle's behalf, but this leaves intact a clear and robust sense in which appetite and spirit are non-rational forms of motivation, and a similarly clear and robust sense in which the cognition involved in these forms of motivation can, and to some extent must, be non-rational.

The expert about ethical and political matters, Aristotle holds, should have some knowledge of the soul, to the extent that such knowledge illuminates the nature of virtue. The *Nicomachean Ethics* therefore includes an outline account of the human soul (*Nicomachean Ethics* 1.13, 1102ª26–1103ª3). In fact, this is the most detailed account of the nature of specifically the human soul in Aristotle's extant writings. According to it, there is a sense in which all of the cognitive and motivating conditions of a mature human being are rational. They all belong to a part or aspect of the soul which in a way can rightly be called rational. However, this part or aspect is twofold. One part of it is rational *strictly speaking*,[2] the other is rational *in an extended sense*,[3] in that it is capable of obeying, and of being influenced by, reason. Looked at in another way, that lower part of human reason is non-rational, because, as we shall see, it is incapable of reasoning in its own right. This lower part of reason is the source of appetitive and spirited desires.

One thing I want to do in the present chapter is to clarify how it is that Aristotle holds human appetite and spirit to be rational in a way. I also want to point out

---

[1] The idea is nicely expressed by H. H. Joachim: 'Thought (intelligence, reasoning), as man's distinctive character, permeates all his being and doing'; from the introduction to his commentary on the *Nicomachean Ethics* (Oxford: Clarendon Press, 1951), 2.

[2] *Nicomachean Ethics* 1.13, 1103ª1–2: 'If one must say that this part, too, has reason [sc. the part that is responsible for appetite and non-rational desire], then reason, too, will be twofold, consisting of one part that has reason strictly speaking and in itself (τὸ μὲν κυρίως καὶ ἐν αὑτῷ), and another part that is capable of listening as if to one's father.' I assume that in writing of 'that which is responsible for desire' (ὀρεκτικόν) at 1102ᵇ30, Aristotle is relying on a use of the word ὄρεξις ('desire') in which it generically picks out *non-rational* desire, rather than desire in all its forms. Parallels include *Eudemian Ethics* 2.8, 1224ᵇ21–4 (cf. 1224ª23–7, 1225ª3); 7.14 (or 8.2), 1247ᵇ34–5; *Politics* 3.16, 1287ª32; *De Anima* 3.9, 433ª6–8; and *Magna Moralia* 1.17, 1189ª1–6.

[3] Note the qualifications at 1102ᵇ13–14 and at 1102ᵇ29–31: the part that is responsible for appetite and (non-rational) desire participates in reason *in a way* (πῇ, πως).

that the rationality of all of a human being's cognitive and motivating conditions leaves intact a robust sense in which some of them are non-rational. In order to see this clearly and in detail, it will be helpful to take a look at some remarks that Aristotle makes in discussing lack of self-control in book 7 of the *Nicomachean Ethics*. Episodes of uncontrolled behaviour involve conflicts between rational motivation on the one hand and appetite or spirit on the other. In discussing such conflicts, Aristotle makes a number of remarks which shed light on how he conceives of the relation between what is strictly speaking reason on the one hand and appetite and spirit on the other. I shall close the chapter with some thoughts about the applicability to human psychology of Aristotle's conception of non-rational cognition, as it emerged in Chapters 8–11.

Aristotle's outline of the human soul, in *Nicomachean Ethics* 1.13, begins with the distinction between one part[4] or aspect of the soul that is non-rational, and another part or aspect that has reason. He adds that, for the purposes of the expert about ethical and political matters, it does not matter 'whether these are delimited like the parts of the body, and like everything that is a thing of parts (μεριστόν), or whether, while they are two in account, they are naturally inseparable, like the convex and the concave in a curved surface' (*Nicomachean Ethics* 1.13, 1102ᵃ28–31). The convex and the concave, Aristotle is implying, are *not* distinct parts of a curved surface—for example, of the surface of a hemisphere. The parts of a composite object are delimited from one another. But the convex and the concave in the surface of a hemisphere are neither delimited nor separable from one another. They are simply two aspects of the same surface.[5] One thing this makes sufficiently clear is that Aristotle's talk of the parts of the soul, in his ethical and political writings, is not meant to indicate a commitment to the view that the items in question have the status of genuine parts, or to the view that the soul really is a composite object.[6] What such talk requires is only that the items in question are distinguishable in account or definition.

Something which the non-rational part quite definitely includes is the part that is responsible for the nutrition and growth of the living organism. This, however,

---

⁴ Note μόριον at 1102ᵇ4.

⁵ Eustratius has worthwhile things to say about the passage. 'He shows by appeal to a curved surface', Eustratius explains, 'that there are things that are not distinct in place, but different in account. The concave and the convex are in their own right (καθ' αὐτό) in the same surface, being distinct from one another only in account and not also in place. Otherwise they could not both be in the same object that is extended in breadth [sc. but not in depth]. For a curved object that is a magnitude without breadth is a line' (112, 32–6). A curved surface, like any surface, has no depth. It is the *limit* of a body—that is, of an object with length, breadth, and depth. If the convex and the concave are both in the same surface, as they plainly are, they cannot have distinct locations.

⁶ Cf. *Eudemian Ethics* 2.1, 1219ᵇ32–6: in the context of an explanation how it is that there are two parts of the soul that possess reason (ὑποκείσθω δύο μέρη ψυχῆς τὰ λόγου μετέχοντα, 1219ᵇ28; cf. 1219ᵇ36–7), Aristotle somewhat abruptly remarks that it actually makes no difference at all whether or not the soul (really) is a thing of parts (διαφέρει δ' οὐδὲν οὔτ' εἰ μεριστὴ ἡ ψυχὴ οὔτ' εἰ ἀμερής). What is important, he adds, is that the soul has different capacities. What warrants talk of the parts of the soul, then, is the fact that the soul has, or is constituted by, distinguishable capacities.

has no share in human virtue and is therefore of no concern to the ethical and political expert (1102^{b}11–12). But as Aristotle explains rather carefully, he does not think that the non-rational part is exhausted by the part responsible for nutrition. He takes it to include in addition to that another part or aspect, which in a way has a share in reason (1102^{b}13–14). This, he thinks, is revealed by both self-controlled and un-self-controlled action. He calls attention to the fact that, in both cases, we praise the person's reason, the rational part of her soul, which impels her to act as she should. But something else in her struggles and exerts itself against reason, impelling her to act in a way that reason opposes.[7] Having shown that what impels self-controlled and uncontrolled characters to act as they should not needs to be *distinguished from* reason, Aristotle next turns to the task of clarifying how it nonetheless shares in reason in a way.

It is, he holds, characteristic of the self-controlled person to have appetitive desires that are both strong and objectionable.[8] He also thinks that it is a fact about the constitution of the human organism that appetitive desires can, all by themselves, get a person to act in pursuit of whatever they are desires for.[9] But in self-controlled action, this is *not* what happens. What happens is that the person in question acts as she should, and as her reason impels her to act. The non-rational part of her soul, the source of her appetites, seems to obey reason at least to the extent of acquiescing in the course of action which reason prescribes and impels her towards. What Aristotle says suggests that the difference between self-control and its lack consists not only in a difference in the motivational structure which a person acquires and maintains over time, with self-controlled characters having stronger rational desires and somewhat less intense appetites than uncontrolled characters. His emphasis on the non-rational part's ability to obey, and to listen to, reason, as well as the reference to admonishing (or warning, νουθέτησις), reprimanding, and encouraging (*Nicomachean Ethics* 1.13, 1102^{b}33–1103^{a}1), indicates an additional point of difference between self-control and its lack. This is the idea that, at the moment of temptation, the self-controlled character affects and influences the non-rational part of his or her soul in a way the uncontrolled character does not. It is part of this idea that the non-rational part of one person's

---

[7] 1102^{b}21: ἐπὶ τἀναντία γὰρ αἱ ὁρμαὶ τῶν ἀκρατῶν ('for the impulses of the un-self-controlled go in opposite directions'). It is worth noting the similarity in thought and language between *Nicomachean Ethics* 1.13 and the argument for tripartition of the soul in *Republic* 4; e.g. ἐπὶ τοῦτο ὁρμᾷ ('it is impelled in this direction'), 439 B 1; ἀνθέλκειν ('pull the other way'), *Republic* 439 B 3; ἀντιτείνειν at *Nicomachean Ethics* 1102^{b}18. Cf. also *De Anima* 3.10, 433^{b}7–8: ὁ μὲν γὰρ νοῦς διὰ τὸ μέλλον ἀνθέλκειν κελεύει, ἡ δὲ ἐπιθυμία διὰ τὸ ἤδη ('the intellect, on account of the future, prompts to pull the other way, while appetite pulls on account of the now').

[8] *Nicomachean Ethics* 7.2, 1146^{a}9–16: the self-controlled character's appetites must be strong and bad (ἰσχυραὶ καὶ φαῦλαι), or else self-control would not be the impressive and praiseworthy disposition that it is. Cf. 7.9, 1151^{b}34–1152^{a}3.

[9] *Nicomachean Ethics* 7.3, 1147^{a}34–5: appetite drives a person to act, 'for it can move each one of the parts [sc. of the body]'. Note also ibid. 3.12, 1119^{b}10: 'if appetites are large and intense, they knock out the person's reasoning' (τὸν λογισμὸν ἐκκρούουσιν). Cf. *Republic* 4, 440 A 9–B 4: appetite can force (βιάζεσθαι) a person to act against his or her reasoning.

soul is more obedient to reason than the non-rational part of another person's soul, just as some children are more obedient to their parents than others.[10] But there is also room for the thought that some people may be better than others at guiding, directing, and influencing the non-rational parts of their souls, just as some people are especially good at directing and influencing others by admonishing, reprimanding, and encouraging them.

Aristotle is somewhat hesitant to speak of what reason may do to the non-rational part as a matter of *persuasion*.[11] This, I suggest, is because he thinks being, properly speaking, open to persuasion requires being rational in the unqualified sense in which only what strictly speaking has reason can truly be said to be rational.[12] The underlying idea, I think, is that being open to genuine persuasion requires having specifically rational abilities such as being able to grasp that one thing follows from another, that this precludes that, or that doing A is a means, or an obstacle, to achieving B. Such abilities, however, are intellectual ones, and their exercise is, in each case, an act of thought. Aristotle has already indicated, in a twofold characterization which plainly anticipates the key distinction of chapter 13's account of the human soul, that acts of thought belong, not to reason's obedient part, but to reason in the strict sense.[13] On the view that I take to be Aristotle's, then, the non-rational part cannot strictly speaking be reasoned with, because it is unable to grasp inferential connections. This, however, leaves open a number of ways in which the non-rational part may be affected and influenced, even in moments of acute temptation. As far as appetite is concerned, its attention may be redirected from the pleasure that seems imminent to some other prospective pleasure ('encouragement'), or to some prospective pain ('admonition' or 'warning'). Similarly, it should be possible to move spirit by drawing its attention to shameful or otherwise unseemly aspects of a course of action ('reprimanding'), or alternatively to fine or admirable aspects (another form of 'encouragement'). In these various ways, an intense occurrent non-rational desire may grow less intense, or may subside altogether.

Aristotle holds appetite and spirit to be rational in a way, then, because they can be influenced and affected in certain ways by what has reason strictly speaking and

[10] *Nicomachean Ethics*, 1103ª3 (cf. 1102ᵇ31–2): the lower part of reason has reason 'as something capable of listening as if to a father'.

[11] Ibid. 1102ᵇ33–4: ὅτι δὲ πείθεταί πως ὑπὸ λόγου τὸ ἄλογον ('that the non-rational part is *in a way* persuaded by reason'). That is Aristotle's way of indicating that this is no ordinary kind of persuasion.

[12] *De Anima* 3.3, 428ª22–4. This is part of an argument for the view that *phantasia* is distinct from belief. Belief always involves conviction, and that always involves having been persuaded. Persuasion, in turn, always requires reason (λόγος). However, whereas some of the brute animals have *phantasia*, none of them has reason. What is denied to the brutes is the faculty of reason; and so it is best to interpret Aristotle as claiming that what is required for persuasion is precisely that faculty.

[13] *Nicomachean Ethics* 1.7, 1098ª3–5: 'There remains a practical sort of life of what possesses reason; and of this, one aspect "possesses reason" in so far as it is obedient to reason, while the other possesses it in so far as it actually has it, *and itself thinks*' (λείπεται δὴ πρακτική τις τοῦ λόγον ἔχοντος. τούτου δὲ τὸ μὲν ὡς ἐπιπειθὲς λόγῳ, τὸ δ᾽ ὡς ἔχον καὶ διανοούμενον).

in itself—that is, by the intellect. In the virtuous person, appetite and spirit have come to be in perfect harmony with reason (1102^{b}28). The virtuous person's appetitive desires are as they are not because reason has managed to persuade the non-rational part to participate fully in the person's pursuit of a flourishing life through activity that expresses the best and most complete virtue. They are as they are because the virtuous person has learned to take pleasure in those things, and only in those things, that one should take pleasure in, and in those ways, and only in those ways, that one should take pleasure in them.[14] The virtuous person's case makes clear that appetite and spirit can be affected and improved by reason over time, as a person cultivates good habits of attention, response, and behaviour. In concrete situations, moreover, reason can influence appetite, and no doubt spirit as well, so as to calm, or cause to subside, intense occurrent non-rational desires. This, I think, is all that Aristotle's general commitment to the rationality of all of a person's cognitive and motivating conditions comes to. In order to see clearly that, so understood, that commitment leaves room for a robust conception of appetite and spirit as non-rational forms of motivation, we should now turn to the discussion of lack of self-control in book 7 of the *Nicomachean Ethics*.

Given Aristotle's conception of lack of self-control, an uncontrolled person is someone who takes excessive pleasure in eating, drinking, or having sex;[15] he or she knows which pleasures of these particular kinds to pursue and which ones not to pursue, and up to what point to pursue those that should be pursued; but such people are unusually bad at resisting pleasures of these kinds in situations in which, as they know, the pleasure in question should not be pursued.[16] In *Nicomachean Ethics* 7.3, Aristotle offers an answer to the question in what way a person who acts without self-control knows that he should not act as in fact he does. Aristotle's analysis of uncontrolled action in that chapter might seem to suggest that he thinks of the psychological conflict involved in such action as always depending on competing chains of practical reasoning. In particular, it might seem to suggest that the appetitive desire that defeats the uncontrolled person in an episode of lack of self-control always depends on intellectual states and activities such as beliefs and inferences—states and activities, that is, which belong, on my view anyhow, to what has reason 'strictly speaking and in itself'. Aristotle does, after all, say that the uncontrolled act results, in a way, from reason and belief (1147^{b}1):

When one universal premiss is in the person preventing tasting, and so is one saying that everything sweet is pleasant—and *this* is sweet (and the latter premiss is active), and there

---

[14] On learning to take pleasure precisely in the things one should and precisely as one should, see M. Burnyeat, 'Aristotle on learning to be good', in A. O. Rorty (ed.), *Essays on Aristotle's Ethics*, 76–7.

[15] Plain or unqualified lack of self-control, Aristotle holds, is connected specifically with those things with which temperance and self-indulgence are concerned (*Nicomachean Ethics* 7.4, 1148^{a}4–11; 1148^{b}10–12). These are said, in *Nicomachean Ethics* 3.10, to be the pleasures that arise through touch and taste, chiefly those obtained by eating, drinking, and having sex (1118^{a}23–32).

[16] That is to say that they tend to be overcome by pleasures of these kinds that most people are able to resist: *Nicomachean Ethics* 7.7, 1150^{a}9–15.

happens to be appetite in the person, then the first one says 'avoid this', but the appetite drives him to it; for it can move each of the parts. So it turns out that the uncontrolled act results, in a way, from reason and belief.   (*Nicomachean Ethics* 7.3, 1147ª31–1147ᵇ1)

The appetite that gets the uncontrolled person to eat the chocolate crème filled doughnut seems to depend on the premises, first, that everything sweet is pleasant, and, secondly, that *this* is sweet. The uncontrolled person no doubt believes both premises, and so concludes, validly, that *this* is pleasant. Once that conclusion is reached, appetite takes over and effects a bit of uncontrolled behaviour. Because the appetite, in this particular case, depends on the uncontrolled person's beliefs, and on an inference to the conclusion that the doughnut is pleasant, it turns out, as Aristotle says it does, that the uncontrolled act results, in a way, from reason and belief. It results from appetite in the first place, but it so happens that the appetite in question results from inference and belief.

Now, it may well be that Aristotle thinks appetitive desires, and non-rational desires in general, *often* depend on beliefs and inferences for information about significant features of the person's current circumstances. That would go some way towards explaining why he describes a case of this kind in his analysis of uncontrolled action in *Nicomachean Ethics* 7.3.[17] He plainly does not think, however, that the formation of appetitive and spirited desires always depends on beliefs and inferences in this way. This becomes perfectly clear in chapter 6 of book 7, where he compares lack of self-control with regard to anger with appetitive lack of self-control. What he wants to show in the context is that lacking control over the type of spirited desire that is anger is less disgraceful than lacking control over appetitive desires (1149ª24–5). His first argument for thinking this is that since spirit follows reason in a way, whereas appetite does not, the person who is overcome by anger is, in a way, defeated by reason, whereas the person who is overcome by appetite is defeated simply by appetite, and not by reason (1149ᵇ1–3).

He begins by comparing spirit to a hasty servant, who hears only part of his master's order and already runs off to fetch what he mistakenly thinks is wanted. Likewise, Aristotle says, spirit rushes off for retaliation, having heard something of what reason says, but without having correctly heard reason's command:

For reason, or *phantasia*, indicates an insult or a slight, and spirit, as if having reasoned that this sort of thing must be fought against, at once gets angry. Appetite, on the other hand, only needs reason or perception to say that something is pleasant for it to rush off to enjoy it.   (*Nicomachean Ethics* 7.6, 1149ª32–ᵇ1)

The comparison between spirit and appetite is supposed to show that spirit follows reason in a way, while appetite does not. The imagery of spirit hearing

---

[17] The deeper and more important reason, I am inclined to think, is that Aristotle wants to emphasize the fact that the appetitive impulses that result in uncontrolled acts do not, as it were, befall a person in unaccountable and mysterious ways. Rather, they are, like other impulses, supported by, and hence explicable in terms of, specifiable cognitive and desiderative states and activities, including such familiar and thoroughly unmysterious items as a person's beliefs and inferences.

something of what reason says, but not properly hearing the whole of it, clearly is supposed to illustrate the particular way in which, Aristotle thinks, spirit follows reason. What spirit does when it follows reason in the relevant way cannot simply be what all of the non-rational part of the soul can do, namely to obey, and to listen to, reason, in the way that Aristotle had in mind in *Nicomachean Ethics* 1.13. Both appetite and spirit can, after all, obey and listen to reason in *that* way.[18] What Aristotle is now adding to the picture is that there is a special way in which spirit, but not appetite, follows reason. Now, the argument is plainly not that it is simply because spirit accepts reason's report about an insult or a slight that it can rightly be said to follow reason in the specific way that Aristotle has in mind here.[19] For he leaves no room for doubt that spirit can receive that information from *phantasia* as well as from reason. Moreover, appetite too can evidently accept reports from reason, and Aristotle means to establish by the present argument that appetite does *not* follow reason in whatever way it is that spirit does.

It is not, then, merely in virtue of accepting reason's report about a particular insult or slight that spirit can rightly be said to follow reason in the way that Aristotle has in mind here. How then is it that spirit follows reason in a way? Having considered spirit's acceptance of reason's report about an insult or a slight, the next thing to turn to is the general evaluative outlook that spirit brings to bear on the particular circumstances, which happen to involve an insult or a slight: namely, that insults and slights are objectionable things that should be responded to in an appropriately hostile and vigorous way. Perhaps it is in virtue of adopting and enacting that evaluative outlook that spirit follows reason in the relevant way? This, I think, is an important part of the correct answer.

Before attempting to spell out the correct answer, however, we should consider one more possibility. This is that spirit follows reason in the relevant way because it does something that is much like practical reasoning. As Aristotle points out, it is as if spirit infers (ὥσπερ συλλογισάμενος) from suitable premisses—one universal, the other particular—that *this* bit of behaviour calls for a hostile response. However, there is good reason to think that the activity of appetite can, on Aristotle's view, be represented by a practical syllogism no less than the activity of spirit. Consider the following passage from *De Motu Animalium* 7:

I must drink, says appetite. *This* is something to drink (τοδὶ δὲ ποτόν), says perception, *phantasia*, or the intellect. And at once the animal drinks. It is in this way, then, that animals are impelled to engage in movement and to act, the proximate cause of movement being desire, and this arises through perception, *phantasia*, or thinking. (*De Motu Animalium* 7, 701ª32–6)

---

[18] Besides, the sort of obedience to reason that Aristotle has in mind in *Nicomachean Ethics* 1.13 is manifested by self-controlled and virtuous character types, but precisely not by uncontrolled ones when they act without self-control. The way in which spirit follows reason in the present context, by contrast, *is* in evidence in acts that express lack of self-control, namely lack of self-control with regard to anger.

[19] I am indebted to the analysis of the argument offered in J. Cooper, 'Reason, moral virtue, and moral value', in M. Frede and G. Striker (eds.), *Rationality in Greek Thought*, 91.

The desire that, in this example, serves as the proximate cause of the act of drinking must be an appetitive desire to drink *this*, which in some way or other incorporates or reflects not only appetite's initial desire for some drink or other, but also the piece of situation-specific information (supplied by perception, *phantasia*, or the intellect) that *this* is something to drink. Appetite, too, then can do something very much like practical reasoning. In the *De Motu* 7 example, it is as if appetite infers from suitable premises that *this* must be imbibed. Moreover, appetite, too, has a general evaluative outlook of its own; this is that whatever currently presents itself as pleasant is to be pursued.[20] It is not clear, then, whether there is good reason to reject on Aristotle's behalf an analysis of appetitive motivation along these lines: reason, *phantasia*, or perception indicate some source of pleasure; and appetite, as if having reasoned that this sort of thing must be pursued, at once drives the person towards enjoyment.

Here, then, is what I take to be the most plausible reconstruction of Aristotle's reason for thinking that spirit follows reason in a way that appetite does not. The central point is that, in appropriately conditioned adults, the functioning of spirit incorporates a general evaluative outlook which derives from correct reason[21] and which partially reflects reason's own evaluative outlook. It is part of reason's own evaluative outlook that insults and slights are objectionable things that one should respond to in an appropriately hostile manner, unless there is good reason not to, as there might occasionally be in the varied circumstances of life. Spirit's evaluative outlook concerning insults and slights is quite simply that they are objectionable things that must be responded to in an appropriately hostile manner.[22]

What Aristotle says in the passage indicates that he thinks that spirit somehow obtains or derives this evaluative outlook from reason. After all, he speaks of spirit as hearing something of what reason says, and as following reason in a way, and also of the person who is overcome by anger as being, in a way, defeated by reason; and we have seen that he cannot, in saying these things, have in mind the piece of situational information that an insult or a slight has occurred. There is no need at all to think, however, that spirit obtains or derives its evaluative outlook from reason all at once—for example, in a particular situation that involves an insult or

---

[20] *De Anima* 3.10, 433^{b}7–10: in conflicts between intellect and appetite, Aristotle says there, the intellect prompts to pull one way on account of the future, whereas appetite, on account of what is immediate, pulls in the opposite direction: 'for what is immediately pleasant (τὸ ἤδη ἡδύ)', he explains, 'appears [sc. to appetite] to be both pleasant without qualification and good without qualification, because it does not see the future'.

[21] By 'correct reason' I am meaning to capture what Aristotle means by ὀρθὸς λόγος: reason as providing the correct practical outlook; this the uncontrolled character has within him or her: *Nicomachean Ethics* 7.4, 1147^{b}31–2.

[22] On my view, then, the relevant part of spirit's outlook is a cruder, and significantly different, version of its analogue in reason's outlook. After all, it is only *in a way* that spirit, on Aristotle's view, follows reason. In this respect, my account differs from Cooper's in 'Reason, moral virtue, and moral value'. According to the latter, spirit and reason *share* the evaluative outlook that 'insults and slights are bad and offensive things, normally to be resisted and retaliated against' (91).

a slight. Spirit's evaluative outlook might well gradually take shape, under reason's influence, over a considerable period of time. At the early stages of that development, moreover, what a maturing person's spirit obtains its outlook from may be correct reason as embodied in others—for example, in family members and in other members of the community. Furthermore, Aristotle may well think that spirit's evaluative outlook in an adult person continues to be sensitive to reason's evaluative outlook concerning such things as insults and slights. Spirit's evaluative outlook may then not only be obtained or derived from reason; it may also stand in need of being reinforced and sustained by reason.

This reconstruction gives Aristotle a suitably sharp contrast between lack of self-control with regard to anger on the one hand and appetitive lack of self-control on the other. The point of contrast is that while anger in a mature and ordinarily conditioned human being depends on, and gives expression to, a general evaluative outlook that derives from, and perhaps is sustained by, correct reason, there is no way at all in which appetite's general evaluative outlook derives from, or otherwise depends on, reason. Appetite's evaluative outlook is that whatever currently presents itself as pleasant is to be pursued. It has this outlook simply as a matter of being constituted the way it is. This outlook is, so to speak, hardwired into appetite.

We are also now in a position to attach force and significance to Aristotle's prominent contrast between spirit's quasi-reasoning on the one hand and appetite's seemingly brute impulse towards enjoyment, which he presents in our text as if it depended on nothing other[23] than some piece of situation-specific information, supplied by reason or perception, to the effect that a source of pleasure is at hand. The point is *not* that the activity of spirit can be represented in terms of practical syllogisms, whereas the activity of appetite cannot. The point is rather that there is a specific way in which, in appropriately conditioned adults, the formation of anger, but not the formation of appetitive impulses, is much like practical reasoning. Much like genuine cases of practical reasoning, the formation of anger, in such adults, involves bringing to bear on a particular situation a general evaluative outlook that is acquired and, at least to some extent, modifiable in light of reasons. Appetitive impulses, by contrast, involve the application of a general evaluative outlook that is inflexibly and unmodifiably built into the constitution, not just of our organisms, but of every animal's organism. It is therefore entirely appropriate, and in fact illuminating, for Aristotle to present appetite as responding mechanically to representations of pleasant things, and to contrast appetite's mode of operation with spirit's quasi-reasoning. In suitably conditioned adults, the formation of anger is not just a mechanical response to certain kinds of situation-specific representations. It so to speak involves two distinct kinds of moving parts that spirit puts together: an acquired and modifiable evaluative outlook on the one hand and a situation-specific belief or representation on the other.

---

[23] Note μόνον at 1149ᵃ35.

It is time to take stock. Aristotle's theory of the human soul sees reason on the one hand and appetite and spirit on the other as interrelated and integrated in a variety of ways. His account of the human soul in *Nicomachean Ethics* 1.13 makes clear that he takes the non-rational part or aspect of the soul that is the origin of appetitive and spirited desires to be capable of obeying, and of listening to, reason. This is illustrated by the way the non-rational part acquiesces in the better course of action when a person acts with self-control. As far as appetite is concerned, I suggested that such 'persuasion' may come about by reason directing appetite's attention away from the pleasure of the moment towards something else that may capture its interest—say, the prospect of a greater and more engaging pleasure, or a prospect of intense pain. (We can now see that this may simply be an exercise of reason's ability to inform appetite about available sources of pleasure.) Aristotle's discussion of lack of self-control, and of its various forms, in book 7 adds two significant details about how he takes reason, appetite, and spirit to be interrelated. First, reason can inform appetite that some source of pleasure is at hand, and it can similarly inform spirit that an insult or a slight has occurred. Secondly, spirit can, and in ordinary circumstances will, derive from reason a general evaluative outlook concerning such things as insults and slights, and presumably also, more broadly, concerning fine and disgraceful forms of behaviour. At the same time, book 7 requires that appetite's general evaluative outlook does not depend on reason in the way spirit's does. Moreover, Aristotle's comparison between lack of self-control with regard to anger and appetitive lack of self-control in 7.6 makes clear that discernment-involving capacities other than thought can supply appetite and spirit with pertinent situation-specific information. For example, *phantasia* can report that an insult has occurred, and perception can report that something pleasant is at hand.

This theory of the human soul leaves intact a clear and robust sense in which appetite and spirit are non-rational forms of motivation. They both belong to a part or aspect of the soul that, Aristotle thinks, can appropriately be called non-rational. That part of the soul can be affected and influenced by reason, and on *this* basis it can be said, in a way, to have a share in reason. Aristotle indicates, moreover, that the non-rational part does not itself engage in thinking (*Nicomachean Ethics* 1.7, 1098ᵃ3–5), and it is safe to assume that he also thinks it does not engage in reasoning, either.[24] For reasoning, as Aristotle conceives of it, is always a matter of thinking. Furthermore, if the non-rational part could itself engage in reasoning, its having *that* ability would plainly be a much stronger basis for attributing a share in reason to it than its being able to obey reason's prescriptions. It is part of Aristotle's theory of the human soul, then, that appetitive and spirited desires stem from a part or aspect of the soul that neither thinks

---

[24] Note the *Eudemian Ethics* passage, 2.1, 1219ᵇ26–1220ᵃ12, which is parallel to *Nicomachean Ethics* 1.13. There the higher part of what participates in reason is picked out by reference to reasoning (λογισμός), and the lower part by reference to desire (ὄρεξις) and affections (παθήματα); 1219ᵇ40–1220ᵃ3.

nor reasons. In the *Eudemian Ethics*, moreover, Aristotle gives further content to this view by indicating that the part or aspect of the soul to which appetite and spirit belong lacks the ability to grasp 'for the sake of' relations. For that ability belongs specifically to the part or aspect of the soul that is capable of deliberation (βούλευσις) and deliberative reasoning (λογισμός).[25] This is the higher part of human reason, the part that in *Nicomachean Ethics* 1.13 is referred to as what has reason strictly speaking and in itself. It should be clear, then, that according to Aristotle's theory of the human soul appetitive and spirited desires stem from a part of the soul that lacks the capacity for practical thought. As we saw in Chapter 12, he conceives of that capacity as crucially involving the capacity for grasping 'for the sake of' relations, and in addition to that, and no doubt dependent on it, also the interrelated capacities for recognizing alternative ways of achieving a goal, and for assessing such alternatives in terms of some standard or other.

When it comes to spirit's attention, then, that a slight or an insult has occurred, it will not, and cannot, generate its distinctive form of response by engaging in a bit of practical thinking. That is to say, it will not, and cannot, form its impulse to act by beginning with the apprehension of a goal (retribution, say, or maintaining one's self-esteem and the esteem of others) and then working out by deliberative reasoning how that goal may best be achieved in the circumstances. As far as appetite is concerned, the availability of some source of pleasure *may* be indicated to it by thought, as when one thinks about how to obtain cigarettes and works out that the thing to do in the circumstances is to go to the shop around the corner and buy a pack of cigarettes there. But Aristotle holds that thought need not be involved in becoming aware of a source of pleasure. Sources of pleasure can also come before the mind by perception, as when you see a chocolate chip muffin in the bakery's window, or by *phantasia*, as when it so happens that a certain scent puts you in mind of making love. It is, moreover, part of Aristotle's theory that appetite can, all by itself, give rise to fully formed impulses to act in pursuit of sources of pleasure that are presented to it in some way or other, for instance by perception.[26] However, when the availability of a source of pleasure is in some way presented to appetite, its response will not, and cannot, be to work out by deliberative reasoning how best to secure and enjoy the pleasure in question. Nor can it be by practical thought that it apprehends the prospective situation it is eager to bring about.

Thus it is not just that Aristotle's theory of the human soul *leaves room* for the occurrence in the domain of human psychology of some forms of non-rational cognition, as when appetite, or spirit, all by itself gives rise to an impulse to act in some specific way or other. In fact, his theory of the human soul *requires* a conception of non-rational cognition that is applicable to the mental lives of ordinarily developed, adult human beings. For in their case, too, he takes appetite and sprit to be able to form and, so to speak, hold in view goals for action, and goals which are relevant to

---

[25] *Eudemian Ethics* 2.10, 1226^{b}25–6; cf. 2.1, 1219^{b}26–1220^{a}12.

[26] *Nicomachean Ethics* 7.6, 1149^{a}34–^{b}1: 'Appetite only needs reason *or perception* to say that something is pleasant for it to rush off to enjoy it.'

the person's circumstances, without themselves being able to think or reason, and without at the time needing to rely on acts of thought or reason in any way at all.

It is, moreover, part of his theory of human psychology that 'passions' like anger, fear, or intense appetitive desire can alter the condition of a person's body, to the extent that he is temporarily unable to employ whatever practical knowledge he may have.[27] This temporary disablement will affect not only the person's decisions, but also pieces of perceptual or situation-specific knowledge, such as the knowledge that *this* is a chocolate chip muffin, or that he should abstain from eating *this*, because it contains chocolate.[28] In effect, Aristotle holds that such psychological states as anger, fear, or appetitive desire can temporarily disable the rational part or aspect of the person's action-producing apparatus. However, it plainly cannot be part of his theory that such psychological states typically cause the person's action-producing apparatus to grind to a halt. On the contrary, he must think that people who are in the grip of such states continue to act with a high degree of goal-directedness, and continue to be sensitive and responsive to their circumstances, as they grasp them by way of their senses. In other words, it must be part of his theory that the non-rational part or aspect of a person's

[27] In this discussion of how it is that the uncontrolled person knows that he should not act as in fact he does, Aristotle identifies a specific kind of psychological state as characteristic of uncontrolled episodes. He marks this kind of state as a special case of having knowledge without exercising it (at *Nicomachean Ethics* 7.3 1147ᵃ10–12), which can correctly be described both as in a way having and as temporarily lacking knowledge (μὴ ἔχειν, 1147ᵃ13; and note ἄγνοια and πάλιν γίνεται ἐπιστήμων at 1147ᵃ6), and which he illustrates by examples of people who are asleep, who are suffering fits of madness, and who are drunk. (It may be worth observing that the early learners and actors, who are mentioned at 1147ᵃ18–24, are plainly not meant to serve as further examples of the psychological state which is characteristic of uncontrolled episodes. They serve to illustrate the separate point that a person can say things that flow from and depend on knowledge without exercising, or even having, knowledge.) Aristotle's choice of examples suggests clearly and strongly that he thinks of the uncontrolled psychological state as a kind of state in which one is not only not currently exercising knowledge but is temporarily prevented by one's physiological condition from employing any knowledge one may have; note especially the repeated comparison with a person who is asleep, along with one who is drunk (*Nicomachean Ethics* 7.3, 1147ᵃ13–14; repeated at 1147ᵇ6–9, and at 7.10, 1152ᵃ14–15; cf. *Physics* 7.3, 247ᵇ13–17 and 248ᵃ5–6). This picture of a comprehensive, though temporary, disablement of reason or the intellect by 'passion' is reinforced by a number of other texts. In his descussion of temperance, Aristotle says that when appetites become large and intense (σφόδραι), they 'knock out' the person's reasoning (καὶ τὸν λογισμὸν ἐκκρούουσιν; *Nicomachean Ethics* 3.12 1119ᵇ10). The term ἐκκρούειν occurs frequently in contexts where Aristotle is describing the impact of one change or activity on another, when the former is more powerful or intense than the latter. Such clashes include ones between sensory or emotional changes on the one hand and intellectual 'motions' on the other (*De Sensu* 7, 447ᵃ14–18; *Rhetoric* 3.17, 1418ᵃ12–15). Note also *Magna Moralia* 2.6, 1202ᵃ5–7: the uncontrolled person is like people who are drunk; 'his passion gains the mastery and brings his reasoning to a standstill' (ἐπικρατῆσαν γὰρ τὸ πάθος ἠρεμεῖν ἐποίησε τὸν λογισμόν). Another text that is relevant is *De Anima* 3.3, 429ᵃ4–8, to which I shall turn presently.

[28] In *Nicomachean Ethics* 7.3, Aristotle refers to a situation-specific belief, such as that one should abstain from *this*, as a piece of perceptual knowledge (1147ᵇ15–17), because he is dealing specifically with uncontrolled action, which involves acting contrary to knowledge rather than, for instance, contrary to an incorrect view of how it is best to act. However, he doubtless thinks that passion can temporarily disable incorrect views about how to act no less than pieces of practical knowledge, and false situation-specific beliefs no less than true ones.

action-producing apparatus can continue to operate while the rational part or aspect is, for one reason or another, not in functioning order. This too makes clear that Aristotle's theory of human psychology not only leaves room for, but in fact requires, a conception of non-rational cognition that is applicable to ordinarily developed, adult human beings.

Furthermore, Aristotle does not think that this non-rational part of a person's action-producing apparatus is, or may be, in operation only when the rational part is unable to function—as it were, as a back-up mechanism. Rather, he thinks that in standard conditions both parts are active and ready to give rise to motivating conditions of the relevant kinds. Ideally, these motivating conditions will fit together harmoniously. In less ideal cases, the non-rational part may compete, and compete successfully, with the rational part. It is part of the ordinary functioning of the latter that it will try to identify the thing to do in the circumstances by relying on practical thought and situation-specific beliefs. The former may, at the same time, yield impulses to act by generating, or activating, suitable *phantasiai*. Aristotle seems to think that the non-rational part tends to operate more rapidly than the rational part, at least in individuals whose constitution renders them especially vulnerable to what he calls impetuous lack of self-control. He characterizes this form of lack of self-control in terms of being especially inclined to follow *phantasia*, so that the person in question tends not to wait for his or her reason to complete the business of working out what should be done in the circumstances, by bringing to bear relevant pieces of practical knowledge, relevant practical commitments, as well as whatever situation-specific beliefs he or she may have: 'Quick-tempered and bilious people, more than others, suffer from lack of self-control in its impulsive variety. Hastiness in the one case, intensity in the other, prevent them from waiting for reason, because their disposition is to follow *phantasia*' (*Nicomachean Ethics* 7.7, 1150^{b}25–8).

It is clear, then, that Aristotle's theory of human psychology, as it is presented and put to use in his ethical writings, requires a conception of non-rational cognition that is applicable to ordinarily developed, adult human beings. This is because he takes it to be a fact of human psychology that people can, and frequently do, form goals for action, and goals that are relevant to their circumstances, without in doing so employing thought or reason in any way at all. What he says about the impulsive form of lack of self-control suggests that he has in mind a conception of non-rational cognition in which *phantasia* plays prominent role. However, his ethical writings do not offer anything like a detailed and specific picture of non-rational Cognition and of the role in it of *phantasia*.

At the end of his discussion of *phantasia* in *De Anima* 3.3, Aristotle indicates that he means to explain the non-rational cognition involved in the motivation by appetite or spirit of adult human beings in much the same way as he means to explain the non-rational cognition involved in non-human animal motivation. He concludes the discussion of *phantasia* by saying that because *phantasiai* persist in the organism and are like perceptions, 'animals do many things in ways that

depend on them [sc. rather than on thought](πολλὰ κατ' αὐτὰς πράττει τὰ ζῷα).
As for the brute animals, this is because they do not have an intellect. With
humans, it is because their intellects are sometimes covered over (ἐπικαλύπτεθαι)
by passion, diseases, or sleep' (*De Anima* 3.3, 429ª4–8).[29]

This remark, I submit, makes the conception of non-rational cognition that I
reconstructed on Aristotle's behalf in Chapters 8–11 applicable to ordinarily
developed, adult human beings. Given that conception, Aristotle is in a position
to explain the continuing goal-directedness of people who are in the grip of, say,
intense desire or anger, as well as their sensitivity and responsiveness to their
circumstances, in terms of non-rational desire, perception, and *phantasia*. He presumably takes it, moreover, that the perceptual system of ordinarily conditioned
humans generates or activates potentially action-inducing *phantasiai* not only
when their intellect has been temporarily disabled, for instance by an intense
emotion. Such *phantasiai* will also be available in standard cognitive conditions,
to play the role, perhaps among others, of presenting to appetite and spirit
prospective situations which they may impel the person to bring about.

It may be worth pointing out that the texts on which I chiefly relied in reconstructing Aristotle's conception of non-rational cognition—the *De Motu Animalium*,
the *De Insomniis*, and in particular the *De Memoria*—are devoted to the explanation of such phenomena as self-locomotion, dreaming, and memory in a way that is
supposed to apply to all those animals which exhibit the phenomena in question,
prominently including humans. It should come as no surprise, then, that Aristotle
takes the conception of non-rational cognition that emerges in considerable detail
in these writings to be applicable to human psychology as well as to the psychology
of the brute animals.

In reconstructing Aristotle's conception of non-rational cognition, I relied
rather heavily on the idea that it is part of the functioning of specifically the
perceptual parts of the souls of suitably constituted animals that sensory impressions are preserved in the animal's perceptual apparatus in orderly ways, with
dispositions obtaining among them such that one specific sensory representation
tends to occur together with, or to be immediately followed by, some other
specific representation. Before closing, I want to draw attention to a passage from
near the end of *De Memoria* 2 in which Aristotle appeals to configurations of
sensory impressions in discussing the representations associated with 'passions'
such as anger and fear. He has just discussed the phenomenon that once one
makes an attempt to recollect something or other, it tends to be difficult to stop
the flow of representations one has set in motion. He is meaning to explain this in
terms of bodily changes that one has initiated and that, once initiated, are no

---

[29] The image Aristotle is employing in this passage is that of the intellect being covered over or
shut down. An ἐπικάλυμμα is a lid or a cover, used to cover or shut something, e.g. a sense-organ or a
passage (cf. *De Anima* 2.9, 422ª2; *Historia Animalium* 2.11, 503ª35; *De Sensu* 2, 437ª25–6). The
image, I suggest, is of the intellect as the eye of the soul, which can be open or shut (cf. *Nicomachean
Ethics* 1.6, 1096ᵇ28–9; 6.12, 1144ª29–30).

longer under one's control. The idea of changes in one's perceptual apparatus that run their course without being under one's control is also supposed to explain why it is that people in the grip of emotional states keep having representations associated with the emotional state in question, even as they try hard to get those representations to subside:

> It is for this reason, too, that anger and fear, once they have initiated some 'change', are not halted, even though the person in question effects counter-changes, but rather the emotional state effects counter-changes in the original direction. What happens is rather like what happens with names, tunes, and sayings, when one such has come to be very much on someone's lips. For after the people have stopped, and without their wishing such a thing, it comes to them to sing it or say it again.   (*De Memoria* 2, 453ª26–31)

In writing of the 'changes' that anger initiates, Aristotle presumably has in mind representations of (say) slights or insults that one takes oneself to have suffered, as well as, perhaps, of prospective acts of retaliation. The context of *De Memoria* 2 makes it clear that Aristotle takes such representations to be, or to consist in, complex patterns of sensory impressions. It is not just that he thinks that emotions can generate, or activate, such representations. He also thinks that when people are in the grip of an emotional state, their perceptual apparatus tends to keep generating or activating such representations, no matter how much they may try to get those representations to subside by generating or activating other representations in an effort to counteract them. This picture of surging and counter-surging sensory affections is, I suggest, the cognitive counterpart of motivational conflict between reason and non-rational desire.[30]

Presumably Aristotle does not think that the expert about ethical and political matters needs to have at his or her fingertips a detailed and specific account of non-rational cognition and of the role in it of *phantasia*. There is every reason to think, however, that Aristotle would direct a theoretically inclined student wishing to gain a deeper understanding of human psychology to the works on which I relied in Chapters 8–11, such as the *De Anima* and the *Parva Naturalia*. I close with a brief and somewhat selective characterization of the overall theory of human psychology which such a student would take away from a suitably careful study of those texts as well as of Aristotle's ethical writings.

Ordinarily developed, adult humans may generate impulses to act in rather sharply contrasting ways. This is because their action-producing apparatus includes two parts or aspects, one rational, the other non-rational. In the course of its functioning, the rational part brings to bear appropriate bits of practical knowledge, relevant decisions (προαιρέσεις), as well as situation-specific beliefs in trying to identify the thing to do in the circumstances in question. The non-rational part is, all by itself, capable of generating and sustaining fully formed impulses to act in specific ways, without the person's reason or intellect being active at the time in any

---

[30] Cf. *Nicomachean Ethics* 1.13, 1102ᵇ21: 'the impulses of the un-self-controlled go in opposite directions'.

way at all—for instance, because it has been disabled temporarily by an intense emotional state, an appetitive desire, or the effects of alcohol. In impelling the person to act, the non-rational part can rely on a system of cognitive capacities which Aristotle assigns to the perceptual part of the soul, and which includes perception and *phantasia*. Because it includes *phantasia* as well as perception, it can account for the occurrence of complex representations that are suited to, and continuous with, the person's current circumstances, as these are grasped by way of the senses. Such representations can prompt and guide action. The occurrence of such representations, Aristotle thinks, requires no more than, on the one hand, perceptual awareness of one's current circumstances and, on the other, the presence in one's perceptual apparatus of appropriate patterns or configurations of sensory impressions. Humans, like many other kinds of animals, are naturally constituted so that such configurations are formed and maintained as a result of ordinary perceptual experience.

This is not to say that, on Aristotle's view, the fact that human beings are reasoning creatures makes no difference to the functioning of the non-rational part or aspect of their action-producing apparatus. On the contrary, it is plainly part of his psychological theory that reason can, and normally does, affect the non-rational part of the soul in a variety of ways. It is a fact about the constitution of the human soul, he seems to think, that spirit can, and normally does, derive from reason a general evaluative outlook about such things as insults and slights. Moreover, he takes the human soul to be integrated in such a way that reason can inform spirit and appetite about salient features of a situation, as when a slight or an insult has occurred, or some source of pleasure is available. He also holds that the non-rational part of the soul is capable of listening to, and in a way of being persuaded by, reason. This commitment may be no more than a corollary of his view that reason can inform appetite and spirit about salient features of a given situation or course of action—for instance, by drawing attention to the availability of some source of pleasure, or to the shameful aspects of some course of action.

In addition to all this, it is clearly part of Aristotle's theory, as I have reconstructed and presented it, that reason makes a profound difference, for better or worse, to the functioning of the non-rational part of a person's soul by quite literally shaping his or her patterns of association. The thoughts and actions of a person will deeply affect what sensory impressions are received and preserved in his or her perceptual apparatus, and how they are related to one another. As a result, what you think and how you act will affect, for better or worse, the very character of your awareness. This, Aristotle thinks, is why wicked people constantly feel the need to drown out the hateful noise of their own memories and expectations by spending their time in the company of others (*Nicomachean Ethics* 9.4, 1166^{b}13–17). And this is why even the dreams of the virtuous may be better than those of the ordinary person (ibid. 1.13, 1102^{b}3–11).

Conclusion

I shall close by calling attention to some significant points of contact between Plato's and Aristotle's conceptions of human motivation. I begin with the parts of the soul. That the embodied human soul has three parts is a central commitment of Plato's psychological theory. An adequate account of that theory requires understanding tripartition and its basis. It only becomes clear, for instance, that the appetitive part really must be non-rational once one appreciates that, being incomposite, it cannot desire something and be averse to it at the same time. Aristotle, as we have seen, accepts Plato's three kinds of desire, but does not accept Platonic tripartition of the soul. His psychological theory, to be sure, appeals to parts or aspects of the soul, but it is somewhat unclear what commitment to such items comes to, and they are in any case not the three parts of Plato's theory. They are conceived of in functional terms, as being responsible for sets of interrelated natural capacities that are distinctive of living things.[1] Thus the part concerned with thinking accounts for understanding and reasoning, the part concerned with perceiving accounts for, among other things, perceiving, *phantasia*, and memory, and the nutritive part is responsible for nutrition, growth, and reproduction.

Can Aristotle accept Plato's three kinds of desire, but avoid Platonic tripartition of the soul? To answer this question, we should recall Plato's argument. The crucial bit is something like this:

(1) The same thing cannot at the same time do or undergo opposites in the same respect and in relation to the same thing.

(2) The soul sometimes does or undergoes opposites in the same respect and in relation to the same thing: it sometimes desires something and is at the same time averse to it.

∴ (3) The soul is a composite.

---

[1] In the ethical writings, as we saw in Ch. 13, pp. 187–90, Aristotle employs a bipartition of the soul into reason (τὸ λόγον ἔχον) and a non-rational part or aspect (τὸ ἄλογον). See, for instance, *Nicomachean Ethics* 1.13, 1102ª18–1103ª10. He makes it very clear, though, that this does not require a commitment to the view that the human soul is in fact a thing of parts: 'whether these are delimited like the parts of the body, and like everything that is a thing of parts (μεριστόν), or whether, while they are two in account, they are naturally non-separate (ἀχώριστα), like the convex and the concave in a curved surface, does not affect the present discussion' (1102ª28–32). The bipartition of the ethical writings, then, requires only that reason and a non-rational aspect of the soul are distinct in account or definition.

Aristotle applies the Principle of Opposites in a passage in *De Sensu* 7, to show that one cannot at the same time perceive opposites such as sweet and bitter:

> If the changes that belong to opposites are themselves opposites, and if opposites cannot simultaneously be in the same indivisible thing (ἅμα δὲ τὰ ἐναντία ἐν τῷ αὐτῷ καὶ ἀτόμῳ οὐκ ἐνδέχεται ὑπάρχειν), and if opposites, e.g. sweet and bitter, come under the same sense, we must conclude that it is impossible to perceive them at the same time. (*De Sensu* 7, 448ª1–5)[2]

The opposites in question being perceptual properties such as sweet and bitter, the qualifications 'in the same respect' and 'in relation to the same thing' are, I take it, inapplicable or irrelevant. Moreover, Aristotle's statement of the principle is more explicit than Plato's in *Republic* 4 in that it specifically restricts its application to indivisible items. A composite object, being divisible,[3] *can* simultaneously be characterized by opposites.

There is reason to think, then, that Aristotle accepts a version of the Principle of Opposites. He also accepts that people sometimes desire something and are at the same time averse to it.[4] Can he, nevertheless, avoid Plato's conclusion?

Aristotle, I suggest, rejects the argument's second step. As we saw, Socrates in *Republic* 4 seems to rely crucially on the idea that desires and aversions involve, or are relevantly like, movements of the soul in opposite directions. He needs an idea of this kind to be able to establish that a desire and a simultaneous aversion are always opposites 'in the same respect'. It may well be part of the idea that since desires bring about large-scale movements—like Leontius' running towards the corpses—they must themselves in some way involve or include movements: since it is the soul that desires and that through its desiring causes large-scale movements, the soul must in its desiring engage in and undergo some sort of movement—say, some sort of rushing forward that in some way or other results in large-scale bodily movement, unless it is impeded by movement in the opposite direction.[5]

In *De Anima* 1.4, Aristotle considers the view that the soul undergoes change because it 'is pained, rejoices, is confident and afraid, is angry, perceives, and thinks' (408ᵇ1–3), and all of these are changes. He is prepared to accept, at least for the sake of the argument, that all these activities *are* changes (408ᵇ5–7). But he insists that none of them are *in the soul* (408ᵇ15). It is in the ensouled body that they take place. 'It is perhaps better', he famously suggests, 'to say, not that *the soul* pities or learns or thinks, but that *the person* does in virtue of the soul' (408ᵇ13–15).

---

[2] *De Anima* 3.2, 426ᵇ29–427ª9, is a similar, but more difficult passage. Note also *Physics* 4.13, 222ᵇ5–6.

[3] Cf. *De Anima* 3.2, 427ª6–7: 'What is the same and undivided is potentially opposites, but not in [sc. actual] being, but in actually coming to be opposites it comes to be divided (διαιρετόν).'

[4] See, for instance, *De Anima* 3.10, 433ᵇ5–10; *Nicomachean Ethics* 1.13, 1102ᵇ21; 7.3, 1147ª31–5.

[5] This, of course, is precisely the sort of picture of how the soul effects movement that Aristotle attributes to his predecessors, including Plato (at 406ᵇ26–8), in *De Anima* 1.3.

It is in fact a central commitment of Aristotle's psychology, and indeed of his physics, that souls are immune from change. Like other principles of change and rest, they play a crucial role in accounting for certain forms of change without themselves engaging in or undergoing change.[6] Something that itself undergoes change could not be a *principle* of change. It is, moreover, fairly clear that Aristotle takes desires to be hylomorphic composites that are constituted by, or realized in, changes of some sort or other.[7] The change that realizes anger, which is a manifestation of spirited desire, is 'boiling of the blood and the hot stuff around the heart' (*De Anima* 1.1, 403ª31–ᵇ1). It is important to note that this physiological change is not, on Aristotle's view, something that merely accompanies anger. It is an integral part of anger. It is, to be more precise, anger's material aspect. To protect his deep and central commitment to the soul's changelessness, Aristotle *must* reject the attribution of anger to the soul. The soul in a certain way accounts for anger, but it is the composite of body and soul—the living thing, in other words—that actually is angry and that undergoes the changes that realize anger. The same goes for the other forms or kinds of desire.

Put in Aristotelian terms, Plato's idea seems to be that desires are realized in movement of some sort, and in desiring the soul itself undergoes at least some of the movement in question. Aristotle, as we have seen, must reject any such view. He accepts that desires are realized in bodily changes, but the changes that realize them occur in and belong to the ensouled body, not the soul. While the soul, on Aristotle's view, does in a certain way account for desire, it is the animal that engages in desiring. The argument for tripartition requires the claim that *the soul* engages in desiring. Since Aristotle rejects that claim, he is not bound to accept tripartition of the soul. He can consistently accept that the human soul accounts for desires of three different kinds, and that desires of these different kinds can conflict in just the ways Plato thought they could, without accepting that the soul must therefore be a composite object. This is because he rejects Plato's idea that the relevant kinds of psychological conflict show that *the soul* sometimes does or undergoes opposites in the same respect and in relation to the same thing. For Aristotle, the soul does not do or undergo anything at all. Whatever is done or undergone in conflicts of these kinds is done or undergone by the person in question, or perhaps by the relevant parts of his or her organism.

It has been one of my purposes to call attention to some Platonic antecedents of Aristotle's concept of *phantasia*. I now want to return briefly to this topic. One precursor to Aristotle's *phantasia* is memory, the preservation of perception, which at *Philebus* 32 B 9–36 C 2 plays the role of putting the depleted animal in

---

[6] M. Frede, 'On Aristotle's conception of the soul', in M. Nussbaum and A. Rorty (eds.), *Essays on Aristotle's* De Anima, 93–107, includes an illuminating discussion of how, on Aristotle's conception of the soul, it enters into the explanations of such natural changes as the formation of anger (99–104).

[7] They are, to use Aristotle's memorable expression, λόγοι ἔνυλοι: *De Anima* 1.1, 403ª25. See *De Anima* 3.10, 433ᵇ16–18, where I accept Torstrik's conjecture ἐνεργείᾳ at 18: 'actual desire is a change' (ἡ ὄρεξις κίνησίς ἐστιν, ἡ ἐνεργείᾳ); *De Motu Animalium* 10, 703ª4–5: 'desire . . . which effects change being changed itself' (ἐστὶν ἡ ὄρεξις τὸ μέσον, ὃ κινεῖ κινούμενον).

cognitive contact with the appropriate replenishing process, so that it can form a desire for something that is opposite to what its body is currently undergoing. Memory also enables humans and other animals alike to apprehend, and take pleasure in, prospective replenishments. As we have seen, a *phantasia*, for Aristotle, is an affection in an animal's perceptual apparatus which is received in an episode of perceiving (*De Anima* 3.3, 429^{a}1–2), which inherits and preserves the character of the perception in question, and which persists (ἐμμένειν, 429^{a}4) beyond the episode of perceiving that generates it. In the production of animal locomotion, the animal apprehends the object of desire either by thought, or by *phantasia* (*De Anima* 3.10, 433^{b}12).

This brings us to a mistake in the *Philebus* that Aristotle tacitly corrects. At *Philebus* 21 C 1–8, Socrates implies that molluscs and shellfish are not equipped with memory. He also, as we have seen, claims that memory is a requirement for desire, on the grounds that desire involves occurrent depletion and cognitive contact with its opposite, replenishment. Plato is overlooking the fact that a desire can occur and persist while replenishment of the appropriate sort is taking place. A subject that is being replenished can have an ongoing desire for replenishment. One can want to keep experiencing what one is experiencing already. One can also want to remain the way one is. It is a mistake, then, to think that desire is always for something that differs in character from, let alone is opposite to, what one is currently experiencing. It is also a mistake to think that a subject whose only form of cognition is perception could not have desires.

Aristotle agrees that there are kinds of animals that lack the capacity for retaining sensory impressions, but he holds that all animals have desires. He recognizes what the *Philebus*' Socrates misses, that perceptual experience can itself be desiderative. To experience something as pleasant, Aristotle thinks, is in itself to be attached to it in a certain way; likewise to experience something as painful is in itself to be averse to it in a way. Such cognitively primitive desiderative states may not be sufficient to support the complex forms of purposive locomotion that many kinds of animals exhibit. But they do not have to. Many kinds of animals are stationary, and the simplest desiderative states may be fully sufficient to explain their behaviour—for instance, a sponge's contracting when someone attempts to remove it from its substratum.

Phantasia can, on Aristotle's view, come about in two rather different ways, 'through thought or through perception' (*De Motu Animalium* 8, 702^{a}19). He also distinguishes between two kinds of *phantasia* (*De Anima* 3.10, 433^{b}29; 3.11, 434^{a}5–10), no doubt based on the different ways in which it comes about. Perceptual *phantasia* comes about through perception. This presumably is the ordinary kind of *phantasia*, which in *De Anima* 3.3 is said to be a change produced by the actuality of perception (429^{a}1–2). Rational or deliberative *phantasia* is a product of the intellect, which represents the course of action that, on the basis of practical thinking, seems best. This, to be sure, is a very special kind of *phantasia*. There must be exercises of the capacity for this kind of *phantasia* which involve more than just the preservation and re-enactment of sensory impressions. It must, after all, be possible to employ deliberative *phantasia* creatively and (precisely) imaginatively in envisaging courses of action which very much go beyond one's past experience. However, Aristotle's discussions of animal locomotion strongly suggest that he takes such reason-generated *phantasiai* to play a crucial role in rational motivation. Desire results in large-scale bodily movement unless it is impeded, but it is arguably only through *phantasia* that reason can bring about the physiological changes that constitute the material aspect of desire.[8] It is *phantasia*'s role, as Aristotle puts it, to 'prepare desire appropriately' (*De Motu Animalium* 8, 702^{a}17–19).

Now, the Aristotelian conception of sensory representations that are generated by reason and that serve to effect a connection between reason and desire seems strikingly close to the *Philebus*' conception of the painter in the soul, whose task it is to illustrate the scribe's accounts. The painter's *phantasmata*, or 'appearances', are exercises of the sensory imagination that accompany, or are involved in, reason's beliefs—crucially including beliefs about prospective pleasures. In the *Timaeus*, *phantasmata* that are in some obscure way generated by reason are supposed to enable it to convey threats and, presumably, agreeable expectations even to the soul's lowest part. The *Philebus*' simile of the illustrated book enables us to see how a story along these lines could work. Aristotle's theory of motivation arguably needs reason-generated *phantasmata* that represent objects of pursuit and avoidance more urgently than Plato's. In Plato's theory, they are needed so that reason can convey messages to the appetitive part, and perhaps to the soul's mortal part in general. They play a much more central role in Aristotle's theory. The *De Motu* account takes them to be involved in every instance of rational motivation. It seems to be at least part of their function to mediate between reason and the ensouled body, enabling thought to affect the organism so that it engages in suitable locomotion. If so, they are in fact required for the very possibility of rational motivation.

It seems, then, that Aristotle's conception of *phantasia* and its role in the production of movement is in a number of ways remarkably, and perhaps surprisingly, close to Plato's last thoughts about the soul. This proximity is somewhat obscured by the fact that Plato's use of the word *phantasia* itself is rather different from Aristotle's. In Plato's use it is a belief of a certain kind, as is clear from the *Sophist*'s account of what it is, at 264 A 4–B 4. It is a belief formed 'through', or on the basis of, perception. The *Sophist* reflects Plato's recognition of belief as a rational capacity, as is clear from the visitor's statement of what a belief is at

---

[8] We should bear in mind that, according to Aristotle's psychological theory, there is no organ of thought (*De Anima* 3.4, 429^{a}24–7), and no change of any sort stands to the activity of thought as matter to form. Thought, on Aristotle's view, is a strictly immaterial activity. Whether or not *phantasia* itself has a material aspect may be controversial, but it is clear, in any case, that it is tied to the perceptual system and, thus, to the ensouled body's locomotion-producing apparatus.

263 E 3–264 A 2.⁹ Thus a *phantasia* as defined in the *Sophist* is a state or disposition of reason, and one which involves acceptance, the silent analogue of assertion or denial (*Sophist* 263 E 12–264 A 1).¹⁰ This of course has little or nothing to do with *phantasia* as Aristotle conceives of it.

It is a striking fact about Aristotle's conception of human motivation that it combines aspects of both Empiricism and Rationalism in one integrated theory.¹¹ Every human being, according to this conception, has a part or aspect that is capable of giving rise to fully formed motivating conditions in a way that puts to use no cognitive resources other than sensory capacities, which are exercised in acts of sense-perception and in the retrieval of suitable sensory impressions. Such motivating conditions can be formed, even as far as adult, ordinarily developed humans are concerned, without reason or the intellect being active at the time *in any way at all*. Every human being also has a part or aspect that can likewise give rise to fully formed motivating conditions, and that, in doing so, employs distinctively rational resources, such as the ability to apprehend intelligible forms or the ability to reason, which crucially includes the ability to grasp 'for the sake of' relations. Furthermore, the human soul's rational and non-rational parts or aspects are integrated so that the former can, perhaps by way of the sensory imagination, communicate with the latter. As a result, reason can share information with appetite and spirit, and it can render non-rational desires less intense, or cause them to subside altogether.

I take myself to have shown that there is a natural and plausible way of reading a number of later Platonic dialogues, especially the *Timaeus* and the *Philebus*, so that a Platonic conception of human motivation emerges which can accurately be described, sentence by sentence, in precisely the way I have in the preceding paragraph described Aristotle's conception. Moreover, this late Platonic conception, I have argued, can be interpreted, naturally and plausibly, as a more precise and careful articulation of the theory of human motivation that is presented in the *Republic*.

---

⁹ Note also 264 B 1, where belief is described as 'the conclusion of thought' (διανοίας ἀποτελεύτησις).

¹⁰ It seems that Plato connects the word φαντασία with the committal use of the expression '. . . φαίνεται . . .' (note *Sophist* 264 B 1), which is standardly translated as '. . . evidently is . . .'.

¹¹ For brief accounts of Empiricism and Rationalism, see Introduction, pp. 4–6.

Bibliography

ANCIENT WORKS

ALEXANDER OF APHRODISIAS, *De Anima Liber cum Mantissa*, ed. I. Bruns (Berlin: Reimer, 1887).

ARISTOTLE, *The Complete Works of Aristotle*, ed. J. Barnes (2 vols.; Oxford: Oxford University Press, 1984).

——. *De Anima*, ed. A. Torstrik (Berlin: Weidmann, 1862).

——. *De Anima*, ed. and trans. R. D. Hicks (Cambridge: Cambridge University Press, 1907).

——. *De Anima*, ed. W. D. Ross (*editio minor*; Oxford: Oxford University Press, 1956).

——. *De Anima, Parva Naturalia* and *De Spiritu*, ed. and trans W. S. Hett (Cambridge, Mass.: Harvard University Press, 1957).

——. *De Anima*, ed. W. D. Ross (*editio maior*; Oxford: Oxford University Press, 1961).

——. *De Anima, Books II and III*, trans. D. W. Hamlyn (Oxford: Oxford University Press, 1968).

——. *De Insomniis* and *De Divinatione per Somnum*, ed. and trans. D. Gallop (Peterborough, Ont.: Broadview Press, 1990).

——. *De Memoria et Reminiscentia*, trans. R. Sorabji (London: Duckworth, 1972).

——. *De Motu Animalium*, ed. and trans. L. Torraca (Naples: Libreria Scientifica, 1958).

——. *De Motu Animalium*, ed. and trans. M. Nussbaum (Princeton: Princeton University Press, 1978).

——. *Historia Animalium*, Books 7–10, ed. and trans. D. M. Balme (Cambridge, Mass.: Harvard University Press, 1991).

——. *Historia Animalium*, ed. D. M. Balme (Cambridge: Cambridge University Press, 2002).

——. *Nicomachean Ethics*, trans. C. Rowe (Oxford: Oxford University Press, 2002).

——. *Parva Naturalia*, ed. W. D. Ross (Oxford: Oxford University Press, 1955).

EUSTRATIUS, *Eustratii et Michaelis et Anonyma in Ethica Nicomachea Commentaria*, ed. G. Heylbut (Berlin: Reimer, 1892).

GALEN, *Three Treatises on the Nature of Science*, trans. R. Walzer and M. Frede (Indianapolis, Ind.: Hackett, 1985).

HIPPOCRATES, Vol. 1, trans. W. H. S. Jones (Cambridge, Mass.: Harvard University Press, 1923).

LEUCIPPUS AND DEMOCRITUS, *The Atomists: Leucippus and Democritus, Fragments*, ed. and trans. C. C. W. Taylor (Toronto: University of Toronto Press, 1999).

MICHAEL OF EPHESUS, *In Parva Naturalia Commentaria*, ed. P. Wendland (Berlin: Reimer, 1903).

PHILOPONUS, *In Aristotelis De Anima Libros Commentaria*, ed. M. Hayduck (Berlin: Reimer, 1897).

PLATO, *Complete Works*, ed. J. Cooper (Indianapolis, Ind.: Hackett, 1997).

——. *Gorgias*, ed. E. R. Dodds (Oxford: Oxford University Press, 1959).

——. *Philebus*, trans. D. Frede (Göttingen: Vandenhoeck & Ruprecht, 1997).

———. *The* Republic *of Plato*, ed. J. Adam (2 vols.; Cambridge: Cambridge University Press, 1920).

———. *Republic*, ed. S. R. Slings (Oxford: Oxford University Press, 2003).

———. *Republic* 10, trans. S. Halliwell (Warminster: Aris and Phillips, 1988)

———. *Theaetetus*, trans. J. McDowell (Oxford: Oxford University Press, 1973).

———. *Theaetetus*, trans. M. Levett (Indianapolis, Ind.: Hackett, 1990).

PLUTARCH, *De Sollertia Animalium*, in *Moralia*, vol. XII, trans. H. Cherniss and W. Helmbold (Cambridge, Mass.: Harvard University Press, 1957).

PORPHYRY, *De Abstinentia*, trans. T. Taylor (London: Centaur Press, 1965).

SIMPLICIUS, *In Libros Aristotelis De Anima Commentaria*, ed. M. Hayduck (Berlin: Reimer, 1882).

THEMISTIUS, *In Libros Aristotelis De Anima Paraphrasis*, ed. R. Heinze (Berlin: Reimer, 1899).

MODERN WORKS

ACKRILL, J. 'Aristotle on *eudaimonia*', *Proceedings of the British Academy*, 60 (1974), 339–59.

ALLEN, J. *Inference from Signs: Ancient Debates about the Nature of Evidence* (Oxford: Oxford University Press, 2001).

ANNAS, J. *An Introduction to Plato's* Republic (Oxford: Oxford University Press, 1981).

———. 'Aristotle on memory and the self', in M. Nussbaum and A. Rorty (eds.), *Essays on Aristotle's* De Anima, 297–311.

ANSCOMBE, E. 'Thought and action in Aristotle', in R. Bambrough (ed.), *New Essays on Plato and Aristotle*, 143–58.

BAMBROUGH, R. (ed.), *New Essays on Plato and Aristotle* (London: Routledge, 1965).

BARNES, J. Review of Aristotle, *De Motu Animalium*, ed. M. Nussbaum, *Classical Review*, 30 (1980), 222–6.

BEARE, J. *Greek Theories of Elementary Cognition From Alcmaeon to Aristotle* (Oxford: Clarendon Press, 1906).

BOBONICH, C. *Plato's Utopia Recast: His Later Ethics and Politics* (Oxford: Oxford University Press, 2002).

BOSTOCK, D. *Plato's* Phaedo (Oxford: Oxford University Press, 1986).

———. *Plato's* Theaetetus (Oxford: Oxford University Press, 1988).

BROWN, L. 'Being in the *Sophist*: a syntactical enquiry', *Oxford Studies in Ancient Philosophy*, 4 (1986), 49–70.

———. 'The verb "to be" in Greek philosophy: some remarks', in S. Everson (ed.), *Companions to Ancient Thought 3: Language*, 212–36.

BURNYEAT, M. 'Plato on the grammar of perceiving', *Classical Quarterly*, 26 (1976), 29–51.

———. 'Is an Aristotelian philosophy of mind still credible? A draft', in M. Nussbaum and A. Rorty (eds.), *Essays on Aristotle's* De Anima, 15–26.

———. 'How much happens when Aristotle sees red and hears middle C?', in M. Nussbaum and A. Rorty (eds.), *Essays on Aristotle's* De Anima, paperback edn., 422–34.

———. 'Culture and society in Plato's *Republic*', in G. Peterson (ed.), *The Tanner Lectures on Human Values* 20 (Salt Lake City: University of Utah Press, 1999), 215–324.

———. 'Plato on why mathematics is good for the soul', in T. Smiley (ed.), *Mathematics and Necessity, Proceedings of the British Academy*, 103 (2000), 1–81.

BURNYEAT, M. 'Aquinas on "spiritual change" in perception', in D. Perler (ed.), *Ancient and Medieval Theories of Intentionality* (Leiden: Brill, 2001), 129–53.

——. '*De Anima* II 5', *Phronesis*, 47 (2002), 28–90.

CALVO, T. AND BRISSON, L. (eds.), *Interpreting the* Timaeus–Critias: *Proceedings of the Fourth Symposium Platonicum* (Sankt Augustin: Academia, 1997).

CASTON, V. 'Why Aristotle needs imagination', *Phronesis*, 41 (1996), 20–55.

CHARLES, D. 'Teleological causation in the *Physics*', in L. Judson (ed.), *Aristotle's* Physics, 101–28.

COOPER, J. 'Plato on sense-perception and knowledge: *Theaetetus* 184–186', *Phronesis*, 15 (1970), 123–46; reprinted in his *Knowledge, Nature, and the Good*, 43–64.

——. *Reason and Human Good in Aristotle* (Indianapolis, Ind.: Hackett, 1975).

——. Review of Aristotle, *De Memoria*, ed. and trans. R. Sorabji, *Archiv für Geschichte der Philosophie*, 57 (1975), 63–9.

——. 'Plato's theory of human motivation', *History of Philosophy Quarterly*, 1 (1984), 3–21; reprinted in his *Reason and Emotion*, 118–37.

——. 'Reason, moral virtue, and moral value', in M. Frede and G. Striker (eds.), *Rationality in Greek Thought*, 81–114; reprinted in his *Reason and Emotion*, 253–80.

——. *Reason and Emotion: Essays on Ancient Moral Psychology and Ethical Theory* (Princeton: Princeton University Press, 1999).

——. *Knowledge, Nature, and the Good: Essays on Ancient Philosophy* (Princeton: Princeton University Press, 2004).

CROMBIE, I. *An Examination of Plato's Doctrines* (2 vols.; London: Routledge, 1962).

DEVEREUX, D. AND PELLEGRIN, P. *Biologie, Logique et Metaphysique chez Aristote* (Paris: Editions du C. N. R. S., 1990).

EVERSON, S. (ed.), *Companions to Ancient Thought 1: Epistemology* (Cambridge: Cambridge University Press, 1990).

——. (ed.), *Companions to Ancient Thought 3: Language* (Cambridge: Cambridge University Press, 1994).

——. *Aristotle on Perception* (Oxford: Oxford University Press, 1997).

FLORIDI, L. 'Scepticism and animal rationality: the fortune of Chrysippus' dog in the history of Western thought', *Archiv für Geschichte der Philosophie*, 79 (1997), 27–57.

FREDE, D. 'The soul's silent dialogue: a non-aporetic reading of the *Theaetetus*', *Proceedings of the Cambridge Philological Society*, 205 (1989), 20–49.

——. 'The cognitive role of *phantasia* in Aristotle', in M. Nussbaum and A. Rorty (eds.), *Essays on Aristotle's* De Anima, 279–95.

FREDE, M. *Essays in Ancient Philosophy* (Oxford: Oxford University Press, 1987).

——. 'Observations on perception in Plato's later dialogues', in his *Essays in Ancient Philosophy*, 3–8.

——. 'An empiricist view of knowledge: memorism', in S. Everson (ed.), *Companions to Ancient Thought 1: Epistemology*, 225–50.

——. 'On Aristotle's conception of the soul', in M. Nussbaum and A. Rorty (eds.), *Essays on Aristotle's* De Anima, 93–107.

——. 'Plato's *Sophist* on false statements', in R. Kraut (ed.), *The Cambridge Companion to Plato*, 397–424.

—— AND STRIKER, G. (eds.), *Rationality in Greek Thought* (Oxford: Oxford University Press, 1996).

FREELAND, C. 'Aristotle on perception, appetition, and self-motion', in M. Gill and J. Lennox, (eds.), *Self-Motion*, 35–63.

FREUDENTHAL, G. *Aristotle's Theory of Material Substance: Heat and Pneuma, Form and Soul* (Oxford: Clarendon Press, 1995).

FREUDENTHAL, J. *Über den Begriff des Wortes* phantasia *bei Aristoteles* (Göttingen: Rente, 1863).

GILL, M. AND LENNOX, J. (eds.), *Self-Motion: From Aristotle to Newton* (Princeton: Princeton University Press, 1994).

HAMILTON, W. 'Contribution towards a history of the doctrine of mental suggestion or association', in T. Reid, *Philosophical Works, With Notes and Supplementary Dissertations by Sir William Hamilton* (Edinburgh: James Thin, 1845; reprinted Hildesheim: Georg Olms Verlag, 1983), 889–910.

HARTE, V. *Plato on Parts and Wholes: The Metaphysics of Structure* (Oxford: Oxford University Press, 2002).

HUFFMAN, K. 'Alcmaeon', in E. N. Zalta (ed.), *The Stanford Encyclopedia of Philosophy* (Summer 2004 Edition).

IRWIN, T. *Plato's Moral Theory* (Oxford: Oxford University Press, 1977).

——. *Aristotle's First Principles* (Oxford: Oxford University Press, 1988).

——. *Plato's Ethics* (Oxford: Oxford University Press, 1995).

JOACHIM, H. H. *Aristotle: The* Nicomachean Ethics, *A Commentary* (Oxford: Clarendon Press, 1951).

JOHANSEN, T. *Aristotle on the Sense-Organs* (Cambridge: Cambridge University Press, 1998).

——. 'Body, soul, and tripartition in Plato's *Timaeus*', *Oxford Studies in Ancient Philosophy*, 19 (2000), 87–111.

——. *Plato's Natural Philosophy: A Study of the* Timaeus–Critias (Cambridge: Cambridge University Press, 2004).

JUDSON, L. *Aristotle's* Physics: *A Collection of Essays* (Oxford: Oxford University Press, 1991).

KAHN, C. 'Some philosophical uses of "to be" in Plato', *Phronesis*, 26 (1981), 105–34.

——. 'Plato's theory of desire', *Review of Metaphysics*, 41 (1987), 77–103.

KANAYAMA, Y. 'Perceiving, considering, and attaining being (*Theaetetus* 184–186)', *Oxford Studies in Ancient Philosophy*, 5 (1987), 29–81.

KENNY, A. *The Anatomy of the Soul* (Oxford: Oxford University Press, 1973).

KRAUT, R. (ed.), *The Cambridge Companion to Plato* (Cambridge: Cambridge University Press, 1992).

KÜHNER, R. AND GERTH, B. *Ausführliche Grammatik der griechischen Sprache, zweiter Teil: Satzlehre* (Hanover: Hahnsche Buchhandlung, 1904).

LABARRIÈRE, J.-L. 'Imagination humaine et imagination animale chez Aristote', *Phronesis*, 29 (1984), 17–49.

——. 'De la *phronesis* animale', in D. Devereux and P. Pellegrin (eds.), *Biologie, Logique et Métaphysique chez Aristote*, 405–28.

LLOYD, G. E. R. *Aristotelian Explorations* (Cambridge: Cambridge University Press, 1996).

LORENZ, H. 'Ancient theories of soul', in E. N. Zalta (ed.), *The Stanford Encyclopedia of Philosophy* (Winter 2003 Edition).

LYCOS, K. 'Aristotle and Plato on "appearing"', *Mind*, 73 (1964), 495–514.

MELE, A. 'Aristotle's wish', *Journal of the History of Philosophy*, 22 (1984), 139–56.

MELE, A. 'Aristotle on the roles of reason in motivation and justification', *Archiv für Geschichte der Philosophie*, 66 (1984), 124–47.

MODRAK, D. 'Perception and judgment in the *Theaetetus*', *Phronesis*, 26 (1981), 35–54.

——. '*Phantasia* reconsidered', *Archiv für Geschichte der Philosophie*, 66 (1986), 47–69.

——. *Aristotle: The Power of Perception* (Chicago: University of Chicago Press, 1987).

MOLINE, J. 'Plato on the complexity of the psyche', *Archiv für Geschichte der Philosophie*, 60 (1978), 1–26.

MORAUX, P. AND WIESNER, J. (eds.), *Zweifelhaftes im Corpus Aristotelicum: Akten des 9. Symposium Aristotelicum* (Berlin: Walter de Gruyter, 1983).

MORAVCSIK, J. AND TEMKO, P. (eds.), *Plato on Beauty, Wisdom and the Arts* (Totowa, NJ: Rowman and Littlefield, 1982).

MORISON, B. *On Location: Aristotle's Concept of Place* (Oxford: Oxford University Press, 2002).

MURPHY, N. *The Interpretation of Plato's Republic* (Oxford: Oxford University Press, 1951).

MURRAY, P. *Plato on Poetry* (Cambridge: Cambridge University Press, 1996).

NEHAMAS, A. 'Plato on imitation and poetry in *Republic* 10', in J. Moravcsik and P. Temko (eds.), *Plato on Beauty, Wisdom and the Arts*, 47–78.

NUSSBAUM, M. 'The "common explanation" of animal motion', in P. Moraux and J. Wiesner (eds.), *Zweifelhaftes im Corpus Aristotelicum*, 116–56.

—— AND RORTY, A. (eds.), *Essays on Aristotle's De Anima* (Oxford: Oxford University Press, 1992; paperback edn., Oxford: Oxford University Press, 1995).

OWEN, G. E. L. 'The place of the *Timaeus* in Plato's dialogues', *Classical Quarterly*, NS 3 (1953), 79–95; reprinted in his *Logic, Science and Dialectic*, 65–84.

——. *Logic, Science and Dialectic. Collected Papers in Ancient Philosophy* (London: Duckworth, 1986).

PENNER, T. 'Thought and desire in Plato', in G. Vlastos (ed.), *Plato II*, 96–118.

——. 'Desire and power in Socrates: the argument of *Gorgias* 466A–468E that orators and tyrants have no power in the city', *Apeiron*, 24 (1991), 182–97.

PERLER, D. (ed.), *Ancient and Medieval Theories of Intentionality* (Leiden: Brill, 2001).

PRICE, A. W. *Mental Conflict* (London: Routledge, 1995).

REEVE, C. D. C. *Philosopher-Kings: The Argument of Plato's Republic* (Princeton: Princeton University Press, 1988).

ROBINSON, R. 'Plato's separation of reason from desire', *Phronesis*, 16 (1971), 38–48.

RORTY, A. (ed.), *Essays on Aristotle's Rhetoric* (Berkeley: University of California Press, 1996).

SCHOFIELD, M. 'Aristotle on the imagination', in M. Nussbaum and A. Rorty (eds.), *Essays on Aristotle's De Anima*, 249–77.

SCOTT, D. *Recollection and Experience: Plato's Theory of Learning and its Successors* (Cambridge: Cambridge University Press, 1995).

——. 'Platonic pessimism and moral education', *Oxford Studies in Ancient Philosophy*, 17 (1999), 15–36.

——. 'Plato's critique of the democratic character', *Phronesis*, 45 (2000), 19–38.

SEDLEY, D. ' "Becoming like god" in the *Timaeus* and Aristotle', in T. Calvo and L. Brisson (eds.), *Interpreting the* Timaeus–Critias, 327–39.

——. *The Midwife of Platonism: Text and Subtext in Plato's* Theaetetus (Oxford: Clarendon Press, 2004).

SEGVIC, H. 'No one errs willingly: the meaning of Socratic intellectualism', *Oxford Studies in Ancient Philosophy*, 19 (2000), 1–45.

SHIELDS, C. 'Simple souls', in E. Wagner (ed.), *Essays on Plato's Psychology*, 137–56.

SILVERMAN, A. 'Plato on perception and "commons"', *Classical Quarterly*, 40 (1990), 148–75.

——. 'Plato on *phantasia*', *Classical Antiquity*, 10 (1991), 123–47.

SOLMSEN, F. 'Greek philosophy and the discovery of the nerves', *Museum Helveticum*, 18 (1961), 150–97; reprinted in his *Kleine Schriften*, vol. 1, 536–82.

——. *Kleine Schriften* (2 vols.; Hildesheim: Georg Olms Verlag, 1968).

SORABJI, R. *Animal Minds and Human Morals: The Origins of the Western Debate* (London: Duckworth, 1993).

——. 'Rationality', in M. Frede and G. Striker (eds.), *Rationality in Greek Thought*, 311–34.

STRIKER, G. *Essays on Hellenistic Epistemology and Ethics* (Cambridge: Cambridge University Press, 1996).

——. 'Emotions in context: Aristotle's treatment of the passions in the *Rhetoric* and his moral psychology', in A. Rorty (ed.), *Essays on Aristotle's Rhetoric*, 286–302.

VLASTOS, G. (ed.), *Plato II: Ethics, Politics and Philosophy of Art and Religion* (Garden City, NY: Anchor Books, 1971).

WAGNER, E. (ed.), *Essays on Plato's Psychology* (Lanham, Md.: Lexington Books, 2001).

WEDIN, M. *Mind and Imagination in Aristotle* (New Haven, Conn.: Yale University Press, 1988).

WHITING, J. 'Locomotive soul: the parts of soul in Aristotle's scientific works', *Oxford Studies in Ancient Philosophy*, 22 (2002), 141–200.

WILLIAMS, B. 'Ethical consistency', in his *Problems of the Self*, 166–86.

——. *Problems of the Self* (Cambridge: Cambridge University Press, 1973).

WOODS, M. 'Plato's division of the soul', *Proceedings of the British Academy*, 73 (1987), 23–47.

General Index

Ackrill, J. 180 n. 13
Acron 5 n. 6
Adam, J. 55, 68 n. 22
Affection 31, 32, 37 n. 4, 75 n. 12, 88 n. 45,
102–5, 116, 119, 124, 133–5, 151–73,
175, 195 n. 24, 200, 205; *see also* Passion
Affinity argument 37
Alcmaeon 5
Alexander of Aphrodisias 132 n. 24, 139 n. 4
Allen, J. 4 n. 4
Anger 3 n. 2, 14–6, 19, 37, 65, 70, 75 n. 7,
98 n. 6, 103, 175, 191–5, 197, 199, 200,
204; *see also* Spirit
Annas, J. 16 n. 5, 43 n. 3
Anscombe, E. 184 n. 18
Appearance 57, 65–8, 71, 72, 99–101, 106–9,
119 n. 19, 143 n. 19, 154, 158, 159, 206;
see also Image, *Phantasia*, Representation,
Sensory appearance, Sensory imagination,
and Sensory impression
Application of predicates 56, 77, 80, 82 n. 29,
87, 90
Aristotle *in* Parts 1 *and* 2 9–11, 13, 27 n. 19,
38–40, 47 n. 14, 51, 55, 67 n. 20, 99 n. 9,
100 n. 10, 102 n. 15
Art 4, 5, 60, 66 n. 17, 69, 70, 72; *see also*
Expertise
Association
between sensory impressions 113, 116, 153,
165, 166, 172–4, 183, 201; *see also*
Ordered sequences of sensory impressions
of ideas 115, 153 n. 8
Atomism 5
Attitude 16, 31, 43, 141
Aversion 9, 10, 15–17, 21, 23, 25–7, 30–3, 37,
41–52, 57, 59, 62, 67 n. 19, 70, 71,
101 n. 12, 131 n. 20, 139–141, 202–5

Barnes, J. 130 n. 19
Beare, J. 153 n. 8, 154 n. 14, 156 n. 22,
164 n. 43
Being (*ousia*) 76–93, 96
Blood 5, 154–6, 175, 204
Bobonich, C. 16 n. 5, 23 n. 11, 24 n. 12,
24 n. 13, 26 n. 18, 27 n. 21, 43 n. 3,
95 n.1, 96 n. 3, 98 n. 8
Bostock, D. 76 n. 13
Brown, L. 79 n. 22
Brute animals, *see* Non-human animals
Burnet, J. 31 n. 30, 68 n. 22, 74 n. 3

Burnyeat, M. 16 n. 5, 27 n. 22, 43 n. 3,
60 n. 3, 63 n. 9, 66 n. 18, 67 n. 21,
70 n. 26, 70 n. 27, 74 n. 1, 76 n. 13,
76 n. 15, 79 n. 23, 80 n. 24, 82, 82 n. 31,
135 n. 30, 190 n. 14

Caston, V. 126 n. 9, 143 n. 19
Character 1, 18, 19, 42, 45 n. 12, 46, 63, 64,
74 n. 1, 110, 188, 192 n. 18, 193 n. 21
Charles, D. 129 n. 17, 140 n. 6
Composite 9, 10, 13, 15, 22–6, 35–40, 42, 44,
49, 70, 71, 93 n. 53, 96 n. 4, 151 n. 3,
187, 202–4; *see also* Incomposite
Conflict
Cognitive 55, 56, 62, 200
Motivational, psychological 1, 2, 9–19, 30,
31, 37, 38, 41–6, 49, 50 n. 17, 59–65,
69–71, 75, 187, 190, 193 n. 20, 200, 204
Cooper, J. 15 n. 3, 16 n. 4, 16 n. 5, 20 n. 3,
41 n. 1, 41 n. 2, 43 n. 3, 43 n. 5, 76 n. 13,
76 n. 14, 77 n. 17, 77 n. 18, 85 n. 39,
88 n. 47, 122 n. 14, 136 n. 33, 180 n. 13,
184 n. 19, 192 n. 19, 193 n. 22

Decision 121 n. 10, 130, 140 n. 5, 148, 176–9,
184, 200
Decomposition 36–9
Deliberation 50 n. 17, 62, 74, 84 n. 34, 121–3,
127, 152 n. 7, 169, 170, 178–84, 196,
205, 206
Democritus 5, 6
Desire, *see also* Impulse *and* Motivating
condition
Bodily 14, 15, 18, 20, 32, 44 n. 9, 47,
102 n. 16, 103 n. 19, 107, 108
First-order 16, 17, 43, 45
Higher-order 17, 43, 49
Non-rational 33, 37, 110, 118, 123 n. 16,
186 n. 2, 186 n. 3, 189–91, 199,
200, 207
Second-order 16, 17, 45
Spirited 1–3, 15, 45, 46, 51 n. 19, 117, 118,
121 n. 10, 122, 130, 138, 143, 148, 176,
177, 186–201, 204, 207; *see also* Anger
Digestion 100 n. 10, 152, 155
Discernment 82 n. 29, 86, 87, 90, 91, 96, 121
n. 10, 128–31, 148, 176 n. 3, 195
Divination 6, 100, 136 n. 34
Dodds, E. R. 86 n. 41
Drama 1, 60–3; *see also* Poetry

Dreams 6, 100, 101, 134 n. 29, 136 n. 34, 151–9, 165, 175, 199, 201

Education 1, 47 n. 14, 48, 64, 75, 88, 91
Empiricism 4–6, 104, 108, 173, 207
Epithumia 39, 42, 45, 46
Esteem 1, 18, 45, 68, 196; *see also* Honour
Eustratius 187 n. 5
Everson, S. 125 n. 4, 125 n. 5, 159 n. 27
Expectation 58, 98, 102–6, 201, 206
Experience 4–6, 150 n. 2, 153, 170, 173, 181, 183, 201
Expertise 4, 5 n. 7, 92; *see also* Art

Fear 18, 42, 58, 75 n. 10, 98, 102–4, 109, 197–200
Final cause 129; *see also* Goal
Frede, D. 76 n. 13, 106 n. 24, 106, n. 25, 126 n. 9, 144 n. 21
Frede, M. 4 n. 3, 5 n. 5, 76 n. 13, 85 n. 37, 204 n. 6
Freeland, C. 125 n. 6, 125 n. 7
Freudenthal, G. 155 n. 16
Freudenthal, J. 134 n. 29, 138 n. 2

Galen 4 n. 3, 5 n. 6
Gallop, D. 136 n. 34, 154 n. 14, 156 n. 22
Glaucon 15, 19, 22, 60–6, 73 n. 31, 74 n. 1
Goal 33, 43, 52, 114, 121, 128–33, 142, 143, 149, 170, 177–84, 196–9
Grief 14, 62–5

Habituation 1, 47, 50 n. 16, 51, 64, 116, 120, 156 n. 22, 164–6, 170–3, 183, 190
Halliwell, S. 67 n. 21
Hamlyn, D. 119 n. 3, 124 n. 2, 139 n. 5, 143 n. 18
Harte, V. 22 n. 8
Heart 37, 71, 154, 155, 204
Hett, W. 156 n. 22
Hicks, R. D. 139 ns. 3–5, 145 n. 25, 146 n. 26
Hippocrates 5 n. 7
Homer 60, 63 n. 8, 71, 132 n. 23
Honour 18, 19, 32, 45–8; *see also* Esteem
Huffman, C. 5 n. 9
Hume, D. 32, 33, 175
Hunger 2, 4, 14, 15, 21 n. 4, 28–31, 37 n. 4, 102–4, 107, 115, 128, 132 n. 23, 150 n. 2, 180

Ideal city 14, 18, 60, 64
Illusion 55, 67
Image 5, 6, 57, 99–101, 105, 107, 109; *see also* Appearance, *Phantasia*, Representation, Sensory appearance, Sensory imagination, *and* Sensory impression
Imitation 55, 56, 60–6, 69–72; *see also* Poetry

Immortality, *see* Soul
Impression, *see* Sensory impression
Impulse 1, 2, 9, 20, 22, 30, 33 n. 32, 35, 50, 59, 89, 102, 114–8, 128, 143, 152, 172, 176 n. 3, 188, 191–201; *see also* Desire *and* Motivating condition
Incomposite 10, 15, 22, 26 n. 18, 35, 36, 39, 40, 44, 51, 60, 65, 71, 202
Inference 90, 175, 189–93
Injustice 29 n. 27, 41, 46, 65, 97, 99 n. 9
Instrumental reasoning, *see* Means-end reasoning
Intellect 1, 6, 38, 60, 87 n. 44, 92, 99, 101, 104, 113, 118, 119 n. 3, 130, 140 n. 5, 142 n. 15, 152 n. 7, 157, 160–2, 166, 167, 170, 171, 177, 184, 188–93, 197–200, 205, 207
Intelligible 4, 6, 76, 83 n. 33, 87 n. 44, 91, 93, 96, 101, 152 n. 6, 160–2, 166, 171 n. 58, 207
Irwin, T. 13 n. 1, 15 n. 3, 16 n. 4, 16 n. 5, 19 n. 1, 25 n. 15, 25 n. 16, 28 n. 23, 41 n. 1, 41 n. 2, 43 n. 3, 43 n. 5, 43 n. 6, 44 n. 7, 45 n. 10, 50 n. 17, 143 n. 19, 144 n. 21, 144 n. 22, 146 n. 27, 184 n. 18

Joachim, H. 186 n. 1
Johansen, T. 36 n. 2, 74 n. 2
Justice 1, 14, 18, 41, 59, 64, 98 n. 7

Kahn, C. 76 n. 13, 79 n. 22, 85 n. 39
Kanayama, Y. 76 n. 13, 79 n. 23, 86 n. 40
Kenny, A. 60 n. 3
Knowledge 4, 5, 20, 27 n. 19, 28, 29 n. 27, 60, 74, 78, 82 n. 29, 91, 93 n. 53, 148, 161 n. 34, 163, 167, 170, 190, 197–200

Labarrière, J.-L. 121 n. 7, 121 n. 9
Lack of self-control 109, 118, 184 n. 18, 187–200
    Plain or unqualified 190 n. 15
    with regard to anger 191–5
Learning 18–22, 27, 28, 48, 89, 163–7, 190
Leontius 9, 16, 17, 32, 43, 45, 59, 70 n. 28, 203
Leucippus 5
Lloyd, G. E. R. 144 n. 20
Locomotion 114–19, 123–33, 137–52, 172, 174, 177–81, 192, 199, 203–6
Logismos 177, 178
Logos 177
Lulofs, D. 154 n. 14

McDowell, J. 76 n. 13, 81 n. 26, 83 n. 32, 84 n. 35, 86 n. 41
Means-end reasoning 11, 16, 32, 43, 44, 47, 48, 52, 113

Means-end relation, *see* Relation
Mele, A. 184 n. 19
Memorist 4 n. 3
Memory 4–6, 55, 69, 102–6, 113, 116,
    132 n. 24, 136, 139 n. 4, 152, 154 n. 12,
    157–75, 201–5; *see also* Recollection
  Dispositional 167–71, 174, 175
Michael of Ephesus 155 n. 21, 163 n. 41
Modrak, D. 76 n. 13, 76 n. 14
Money 15, 18–22, 33, 41–8, 52, 75, 107; *see*
    also Wealth
Morison, B. 27 n. 19
Motivating condition 2, 6, 9, 20–8, 33, 35, 49,
    50, 55–9, 95–9, 104, 108, 117, 140 n. 7,
    178, 186, 187, 190, 198, 207; *see also*
    Desire *and* Impulse
Murphy, N. 28 n. 23, 60 n. 3
Murray, P. 67 n. 21

Nehamas, A. 60 n. 3, 61 n. 5, 66 n. 17,
    67 n. 21
Non-human animals 2, 31, 38, 58, 59, 77,
    91 n. 51, 97, 100–5, 113–57, 169–85,
    189 n. 12, 198, 199, 201, 205
Non-rational
  belief 4, 56, 71–3
  desire, *see* Desire
  part of the soul, *see* Part of the soul
  thought 4, 59, 62
Nussbaum, M. 124 n. 4, 128 n. 13, 130 n. 19

Odysseus 37, 71
Oligarch 41–8, 59, 98 n. 8, 109
Opposites 10, 21–7, 31, 37 n. 4, 56, 61, 62,
    65–71, 86–91, 102 n. 16, 103, 116, 164,
    165, 169 n. 53, 188 n. 7, 193 n. 20,
    200–5; *see also* Principle of Opposites
Opposition 21–6, 61–3, 67, 68, 72, 76,
    86–93, 96, 165
Ordered sequences of sensory representations
    116, 153, 154, 157, 164–9, 172, 175; *see*
    also Association
Ousia, see Being

Pain 32, 33, 49, 51, 61, 69 n. 25, 70, 75 n. 10,
    98–110, 118, 125 n. 6, 125 n. 7, 126,
    131 n. 20, 138–43, 176 n. 3, 189, 195,
    203, 205
Painter in the soul 101 n. 14, 105–7,
    161 n. 34, 206; *see also* Sensory imagination
    and Simile of the illustrated book
Painting 55, 60–6, 69–71, 109, 134 n. 29,
    161 n. 34
Partition, *see* Soul
Part of the soul
  Appetitive (appetite) *passim in* Parts 1 *and* 2
    202, 206

Mortal 38, 74, 75 n. 7, 75 n. 12, 99, 101–4,
    107, 108, 206
  Non-rational 9, 47 n. 14, 52, 55–65, 68–73,
    93–101, 104, 108, 109, 118, 187–92,
    195, 198–202, 207
  Perceptual 116, 140, 151–4, 157–60, 171,
    174, 175, 199, 201
  Spirited (spirit) 11, 14–19, 22 n. 8, 31, 32,
    37, 38, 45–7, 51 n. 19, 57, 59, 62–5, 70,
    71, 74, 75, 97–101, 108, 207
Passion 32, 33, 63, 142 n. 15, 197, 199;
    see also Affection
Penner, T. 28 n. 23, 29 n. 27
Perceptible 4, 6, 27 n. 22, 76, 81, 91, 93 n. 53,
    96 n. 4, 132, 160, 166
Perceptual
  apparatus 116, 152–8, 162–75, 183,
    199–201, 205
  belief 76–9, 93 n. 53, 105
  features 56, 86, 87, 90
  part of the soul, *see* Part of the soul
  phantasia, see Phantasia
  system 116, 199
Persuasion 109, 189, 190, 195, 201
Phantasia outside Part 3 3, 4, 99 n. 9, 202–7;
    see also Appearance, Image, Representation,
    Sensory appearance, Sensory imagination,
    and Sensory impression
  Deliberative, *see Phantasia*, Rational
  Perceptual 121, 122, 125, 205
  Rational 121–3, 127, 182, 205, 206
Philoponus 6 n. 12, 139 n. 4, 139 n. 5, 141 n. 8
Philosopher 18, 45, 85 n. 39
Plato *in* Part 3 113, 120 n. 4, 131, 132 n. 24,
    136, 154 n. 12, 158–64, 177 n. 7,
    188 n. 7, 188 n. 9
Pleasure 1–3, 9, 20, 25 n. 16, 27, 31–3, 45–51,
    58, 61, 65, 69, 70, 75 n. 10, 98–110,
    118–122, 125 n. 6, 125 n. 7, 126,
    129–43, 149, 150 n. 2, 163 n. 39, 172,
    189, 190–6, 201, 205, 206
  of anticipation 58, 102–8, 131, 136, 137,
    149, 172
Plutarch 176 n. 3
Pneuma 155 n. 16
Poetry 1, 55, 60
  Imitative 55, 56, 60–5, 69, 70
Polus 5 n. 7
Porphyry 176 n. 3
Practical syllogism 192, 194
Preservation
  of perception 4, 102 n. 15, 103, 106, 136,
    154 n. 12, 158, 204
  of sensory impressions 55, 58, 103–8, 113,
    116, 153–8, 161, 162, 166–8, 171, 172,
    175, 199, 201, 206; *see also* Retention of
    sensory impressions

Price, A. 16 n. 4, 16 n. 5, 25 n. 15, 41 n. 1,
     43 n. 3, 43 n. 5, 43 n. 6, 44 n. 7,
     66 n. 18
Principle
     of change and rest 204
     of Opposites (**PO**) 10, 14, 21–8, 41–4, 47,
     48, 62, 66–8, 90 n. 50, 203
     of unity 10, 39
Proper subject 10, 20–8, 35, 37, 49,
     103 n. 19
Prospective situation or course of action,
     Prospect 3, 58, 100, 105–9, 114–18,
     131–3, 136, 137, 141–3, 149–53, 174,
     180, 181, 189, 195, 196, 199, 200, 205,
     206

Rapp, C. 141 n. 12
Rationalism 4, 6, 207
Rationality 1, 16, 17, 51, 95, 113, 176 n. 3,
     177, 186, 187, 190
     Practical 51, 113
Recollection 116, 134 n. 29, 153 n. 11,
     156 n. 22, 157, 162–72, 199; *see also*
     Memory
     Theory of 162, 163
Re-enactment of sensory impressions 55, 58,
     113, 156, 158, 206; *see also* Retrieval of
     sensory impressions
Reeve, C. D. C. 13 n. 1, 21 n. 5
Relation
     'For the sake of' 11, 113, 117, 179, 180–4,
     196, 207
     Means-end 6, 11, 48–52, 113, 120, 180,
     183
Remembering, *see* Memory
Replenishment 4, 31, 103, 104, 107, 136, 158,
     205
Representation 3, 49–51, 55, 56, 82, 93, 97,
     100, 101, 106, 109, 113–23, 127, 136,
     137, 140 n. 7, 150, 153, 156–75, 181,
     194, 199–201, 205, 206; *see also*
     Appearance, Image, *Phantasia*, Sensory
     appearance, Sensory imagination, *and*
     Sensory impression
     Action-guiding, behaviour-guiding 51, 104,
     113, 116, 181, 183, 201
Representational 93, 97, 159, 161, 162
Retaliation 3 n. 2, 191, 193 n. 22, 200
Retention of sensory impressions 3–6, 132–7,
     150–4, 161, 166–74, 205; *see also*
     Preservation
Retrieval of sensory impressions 3, 6, 158, 161,
     207; *see also* Re-enactment of sensory
     impressions
Robinson, R. 35 n. 1
Ross, W. D. 139 n. 5, 145 n. 25, 146 n. 26,
     154 n. 14, 163 n. 41

Schofield, M. 128 n. 12
Scott, D. 45 n. 12, 64 n. 11, 137 n. 36
Sedley, D. 36 n. 2, 60 n. 3
Segvic, H. 28 n. 25, 29 n. 27
Self-control 41, 42, 46, 62, 63, 98 n. 8, 101,
     188, 192 n. 18, 195
Self-indulgence 131, 163 n. 39, 190 n. 15
Sense-organ 5, 81, 82, 134 n. 29, 135 n. 30,
     152–5, 199 n. 29
Sensory
     appearance 66–8, 71, 101; *see also*
     Appearance, Image, *Phantasia*, and
     Representation
     experience 4, 6, 101, 154, 170
     imagination 57, 101, 106–9, 113, 118, 160,
     206, 207; *see also* Painter in the soul
     impression 3, 6, 55, 58, 103, 104, 108, 113,
     116, 132–7, 150–3, 159, 160, 172–5,
     183, 199–201, 205–7
     memory 4
     representation, *see* Representation
     system 113, 206 n. 8
Sex 20, 32, 42–7, 52, 59, 68, 70, 75, 190
Sexual arousal 14, 15
Shields, C. 13 n. 1
Silverman, A. 76 n. 13
Simile of the illustrated book 57, 58, 102–5,
     108, 118, 206; *see also* Painter in the soul
Simplicius 139 n. 4, 139 n. 5
Sleep 59, 100, 136 n. 32, 142 n. 15, 151 n. 4,
     155, 165 n. 47, 197 n. 27, 199
Slings, S. 31 n. 30, 68 n. 22
Socrates 13 n. 1, 28–30
Socratic intellectualism 29 n. 27
Solmsen, F. 155 n. 16
Sophonias 155 n. 21, 163 n. 41, 164 n. 43
Sorabji, R. 121 n. 7, 135 n. 32, 136 n. 33,
     163 n. 37, 163 n. 38, 163 n. 41, 164 n. 43,
     167 n. 48, 167 n. 51, 176 n. 3
Soul
     Bipartition of 65, 202n. 1
     Immortality of 36–8
     Partition of 9–11, 14–17, 26 n. 18, 30,
     34–49, 67, 151 n. 3
     Tripartition of 1–6, 9–11, 14, 19–22, 25,
     28–31, 34–41, 44, 47–51, 56, 57, 60–2,
     65, 66, 71, 74, 75, 95, 97–9, 188 n. 7,
     202, 204
     World 93 n. 53, 96 n. 4, 97
Spirit, *see* Desire *and* Part of the soul; *see also*
     Anger
Sponge 141, 205
Striker, G. 122 n. 15

Taylor, C. C. W. 6 n. 11
Temperance 59, 73 n. 31, 98 n. 8, 109, 131,
     190 n. 15, 197 n. 27

Themistius 126 n. 9, 139 n. 4
Thirst 4, 14, 15, 21, 27–32, 37 n. 4, 62, 102–4, 107, 158
Thrasymachus 45
Torraca, L. 130 n. 19
Torstrik, A. 139 n. 4, 139 n. 5, 204 n. 7
Tripartition, *see* Soul

Understanding 1, 20, 52, 62 n. 6, 88–100, 177, 202
Unity
  of the person 26 n. 18
  of the soul 22, 26 n. 18, 39, 59, 64

Vice 1, 38, 131
Virtue 1, 2, 42, 98 n. 8, 101, 109, 110, 131, 186, 188, 190, 192 n. 18, 201

Wealth 18, 33, 41, 44–7, 93, 107; *see also* Money
Wedin, M. 125 n. 6, 125 n. 7, 127 n. 11
Whiting, J. 152 n. 7
Wisdom 18, 38, 46, 60 n. 4, 66, 69, 74
Wish 3 n. 2, 121 n. 10, 130, 138, 143, 148, 176, 184 n. 18
Woods, M. 15 n. 3, 41 n. 2

Index Locorum

ARISTOTLE

DE ANIMA

403a25	204 n. 7
403a31–b1	204
403b24–8	128 n. 14
404a27–31	5 n. 10
405a8–13	5 n. 10
406b26–8	203 n. 5
408b1–3	203
408b5–7	203
408b13–8	151 n. 5
408b13–5	203
408b15	203
408b15–8	134 n. 29
408b17–8	153 n. 11
411a26–b3	39
411b5	39
411b5–6	39
411b5–14	38, 39, 151 n. 3
411b9	39
411b11	39
412a22–3	167 n. 49
413a32	127 n. 10
413b2–4	133 n. 25
413b11–6	151 n. 3
413b21–4	125 n. 6, 126 n. 8, 138 n. 2
413b22	134 n. 4
414b1–6	125 n. 6, 138, 141, 141 n. 11, 143, 146
414b2	3 n. 2
414b3–6	3 n. 2, 126 n. 8
414b14–7	133 n. 25
414b14–9	144 n. 20
414b15–7	138 n. 1
415a8–11	124 n. 3
415a9	127 n. 10
415a10–11	138 n. 2
415a18–20	159 n. 28
417a21–417b2	167 n. 49
417b22–4	170 n. 57
422a2	199 n. 29
425b24–5	134 n. 29
426b29–427a9	203 n. 2
427a6–7	203 n. 3
427a17–b8	5 n. 10
428a8–11	124 n. 3, 126, 139, 139 n. 2, 144
428a9–11	144 n. 21
428a19–24	67 n. 20, 138 n. 2
428a22–4	189 n. 12
428b10–7	135, 136 n. 33
428b12–3	135 n. 31
428b25–30	134 n. 29
429a1–2	205
429a1–5	153
429a2–4	119 n. 1
429a4	134, 205
429a4–8	135, 142 n. 15, 176 n. 4, 197 n. 27, 199
429a22–7	162
429a24–7	206 n. 8
431a8–14	141 n. 11
431a8–16	140
431a12	139 n. 5
431a16–7	127
431b2–3	127 n. 11
432a3–10	127 n. 11
432a7–8	145
432a15–8	128
432a15–22	145 n. 24
432a17	144 n. 23
432a18	144 n. 23
432a18–9	145
432b3–7	125 n. 6
432b4–7	122 n. 15
432b5–6	3 n. 2
432b7–8	145, 145 n. 24
432b8	144 n. 23
432b13–4	142 n. 13, 145, 145 n. 24
432b13–7	128
432b19–21	132 n. 25, 144, 146
432b19–26	146
432b25–6	142 n. 13
432b28	144 n. 23
433a6–8	186 n. 2
433a7	144 n. 23
433a9	144 n. 23
433a9–10	121 n. 9
433a9–12	117
433a9–13	145
433a9–14	148
433a10–12	120 n. 4
433a11–12	120, 176 n. 4
433a12	120 n. 4
433a13	144 n. 23
433a13–15	121 n. 10, 177
433a13–17	179
433a14	178 n. 11
433a15–16	119 n. 3

433a16	177 n. 6	459a26	153 n. 10
433a18	144 n. 23, 177 n. 6	459a26–7	153 n. 11
433a24	120 n. 4	459b1–7	154
433a25	120 n. 4	459b5	153 n. 10
433a25–6	122 n. 14, 123 n. 16,	459b5–7	153 n. 11
	125 n. 6	459b10–11	155 n. 17
433a31–b1	145, 146	460a32–b3	134 n. 29
433b5–10	177 n. 8, 203 n. 4	461a8–11	154
433b6	120 n. 4	461a14–25	155
433b7–8	188 n. 7	461a18–9	154 n. 13
433b7–10	193 n. 20	461a25–6	156 n. 24
433b11–12	119, 126, 146	461a25–b1	154
433b12	205	461a26	154 n. 13
433b16–18	204 n. 7	461a27	154 n. 14
433b27	145	461b11–24	156
433b27–8	145, 146 n. 26	461b13–5	156 n. 22
433b27–9	125, 125 n. 6, 143, 144	461b16–21	155 n. 17
433b27–30	124	462a2–8	155 n. 18
433b27–434a5	127, 143, 145	462a3	135 n. 32
433b28	146 n. 26	462a5–7	156
433b28–9	145, 146 n. 26, 147	462a9	153 n. 11
433b28–30	125 n. 5	462a28–9	156
433b29	178 n. 10, 205		
433b29–30	121	DE IUVENTUTE	
433b31	125 n. 6	469a5–7	154
433b31–434a5	102 n. 15, 125, 125 n. 6		
433b31–434a7	144 n. 21	DE MEMORIA	
434a4	125 n. 6	449b4	163 n. 41
434a4–5	125	449b4–5	159
434a5	125 n. 7	449b13–5	132
434a5–10	205	449b15	158 n. 25
434a7	122, 178 n. 10	449b15–23	160
434a7–10	122, 127, 143 n. 16, 178	449b18–23	258
	n. 11, 182	449b19	159 n. 28
434a8	120 n. 4	449b27–8	158 n. 25
434b11–8	141 n. 11	449b30–1	153 n. 9
		449b30–450a9	127 n. 11
DE DIVINATIONE PER SOMNUM		449b31–450a1	158 n. 26
463a21–30	156	450a4–5	160 n. 31
463a23–7	155 n. 19	450a12–13	160
463b12–13	156 n. 23	450a12–14	152 n. 6
463b31–464a24	6	450a13–14	160
		450a15–16	171
DE INSOMNIIS		450a16–17	152 n. 7
458a33–b2	151	450a19–21	158
458b2	151 n. 4	450a22–3	159 n. 29, 171, 171 n. 58
458b2–3	151 n. 5	450a22–5	152 n. 7
458b15–20	156	450a23–5	160 n. 32
458b25	156	450a25–7	158
459a8–9	152 n. 7	450a27–32	162 n. 34
459a10–1	152 n. 7	450a28–9	153 n. 11
459a11–4	151 n. 4	450a29–30	134 n. 29
459a13–5	156 n. 23	450a29–32	161 n. 34
459a14–8	153 n. 9	450a31	134 n. 29
459a14–22	151	450b5	153 n. 10
459a21–2	151, 152 n. 7	450b10	158 n. 26
459a24–8	134 n. 29, 155 n. 17	450b10–11	134 n. 29

450b11–15	158
450b11–451a17	158 n. 26
450b12	153 n. 10
450b18	153 n. 10
450b20–7	159
450b27–451a2	159
451a10	158 n. 26
451a14–15	163 n. 41
451a16–17	159 n. 29, 171 n. 58
451a31–452b2	169 n. 54
451b2–3	163 n. 40
451b5	163 n. 41
451b2–6	163
451b9–10	164
451b10–14	156 n. 22, 173
451b10–25	164
451b16–8	168 n. 52
451b18–9	169 n. 53
451b18–20	170
451b18–22	168 n. 52
451b23–4	165 n. 46
451b28–30	165
451b28–452a2	166
451b29–31	168 n. 52, 170 n. 56
451b30	164 n. 43
452a4–6	168 n. 52
452a4–10	166
452a6–7	167
452a8	164 n. 43
452a8–10	168 n. 52
452a10–12	167
452a12–16	168 n. 52
452a13–16	165 n. 46
452b23–453a4	158
452b26–8	165
452b30–453a2	136 n. 33
453a4–14	169
453a12	164 n. 43
453a12–14	170
453a15	163 n. 39
453a15–16	164 n. 43, 169
453a24	153 n. 11
453a26–31	200
453b8–9	163 n. 41
453b8–10	171 n. 58

DE MOTU ANIMALIUM
698a4–7	128, 130, 142 n. 14
700a7–11	144 n. 20
700a8	130 n. 19
700a21–5	144 n. 20
700a26	130 n. 19
700b15–29	129
700b17	130 n. 19
700b17–18	176
700b17–22	121 n. 10, 130, 148
700b22	125 n. 6

700b23	140 n. 5, 176 n. 4
701a19	130 n. 19
701a15–6	128
701a32–6	192
701b13–22	134
701b33–5	126
702a15–17	124 n. 1, 142
702a17–19	114, 119, 124, 206
702a19	205
702a20	130 n. 19
703a4–5	204 n. 7
703b18–20	188
703b20–6	100 n. 10

DE SENSU
436a5–17	165 n. 47
447a14–8	197 n. 27
448a1–5	203

DE SOMNO
453b17–20	151 n. 4, 165 n. 47
454a11–9	151 n. 4
454b9–12	151 n. 4
454b29–31	138 n. 1

EUDEMIAN ETHICS
1219b26–1220a12	195 n. 24, 196 n. 25
1219b28	187 n. 6
1219b32–6	187 n. 6
1219b36–7	187 n. 6
1219b40–1220a3	195 n. 24
1223a26–7	125 n. 6
1224a23–7	186 n. 2
1224b21–4	186 n. 2
1225a3	186 n. 2
1225b24–26	3 n. 2
1225b26–7	177 n. 5
1226b9–13	179
1226b14–7	184 n. 18
1226b17	184 n. 17
1226b21–3	182 n. 16
1226b21–30	178 n. 11, 179
1226b25–6	196 n. 25
1227a3–5	184 n. 17
1247b34–5	186 n. 2

HISTORIA ANIMALIUM
487b6–12	141 n. 10
487b7–11	144 n. 22
487b10–2	141 n. 9
488b25–6	171 n. 59
488b26	169 n. 55
503a35	199 n. 29
548b10–15	141
608a13–7	121 n. 7
611a15–b23	120
611a20–1	172

612a2–5   175 n. 2
612a3–5   121
612a16–21   175 n. 2
614b18–27   175 n. 2
629b24–7   175 n. 2
631b27–31   175 n. 2

MAGNA MORALIA
1189a1–6   186 n. 2
1202a5–7   197 n. 27

METAPHYSICS
980a27–980b25   39 n. 4
980b1–5   121 n. 7
980b21–7   171 n. 59
980b25–8   120 n. 4
981a3–5   5 n. 7
1072b19–21   126 n. 10

NICOMACHEAN ETHICS
1098a3–5   189 n. 13, 195
1102a18–1103a10   202 n. 1
1102a26–1103a3   186
1102a28–31   187
1102a28–32   202 n. 1
1102b3–11   201
1102b4   187 n. 4
1102b11–12   188
1102b13–14   186 n. 3, 188
1102b18   188 n. 7
1102b21   188 n. 7, 200 n. 30,
             203 n. 4
1102b28   190
1102b29–31   186 n. 3
1102b30   186 n. 2
1102b31–2   189 n. 10
1102b33–4   189 n. 11
1102b33–1103a1   188
1103a1–2   186 n. 2
1103a3   189 n. 10
1111b6–9   176 n. 4
1111b10–26   3 n. 2
1111b12–13   176 n. 4, 177 n. 5
1111b13–15   184 n. 18
1112b11–20   181
1113a2–5   184 n. 17
1118a12–3   163 n. 39
1118a18–23   131, 149
1118a20–3   128 n. 15
1118a23–6   131
1118a23–32   190 n. 15
1119b7–10   2 n. 1
1119b10   188 n. 9, 197 n. 27
1136b7–9   3 n. 2
1139a3–15   177
1139a5–6   177 n. 6
1139a12–3   178 n. 10
1139a23   184 n. 17

1139b1–2   177 n. 6
1139b4–5   140 n. 5, 176 n. 4
1139b12   177 n. 9
1141a26–8   121 n. 8
1142b18–20   184 n. 18
1144a29–30   199 n. 29
1146a9–16   188 n. 8
1147a10–12   197 n. 27
1147a13   197 n. 27
1147a13–14   197 n. 27
1147a18–24   197 n. 27
1147a31–5   203 n. 4
1147a31–b1   191
1147a34–5   123 n. 16, 188 n. 9
1147b1   190
1147b31–2   193 n. 21
1147b6   197 n. 27
1147b6–9   197 n. 27
1147b15–17   197 n. 28
1148a4–11   190 n. 15
1148b10–12   190 n. 15
1149a24–5   191
1149a24–b26   3 n. 2
1149a32–b1   99 n. 9, 191
1149a34–b1   196 n. 26
1149a35   194 n. 23
1149b1–3   191
1150a9–15   190 n. 16
1150b25–8   198
1151b34–1152a3   188 n. 8
1152a14–15   197 n. 27
1166b13–17   201
1166b15   163 n. 38
1170a25–b8   136 n. 32

PARTS OF ANIMALS
681a16–18   141 n. 10
683b9–10   133 n. 25, 199 n. 160

PHYSICS
184a21–b14   137 n. 36
194b32–5   129
195a23–6   129 n. 16
197b22–6   129 n. 18
209a31–b1   27 n. 19
210a26–7   27 n. 19
210a29–30   27 n. 19
254b7–14   27 n. 19, 142 n. 13
261a15–17   133 n. 25, 144 n. 20

POSTERIOR ANALYTICS
99b36–7   133 n. 27
99b36–100a1   124 n. 3, 132, 138 n. 2
99b39–100a1   133 n. 27

RHETORIC
1369a2   122 n. 15
1369a3–4   3 n. 2

1369a4	122 n. 15
1370a27–8	136 n. 32
1418a12–5	197 n. 27

PLATO

APOLOGY
29D7–E3	18

GORGIAS
460A5	86 n. 41
462B10–C3	5 n. 7
465A2–6	5 n. 7
468B1–E5	28 n. 24, 29 n. 27

MENO
77B6–78B2	28 n. 24
77C1–2	29 n. 29
77D6–E4	29 n. 27
81C5–86C2	162 n. 35
85D6–7	163 n. 36, 163 n. 40
86B4	163 n. 36

PHAEDO
68B8–C3	18
69E6–70B4	36
72E1–77A5	162 n. 35
73C6–74A7	163 n. 38
73D10	163 n. 39
73D10–1	163 n. 38
73E1	163 n. 39
73E6–7	163 n. 38
74A2	163 n. 39
74A5	163 n. 38
75E2–7	163 n. 36
75E4	163 n. 40
77B3–6	36
78C1–4	36
78C6–79E6	37
82B10–C8	18
94B7–C1	37 n. 4
94D7–E1	37
96A5–7	46
96B3–9	5

PHILEBUS
11B4–6	101
21C1–8	102 n. 15, 132 n. 24, 205
31E3–4	102 n. 16
31E6–32A8	102 n. 16
32B9–C2	102
32B9–36C2	58, 95 n. 2, 102, 105, 108, 136, 204
32C3–5	102
32C4–5	102
32E4	102 n. 15
33C5–6	103, 106
33C6	103 n. 18
33C6–7	146 n. 179
33D2–34A5	103
33D5	154 n. 12
33E11	154 n. 12
34A3	154 n. 12
34A4	154 n. 12
34A10–11	102 n. 15, 103, 154 n. 12, 158
34A10–35D6	4
34B6–8	163 n. 40
34D10–E1	102 n. 16
34D10–35D6	102 n. 16
35A6–9	104
35B6–7	103
35B11–C1	103
35C6–7	103 n. 19
35C8	103 n. 19
35C9–10	102 n. 15, 102 n. 16
35D1–2	104
35D1–3	102
35D3	102 n. 15
35D5–6	103 n. 19
35E3	102 n. 15
36A7–B1	104
36A7–B2	105
36B4	104
36B4–6	104
36B8–9	102 n. 15
38C5–E7	105
38E6–7	105
38E12–13	105
38E12–40C6	58, 95 n. 2, 99, 102, 105, 108
39A3–7	105
39B6–7	105
39B9	105
39B9–C1	105 n. 22
39C1–2	106
39C4–5	105
39D1–3	102 n. 17
39D7–E2	105
39E4–5	105
40A9	101 n. 14, 106 n. 23
40A9–12	106
40D7–10	104
42A7–9	104
50E5–52B8	102 n. 16
55E1–3	95 n. 93

PROTAGORAS
356A5–E4	106
358B6–D4	28 n. 24

REPUBLIC
328D3–5	45

338A5–7	45
372E–434C	14
375C6–D1	90 n. 50
377A11–378E4	47 n. 14
377B1–2	48
378D7–E2	47 n. 14
387D4–E8	62
390E8–391C6	48
434E4–435A4	14
435D9–436A3	15 n. 2, 19
436A1–3	47 n. 13
436A8–B4	20, 22, 27, 39
436A10	20 n. 2
436A10–B2	75 n. 11
436B3	20
436B6–437A8	48
436B6–441C7	35
436B8–9	22
436B9–C2	90 n. 50
436C1–2	22 n. 7
436C6–10	21 n. 6
436C9	90 n. 50
436C9–437A9	90 n. 50
436C12–D1	21 n. 5
436D1	23 n. 9
436D4–5	23
436D5	24 n. 14
436D9–E1	24 n. 14
437B1	67
437C2	26 n. 17
437C8	26 n. 17
437D9–E2	28 n. 26
438A1–5	29
439A5–6	29 n. 28
439A9–B1	30
439A9–B3	21
439A9–D2	44
439B1	188 n. 7
439B3	25, 26 n. 17, 188 n. 7
439B3–4	21
439B3–D2	33
439B4	21, 26 n. 17, 31 n. 30
439B5–6	27, 27 n. 21
439B8–C1	21, 23 n. 9
439B10	23 n. 9
439B10–C1	26 n. 17
439C3–4	37 n. 4
439C5	61
439C8	25, 44
439C10–D8	31
439D1	26 n. 17, 120 n. 4
439D1–2	21, 32
439D4	44
439D4–8	27 n. 20
439D6–7	75 n. 11
439D6–8	9, 21 n. 4
439D7	44 n. 8
439E2–4	15
439E5–440A4	9, 16, 43
440A3–4	43
440A5–7	15
440A9–B4	32, 188 n. 9
440A9–B7	177 n. 7
440B1	120 n. 4, 177 n. 7
440B3	75 n. 9, 120 n. 4, 177 n. 7
440B5	120 n. 4, 177 n. 7
440B9–C4	12
440E1	15
440E3–4	75 n. 9
440E6–8	70
440E6–441C6	70
441A2–3	2
441A7–B1	47 n. 14, 98 n. 6
441A9	120 n. 4
441B3–C2	3 n. 2, 37
441B6–C2	71
441E4–5	2
441E5	74 n. 6
442A4–B3	2, 101 n. 12
442A6–7	15 n. 2, 47 n. 13
442A7	47
442A7–8	2
442B10	20 n. 2, 35
442B10–C2	75 n. 10
442C2	74 n. 5
442C4	20 n. 2, 35
442C4–7	74
442C5	74 n. 5
442C9–D2	59, 73 n. 31, 109
442D3–4	73 n. 31
443D6–E2	22 n. 7, 22 n. 8
443D7–8	15
443E1	22 n. 8
443E1–2	25 n. 16
475B4–6	45
509D1–511E5	91
522A3–9	47 n. 14
524A6	88
524A7	88, 93
524B3–5	88
524B7–8	89 n. 49
524B10–C1	88
524C6–8	89 n. 48
524C13	83 n. 33
548D8–9	63 n. 7
553A1–555B2	10, 11, 15, 41
553C4–D4	33
553C5	41, 47 n. 13
553D2–4	44 n. 9
554B7–E6	44
554C12	41
554C12–D1	69
554C12–D3	109

554D1	75 n. 8
554D2	109 n. 27
554D6–7	44
554D9–E1	22 n. 7, 44
554D9–E6	42
554E1–2	46
554E2	44
555B9–11	93
555B10–11	46
555B11	44 n. 9
558D4–6	41
558D7–8	37 n. 24
560B7	74
561D3	45 n. 12
571B3–C1	101 n. 12
571C5–D5	59
571D1–5	4
571D2	25 n. 16
572B2–7	101 n. 12
580D6–7	25 n. 16, 33
580D10–E5	46
580D10–581A1	42
580E2–5	75 n. 11
580E2–581A1	47
580E5–581A1	15 n. 2
581A3–7	15 n. 2, 47 n. 13, 48 n. 15
581A6	20 n. 2
581A9–B1	45 n. 11, 75
581B6–7	67, 89
581C4–5	18
581C5	75
581C11–D3	48
586D4–5	15 n. 2
588B10–E1	31 n. 30
588C7	31 n. 30
588C7–E2	2
588D5–6	22 n. 7
588E6	31 n. 30
589A1	64 n. 10
589A6–B6	2, 101 n. 12
590B6–9	47 n. 14
590B7	31 n. 30
591B2	31 n. 30
595A5–B1	60
595B1	71 n. 29
595C8–602C2	60
598A5	66 n. 14
598B2–3	66 n. 14
602B6–8	65
602C1–2	63, 69
602C4–5	60, 61 n. 5
602C4–603B3	55, 59, 60, 64 n. 9, 65, 69, 70, 71
602C4–606D7	60
602D6–7	66 n. 16
602D6–9	68
602E4–6	55
602E4–9	66
602E4–603A2	71
602E6	66 n. 16, 68 n. 22, 68 n. 23
602E8–9	71 n. 29
602E8–603D2	59 n. 1
603A1	71
603A1–2	4, 25 n. 16
603A4	67 n. 20
603A4–5	68
603A9–B3	60 n. 4, 69
603B1–2	66 n. 17
603B1–3	61 n. 5
603B7–605A6	61 n. 5
603B10–C3	61 n. 5
603C1–2	59, 93
603C2–3	63
603C5–8	61
603C5–605C3	61
603C11	59 n. 2
603C11–D1	61
603D1–3	61
603D3–6	69, 71 n. 29
603D5–6	61
603E4	64
604A3	63 n. 7
604A4	62, 63 n. 7
604A6	63
604B1–2	62
604B4–C3	63
604D4–5	62, 69
604D7–9	25 n. 16, 69
604E1–3	63
605A3	69 n. 25
605A8–C3	61 n. 5
605B2–3	64
605B5–7	65 n. 12
605B7	66 n. 17, 69 n. 25
605B7–C1	96
605B7–C3	64, 64 n. 9, 69, 70 n. 26, 71
605C1–2	25 n. 16
605C5–7	64
605C5–606D7	64
605D3–4	64
605E4	63
605E5	69 n. 25
606A3–6	69
606A3–7	25 n. 16
606A5–6	64
606A7	69 n. 25
606A7–B1	64
606B3–7	64
606B4	69 n. 25
606B5–8	65 n. 12
606C2–9	65

606C3 — 65 n. 12
606D1 — 65
606D1–7 — 70
606D2 — 69 n. 25
606D4–7 — 65 n. 12
607A2–3 — 63 n. 8
608B4–5 — 65
610B4–6 — 25 n. 16
611A10–B7 — 36, 37
611B5–7 — 10, 22
611D3–5 — 38
611D8–612A5 — 38
612A5–6 — 38

SOPHIST
256E6–7 — 85 n. 37
261D1–263D4 — 92 n. 52
262C2–5 — 85 n. 37
263B11–12 — 85 n. 37
263D6–264B4 — 92
263E3–5 — 92
263E3–264A2 — 207
263E10–264A2 — 92
263E12–264A1 — 207
264A4–B4 — 206
264B1 — 92, 207 n. 9, 207 n. 10

THEAETETUS
172C–177C — 85 n. 39
173D3–4 — 85 n. 39
173E4–5 — 85 n. 39
173E6–174A2 — 85 n. 39
174B1–4 — 85 n. 39
177D2 — 85
177D4 — 85 n. 38
177E5 — 85
178A5–10 — 85
179C2–D1 — 78 n. 20
183C1–3 — 78 n. 20
184–7 — 56, 76, 88 n. 47, 89, 92, 93, 97
184B7–8 — 81
184B8 — 81
184B8–E1 — 76 n. 15
184C1–D5 — 27 n. 22
184E2 — 81
184E4–185B9 — 81
184E4–185E9 — 81
184E4–186A1 — 78
184E5 — 81
184E8–185A2 — 80
184E8–185A3 — 81, 83 n. 32
185–6 — 90
185A3 — 80
185A4–9 — 83 n. 32
185A8–9 — 84
185A8–B5 — 79 n. 22, 85

185A9 — 79, 79 n. 22, 81 n. 27, 84
185A11 — 82
185A11–12 — 84
185A11–B5 — 79
185B2 — 81 n. 27, 84
185B4 — 81 n. 27
185B4–5 — 83, 84
185B7 — 81 n. 27
185B8 — 78
185B9–C2 — 78
185B9–E2 — 82
185B9–186A1 — 85 n. 36
185B10 — 82 n. 29, 84
185C1 — 79 n. 21
185C4–7 — 79
185C4–D3 — 81
185C9 — 78, 84
185D1–2 — 83 n. 33
185D6–7 — 79 n. 21
185D6–E2 — 80
185D7–8 — 81
185D8–E2 — 81
185E1–2 — 83 n. 32
185E5–7 — 80
185E6–7 — 77, 77 n. 19, 81
185E7 — 77
185E7–9 — 81 n. 28
186A1 — 77
186A2 — 78, 83
186A2–7 — 84
186A2–C5 — 90
186A6–7 — 86
186A6–8 — 86
186A9 — 86
186A10 — 84 n. 35
186A10–11 — 86, 87 n. 42
186A10–B1 — 84, 85, 87, 88
186A11 — 85 n. 37
186B2 — 86 n. 41
186B2–3 — 87 n. 44
186B2–9 — 91
186B6 — 85 n. 37, 88 n. 46
186B6–7 — 87 n. 42, 87 n. 44
186B6–9 — 86, 87 n. 44, 89, 90
186B7 — 85 n. 37, 88 n. 46
186B8 — 87 n. 42
186B10 — 86
186B11–C2 — 77
186C1 — 91 n. 51
186C2–3 — 84 n. 34
186C2–5 — 91
186C3 — 85 n. 38, 87 n. 43, 88, 88 n. 46
186D2–3 — 87 n. 43
186D2–5 — 77, 88 n. 45
186D10–E1 — 77
187A5–6 — 77, 77 n. 19

187A7–8	77	70A5–6	75 n. 8
187C7–200D2	91	70A6	74
188C10–D1	92 n. 52	70A6–7	98
189C11–D3	90 n. 50	70A7–B3	75
189E4–190A7	92	70B4	74 n. 5
189E6–190A2	92	70B4–5	97 n. 5
190A2–7	92	70B6–8	100 n. 10
191D4–8	162 n. 34	70B7	75 n. 8
192D3–8	82 n. 29	70D7–8	75
197B1–4	159 n. 28	70D7–E5	75
197C9	159 n. 28	71A1–2	74
197D1	164 n. 42	71A3–5	99, 109
198A2	164 n. 42	71A3–D4	108
198A7	164 n. 42	71A3–E2	57, 95 n. 2, 99
		71A5–7	109
TIMAEUS		71B3–5	99, 107
27A3–6	75	71B7	100
27A7–B6	75	71B7–8	100
35A1–6	96 n. 4	71C3–4	100, 101 n. 13
35A1–8	93 n. 53	71C4–5	107
36B6–D7	97	71D1–2	109 n. 27
37A2–C3	96 n. 4	71D3–4	100
37A2–C5	93 n. 53	71E4–6	100
41D8–42A3	38	71E7	100
42E6–43B2	93 n. 53	71E8	100
44A7–B7	98	72A1–2	100
69C5–D4	58	72B6–7	100 n. 11
69C5–D6	38, 104	72B7–D3	100
69C5–72D3	74	77B3–6	56, 75
69C7–D6	75 n. 12	77B5	44 n. 8, 94
69D1–4	98	89E3–90A2	36
69D1–6	103	90B2	75
69D4–6	101	90E1–91D6	75
70A2–6	108 n. 26	90E6–91D6	100 n. 10
70A2–7	75 n. 7, 99	91B4–7	100 n. 10
70A2–C1	2	91B7–C2	100 n. 10
70A5	74 n. 6, 75 n. 8	91E2–6	97